The European Union and China's Belt and Road

This book explores key elements of European Union (EU) engagement with the Belt Road Initiative (BRI), drawing on the expertise of leading practitioners and scholars of EU-China relations.

Under the theme of discerning the BRI and its nexus with the EU, chapters examine the nature of the BRI as China's approach to global governance and consider how BRI intersects with the EU as a very different regional integration project. Under the theme of BRI factors in EU law and policy, chapters examine the BRI as a factor in specific domains of EU law and policy, including investment, finance, the environment and the COVID-19 pandemic and consider EU responses. Under the theme of EU Member State experiences, chapters present a series of case studies of individual Member States, their engagement with the BRI and ongoing policy debates.

This book will be of interest to scholars and students of International Relations, EU external relations, Chinese public policy and foreign relations, European studies and security studies as well as policymakers dealing with China in EU and Member State institutions.

Vassilis Ntousas is Senior International Relations Policy Advisor at the Foundation for European Progressive Studies and an Academy Associate at Chatham House.

Stephen Minas is Associate Professor of Law at the School of Transnational Law, Peking University, China, and Senior Research Fellow at the Transnational Law Institute, King's College London, UK.

Routledge Studies in European Foreign Policy

This series addresses the standard range of conceptual and theoretical questions related to European foreign policy. At the same time, in response to the intensity of new policy developments, it endeavours to ensure that it also has a topical flavour, addressing the most important and evolving challenges to European foreign policy, in a way that will be relevant to the policy-making and think-tank communities.

Series Editors: *Richard Whitman, University of Kent, UK, and Richard Youngs, University of Warwick, UK.*

The Proliferation of Privileged Partnerships between the European Union and its Neighbours
Edited by Sieglinde Gstöhl and David Phinnemore

EU–Turkey Relations
Civil Society and Depoliticization
Özge Zihnioğlu

The Politics of the European Neighbourhood Policy
Agnieszka K. Cianciara

European Identities and Foreign Policy Discourses on Russia
From the Ukraine to the Syrian Crisis
Marco Siddi

The EU in Southeast Asian Security
The Role of External Perceptions
Ronja Scheler

EU Regional Trade Agreements
An Instrument of Promoting the Rule of Law to Third States
Maryna Rabinovych

The European Union and China's Belt and Road
Impact, Engagement and Competition
Edited by Vassilis Ntousas and Stephen Minas

The European Union and China's Belt and Road

Impact, Engagement and Competition

Edited by Vassilis Ntousas and Stephen Minas

Routledge
Taylor & Francis Group
LONDON AND NEW YORK

First published 2022
by Routledge
2 Park Square, Milton Park, Abingdon, Oxon OX14 4RN

and by Routledge
605 Third Avenue, New York, NY 10158

Routledge is an imprint of the Taylor & Francis Group, an informa business

British Library Cataloguing-in-Publication Data
A catalogue record for this book is available from the British Library

Library of Congress Cataloging-in-Publication Data
Names: Ntousas, Vassilis, editor. | Minas, Stephen, editor.
Title: The European Union and China's Belt and Road : impact, engagement and competition / edited by Vassilis Ntousas and Stephen Minas.
Description: Abingdon, Oxon ; New York, NY : Routledge, 2021. | Includes bibliographical references and index. Identifiers: LCCN 2021004852 (print) | LCCN 2021004853 (ebook) | ISBN 9780367422905 (hardback) | ISBN 9781032045467 (paperback) | ISBN 9780367853235 (ebook)
Subjects: LCSH: European Union. | Yi dai yi lu (Initiative : China) | European Union countries--Foreign economic relations--China. | China--Foreign economic relations--European Union countries. | European Union countries--Economic policy. | China--Economic policy.
Classification: LCC HC240.25.C6 .E97 2021 (print) | LCC HC240.25.C6 (ebook) | DDC 337.1/420951--dc23
LC record available at https://lccn.loc.gov/2021004852
LC ebook record available at https://lccn.loc.gov/2021004853

ISBN: 978-0-367-42290-5 (hbk)
ISBN: 978-1-032-04546-7 (pbk)
ISBN: 978-0-367-85323-5 (ebk)

Typeset in Times New Roman
by MPS Limited, Dehradun

To my grandparents

-Stephen Minas

To my parents, Elpida and Panagiotis

-Vassilis Ntousas

Contents

List of Illustrations

Figures

Tables

Contributors

Alessia Amighini, Co-Head of Asia Centre and Senior Associate Research Fellow, ISPI; Associate Professor of Economic Policy, Università del Piemonte Orientale (Novara, Italy).

Ugo Armanini, Research Assistant, Elcano Royal Institute.

Jens Bastian, Senior Policy Advisor, Hellenic Foundation for European & Foreign Policy (ELIAMEP); Independent Financial Sector Analyst & Economic Consultant.

Steven Blockmans, Director of Research, CEPS; Professor of EU External Relations Law and Governance, University of Amsterdam.

Hui Chen, Post-Doctoral Fellow, Faculty of Law, University of Hong Kong.

Angelos Chryssogelos, Lecturer in Politics and International Relations, School of Social Sciences, London Metropolitan University; Associate Fellow, Chatham House.

Thanos Dokos, Member of the Advisory Board, Hellenic Foundation for European & Foreign Policy (ELIAMEP).

Paulo Afonso B. Duarte, Collaborative Member, Research Centre in Political Science (CICP), University of Minho.

Mario Esteban, Senior Lecturer, Centre for East Asian Studies, Autonomous University of Madrid; Senior Analyst, Elcano Royal Institute.

Laura C. Ferreira-Pereira, Professor of Political Science and International Relations, University of Minho; Integrated Member, Research Centre in Political Science (CICP), University of Minho.

Weinian Hu, Research Fellow in the GRID (Global Governance, Regulation, Innovation, Digital Economy) unit, CEPS.

Dimitri Kokoromytis, PhD Student, Department of Political Science, University of Utah; Junior Research Associate, Hellenic Foundation for European and Foreign Policy.

Stefan Mair, Director and CEO, SWP (German Institute for International and Security Affairs).

Jing Men, Professor, School of International Relations and Area Studies, East China Normal University.

Stephen Minas, Associate Professor, School of Transnational Law, Peking University; Senior Research Fellow, Transnational Law Institute, King's College London.

Françoise Nicolas, Director, Center for Asian Studies, French Institute of International Relations.

Vassilis Ntousas, Senior International Relations Policy Advisor, Foundation for European Progressive Studies; Academy Associate, Chatham House.

Ferdinand Schaff, Senior Manager - Greater China, BDI (Federation of German Industries).

Francis Snyder, C.V. Starr Professor of Law, School of Transnational Law, Peking University.

Alexandr Svetlicinii, Associate Professor, University of Macau, Faculty of Law.

Su Xueji, PhD Student, Faculty of Law, Chinese University of Hong Kong.

Yun Zhao, Professor and Head of Department of Law, University of Hong Kong.

Foreword

The EU and China's Belt and Road: Strategic dilemmas for the Union

Thanos Dokos

Member of the Advisory Board (and former Director-General), Hellenic Foundation for European & Foreign Policy (ELIAMEP)

There is increasing agreement among experts and policymakers that the future international political system will be multipolar, with the US probably as *primus inter pares,* but with China (already the second largest global economy and projected to surpass the US sometime in the next 10 years), India, Japan, the European Union, Russia and a number of regional powers playing increasing roles. In combination with the financial and political crises of the past decade and of other global challenges, such as the evolving COVID-19 pandemic, this raises questions of global security and governance.

China is generally perceived as an emerging superpower, and its spectacular rise raises a number of very important questions regarding the global balance of power, China's foreign policy and its relations with the rest of the world. Some of these questions are being addressed in the rapidly expanding literature published over the past few years. To start with, many scholars seek to answer the "one million dollar" question: what does China want? Kerry Brown (2017) is attempting to answer the question from a Chinese perspective, focusing on Chinese leaders, their beliefs and their instincts. Daniel Lynch presents a very interesting debate of Chinese elites debating economics, politics and foreign policy and outlines "two fundamentally different, completely disjointed Chinas floating in the[ir] minds" (2015, 248). One is a China so spectacularly successful that this ancient civilization returns to centrality in international relations and world history. The other is a China whose rise is, even now, slowly grinding to a halt: a country that could even be on the verge of failing tragically in multiple, crisscrossing cascades. David Shambaugh (2016) argues that China is at a critical juncture in the development of its economy, society, polity, national security and international relations and that the direction the nation takes at this turning point will determine whether it stalls or continues to develop and prosper. He believes that these potential pathways are all possibilities—but they depend on key decisions yet to be made by China's leaders, on different pressures from within Chinese society, as well as on actions taken by other nations.

The impact of China's rise on regional and global security and stability is the focus of numerous studies. Gideon Rachman argues that the "West's centuries-long domination of world affairs is now coming to a close … [a]nd the consequences are now being felt in global politics" (2016, 3). Michael Auslin presents a different narrative, namely that "trends and events, from China's slumping economy to war clouds over the South China Sea, from environmental devastation to demographic crisis, indicate that Asia's future is highly uncertain" (2017). In a 2011 Munk debate on China, Niall Ferguson and David Li supported the motion that the 21st century belongs to China, whereas Henry Kissinger and Fareed Zakaria disagreed.

Kishore Mahbubani (2020) describes the defining geopolitical contest of the 21st century as between China and the US and attempts to answer the questions: Is it avoidable? And if it happens, is the outcome already inevitable? Christopher Coker (2015) explains why even though the next global conflict may be played out in the new spheres of cyberspace and outer space, like all previous wars, it will have devastating consequences. Such a war between the US and China looks less "improbable" with every passing year. On the same topic, Graham Allison (2017) makes a convincing case that China and the US are heading toward a war neither wants because of "Thucydides' Trap": the phenomenon of a rising power threatening to displace a ruling one. Although he claims that we are close to the unthinkable, he stresses that war is not inevitable if the US and China take a number of painful steps. Finally, Thomas Christensen (2015) argues that the real challenge lies in dissuading China from regional aggression while eliciting its global cooperation. He describes how we might shape China's choices in the coming decades so that it contributes more to the international system from which it benefits.

Although the EU is not a major player in the geopolitical competition taking place in East Asia and the Pacific, it has a very high volume of trade with China, and Beijing has in recent years spectacularly increased its economic footprint not only in Europe's immediate neighborhood but also in EU Member States through the Belt and Road Initiative (BRI) and other multilateral (17+1) and bilateral arrangements, as well as direct investment in various countries.

Indeed, changes in the global balance of power are already being reflected at the regional level as well. Although the US will remain the dominant player in the Middle East and the Eastern Mediterranean for the foreseeable future and the EU is expected to remain an influential actor, despite its current problems, it would be fairly safe to predict that the Mediterranean and the wider Middle East will gradually evolve into a multi-player security system. The expected substantial reduction in US energy dependence from the Middle East, which has affected US regional policies, and the more general trend for a US pivot towards the Asia-Pacific region will have a substantial impact on the evolution of the regional security system. China has adopted a policy of close relations with resource-rich states in Africa and the Gulf region and has limited its regional involvement to the economic sector, presently satisfied with the US guarantee of the safety of supply lines. But this may change, given Beijing's growing energy dependency. As this author has previously observed: "Through initiatives and projects such as "Belt and Road", ["17+1"], the acquisition of ports and other strategic infrastructure assets across the Mediterranean, China is continuously increasing its economic, but also political footprint in the above-mentioned regions … On the other hand, there are no signs so far that China is interested in acting as a security provider in this region" (Dokos 2018).

As a result of these developments, its overall relationship with China has become a matter of rising importance for the EU. In a 2019 European Commission communique, it is noted that "there is growing appreciation that the balance of challenges and opportunities presented by China has shifted" and that China is "simultaneously, in different policy areas, a cooperation partner with whom the EU has closely aligned objectives, a negotiating partner with whom the EU needs to find a balance of interests, an economic competitor in the pursuit of technological leadership, and a systemic rival promoting alternative models of governance. This requires a flexible and pragmatic whole-of-EU approach enabling a principled defence of interests and values" (2019, 1). It is also mentioned that the 2016 Strategy on China remains the cornerstone of EU engagement, providing the basis for delivering a further EU policy shift towards a more realistic, assertive, and multi-faceted approach and that "neither the EU nor any of its Member States can effectively achieve their aims with China without full unity" (Ibid, 2).

Relations with China have become an issue of increasing importance for countries in Southern Europe, such as Greece, as Beijing is apparently viewing her as a regional hub for enlarging its economic (and perhaps in the future political) footprint in the wider region. Whereas foreign direct investment is generally welcomed, this creates a number of policy dilemmas for Greece and the EU, as the situation has become more complicated because of the impact of the COVID-19 pandemic on major power relations and of the 5G controversy. This has led to, *inter alia*, calls for closer scrutiny on foreign investment in critical infrastructure in EU countries.

This important and timely edited volume is addressing issues such as the contested characterizations of BRI (as opportunity, challenge or threat), the diverging policy responses from EU institutions and Member States, the shift from an earlier focus on economic opportunities to a more realist response, efforts for a united EU position, China's approach to global governance, its grand strategy, the external dimension of Xi Jinping's 'China Dream' and the terms of the Sino-EU relationship. The book is attempting to answer the following questions: What have been the respective roles of EU institutions and Member States in responding to the Belt and Road, and what is the prospect for a unified position? How can the EU manage the risks presented by the Belt and Road? What is the potential for EU engagement in the Belt and Road to contribute to positive Sino-EU cooperation on shared priorities? In addressing these critical questions, the book is making an important contribution to an evolving debate of increasing significance for Europe.

References

Allison, Graham, 2017. Destined for War, Scribe, Melbourne.
Auslin, Michael, 2017. The End of the Asian Century, Yale University Press, New Haven.
Brown, Kerry, 2017. China's World. What Does China Want?, I.B. Tauris, London.
Christensen, Thomas J, 2015. The China Challenge, W.W. Norton & Company, New York.
Coker, Christopher, 2015. The Improbable War. China, the United States and the Logic of Great Power Conflict, Hurst & Company, London.
Dokos, Thanos, 2018. Contested Mediterranean? NATO's Maritime Role Amid Shifting Balances, Italian Institute for International Political Studies, https://www.ispionline.it/en/pubblicazione/contested-mediterranean-natos-maritime-role-amid-shifting-balances-20936
European Commission, 2019. EU-China – A Strategic Outlook, European Commission, Strasbourg, 12.3.2019, JOIN 5 final.
Lynch, Daniel, 2015. China's Futures: PRC Elites Debate Economics, Politics, and Foreign Policy, Stanford University Press, Stanford.
Mahbubani, Kishore, 2020. Has China Won? Public Affairs, New York.
Rachman, Gideon, 2016. Easternisation. War and Peace in the Asian Century, The Bodley Head, London.
Shambaugh, David, 2016. China's Future, Polity, Cambridge.

Acknowledgements

This book has its origins in a conversation over coffee near Place Flagey in Brussels in 2018, but is also linked to several trips to as well as discussions in and on China we have had over the years. Our shared interest and curiosity to map and explore the Belt and Road Initiative's interconnections with Europe's evolving hopes and concerns regarding China led us to an exciting two-year-old (research) journey, the outcome of which you are holding in your hands today.

As such, there is a number of co-travellers whom we are grateful to and would therefore like to acknowledge, beginning with the impressive line-up of authors who have contributed to this book, both from Europe and China. We are truly thankful to them for an excellent and particularly productive collaboration. It has been our honour and privilege to help steer the work of such a diverse set of scholars and analysts, who are all intently focused on fostering a more meaningful understanding of the critical and timely topics discussed in this book.

We also gratefully recognise the team at Routledge, who commissioned this book and then expertly guided it to maturity and completion.

One a more personal level, Vassilis Ntousas wishes to express his great appreciation for several colleagues at Chatham House in London and the Foundation for European Progressive Studies in Brussels for their valuable and constructive suggestions throughout this process. Gratitude is also owed to many friends, including Vangelis Koloptas, Hedwig Giusto and Maria Freitas, for their continuous encouragement and support.

Stephen Minas gratefully acknowledges his main professional home during the period of this book project, Peking University's School of Transnational Law, for its support for research collaborations and commitment to academic freedom. Engagement with a broader circle of colleagues and friends working on EU-China matters has also been greatly valued, especially during the pandemic.

To all involved in this rewarding project, thank you and 谢谢大家.

Vassilis Ntousas and Stephen Minas

Part I

Introduction

1 Introduction: Facing the Belt and Road from the European Union

Vassilis Ntousas and Stephen Minas

Decades of rapid economic growth in China have transformed the global economy and are also bringing political consequences, as a wealthier China becomes more assertive. Since 2013, under President Xi Jinping, China has expanded its investment, trade and political relationships under the rubric of the Belt and Road Initiative (BRI). For the European Union, the BRI has over time raised profound questions concerning the bloc's relationship with China. These include the environmental and social impacts of Chinese investments in the EU, the ability of the EU to speak with one voice and act in unison concerning Beijing and competition to influence economic and political developments in broader Eurasia and globally. Concurrently, however, a number of EU Member States have welcomed BRI-related investments, while some take the view that the BRI may encompass new opportunities for EU-China cooperation on issues of common concern. Historically, the EU has not taken an overall strategic approach to relations with China. Given that the EU has long viewed China primarily as a trading and economic partner, the BRI requires getting to grips with broader elements of large power relations.

The contested characterisations of the BRI as opportunity, challenge and threat, and the different perceptions and interests of various EU institutions and Member States, have driven diverging policy responses. The longstanding willingness of a number of EU members to upgrade bilateral relationships with China to reap financial and other benefits at times translated into an open stance based on positive appraisals of the BRI. This was more pronounced in southern Europe, partly because of the need for economic support in face of the eurozone crisis. Regardless of the country specifics, however, the early years of the BRI were characterised by efforts to vie for (in)direct Chinese support at Member State level. This made the crystallisation of a unified EU approach vis-à-vis the initiative a difficult undertaking.

As BRI gradually morphed into a more concrete initiative and its terms and contours became more visible, the approaches of Member States became more balanced. This allowed the EU to make some progress towards a more united stance. This, however, has not negated the continuing importance attached by certain Member States, such as Portugal, to attracting Chinese investments, even beyond the parameters of the 'strategic' approach newly favoured in Brussels.

In March 2019, the European Commission signalled a shift in its approach, describing China as 'simultaneously, in different policy areas, a cooperation partner with whom the EU has closely aligned objectives, a negotiating partner with whom the EU needs to find a balance of interests, an economic competitor in the pursuit of technological leadership, and a systemic rival promoting alternative models of governance' (European Commission 2019, 1). Although criticising China's widespread outbound financing of fossil-fuel projects (by far the largest component of Chinese outbound energy financing: Brown University 2020), the Commission declined to address the BRI directly (European Commission 2019, 3). This formulation, since adopted by the new Commission (von der Leyen 2020), was an important intervention in the EU debate on relations with China. Nonetheless, it can hardly be perceived as the final word, not least due to ongoing Member State differentiation in approaching this 'partner, competitor, rival' schema and the concomitant need for the Commission to clarify how its approach can be implemented.

The complexity of framing a response to the BRI is not solely due to the EU's *sui generis* nature and intricate decision-making processes. The EU faces a changing Belt and Road, emanating from a changing China. The years since Xi announced the BRI have seen arguably the most consequential changes in China's internal politics and international stance since the fall of the 'Gang of Four' and the pivot to 'reform and opening up' under Deng Xiaoping. These changes have included Xi's consolidation of personal power, ending decades of 'collective leadership' and symbolised by the 2017 abolition of presidential term limits. The leadership role of the Chinese Communist Party (CCP) has been reasserted over government and economy. Under Xi, China simultaneously presents itself as a champion of multilateral cooperation and vigorously pursues its (increasingly broadly defined) 'core interests'. The BRI, endorsed in the Party constitution since 2017, is a key instrument for achieving China's national aims as defined by its president.

But what is the Belt and Road? Since 2013, it has been variously explained as China's approach to global governance; Chinese grand strategy; the external dimension of Xi's 'China Dream'; an economic plan for exporting Chinese excess capacity and low–value-added activities; and a slogan applied indiscriminately to multiple disconnected projects. Debate continues over the BRI's nature, and this volume will demonstrate that EU perceptions of it have changed considerably in a few short years. While in 2017 an EU official might have still thought '[i]t's about selling their stuff' (quoted in Frankopan 2018, 120), the increasingly dominant view in EU policy circles in the last few years is that BRI is not just, or even primarily, a commercial project. Gone, too, is the implausible notion that the EU could perform a 'scrutinizing role' in the BRI (another EU official, quoted in Maçães 2018, 145). The BRI is better understood as 'a vector for generally internationalizing Chinese priorities' (Ekman 2019, 24), and indeed as 'China's global development policy' (Maçães 2018, 78). The BRI's scale and complexities challenge the EU to develop sophisticated responses.

Much is at stake. Through the BRI, China is competing to set the standards of global economic activity — a field in which the EU has long excelled, often in partnership with the United States and other democracies. Such competition entails not just an economic contest for technology leadership, third-party markets and global value chains, but also normative choices. Many BRI projects have sharply diverged from EU values concerning environmental sustainability, social standards and labour rights. These divergences have been identified in BRI projects in the EU's near-abroad and even in some Member States, testing EU unity and its ability to consolidate the European space through shared norms. More broadly, the BRI has served as a factor in the constantly developing terms of the overall EU-China relationship. The prospects for an improved and more reciprocal economic relationship, and for enhanced cooperation on mutual priorities such as climate change, are at stake.

Compounding these complexities, EU-China relations are developing in the context of multiple crises: the Brexit crisis, which brought a sustained and coherent response from the EU; the crisis of great power relations, with the Sino-US 'trade war' feeding generalised confrontation and hostility; the COVID-19 pandemic, which has both jolted EU-China relations and put much of conventional diplomacy on hold; and the ever-worsening crisis of climate change, amongst many.

This book makes a targeted intervention in the vast policy and academic debate concerning BRI. Already, the BRI has spawned a voluminous literature. Multiple monographs (e.g. Rolland 2017; Maçães 2018; Drache, Kingsmith and Qi 2019) and edited volumes (e.g. Zhang, Alon and Lattemann 2018; Leandro and Duarte 2020) have sought to answer the riddle of the BRI. Other studies have approached the BRI from particular academic perspectives, from normative readings (Shan, Nuotio and Zhang 2018) to the perspectives of international law and global governance (Zhao 2018). There is also a growing number of publications that suggest BRI policy changes or law reform, such as Wang, Lee and Leung's (2020) proposals for a new BRI dispute settlement system. Publications concerning Europe and the BRI have tended to focus on the tensions between economic and national security concerns in shaping EU responses to the BRI (e.g. Van der Putten et al. 2016; Le Corre 2018). Chinese state think-tanks have also published research on the EU-BRI nexus, some of which is available in English (see, e.g. Liu 2017, identifying the EU as 'the very focus of' the BRI).

Despite this proliferation of publications, no previous book has explicitly focused on examining BRI for an audience of EU policymakers, scholars and students, with chapters dedicated to the key considerations, from EU perspectives, of the BRI. This volume addresses that gap in the literature. Our book does not attempt to describe the 'whole elephant' of the BRI. Rather, chapters focus on different moving objects in the 'BRI kaleidoscope' (borrowing Snyder's metaphor, Chapter 4) that are particularly salient to Sino-EU relations.

This book explores key elements of EU engagement with the BRI by drawing on the expertise of leading practitioners and scholars of EU-China relations. The EU is the main geographic focus. Some chapters also discuss the EU's near-abroad of the Western Balkans, regarding the interface of BRI and EU priorities. Finally, elements of the book address the entirety of the BRI, in order to introduce the BRI and appraise its significance to the EU.

To assess the BRI's significance to the EU, we assembled a group of both Europe- and China-based scholars and practitioners, from disciplines including law, economics, international relations and political science. Authors were asked to address a set of interrelated questions: What have been the respective roles of EU institutions and Member States concerning the BRI, and what is the prospect for a unified position? How can the EU utilise law, regulation and standards to respond to BRI and protect EU interests? How can the EU manage risks presented by the BRI? Is there potential for EU engagement in the BRI to contribute to positive Sino-EU cooperation on shared priorities?

The book is structured as follows. Section 2 examines the nature of the BRI as China's approach to global governance, and considers how BRI intersects with the EU as a very different regional integration project. Section 3 examines the BRI as a factor in specific domains of EU law and policy and considers EU responses. Eschewing any attempt to be comprehensive, chapters focus on important policy areas of financial and economic relations, the environment and health. Section 4 presents a series of case studies of individual Member States, their engagement with the BRI and ongoing policy debates. The conclusion summarises the book's contribution and distils key messages for the EU's future approach to the BRI.

Section 2: Discerning the BRI and its crossroads with the European Union

Zhao and Chen present the Belt and Road as China's approach to global governance, which the authors contend is a 'development strategy with its origin from China's reform and opening up policy', building on existing bilateral, regional and multilateral cooperation mechanisms. The BRI profoundly affects China-EU relations while, at the same time, the EU will have a 'significant impact' on the BRI. Zhao and Chen acknowledge different Member State perspectives on the BRI and make suggestions for improving cooperation on a 'reciprocal and rules-based basis'.

Men tracks the BRI as a factor in China-EU diplomacy, situating the initially positive EU response to the BRI in the aftermath of the eurozone crisis, when both the Juncker Commission and Member States looked to attract investment to support economic recovery. However, EU institutions soon adopted a more sceptical stance, a change which Men attributes to growing awareness of the different standards promoted through the BRI, the 'Made in China 2025' industrial policy and concerns over Chinese acquisition of 'cutting-edge' European technologies. Men concludes that a united approach to China continues to elude the EU.

The BRI challenges the EU in the domain of law as well as diplomacy. **Snyder** observes that the EU is constrained in developing a general approach to the BRI because relevant legal competences are divided, and shared, between the EU and Member States. However, Snyder also locates in the EU's 'legal pluralism' the potential for the EU to pursue its own interests in the BRI. EU law, national law and European 'soft law' can all be utilised to promote EU norms in the BRI. Importantly, Snyder notes that these legal processes are not limited to governments, with the private sector an important driver of policies and norms.

Blockmans and Hu analyse legal considerations from another perspective, in their discussion of the EU's legal bulwarks and regulatory responses to address concerns about economic and national security triggered by BRI investments. They suggest that, while a more realistic and assertive EU approach toward Chinese market behaviour is welcome, the EU should take China up on BRI 'soft connectivity', i.e. a legal infrastructure, to truly achieve 'win-win' cooperation, rather than risk mutual harm by adopting too protectionist a stance.

Section 3: Belt and Road factors in EU law and policy

Bastian's chapter analyses the BRI's financial underpinnings in Europe, with a focus on EU Member States and candidate countries in south-eastern Europe. Bastian presents a nuanced picture of China's financing activities in the region; many projects were underway before the launch of the BRI, and *ad hoc* initiatives have gradually transformed into a more strategic approach. Alongside money, China has also hazarded its 'reputational capital', as environmental impacts conflict with commitments to a 'green Belt and Road'. The EU has responded to growing Chinese investment with enforcement of procurement norms and new investment-screening rules. However, the EU's ability to mainstream this approach to non-members in the 17+1 group (16+1 following Lithuania's withdrawal)[i] is unclear.

Svetlicinii's chapter continues the examination of investment, focusing on one of the 'pillars' of the BRI: Chinese state-owned enterprises (SOEs). Svetlicinii portrays the BRI as less grand strategy and more a response to China's domestic economic challenges, with the EU an attractive outlet for excess capacity. Svetlicinii identifies the central role of SOEs in the global expansion of Chinese commerce, before detailing their EU acquisitions. The ongoing debate concerning regulatory responses to contentious Chinese SOE acquisitions in Europe illustrates the tension between orthodox competition policy targeting economic efficiency and a more politicised approach.

Some of the clearest divergences between EU norms and the BRI lie in the field of environmental and social standards. **Su** notes that the EU and China share a high-level commitment to 'sustainable development' but have sharply diverged over what this means in practice. The BRI, 'constructed upon China's developmental experience', continues this divergence. However, Su suggests that China has responded to widespread criticism of the BRI's environmental and social impacts with new policies and safeguards and highlights the scope for pragmatic EU-China collaboration on sustainability.

Esteban and Armanini contend that the COVID-19 pandemic has undermined the BRI's appeal in Europe. While the EU and China engaged in reciprocal emergency assistance during the pandemic, Chinese attempts to revitalise its 'Health Silk Road' were unsuccessful. Moreover, assertive Chinese pandemic diplomacy alienated both EU leaders and citizens. The authors suggest that Chinese authorities have adjusted to these reactions with a strategy to 'avoid [further] deterioration of the standing of the BRI in this region, instead of a growth strategy'.

Section 4: EU Member State experiences and debates

Nicolas investigates the historical foundations of the relationship between France and China and the clear shift in France's approach in recent years, away from 'naivety' and towards more firmness. Following a logic of conditional engagement, she argues that French authorities are favourable to the BRI's overall objective of connectivity enhancement but refuse to endorse the project in its entirety.

Presenting the case of Germany, **Mair and Schaff** survey the development of the country's China policy and its consistent focus on economic relations. This approach was not solely based on the huge economic benefits that the rise of China had for Germany but was reinforced by the idea that engaging China economically would also help to nudge the country towards political and economic liberalisation, not to say deeper integration into the liberal international order. Despite its evolution, the authors hold that Berlin's current policy vis-à-vis Beijing is ill-equipped to address the complex geopolitical and geo-economic challenges related to BRI and is consequently in need of rethinking.

Kokoromytis and Chryssogelos discuss the case of Greece as an example of how BRI has served Beijing's economic and political goals. By exploring the (geo-)political and economic dimensions of the Sino-Greek relationship and focusing on the emblematic Chinese investment in the port of Piraeus, the chapter also examines the rationale behind Greece's evolving orientation towards BRI and situates this development in the wider European context.

Amighini explores the domestic political dynamics in Italy that led Rome to sign its BRI Memorandum of Understanding (MoU) with Beijing in March 2019. As she indicates, the country was the first NATO and G7 member to do so, sparking lively debate about this move's geopolitical implications at European and global levels, some of the key elements of which are also discussed in this contribution.

Ferreira-Pereira and Duarte offer an account of China's presence and investments in Portugal under the BRI aegis. Their contribution delves into the Portuguese authorities' growing realization of opportunities resulting from an ever-closer relationship with China, in particular after the 2008–2009 financial and economic crisis, as well as Lisbon's arguably accommodating stance toward Beijing. This stance is not without consequences in foreign policy, given the country's traditional orientation towards the United States and EU.

References

Brown University, 2020. China's Global Energy Finance, https://www.bu.edu/cgef/#/all/Country.

Drache, D., Kingsmith, A.T., Qi, D., 2019. One Road, Many Dreams: China's Bold Plan to Remake the Global Economy. Bloomsbury China, London.

Ekman, A., 2019. China's Belt & Road and the World: Competing Forms of Globalization. Ifri, Paris.

European Commission, 2019. EU-China – a strategic outlook, Strasbourg, 12.3.2019, JOIN. https://ec.europa.eu/info/sites/default/files/communication-eu-china-a-strategic-outlook.pdf

Frankopan, P., 2018. The New Silk Roads: The Present and Future of the World. Bloomsbury Publishing, London.

Le Corre, P., 2018. Chinese Investments in European Countries: Experiences and Lessons for the "Belt and Road" Initiative, in: Mayer, M. (Ed.), Rethinking the Silk Road: China's Belt and Road Initiative and Emerging Eurasian Relations. Palgrave, Singapore, pp. 161–175.

Leandro, F.J.B.S., Duarte, P.A.B. (Eds.), 2020. The Belt and Road Initiative: An Old Archetype of a New Development Model. Palgrave Macmillan, Singapore.

Liu, Z., 2017. Europe and the Belt and Road Initiative: Responses and Risks. China Social Sciences Press.

Maçães, B., 2018. Belt and Road: A Chinese World Order. Hurst & Company, London.

Rolland, N., 2017. China's Eurasian Century? Political and Strategic Implications of the Belt and Road Initiative. National Bureau of Asian Research, Washington, DC.

Shan, W., Nuotio, K., Zhang, K. (Eds.), 2018. Normative Readings of the Belt and Road Initiative: Road to New Paradigms. Springer, Cham.

Van der Putten, F.-P., et al., 2016.The Geopolitical Relevance of Piraeus and China's New Silk Road for Southeast Europe and Turkey (Clingendael Report). https://www.clingendael.org/sites/default/files/pdfs/Report_the%20geopolitical_relevance_of_Piraeus_and_China's_New_Silk_Road.pdf

Von der Leyen, U., 2020. State of the Union Address by President von der Leyen at the European Parliament Plenary, European Commission, https://ec.europa.eu/commission/presscorner/detail/en/SPEECH_20_1655.

Wang, G., Lee, Y.-L., Leung, M.-F., 2020. Dispute Resolution Mechanism for the Belt and Road Initiative. Zhejiang University Press/Springer, Singapore.

Zhang, W., Alon, I., Lattemann, C. (Eds.), 2018. China's Belt and Road Initiative: Changing the Rules of Globalization. Palgrave Macmillan, Cham.

Zhao, Y. (Ed.), 2018. International Governance and the Rule of Law in China under the Belt and Road Initiative. Cambridge University Press, Cambridge.

Part II

Discerning the BRI and its intersections with the European Union

2 The Belt and Road Initiative in China's approach to global governance: Implications for China-EU relations and economic cooperation

Yun Zhao and Hui Chen

1 Introduction

China launched the Belt and Road Initiative (BRI) as a significant step to contribute to global governance, in particular economic cooperation among its trading partners. China has signed 197 cooperative agreements with 137 countries (including 27 European countries and 17 EU member states)[i] and 30 international organizations since Chinese President Xi Jinping put forward the BRI framework in 2013 (Belt and Road Portal 2019).

China has been expanding its political and economic influence through bilateral and regional talks with the BRI countries, with the aim of playing a more active role in global governance, in the forms of increasing mutual understanding, strengthening pragmatic cooperation, and promoting collaboration in economic, national security and environmental protection among the BRI countries (Belt & Road News 2020). The EU, as an indispensable participant and the geographical end of the BRI, will have a significant impact on the development and success of the BRI. As such, it is important to study how to incentivize the EU and other nations to participate in the BRI. As far as the China-EU relationship is concerned, it is necessary to examine how to balance the cooperation and competition between China and the EU (and the EU member states separately) and how to use laws and regulations in managing the China-EU relations. This chapter takes up the task of studying possible contributions China can make in enhancing global governance and examines how to further the collaboration between China and the EU in the context of the BRI.

2 China's vision and modalities to enhance global governance

2.1 The BRI and China's vision of global governance

The Belt and Road Initiative (BRI) is a development strategy with its origin in China's opening up and reform policy. The BRI calls for stimulating shared growth via strengthening the connectivity of economy, strategy, and culture along the six economic corridors (OECD Business and Finance

Outlook 2018, p. 11).[ii] The priorities of the BRI lie in the infrastructure projects and funding, while the motivations cover 'openness', 'sustainable development', 'energy and food security' and 'more balanced regional development'(OECD Business and Finance Outlook 2018, pp. 13–15). According to the official document of 'Vision and Actions on Jointly Building Silk Road Economic Belt and 21st-Century Maritime Silk Road', the prioritized cooperation areas of China's BRI projects include policy coordination, facilities connectivity, unimpeded trade, financial integration, and people-to-people bonds (Chinese Embassy in UK (CEUK) 2015). China upholds the UN Charter and the Five Principles of Peaceful Coexistence and insists on the principles of 'open for cooperation', 'harmonious and inclusive', 'following of market operation', and 'seeking mutual benefit' in the undertaking of BRI projects (Chinese Embassy in UK (CEUK) 2015). The existing multilateral and bilateral cooperation platforms provide the basis and starting point for the cooperation in BRI projects. China has signed documents, such as Memorandums of Understanding (MoUs) and plans for pilot projects with trading partners to strengthen bilateral cooperation. In the meantime, China makes full use of the existing platforms (e.g., Shanghai Cooperation Organization (SCO), Asia-Pacific Economic Cooperation (APEC), Boao Forum for Asia, Asia-Europe Meeting (ASEM), China-Eurasia Expo, and Euro-Asia Economic Forum) to promote multilateral and regional cooperation and strengthen connectivity among BRI countries (Chinese Embassy in UK (CEUK) 2015).

In June 2017, China synchronized the BRI development plans and released the document 'Vision for Maritime Cooperation under the Belt and Road Initiative', putting forward maritime-related cooperation priorities and project updates (State Council 2017).[iii] China reiterates in this document the importance of bilateral, multilateral, and regional cooperation in opening up on a peaceful and reciprocal basis. Meanwhile, China respects cultural diversity and encourages the voluntary participation of BRI countries, with the projects undertaken adhering to market rules and international standards.

2.2 The modalities of China to enhance global governance

As mentioned above, the BRI aims to enhance China's role in global governance through upgrading, instead of replacing, the existing bilateral, multilateral, and regional economic cooperation mechanisms (United Nations ESCAP 2017, p. 2).

First of all, China pursues an incremental approach to increase its political and economic impact on the international community (Belt & Road News 2019). For example, in recent discussions regarding World Trade Organization (WTO) reform, China shared similar positions with the majority of WTO members in tackling the Appellate Body crisis by incrementally fixing the procedural and systematic problems on an issue-by-issue basis (World Trade Organization 2018). In the meantime, as the US is playing a different role in the international community with its changing attitude towards multilateralism, China undertakes both regional and bilateral negotiations to protect the multilateral trading system. Against this backdrop, China, the EU, and Japan would play more significant roles in safeguarding the international trading order (Stiftung 2018, p. 44).

The BRI projects would gradually strengthen plurilateral cooperation and economic growth, provide proper arrangements to reduce distortive trade measures, and level the playing field for foreign investment (Stiftung 2018, p. 44). China utilizes the bilateral investment treaties (BITs) as significant instruments to facilitate investment and trade in the BRI countries, although it has been argued that some BITs with BRI countries are either relatively low quality or outdated (Shi 2018, pp. 28–30). In addition, the conclusion of free trade agreements (FTAs) with BRI countries has been used as a more comprehensive means to promote cooperation in foreign investment and trade. It is to be noted that the newly formulated strategy of Chinese FTAs is 'to start from neighboring countries, then expand to BRI nations, and further to the globe' (Shi 2018, pp. 28–30).

When it comes to China-EU cooperation, China recently reached a consensus with France, Italy, and Monaco in protecting multilateralism and deepening bilateral cooperation (Belt & Road News 2020). Italy became the first G-7 country to sign an MoU with China endorsing BRI projects (Miner & Abellan-Matamoros 2019, also see Chapter 13 in this book). The strategic partnership between China and Italy covers a wide range of economic cooperation areas, deemed as one initial step (starting from the central and southern periphery of the EU) to incrementally increase China's influence in the 'core economies' of Europe (Zeneli 2019).[iv]

Secondly, China adopts a balanced approach between the top-down and bottom-up approaches. The traditional top-down (normalization) approach seeks to establish unified arrangements of actions, institutions, or implementation before actual actions (Zhang 2017, pp. 183–185).[v] In addition to the top-down approach, the BRI adopts a bottom-up approach and combines the two approaches to encourage voluntary actions from trading partners (Zhang 2017, pp. 183–185). China advocates the principles of broad consultations on an equal footing and joint contribution in building a community of shared interests in the BRI development (Wang & Li 2019, pp. 99–105). Apart from the bilateral and regional MoUs and FTAs signed between China and its BRI partners, the bottom-up approach is supported by a range of BRI financial institutions (Zhang 2017, pp. 185–186). The funding sources for BRI projects include the China Development Bank, China Export-Import Bank, Bank of China, the Silk Road Fund, Industrial and Commercial Bank of China, China Construction Bank, China Export and Credit Insurance Corporation, and the China-based multilateral financial institutions New Development Bank (NDB) and Asia Infrastructure Investment Bank (AIIB) (Stiftung 2018, p. 20).[vi]

China also emphasizes its peaceful mindset in global governance by improving rather than challenging the current global economic and trading order. For instance, China put forward the concept of a 'Community of Common Destiny for Mankind' in January 2017, which was later incorporated into a UN resolution entitled 'Social Dimensions of the New Partnership for Africa's Development' (Zhang 2018, pp. 196–207). China's promotion of this concept is regarded as an effort to ease the growing tension with its neighboring states over territorial conflicts, while sustaining a favourable external environment for comprehensive economic cooperation (Zhang 2018, pp. 196–207). However, since the balanced approach calls for voluntary actions from BRI partners, the effectiveness of this approach depends very much on the progress of China's efforts in carrying forward the 'comprehensive strategic partnership' and the attitude of other BRI countries on China's proposals (Tobin 2018, pp. 155–166).

Last but not least, while emphasizing the convergence of different legal systems, China also upholds the principle of reciprocity and synergies in economic cooperation.

The BRI projects cross vastly different regulatory systems. The involved jurisdictions consist of the common law system, the civil law system, and the Islamic law system. On the one hand, regulatory risks arise when multinational corporations are involved in the BRI projects, particularly when multinational investigation (sometimes across BRI and non-BRI countries) on misconduct or other illegal misbehaviors is required (Wu et al. 2019, pp. 10–11). On the other hand, investment and trade along the BRI economic corridors have inevitably led to more international commercial disputes between the actors. It was reported that trade dispute cases involving a foreign party increased by nearly 10% in China in 2016 (OBOReurope 2018).

To address the potential legal risks raised from BRI projects, the Chinese government has introduced a series of arrangements and measures. For instance, China has established the National Supervision Commission (NSC) to enforce anti-graft measures on all officials in the government, state-owned enterprises, and multinational corporations (Wu et al. 2019, p. 11). In 2018, China adopted the Supervision Law of the People's Republic of China – Chapter VI, International Cooperation Against Corruption, Order of the President (No. 3) to strengthen communication and cooperation on anti-corruption enforcement between different regulators.

On 29 June 2018, China's Supreme People's Court (SPC) established (the First and Second) China International Commercial Courts (CICC), based in Shenzhen and Xi'an. Both courts are supervised by the SPC (Wiendieck & Stark 2018). The CICC Shenzhen Court (the First CICC court) focuses on commercial disputes related to BRI sea routes, while the one in Xi'an (the second) is responsible for commercial disputes along the new Continental Silk Roads (OBOReurope 2018). Unlike international commercial courts in other countries, the CICC provides a 'one-stop' dispute resolution platform to coordinate mediation, arbitration, and litigation for disputing parties (Liu 2019). Two international commercial mediation institutions (China Council for the Promotion of International Trade Mediation Center and Shanghai Commercial Mediation Center (SCMC)) and five international commercial arbitration institutions (China International Economic and Trade Arbitration Commission (CIETAC), Shenzhen Court of International Arbitration (SCIA), Beijing Arbitration Commission (BAC), China Maritime Arbitration Commission (CMAC), and Shanghai International Economic and Trade Arbitration Commission (SHIAC)) have been incorporated into the 'one-stop' Diversified International Commercial Dispute Resolution Mechanism (Liu 2019). The CICCs, combined with the listed mediation and arbitration institutions, collectively seek to provide disputing parties with convenience for international commercial dispute settlement and multiple choices at lower costs. More importantly, the 'one-stop' dispute settlement platform also provides a 'direct train' to the SPC for disputing parties, as it avoids potential local protectionism by removing the barriers of traditional territorial and jurisdictional levels (Liu 2019). On 27 December 2019, the SPC further released 'Judicial Interpretation Applicable to the Foreign Investment Law' and 'Guidelines for Belt and Road Initiative Construction' to advance the building of the rules-based business environment and improve the legal mechanisms for the commercial dispute settlement between BRI countries (China's Supreme People's Court 2019).

3 The implications of China's global governance for the China-EU cooperation

3.1 The legislation competence and the decision-making mechanism of the EU institutions

As per articles 3, 4, and 5 of the Treaty on the Functioning of the European Union (TFEU), the competences of the EU are divided into three categories based on the areas of legislation, i.e. exclusive competencies, shared competencies, and supporting competencies (see Snyder, Chapter 4, for further discussion).

In addition, two decision-making methods are applied in the EU for different legislation areas—community method and the intergovernmental method (Schuette 2019). Around 80% of EU pieces of legislation are adopted through the 'community method' (European Council, Council of the European Union 2019), which refers to the adoption of binding acts through qualified majority voting (QMV), i.e. the required votes representing at least 55% of member-states and 65% of the EU population (Official Journal of the European Union 2012).[vii]

The 'intergovernmental method' requires the unanimity of all member states (with very few exceptions). For example, the legally binding acts on Common Foreign and Security Policy (CFSP) and Common Security and

Defense Policy (CSDP) should be adopted through the 'intergovernmental method' (by consensus) (Schuette 2019).

3.2 The impact of BRI projects on China-EU relations

In light of the five cooperation priorities in the BRI framework,[viii] China-EU cooperation primarily covers the following areas: i) infrastructure building; ii) foreign trade, investment, and financial cooperation; and iii) the exchange of knowledge and understanding of cultural backgrounds (people-to-people bonds) (Wang 2019, pp. 64–77). According to the competencies mentioned in the last section, the EU is conferred with exclusive competencies in adopting legislation on foreign trade, investment, and financial cooperation (e.g. monetary policy for Euro area countries) (Killick et al. 2017, p. 1).[ix] For infrastructure building, such as the infrastructure of 'transport', 'trans-European networks', and 'energy', the EU shares the legislative competencies with its member states. As per articles 170, 171, and 172, the binding Acts on infrastructure building of the EU shall be adopted through 'community method' or QMV (Official Journal of the European Union 2012). However, for people-to-people bonds, such as the exchange and cooperation on 'culture', 'tourism', 'education, vocational training, youth, and sport', the EU can only support, coordinate, or supplement legislation actions of member states in these areas.

For the BRI cooperation between China and the EU, there are two major forms of cooperation. First of all, the cooperation between China and the EU institutions as a whole shall satisfy at least three prerequisites: adherence to international and EU market standards; generally supportive positions of the EU member states; and operational strategies and approaches at a regional level (European Commission 2016, pp. 2–19).[x] Alternatively, the EU would be engaged in BRI projects in the form of bilateral consultation between individual EU Member States and China. According to the 2018 study report from Steer Davies Gleave, BRI cooperation between China and the EU is undertaken primarily through bilateral discussion (Cosentino et al. 2018, p. 16).

As early as 2012 (one year before the launch of BRI), China initiated the '16+1 platform' to strengthen cooperation with Central and Eastern European countries (CEECs), including 11 EU member states and 5 Balkan countries (17+1 after Greece joined in 2019) (Hillman & McCalpin 2019, see also Snyder, Chapter 4). China values the geostrategic position of the 17 CEECs as a bridgehead to the EU market, as well as a crucial transit corridor for the BRI cooperation (Grieger 2018). The '17+1 platform' approach reflects China's vision and innovative approach to strengthen economic cooperation with CEECs and EU countries. The sectoral cooperation under the 17+1 format is conducted on a voluntary basis, and incorporated into the BRI based on the specialization of each CEEC (Grieger 2018). As an observer of the '17+1 platform', the EU promotes a sense of caution for

China's BRI cooperation with the CEECs. In 2016, the EU released a joint communication report concerning the new EU strategy towards China, expressing the EU's concerns that 'China could undermine the unity of the EU' (European Commission 2016). The new EU strategy provides that the China-EU relation must be built on a reciprocal basis (in both economic and political terms) and that China would be expected to comply with the international standards and the EU market rules (European Commission 2016). In particular, this report stresses that each member state should cooperate with the EU institutions to ensure that the regional and bilateral cooperation (e.g. the 16+1 format) with China would not harm the unity and the interests of the EU as a whole (European Commission 2016). The 'reciprocal, rule-based, and no prejudice to the unity' position of the EU on the regional and bilateral cooperation with China is reiterated in the 2018 resolution of the European Parliament on China-EU relations (European Parliament 2018).

3.3 The strategies and approaches to strengthen the BRI cooperation between China and the EU

With more and more European countries involved in BRI projects, concerns were raised that China may have become (intentionally or accidentally) a 'full-fledged' European power (Kavalski 2019). In April 2019, the '16+1' format was further expanded to the '17+1 platform', as Greece was invited to join the China-CEECs cooperation (Kavalski 2019). In the context of China's expanded political and economic impact on the European countries, the EU should also consider its evolving relation with China beyond the debate of 'friend or rivalry' (Kavalski 2019). Both China and the EU should be engaged to improve the pattern of cooperation on the basis of exploring more mutual benefits while addressing their own concerns.

First, in addition to the expansion of bilateral and regional cooperation between China and the EU member states, both China and the EU should consider strengthening their dialogue platform, i.e. the 'EU-China Connectivity Platform', in order to have a better understanding of specific BRI projects, e.g. the connection of specific Trans-European Transport Network and the BRI economic corridors (Cosentino et al. 2018, p. 18; see also Su, Chapter 8). Communication and consultation through dialogues shall increase the clarity and transparency of BRI projects. The dialogues provide the EU with more detailed information on the projects and the opportunities to assess whether the projects comply with the core interest of the EU as a whole (e.g. the compliance with the EU laws and market rules, and the impact on the unity of the EU). The deepened dialogue platform between China and the EU institutions could also play a significant role in addressing misconceptions concerning China's approach and vision of global governance and fostering mutually beneficial relations with the EU.

Secondly, China and the EU need to negotiate and conclude more agreements over specific cooperative projects. As mentioned earlier, the EU has exclusive legislation power in areas such as competition rules, monetary policy, and common commercial policy (article 3 of TFEU). Although China could promote the 17+1 format to strengthen bilateral cooperation with individual EU member states, such cooperative arrangements are restricted to the areas where the EU institutions have shared or supporting competencies. Therefore, China should work with the EU to deepen economic cooperation over the areas where the EU is conferred with exclusive competence. Even in the areas where individual EU member states are conferred with shared and/or supporting competence, the China-EU cooperative agreements could potentially reassure the EU as a whole that specific BRI projects are not detrimental to the EU common interests, the unity of policymaking, and the rule-based internal market order.

Thirdly, both China and the EU should take into account possible different positions of EU member states in the BRI cooperation. Mixed attitudes and positions are demonstrated by various member states in terms of BRI cooperation. Some major EU member states, such as Germany and France, despite having signed bilateral cooperation agreements with China, have become increasingly skeptical about the BRI. Some member states (such as Italy), on the contrary, have been actively engaged in the BRI cooperation with China and supportive of expanding the cooperative projects in infrastructure building, transportation, and culture (Brattberg & Soula 2018). Yet some other EU member states (such as Hungary and Greece) rely heavily upon bilateral cooperation with China to alleviate their economic and debt crises (Brattberg & Soula 2018). Consequently, the BRI cooperation between China and the EU calls for the political and legal recognition from each individual member state to strengthen the linkages and synergies.

Fourthly, given the new EU strategy on its connection with Asia, both China and the EU should consider how to proceed with the formulation of operational strategies and approaches at a regional level. In September 2018, the EU institutions adopted a new comprehensive strategy on connecting Europe and Asia, which sets out the EU's vision on strengthening the EU-Asia cooperation (European Commission 2018). The new strategy reflects the common understanding of all the EU member states on the objectives of building the EU-Asia connectivity: creating cross-border (transport, energy, and digital) networks and human connections; developing strong partnerships with Asian countries in a sustainable and rules-based model; and promoting sustainable finance through various financial tools (European Parliament 2018). Against this backdrop, the China-EU operational strategies and approaches in the BRI cooperation could take into account the following aspects: i) encouraging the innovative expansion of cross-border networks by taking full advantage of BRI resources (Wang & Picciau 2018, p. 30);[xi] ii) promoting cooperation in the areas of urbanization and new energy (Wang & Picciau 2018, p. 30);[xii] and iii) allocating specific and sufficient funds for each project to build capacity and establish networks across the Eurasian region (Brattberg & Soula 2018).[xiii]

Fifthly, both China and the EU should consider their evolving relations with the US in their BRI cooperation. China proposed 'a new type of major-country relationship' between China and the US to strengthen bilateral cooperation and connectivity in 2012, but the positive trend has been eroded in the last few years due to the rising of China and the change of attitude from the US (Sun 2015). With different interpretations of the 'new major-country relationship' concept, China and the US failed to build the ideal bilateral relationship as planned, particularly in the areas of some sensitive issues (Ku 2015, pp. 17–42).[xiv] In response, China has altered its strategy on diplomacy discourse to enhance its international relations with non-major powers (a new type of international relations), while expanding the new model of major-country relationships to other major powers in Europe (Ku 2015, pp. 17–42). The objective of China's foreign policy strategy is to deepen the understanding of other countries on China's vision of global governance and to build mutual trust in furthering economic cooperation. China's position is confirmed in a dialogue between the US and China in the 2016 China Development Forum, in which former State Councilor Dai Bingguo had a dialogue with former US Secretary of State Henry Kissinger to stress China's principles of 'peaceful development and non-alignment' (Ministry of Foreign Affairs of the People's Republic of China (FMPRC) 2016). China also recognizes the impact of US-China relations on 'the BRI development', 'the stability and prosperity of the Asia-Pacific region', and 'the strengthening and improving international order' (Ministry of Foreign Affairs of the People's Republic of China (FMPRC) 2016).

To a certain extent, the EU shares a similar skepticism with the US on China's expanding impact on global politics and economies. The EU and the US have been working together to address trade practice concerns over China since 2017 (USTR 2017). However, the EU and the US have some significant divergence in the path of WTO reforms and safeguarding the multilateral trade system (Schneider-Petsinger 2019). As the China-US relation is severely affected by the escalating trade war, the EU should be extremely cautious (and unlikely in the near future) in making a one-sided general choice between the US and China (González & Véron 2019). Nevertheless, the EU shares a similar interest with China in maintaining the multilateral trade system and resisting the protectionism and unilateralism promoted by the US (González & Véron 2019). In this regard, since the topic of a new type of major-country relationship cannot be avoided, both China and the EU should work closely to find shared interests in terms of managing their respective relations with the US in the BRI cooperation.

Last but not least, the EU and China should further negotiate an agreement for BRI dispute settlement. All the existing international dispute settlement mechanisms have their own limitations and cannot fully fit in the dispute settlement for BRI countries. The WTO is now facing a severe

Appellate Body crisis and cannot efficiently address the international trade disputes among BRI countries. The International Centre for Settlement of Investment Disputes (ICSID) mechanism does not apply to all the BRI countries. Furthermore, this mechanism is not without criticism. For example, criticisms were raised that the ICSID rulings are not coordinated and conflict, and that its arbitration awards are difficult to enforce (Ren 2019, p. 448). The Asian Infrastructure Investment Bank (AIIB) could be utilized as a platform for BRI dispute settlement (Hu & Huang 2018, pp. 815–837), but not all EU member states are members of the AIIB (Stanzel 2017).[xv] However, in view of the development of the Singapore Mediation Convention in 2019, it is noted that AIIB officials have discussed possibly utilizing mediation for dispute settlement. On 31 March 2019, the AIIB established the Project-affected People's Mechanism (PPM). The dispute resolution system of the PPM includes the creation of a mediation mechanism or other mutually acceptable dispute resolution methods between the concerned parties (Asian Infrastructure Investment Bank 2019, p. 15). Some multinational companies may resort to international commercial arbitration since 92% of the BRI countries are members of the 1958 New York Convention on the Recognition and Enforcement of Foreign Arbitral Awards (Eurobiz 2019). However, it is also noted that China, while a member of the New York Convention, has not recognized and enforced all foreign awards, with the recognition and enforcement rate at approximately 70% (Sausmikat & Sprick 2019, p. 16).

Domestically, China established the CICC in 2018 to provide a one-stop diversified dispute settlement platform for the BRI dispute settlement. The CICC jurisdiction is nevertheless constrained by the existing national legislation (Erie 2018). It remains to be seen whether all BRI-related cases are under the jurisdiction of the CICC, and whether the CICC has sufficient discretion to develop the jurisprudence through its judicial decisions (Erie 2018). Moreover, it is uncertain whether the parties shall specify the CICC exclusive jurisdiction in their contracts (Erie 2018), and whether the parties are willing to do so in practice.

In view of the limitations of all the existing mechanisms, China and the EU should consider reaching a bilateral agreement on judicial cooperation, information sharing, and recognition and enforcement of foreign awards. In the short term, the bilateral agreement could address the uncertainties of the BRI dispute settlement between the disputing parties in China and the EU. In the long run, the CICC could be improved and used more widely through its future reforms by making reference to the experience of the bilateral dispute settlement mechanism and international commercial courts in other jurisdictions.

4 Conclusion

To sum up, China upholds a peaceful, reciprocal, and opening-up position to develop its bilateral, multilateral, and regional economic cooperation with its BRI partners. China proactively participates in global governance to strengthen, instead of replacing, the existing cooperative platforms. China's modalities of global governance include an incremental approach to increase its political and economic impacts on the international community, a balanced 'top-down' and 'bottom-up' approach, to encourage voluntary BRI cooperation and the promotion of convergence of different legal systems.

Both the two forms of BRI cooperation between China and the EU, i.e. bilateral (China and individual EU member states) and regional (China and the EU as a whole) cooperation, should be conducted on a reciprocal and rules-based basis. Such cooperation shall have no prejudice to the unity of EU policymaking, while taking into account the different positions of EU member states. In addition, China and the EU should engage to improve the existing pattern of BRI cooperation through the following measures: i) deepening communication and consultation through the 'EU-China Connectivity Platform'; ii) negotiating on specific cooperative projects; iii) formulating operational strategies and approaches at a regional level; iv) working closely to find shared interests in terms of managing their respective relations with the US; and v) concluding a bilateral agreement for BRI dispute settlement.

Notes

i The 17 EU member states are Cyprus, Austria, Greece, Poland, Czechia, Bulgaria, Slovakia, Croatia, Estonia, Lithuania, Slovenia, Hungary, Romania, Latvia, Portugal, Italy, and Luxembourg.

ii The six BRI economic corridors consist of i) New Eurasia Land Bridge (involving rail to Europe); ii) China, Mongolia, Russia Economic Corridor; iii) China, Central Asia, West Asia Economic Corridor; iv) China Indochina Peninsula Economic Corridor; v) China, Pakistan Economic Corridor; and vi) China, Bangladesh, India, Myanmar Economic Corridor.

iii The maritime-related cooperation priorities consist of 'green development', 'ocean-based prosperity', 'maritime security', 'innovative growth', and 'collaborative governance'.

iv The cooperation areas between China and Italy include infrastructure, investment, trade, finance, transportation, logistics, and cooperation with third countries (the area of telecommunications was left out).

v Top-down normalization approach is applied in the global governance of climate change, anti-terrorism, and epidemics control. However, the approach has its limitations at the practical level: e.g. the implementation difficulties without an international government, and the rule-making lags behind the changes and weakened by the global power diffusion.

vi The main funding source comes from the China development banks, the Silk Road Fund, and the state-owned commercial banks. Although the Asia Infrastructure Investment Bank (AIIB) is not a major funding source of the BRI projects, all of the AIIB infrastructure projects are located in the BRI countries.

vii The 'double majority rule' is for the decision-making of adopting EU legislation. For non-legislation matters, the simple majority rule is applied (14 out of 27 member states). In addition, a 'reinforced qualified majority' (representing at least 72% council members and 65%t EU population) is applied when the legislative proposal is not raised by the European Commission or the High Representative of the Union for Foreign and Security Police.

viii The five cooperation priorities consist of policy coordination, facilities connectivity, unimpeded trade, financial integration, and people-to-people bond.

ix However, it is noted that the EU does not have the exclusive competence in two significant areas, i.e. the "non-direct foreign investment" and "the ISDS regime".

x For example, according to the 2016 Joint Communication to the European Parliament and the Council, the EU's engagement with China should be reciprocal, practical, pragmatic, and adhere to the rules of the EU markets and international standards. The EU must project a strong, clear, and unified voice in its approach to China. Also, it is noted in the Joint Communication that the Chinese involvement in the EU's Eastern and Southern neighbourhoods helps reinforce rules-based governance and regional security, while the EU should continue to contribute actively to regional security in the Asia-Pacific and further develop its partnerships in the region.

xi For example, the utilization of existing BRI trade platforms and the building of new ones, and developing exclusive BRI tourism products, which further generate opportunities for jobs creation, infrastructure building, and people-to-people bonds between China and the EU.

xii China could learn from the EU on the advanced experience and innovative technologies in its urban development and the application of sustainable new energy.

xiii For the development of EU-Asia connectivity projects, the uncertainty remains as to how the EU will allocate its funding for the next multiannual budget (2021 to 2027).

xiv For example, the relationship between China and the US has faced many obstacles, and major differences continue to exist on some sensitive issues such as human rights, cybersecurity, and maritime disputes in the South China Sea.

xv 17 out of 27 EU member states have joined the AIIB.

Bibliography

China Issues Judicial Interpretation to Better Protect Foreign Investors' Interests. China's Supreme People's Court, 30 December 2019. <http://english.court.gov.cn/2019-12/30/content_37530686.htm> accessed 10 January 2020.

Communication from the European Union, China, Canada, India, Norway, New Zealand, Switzerland, Australia, Republic of Korea, Iceland, Singapore, Mexico, Costa Rica, and Montenegro to the General CouncilWorld Trade Organization, WT/GC/W/752/Rev.2, 11 December 2018, <https://docs.wto.org/dol2fe/Pages/SS/directdoc.aspx?filename=q:/WT/GC/W752R2.pdf&Open=True>, accessed 18 May 2021.

Consolidated Version of the Treaty on the Functioning of the European Union. Official Journal of the European Union, 26 October 2012. <https://eur-lex.europa.eu/LexUriServ/LexUriServ.do?uri=CELEX:12012E/TXT:EN:PDF> accessed 8 December 2019.

Enhancing Regional Economic Cooperation and Integration in Asia and the Pacific. United Nations ESCAP, ST/ESCAP/2781, 2017. <https://www.unescap.org/sites/default/files/Asia-Pacific%20RECI%20Report.pdf> accessed 16 December 2019.

Erie, Matthew S. The China International Commercial Court: Prospects for Dispute Resolution for the "Belt and Road Initiative". (2018) American Society of International Law, 22, 11, 31 August. <https://www.asil.org/insights/volume/22/

issue/11/china-international-commercial-court-prospects-dispute-resolution-belt> accessed 16 July 2020.

EU Steps Up Its Strategy for Connecting Europe and Asia. European Commission, 19 September 2018. <https://ec.europa.eu/commission/presscorner/detail/en/IP_18_5803> accessed 14 January 2020.

Full text of the Vision for Maritime Cooperation under the Belt and Road Initiative. State Council, 20 June 2017. <http://english.www.gov.cn/archive/publications/2017/06/20/content_281475691873460.htm> accessed 13 January 2020.

Hu, Jiaxiang, and Jie Huang. Dispute Resolution Mechanisms and Organizations in the Implementation of 'One Belt, One Road' Initiative: Whence and Whither. (2018) Journal of World Trade, 52, 5.

Joint Communication to the European Parliament and the Council - Elements for a New EU Strategy on China. European Commission, High Representative of the Union for Foreign Affairs and Security Policy, Brussels, 2016, <https://eeas.europa.eu/archives/docs/china/docs/joint_communication_to_the_european_parliament_and_the_council_-_elements_for_a_new_eu_strategy_on_china.pdf>, accessed 18 May 2021.

Joint Statement by the United States, European Union and Japan at MC11. USTR, 12 December 2017. <https://ustr.gov/about-us/policy-offices/press-office/press-releases/2017/december/joint-statement-united-states> accessed 14 January 2020.

Ku, Minseon. The Motives and Effects of China's "New Model of Major Country Relations" in China-U.S. Relations. (2015) Journal of International Relations and Foreign Policy, 3, 1, June.

On Building a New Model of Major-Country Relations Between China and the United States - A Dialogue Between Dai Bingguo and Former US Secretary of State Henry Kissinger on How to Avoid the "Thucydides Trap". Ministry of Foreign Affairs of the People's Republic of China (FMPRC), 20 March 2016. <https://www.fmprc.gov.cn/mfa_eng/zxxx_662805/t1350752.shtml> accessed 14 January 2020.

Ren, Hu. Treaties on the International Trade Dispute Settlement and the China "Belt and Road" Initiative. (2019) Beijing Law Review, 10.

Rules of Procedure of the Project-Affected People's Mechanism Issued by the Managing Director, Complaints-resolution, Evaluation and Integrity Unit (CEIU). Asian Infrastructure Investment Bank (AIIB), 13 June 2019. <https://www.aiib.org/en/policies-strategies/_download/project-affected/PPM-RofP.pdf> accessed 27 July 2020.

Shi, Jingxia. 2018 "The Belt and Road Initiative and International Law an International Public Goods Perspective." In Zhao Yun (ed.), International Governance and the Rule of Law in China under the Belt and Road Initiative. Cambridge: Cambridge University Press.

Supervision Law of the People's Republic of China – Chapter VI, International Cooperation Against Corruption, Order of the President (No. 3). Standing Committee of the Thirteenth National People's Congress of the People's Republic of China, 20 March 2018. <https://www.legal-tools.org/doc/ef4c4d/pdf/> accessed 10 January 2020.

Text Adopted by Parliament, Single Reading. European Parliament, 2017/2274(INI), 09 December 2018. <https://oeil.secure.europarl.europa.eu/oeil/popups/summary.do?id=1552113&t=d&l=en > accessed 12January2020.

The List of Countries That Signed Cooperation Documents with China on Belt and Road Initiative. Belt and Road Portal, October 2019. <https://www.yidaiyilu.gov.cn/info/iList.jsp?tm_id=126&cat_id=10122&info_id=77298> accessed 20December2019.

Tobin, Liza. Xi's Vision for Transforming Global Governance: A Strategic Challenge for Washington and Its Allies. (2018) The Strategist, 2, 1, November.

Vision and Actions on Jointly Building Silk Road Economic Belt and 21st-Century Maritime Silk Road. Issued by National Development and Reform Commission, Ministry of Foreign Affairs and Ministry of Commerce of the People's Republic of China, with State Council Authorization. Chinese Embassy in UK (CEUK), 28 March 2015. <http://www.chinese-embassy.org.uk/eng/zywl/t1251719.htm> accessed 13 January 2020.

Voting System - Qualified Majority. European Council, Council of the European Union, 03 September 2019. <https://www.consilium.europa.eu/en/council-eu/voting-system/qualified-majority/> accessed 12 December 2019.

Wang, Weidong, and Simona Picciau. How to Strengthen EU-China Cooperation Based on 'the Belt and Road'? Revista de Relaciones Internacionales. (2018) Estrategia y Seguridad, 13, 1.

Wang, Yuzhu, and Shicheng Li. 2019 "The Belt and Road Initiative Framework." In Cai Fang and Peter Nolan (eds.), Routledge Handbook of the Belt and Road. Routledge, London.

Wang, Zhenling. EU Institutions' Perceptions towards BRI and China's Coping Measures: Multilevel Alignment Based on EU Perceptions and Competences. (2019) Pacific Journal, 4. "王振玲. 欧盟机构对"一带一路"倡议的认知以及中国的应对策略——认知与权限类别基础上的多重对接. 太平洋学报, 2019年04期."

Zhang, Chun. The Belt and Road Initiative and Global Governance in Transition. (2017) China Quarterly of International Strategic Studies, 3, 2.

Zhang, Denghua. The Concept of 'Community of Common Destiny' in China's Diplomacy: Meaning, Motives and Implications. (2018) Asia & the Pacific Policy Studies, 5, 2, 1 March.

Stiftung, Bertelsmann. Revitalizing Multilateral Governance at the World Trade Organization: Report of the High-Level Board of Experts on the Future of Global Trade GovernanceGlobal Economic Dynamics (GED), 2018, <https://cadmus.eui.eu/bitstream/handle/1814/60580/MT_Report_Revitalizing_Multilateral_Governance_at_the_WTO.pdf?sequence=1&isAllowed=y>, accessed 18 May 2021.

Brattberg, Erik, and Etienne Soula. Europe's Emerging Approach to China's Belt and Road Initiative. Carnegie Endowment for International Peace. 19 October 2018. <https://carnegieendowment.org/2018/10/19/europe-s-emerging-approach-to-china-s-belt-and-road-initiative-pub-77536> accessed 12 December 2019.

BRI: Dispute Resolution and Jurisdictional Issues. Eurobiz, 3 January 2019. <https://www.eurobiz.com.cn/bri-dispute-resolution-and-jurisdictional-issues/> accessed 14 January 2020.

China's Belt & Road for Better Global Governance & Growth. Belt & Road News, 1 January2020. <https://www.beltandroad.news/2020/01/01/chinas-belt-road-for-better-global-governance-growth/> accessed 5 January 2020.

China's Belt and Road Initiative in The Global Trade, Investment and Finance Landscape. OECD Business and Finance Outlook, 2018. <https://www.oecd.org/finance/Chinas-Belt-and-Road-Initiative-in-the-global-trade-investment-and-finance-landscape.pdf> accessed 16 December 2019.

Cosentino, Bianca et al. (Steer Davies Gleave). Research for TRAN Committee: The New Silk Route – Opportunities and Challenges for EU transport, European Parliament, Policy Department for Structural and Cohesion Policies, Brussels, 2018. <https://www.europarl.europa.eu/RegData/etudes/STUD/2018/585907/IPOL_STU(2018)585907_EN.pdf> accessed 12 December 2019.

González, Anabel, and Nicolas Véron. EU Trade Policy Amid the China-Us Clash: Caught in the Cross-Fire? Bruegel, Working Paper, Issue 7, 16 September 2019. <https://www.bruegel.org/2019/09/eu-trade-policy-amid-the-china-us-clash-caught-in-the-crossfire/> accessed 12 January 2020.

Grieger, Gisela. China, the 16+1 Format and the EU. European Parliamentary Research Service, September 2018. <https://www.europarl.europa.eu/RegData/etudes/BRIE/2018/625173/EPRS_BRI(2018)625173_EN.pdf> accessed 12January2020.

Hillman, Jonathan E., and Maesea McCalpin. Will China's '16+1' Format Divide Europe? Centre for Strategic and International Study, 11 April 2019. <https://www.csis.org/analysis/will-chinas-161-format-divide-europe> accessed 12 January 2020.

Kavalski, Emilian. China's "16+1" Is Dead? Long Live the "17+1." The Diplomat, 29 March 2019. <https://thediplomat.com/2019/03/chinas-161-is-dead-long-live-the-171/> accessed 12 January 2020.

Killick, James et al. EU Court Confirms EU Competence on Wide Range of Trade Areas in Opinion on EU-Singapore FTA. White & Case, 17 May 2017. <https://www.whitecase.com/publications/alert/eu-court-confirms-eu-competence-wide-range-trade-areas-opinion-eu-singapore-fta> accessed 15 July 2020.

Liu, Tingmei. The China International Commercial Court (CICC) in 2018. China International Commercial Court, 22 July 2019. <http://cicc.court.gov.cn/html/1/219/208/209/1316.html> accessed 10 January 2020.

Miner, Louise, and Cristina Abellan-Matamoros. China's Belt and Road Plan: Why Did Italy Sign It and Why Is Brussels Worried? Euronews, 09 April 2019. <https://www.euronews.com/2019/03/24/china-and-italy-sign-silk-road-project> accessed 5 January 2020.

New Courts for the Belt and Road Initiative. OBOReurope, 2 June 2018. <https://www.oboreurope.com/en/bri-courts/> accessed 10 January 2020.

Sausmikat, Nora, and Daniel Sprick. China's International Commercial Courts for the 'Belt & Road': A Gateway for Beijing's Bigger Role in Global Rules Setting. The Greens/EFA Group of the European Parliament, July 2019. <https://urgewald.org/sites/default/files/Study%20CICCs%20final.pdf> accessed 10 January 2020.

Schneider-Petsinger, Marianne. The Path Forward on WTO Reform. Chatham House, 7 May 2019. <https://www.chathamhouse.org/expert/comment/path-forward-wto-reform> accessed 14 January 2020.

Schuette, Leonard. Should the EU Make Foreign Policy Decisions by Majority Voting? Centre for European Reform, Policy Brief, 15 May 2019. <https://www.cer.eu/publications/archive/policy-brief/2019/should-eu-make-foreign-policy-decisions-majority-voting#section-4> accessed 12 December 2019.

Stanzel, Angela. A German View of the Asian Infrastructure Investment Bank. European Council on Foreign Relations, 21 April 2017. <https://www.ecfr.eu/article/commentary_a_german_view_of_the_aiib_7275> accessed 12 December 2019.

Sun, Chenghao. A New Type of Major-Country Relationship: Challenges and Opportunities. China-US Focus, 09 September 2015. <https://www.chinausfocus.

com/foreign-policy/a-new-type-of-major-country-relationship-challenges-and-opportunities> accessed 14 January 2020.

Three lessons China Has Learned About Global Governance. Belt & Road News, 27 September 2019. <https://www.beltandroad.news/2019/09/27/three-lessons-china-has-learned-about-global-governance/> accessed 12 December 2019.

Wiendieck, Sebastian, and Peter Stark. China Has Established International Commercial Court for Commercial Disputes Under BRI. Rödl & Partner in China, 25 September 2018. <https://www.roedl.com/insights/china-international-commercial-court-commercial-disputes-bri> accessed 4 December 2019.

Wu, Shaun Z. et al. How MNCs Should Navigate the Risks. In Asian Legal Business - Guide to The Belt and Road Initiative 2019. Thomson Reuters, 2019. <https://www.legalbusinessonline.com/sites/default/files/e-magazines/ALB-BRI-2019/528F1B3DAB37AC56593D152596C906EE/Guide%20To%20The%20BRI%202019.pdf> accessed 5 January 2020.

Zeneli, Valbona. Italy Signs on to Belt and Road Initiative: EU-China Relations at Crossroads? 03 April 2019. <https://thediplomat.com/2019/04/italy-signs-on-to-belt-and-road-initiative-eu-china-relations-at-crossroads/> accessed 5 January 2020.

3 The EU-China diplomacy and the Belt and Road Initiative

Jing Men

Introduction

The EU-China relationship has undergone noticeable changes in recent years. Since Xi Jinping became General Party Secretary of the Chinese Communist Party in November 2012 and President of China in March 2013, Chinese foreign policy has been further adjusted from "not taking the lead" to becoming more active and even more assertive. Based on its economic success during the years of reform, China has become increasingly confident in its development model and eager to promote international cooperation with Chinese characteristics. Against this background, the Belt and Road Initiative was put forward as a "proactive" plan for China (Men 2015, p. 12) to realise the "Chinese dream" and to achieve its centennial goals. The idea of the Silk Road Economic Belt (One Belt) and the Maritime Silk Road (One Road) was first introduced by Chinese President Xi Jinping during his visits to Kazakhstan and Indonesia in late 2013. The official term of the Belt and Road Initiative (BRI) was adopted when the Chinese government published the document "Action plan on the Belt and Road Initiative" in March 2015.

The EU used to perceive China's rise as a good opportunity for mutual benefit: the EU published in 1995, 1998 and 2003 respectively its China policy papers, which positively addressed China's reform achievements and actively pushed forward the strategic partnership. Yet, as its trade deficit with China steadily grew in the early 21st century, the EU gradually lost its patience and referred to China as "the single most important challenge for EU trade policy" in its China policy paper published in 2006 (European Commission 2006, p. 3). In the decade thereafter, the EU was kept busy with the financial crisis, the economic crisis and the refugee crisis as well as internal institutional reform (with the ratification of the Lisbon Treaty), with the result that the China policy paper was only updated in 2016. There were, however, other important developments in EU-China relations during this period, such as the establishment of the High-Level Strategic Dialogue (2010) and the EU-China Strategic Agenda for Cooperation (2013).

When China promoted the BRI to the world in early 2015, the Juncker Commission had just taken office and was looking for funding for the Investment Plan for Europe. At the EU-China summit held in June that year, the two sides were pleased to find common ground in cooperation and reached several agreements in developing synergies between the Juncker Plan and the BRI. Yet, the synergies were not explored very successfully in the following years, and the BRI somehow is now perceived with greater doubts and suspicion in the EU. This is partially due to the EU's increasingly negative perception of its relationship with China. In 2015, the Chinese government agreed to invest to the Juncker Plan but refused to sign an agreement in 2016 at the EU-China summit of that year, which made the EU rather disappointed. The EU and China held many rounds of discussion on the selection of connectivity projects in both the EU and China, but the progress was very slow. EU-China summits were held annually, but joint statements were only issued in 2015, 2018 and 2019. The BRI appears in all three joint statements, but the EU is less enthusiastic than before. In 2017 and 2019, when China organised the first and the second Belt and Road Forums respectively, the EU sent its representative to speak at them and highlighted its own principles of cooperation, which are different from the Chinese BRI design. Furthermore, in the years 2016 and 2017, when the EU and China failed to reach a joint statement at the summit, the European Council President Donald Tusk made a speech after each meeting in which the BRI was not mentioned at all. In order to counter China's growing influence and its BRI promotion in Europe, one of the countermeasures that the EU has taken is to develop its own strategy of Eurasian connectivity. All the policies and actions taken by the EU in recent years demonstrate that China's proactive strategy of the BRI is not supported by the EU. As a consequence, the EU is getting more defensive and more protective of its own model of development and its market. In this paper, the author will first review the EU's changing attitude toward the BRI and examine how the EU gradually shaped its perception of the BRI. The author will then analyse why such changes occurred and finally conclude with some tentative remarks on how the EU-China relationship might further evolve.

The declarations of the EU–China Summit (2015, 2018, 2019) and the EU's position on the BRI

As mentioned earlier, China and the EU started to talk about establishing synergies between the Juncker Plan and the Belt and Road Initiative in 2015 at the summit, and both sides were enthusiastic about the prospect for cooperation. In the six-page-long document, the joint statement after the summit mentioned the BRI three times. It confirmed that in order to develop synergies and explore business and investment opportunities for mutually beneficial cooperation, the two sides would establish a "China-EU co-investment vehicle", and a "new Connectivity Platform" to improve their infrastructure links (see Su, Chapter 8). When addressing the connectivity possibilities, the two sides mentioned very clearly the cooperation opportunities "between the Trans-European Networks and the Belt and Road Initiative" and the "sustainable and inter-operable cross-border infrastructure networks in countries and regions between the EU and China" (Council of the European Union 2015, p. 1).

The EU and China failed to issue a joint statement after the summit in 2016 and in 2017. When the summit joint statement was made in 2018, the atmosphere for cooperation had further deteriorated and the European leaders believed that China's BRI was promoting a different set of rules and practices. In the joint statement, while both sides repeated that they would continue to forge synergies and develop a connectivity platform, the EU stressed that "cooperation should abide by the shared principles of market rules, transparency, open procurement and a level playing field for all investors, and comply with established international norms and standards, respective international obligations, as well as the law of the countries benefitting from the projects, while taking into account their policies and individual situations" (Council of the European Union 2018, p. 3). This paragraph demonstrates that the EU tried to push its own principles and norms in cooperation with China and suggests that the joint statement is a compromise between the Chinese and the European leadership.

Before the EU and China had their 21st summit meeting in April 2019, the EU published its strategy to connect Europe and Asia in September 2018 (European Commission 2018) (see Zhao and Chen, Chapter 2). This Eurasian connectivity strategy was developed to compete with China's BRI, which pushes connection westward from East Asia all the way to Europe. The release of the strategy showed that the EU intends to be a more influential geopolitical player on the Eurasian continent in terms of principles and standards. As a matter of fact, the EU has been engaged in huge infrastructure projects across the Eurasian continent since as early as the 1990s, and thus is rich in experience in regional/transnational cooperation (Men 2020). Against this background, in the 2019 EU-China summit joint statement, apart from repeating what was mentioned in the two documents mentioned previously, the EU stressed the synergies between its strategy on connecting Europe and Asia as well as the EU Trans-European Transport Networks and China's BRI, and the joint study on sustainable railway-based corridors between Europe and China (Council of the European Union 2019, p. 6).

Thus, a review of the three summit joint statements demonstrates a clear tendency whereby the EU changed from an active partner interested in benefiting from China's BRI to a player trying to distance itself from China's initiative and in the meantime vigorously developing its Eurasian connectivity strategy backed by its distinctive norms and values. Up until now, the EU has not expressed openly its overall objections to China's BRI, but has criticised on many occasions that the BRI is not in line with many principles that the EU embraces.

Perception shaping of the BRI in the EU

Different EU institutions, including the European Parliament, the European External Action Service, as well as think tanks of the member states have published a number of resolutions, speeches and reports, which contributed to the EU's perception shaping on China's BRI.

As mentioned earlier, when China promoted the BRI to the EU in early 2015 and reached a consensus with Brussels that the synergy between the BRI and the Juncker Plan would be developed, the European institutions were interested in such cooperation. Such a positive attitude was also reflected in the European Parliament resolution published at the end of 2015. The resolution:

> highlights the vigorous growth of the Chinese economy in the last twenty years and underlines that EU Member States should take greater advantage of the opportunities offered by this economic development; notes the Chinese interest in strategic infrastructure investments in Europe, and underlines the need to cooperate with China and other countries in the region in this respect on projects such as China's Belt and Road Initiative and the EU's Juncker Investment Plan, including rail links, seaports and airports;... (European Parliament 2015, p. 8).

The Europeans were interested in the BRI in 2015 because of the opportunities for attracting Chinese investment to Europe, but neither the EU nor its member states developed "a comprehensive strategic approach in responding to the impact of OBOR on regional dynamics and the way in which European engagement should be developed" (van der Putten et al. 2016, p. 10). This is partially due to the fact that the BRI is unclearly defined. Inside the EU, as the report made by the European Think-tank Network on China (ETNC) in 2016 pointed out, "there is hardly a European country where the Chinese initiative has not stirred debate in policy-making circles about China's motivations, the feasibility and challenges of OBOR, as well as potential opportunities for EU member states and business" (van der Putten et al. 2016, p. 9). Thus, most of the member states adopted a wait-and-see attitude.

In 2017, when China held its first BRI forum, the EU was invited to send its representative to Beijing. The short speech by Mr Katainen, then European Commission Vice President, at the forum, demonstrated that the EU had already developed a distinct understanding and an independent approach to the BRI. Mr Katainen stressed the importance of international rules, multilateral cooperation and sustainable development, and highlighted nine principles that should be followed in the connectivity projects. Noticeably in his speech, Mr Katainen not only addressed cooperation with China, but intentionally included other partners, particularly other Asian countries in such schemes of connection (European External Action Service 2017).

In 2018, the European Parliament formed a very critical position on the BRI when it published another resolution on China. The resolution pointed out six challenges brought by the BRI: a bilateral rather than a multilateral approach to BRI governance; very little employment of local labour; extremely limited involvement from host-country and third-country contractors; construction materials and equipment imported from China; lack of transparency on tender; and the potential use of Chinese standards instead of international standards (European Parliament 2018, p. 10). The change of the European Parliament's attitude on the BRI was explained in the Briefing published in early 2019, by one of its analysts:

> With the BRI, China seeks to build geopolitical influence and shape third markets in line with China's interests and terms, which reveals a China-centric rather than multilateral approach to global governance as embraced by the EU. Moreover, the current Chinese leadership's bold rhetoric suggests that China considers its authoritarian and algorithmic governance model an attractive alternative to the Western liberal governance model and encourages its emulation by other countries (Grieger 2019).

As a matter of fact, the 2018 European Parliament resolution was published after the EU ambassadors in Beijing jointly made a report in April that year which warned that China's BRI "runs counter to the EU agenda for liberalizing trade and pushes the balance of power in favor of subsidized Chinese companies" (quoted in Heide et al. 2018). The report served as part of the preparations not only for the EU-China summit scheduled in July, but also for the EU to draft its own Eurasian strategy which was published in September. Three years after China's BRI was introduced to the EU, it was getting clear to Brussels that the development model promoted by the BRI is in contradiction to the European model and therefore needs to be dealt with cautiously.

In spring 2019, when China held its second BRI forum, Mr Maroš Šefčovič, as a European Commission Vice President, went to Beijing and delivered a speech which could be regarded as an extension of the speech by Mr Katainen two years prior and which confirmed the principles of multilateralism, rule-based international system and sustainability, and emphasized Europe's rich experience in sustainable connectivity (Šefčovič 2019). Mr Šefčovič made this speech two weeks after the EU-China summit was held in Brussels. To a certain degree, the Forum offered another platform for the EU to promote its own Eurasian connectivity strategy and to exert its influence on rule-making in EU-China cooperation. While trying to provide Eurasian connectivity with a European brand, the EU declined to endorse the BRI.

Although some of the EU member states signed the BRI-related Memorandum of Understanding (MoU) with China, the EU as a bloc never did so (Valero 2019). When Italy, a G7 country, planned to sign such an MoU with China, the European Commission got alarmed. Mr Katainen was afraid that the EU's position would be weakened if the member states did not deal with China with unity. In one of his speeches, he stressed again that, "All the member states, and also Belt and Road operators, must comply with our regulations and rules, which we have when it comes to competition and transparency" (quoted in von der Burchard 2019).

Why is the BRI perceived negatively by the EU?

As mentioned earlier, when the BRI was promoted by the Chinese government to the EU in 2015, Brussels was rather interested in cooperation with Beijing in order to benefit from this initiative. Fourteen EU member states signed a bilateral MoU with Beijing for cooperation in the framework of BRI. However, as time went on, the EU became increasingly suspicious of the BRI and more defensive in dealing with China. The changing attitude may have been due to the following reasons.

First of all, with regards to the BRI itself, European observers found out that the BRI implements a different set of rules and a different development model; with Chinese investment in a large number of infrastructure projects worldwide, the BRI tries to promote China's soft power with strategic purposes (García-Herrero and Xu 2019). China is believed to be "an exporter of influence" and increasingly presents itself as an alternative to the Western democratic model (Le Corre 2018, p. 2). Furthermore, although the Chinese government declares that the BRI is aimed at multilateral cooperation, the multilateral image fades when one takes a close look at the BRI projects, as China always maintains control over their finance and implementation (Klose et al. 2017, p. 2). The other principles which are embraced by the EU, including high transparency and sustainability standards, are put in question as well. In several projects, China was accused of conducting "debt-trap diplomacy" through stringent loan-repayment conditions. In particular, the highway project in Montenegro sent the country's debt soaring from 63% of gross domestic product in 2012 to almost 80%, which caused serious concern in the EU (Hopkins and Kynge 2019). The report produced by the EU Chamber of Commerce in China in early 2020 revealed European disappointment that "European businesses have continuously sought ways to contribute in order to introduce greater competition … However, they have come up against a variety of barriers to participation, including, at the most basic level, being unable to access information on project tenders" (EU Chamber of Commerce in China 2020, p. 2).

Secondly, the Chinese government in 2015 announced *Made in China 2025* (MIC2025), which is a strategic plan to strengthen China's technological innovation and to upgrade its industrial and manufacturing capability. The EU Chamber of Commerce expressed its concern in a report published in 2017 that the role of the Chinese government disturbs market operation and European businesses face serious pressure in the Chinese market because the Chinese government makes policies in favour of its domestic companies. Although in the short- and medium-term, European businesses in partnerships with Chinese companies may get attractive opportunities in China, in the long term, the Chinese market would shrink for European businesses where Chinese companies are able to close the technology gap (EU Chamber of Commerce in China 2017). The European Commission echoed such conclusions and pointed out that the Chinese government made this strategy in order to achieve industrial modernisation, which would lead to a further deterioration of the competitive position of European companies in China and also increasingly complained that EU investments would suffer from reciprocity concerns, that China is an uneven playing field for European companies (Nadir et al. 2019, p. 9).

Thirdly, directly related to the strategic objectives of the BRI and the MIC2025, the Chinese government provided fiscal and policy support to encourage its enterprises to invest in Europe in order to acquire cutting-edge technology. The joint report made by MERICS and Rhodium Group in 2015 found out that the first wave of Chinese capital deployed for this purpose had already arrived in Europe (Hanemann and Huotari 2015, p. 5). Then in a report in 2016, the same group of authors stated that Europe had emerged as a main destination for Chinese foreign direct investment. According to this report, Chinese companies invested EUR 20 billion in the EU in 2015, a 44% increase compared to the previous year's EUR 14 billion (Hanemann and Huotari 2016, p. 3). The authors continued to follow the growth of Chinese foreign direct investment (FDI) in the EU and reported in 2017 that such investment totalled more than EUR 35 billion in 2016, an increase of 77% from 2015. Yet, the investment from the EU to China continued to decrease for the fourth consecutive year to only EUR 8 billion in 2016, less than one third of the combined value of all Chinese investments in Europe. One noticeable feature of Chinese investment is that it is particularly interested in high technology and strategic assets. Together with the growing gap in two-way investment, the EU complained about a lack of reciprocity between the EU and China and embarked on a debate about potential risks from Chinese investment (Hanemann and Huotari 2017, pp. 4–5).

As a countermeasure against Chinese investment in order to defend its strategic interests, the European Commission took the initiative to propose a framework for screening foreign direct investment in September 2017 (entered into force in April 2019). In the State of the Union speech in 2017, Mr Juncker explained why it was necessary to introduce the new regulation: "[i]f a foreign, state-owned company wants to purchase a European harbour, part of our energy infrastructure or a defence technology firm, this should only happen in transparency, with scrutiny and debate. It is a political responsibility to know what is going on in our own backyard so that we can protect our collective security if needed" (Juncker 2017). Although the

European Commission did not admit that the newly introduced screening mechanism was targeted at China, the European Parliament indeed addressed the debate on the creation of an EU-wide FDI screening mechanism in a Briefing published in May 2017 and held that the debate was triggered by China's record FDI flows to the European market and unfair competition from China (Grieger 2017).

EU–China diplomacy

The changes in the EU's perception and discourse on China, as examined above, show that EU–China diplomacy is increasingly troubled. Due to the fact that the EU is increasingly suspicious of China's rise and political influence on its member states, the European Commission openly addressed China as "a systemic rival" for the first time in its most recently published China policy paper in March 2019. For the EU, China is simultaneously a partner, competitor and rival (see Bastian, Chapter 6). This narrative reveals the mounting complexity of EU–China relationship: "There is a growing appreciation in Europe that the balance of challenges and opportunities presented by China has shifted" (European Commission 2019, p. 1). In the past, while the EU kept a critical eye on China's human rights record and the lack of a level playing field in trade and economic relationship, the EU was hopeful to promote political transformation in Chinese society based on its own model. Yet, China's rapid rise in the world with unprecedented scale and speed, coupled with an increasingly assertive foreign and economic policy pushed the EU to drop its unrealistic expectations on China and instead, to approach China with a more pragmatic and realistic policy.

In the above-mentioned policy paper, the European Commission also listed ten action proposals that could only be taken with efforts from both the EU and China. Apart from systemic rivalry, the EU deems China as an important partner/competitor for its economic and trade interests. In the field of trade, the EU modified the relevant regulations and introduced new anti-dumping and anti-subsidy measures in 2017 in order to maintain the defensive instruments against Chinese exports to the European market. In the field of investment, apart from implementing the screening mechanism to keep Chinese companies away from strategic European assets, the EU is actively engaged in negotiations with China for the conclusion of a bilateral comprehensive investment agreement in order to open the Chinese market for European products. In the field of transport connectivity, the EU promotes the EU–Asia connectivity strategy in order to strengthen its geopolitical influence. As German EU Ambassador Michael Clauß said, "It's high time to walk the talk in order to promote our European vision of a rules and values-based globalisation as well as fair trade competition" (quoted in Eder 2020).

China is the EU's biggest source of imports and its second-biggest export market. EU–China trade on average is over €1 billion per day. The EU has a strong degree of interdependence with China and is thus seriously concerned about China's rise. The Chinese government devotes itself to the realisation of the "Chinese dream"—a dream of power and prosperity exemplified by its two centennial goals—when the Chinese Communist Party celebrates its centenary in 2021, China should be built into "a moderately prosperous society in all respects", and when the People's Republic of China celebrates its centenary in 2049, the country should be built into "a modern socialist country that is prosperous, strong, democratic, culturally advanced and harmonious" (Xinhuanet 2017).

China's adherence to a "socialist road with Chinese characteristics" increased the EU's mistrust of the Chinese government in recent years and has motivated the new European Commission, which took office at the end of 2019, to decide to compete in digital leadership with China and to diversify supply chains, and in the meantime to push forward geopolitical strategy in its external relations, in particular, to strengthen cooperation with "like-minded" Asian partners including Japan and South Korea (see, for example, European Commission 2020; Renard 2015).

In recent months, COVID-19, which first broke out in China and then developed into a pandemic all over the world, has become an important testing ground for EU–China relations. When the EU member states were struck seriously by the coronavirus, China actively engaged with the EU by providing masks and other medical facilities to Europe. However, China's moves were labelled "mask diplomacy" or "politics of generosity" by some European media (see, for example, Chapter 9 in this book, and Silva 2020), suggesting that Beijing had hidden intentions. European Commission Vice-President Vestager warned of the risks for vulnerable European companies to be taken over by Chinese bids. The Commission's position was that "[p] eople are more than welcome to come do business in Europe but not to do that with unfair competitive means" (quoted in Espinoza 2020), implying that those companies, including Chinese companies, which do not play by the same rules as the Europeans, are therefore not welcome in Europe. The European External Action Service scrutinised media publications inside and outside the EU during those months and criticised Chinese media for disinformation, stating that China tried "to deflect blame, to use the pandemic to promote their own governmental system and enhance their image abroad" (European External Action Service 2020). Josep Borrell, the Union's High Representative for Foreign Affairs and Security Policy, talked about China several times recently. In his op-eds, he admitted that China's rise led to changes in EU–China relations; the diversity of the relationship requires that the EU's approach cannot be reduced to one single perspective; and that the EU should achieve unity when dealing with China "based on a realistic assessment of China's strategic intent and the EU's common interests" (Borrel 2020a). At the annual German Ambassadors' Conference, Mr Borrell stressed again the changing nature of EU–China relations and maintained that the EU needs to develop "a more robust strategy for China" based on its "own interests and values", otherwise the EU would be instrumentalised in the rivalry between the US and China as the EU faces increasing pressure to choose sides. He also pointed out that China is getting more powerful, but its rise not only "triggers respect, but also many questions and fears" (Borrel 2020b). Due to COVID-19, almost all the originally planned bilateral meetings have been postponed. The increasing distrust of China in the EU is worsened by the lack of bilateral exchanges. Covid-19 brings uncertainty not only to public health but also to EU–China relations.

Before Germany took the rotating presidency of the EU, the German government already announced that the Leipzig 27+1 EU-China Summit scheduled for autumn 2020 would have to be postponed. Although the summit was finally held online in September between EU leaders, the German President and the Chinese President, its outcomes were reportedly insubstantial. The Chinese side seems to be more eager to discuss the Strategic Agenda for Cooperation 2025, but the European side insisted on the priority of the CAI and did not want to consider the new agenda before "significant progress ha[d] been made in the negotiations" on the CAI (Council of the European Union 2020).

Concluding remarks

This chapter examines the EU's negative perception of China's BRI and why the EU has adjusted its China policy in recent years. For the EU, China presents more challenges than opportunities. But the EU is uncertain whether it can successfully manage its relationship with China and how to deal with China's rise. Borrell's call for a more robust China strategy and a united EU approach reveals exactly what is missing in the EU's China policy.

The EU leaders have called for unity among its member states in their China policy and stress both their values and interests in the relationship with China. Labelled as a "systemic rival" to the EU, China is a very different player in the international system. However, for the Europeans, despite increasing differences, it needs to cooperate with China in many fields and at different levels. By addressing China both as a rival and a partner, the EU has somehow entered into uncharted waters. The EU is a normative power as well as a pragmatic player. Whether norms are more important than pragmatic interests is a difficult question. The complexity of the question itself brings uncertainty to the EU's relationship with China. What is clear is that while the EU is developing a new China strategy and the EU and China will finalise a new agenda for cooperation, the working environment has been changing and challenges are increasing. Both the EU and China need to be more cautious in engaging with each other in order to maintain a workable partnership.

Bibliography

Borrel, J. (2020a). Trust and reciprocity: the necessary ingredients for EU-China co-operation. 15 May. Available at: https://eeas.europa.eu/headquarters/headquarters-homepage_en/79355/Trust%20and%20reciprocity:%20the%20necessary%20ingredients%20for%20EU-China%20cooperation (Accessed 15 May 2020).

Borrel, J. (2020b). Annual German Ambassadors' Conference 2020: Opening remarks. 25 May. Available at: https://eeas.europa.eu/headquarters/headquarters-homepage/79817/annual-german-ambassadors%E2%80%99-conference-2020-opening-remarks-high-representative-vice-president_en (Accessed 25 May 2020).

Council of the European Union (2015). EU-China Summit joint statement: The way forward after forty years of EU-China cooperation. 29 June, Available at: https://www.consilium.europa.eu/media/23732/150629-eu-china-summit-joint-statement-final.pdf (Accessed 12 April 2020).

Council of the European Union (2018). Joint statement of the 20th EU-China Summit. 16 July. Available at: https://www.consilium.europa.eu/media/36165/final-eu-cn-joint-statement-consolidated-text-with-climate-change-clean-energy-annex.pdf (Accessed 12 April 2020).

Council of the European Union (2019). EU-China Summit joint statement. 9 April. Available at: https://www.consilium.europa.eu/media/39020/euchina-joint-statement-9april2019.pdf (Accessed 12 April 2020).

Council of the European Union (2020). EU-China leaders' meeting via video conference. 14 September. Available at: https://www.consilium.europa.eu/en/meetings/international-summit/2020/09/14/ (Accessed 14 September 2020).

Eder, F. (2020). Spy fallout — American reset — China's all belt, no road. *Politico Brussels Playbook*, 17 January. Available at: https://www.politico.eu/newsletter/brussels-playbook/politico-brussels-playbook-spy-fallout-american-reset-chinas-all-belt-no-road/ (Accessed 2 April 2020).

Espinoza, J. (2020). Vestager urges stakebuilding to block Chinese takeovers. *Financial Times*, 12 April. Available at: https://www.ft.com/content/e14f24c7-e47a-4c22-8cf3-f629da62b0a7 (Accessed 12 April 2020).

EU Chamber of Commerce in China (2017). China manufacturing 2025: Putting industrial policy ahead of market forces. Available at: https://static.europeanchamber.com.cn/upload/documents/documents/CM2025_EN_final_version_0301[473].pdf (Accessed 19 March 2020).

EU Chamber of Commerce in China (2020). The road less travelled: European involvement in China's Belt and Road Initiative. January. Available at: https://static.europeanchamber.com.cn/upload/documents/documents/The_Road_Less_Travelled[762].pdf (Accessed 10 March 2020).

European Commission (2006). Accompanying COM (2006) 631 final: Closer partners, growing responsibilities: A policy paper on EU-China trade and investment: Competition and partnership. Brussels, 24 October, COM (2006) 632 final, https://eur-lex.europa.eu/legal-content/EN/TXT/PDF/?uri=CELEX:52006DC0632&from=EN

European Commission (2018). Connecting Europe and Asia -Building blocks for an EU strategy. 19 September, JOIN (2018) 31 final. Available at: https://eeas.europa.eu/sites/eeas/files/joint_communication_-_connecting_europe_and_asia_-_building_blocks_for_an_eu_strategy_2018-09-19.pdf (Accessed 3 April 2020).

European Commission (2019). EU-China – A strategic outlook. Strasbourg, JOIN (2019) 5 final. Available at: https://ec.europa.eu/commission/sites/beta-political/files/communication-eu-china-a-strategic-outlook.pdf (Accessed 12 March 2020).

European Commission (2020). Shaping Europe's digital future. Available at: https://ec.europa.eu/info/sites/info/files/communication-shaping-europes-digital-future-feb2020_en_4.pdf (Accessed 12 March 2020).

European External Action Service (2017). European Commission Vice-President Jyrki Katainen speech at Belt and Road Forum Leaders' Round Table. 16 May. Available at: https://eeas.europa.eu/delegations/china/26154/european-commission-vice-president-jyrki-katainen-speech-belt-and-road-forum-leaders-round_en (Accessed 12 April 2020).

European External Action Service (2020). Covid-19 Disinformation EEAS Special Report. 23 April–18 May. Available at: https://euvsdisinfo.eu/eeas-special-report-update-short-assessment-of-narratives-and-disinformation-around-the-covid19-pandemic-updated-23-april-18-may/?highlight=China (Accessed 30 April 2020).

European Parliament (2015). Resolution on EU-China relations. 16 December. Available at: https://www.europarl.europa.eu/doceo/document/TA-8-2015-0458_EN.pdf (Accessed 1 April 2020).

European Parliament (2018). Resolution on the state of EU-China relations (2017/2274(INI)). 12 September. Available at: https://www.europarl.europa.eu/doceo/document/TA-8-2018-0343_EN.pdf (Accessed 12 April 2020).

García-Herrero, A. and Xu, J. (2019). The next step of the Belt and Road Initiative: Multilateralisation with Chinese characteristics. 18 April. [Blog] Bruegel Blog Post. Available at: https://www.bruegel.org/2019/04/the-next-step-of-the-belt-and-road-initiative-multilateralisation-with-chinese-characteristics/ (Accessed 12 March 2020).

Grieger, G. (2017). Foreign direct investment screening: A debate in light of China-EU FDI flows. European Parliament Briefing, May. Available at: https://www.europarl.europa.eu/RegData/etudes/BRIE/2017/603941/EPRS_BRI(2017)603941_EN.pdf (Accessed 14 March 2020).

Grieger, G. (2019). State of play of EU-China relations. Briefing, PE 633.149, January. Available at: https://www.europarl.europa.eu/RegData/etudes/BRIE/2019/633149/EPRS_BRI(2019)633149_EN.pdf (Accessed 10 March 2020).

Hanemann, T. and Huotari, M. (2015). Preparing for a new era of Chinese Capital: Chinese FDI in Europe and Germany. Joint Report by MERICS and Rhodium Group, June. Available at: https://www.merics.org/sites/default/files/2018-07/COFDI_2015_EN_web.pdf (Accessed 14 March 2020).

Hanemann, T. and Huotari, M. (2016). A new record year for Chinese outbound investment in Europe. Joint Report by MERICS and Rhodium Group, February. Available at: https://www.merics.org/sites/default/files/2018-07/COFDI_2016_web.pdf (Accessed 14 March 2020).

Hanemann, T. and Huotari, M. (2017). Record flows and growing imbalances: Chinese investment in Europe in 2016. Joint Report by MERICS and Rhodium Group, January. Available at: https://www.merics.org/sites/default/files/2018-07/MPOC_3_COFDI_2017_web.pdf (Accessed 14 March 2020).

Heide, D. et al. (2018). EU ambassadors band together against Silk Road. *Handelsblatt*, 17 April. Available at: https://www.handelsblatt.com/today/politics/china-first-eu-ambassadors-band-together-against-silk-road/23581860.html?ticket=ST-3246488-twsJ9o5cTLYNbHumNyuo-ap6 (Accessed 12 March 2020).

Hopkins, V. and Kynge, J. (2019). Montenegro fears China-backed highway will put it on road to ruin. *Financial Times*, 10 April. Available at: https://www.ft.com/content/d3d56d20-5a8d-11e9-9dde-7aedca0a081a (Accessed 12 March 2020).

Juncker, J. C. (2017). State of the Union 2017. 13 September. Available at: https://ec.europa.eu/commission/sites/beta-political/files/state-union-2017-brochure_en.pdf (Accessed 14 March 2020).

Klose, S. et al. (2017). An uphill struggle? Towards coordinated EU engagement with China's Belt and Road Initiative. European Policy Brief, EGMONT Royal Institute for International Relation, No. 48. Available at: http://www.egmontinstitute.be/content/uploads/2017/11/EPB-48.pdf?type=pdf (Accessed 13 March 2020).

Le Corre, P. (2018). China's Rise as a geoeconomic influencer: Four European case studies. Carnegie Endowment for International Peace. Available at: https://carnegieendowment.org/2018/10/15/china-s-rise-as-geoeconomic-influencer-four-european-case-studies-pub-77462 (Accessed 19 March 2020).

Men, J. (2015). China's new Silk Road and EU-China relations. *EU-China Observer*, 1, pp. 12–15.

Men, J. (2020). China-Europe railway connectivity: Opportunities and challenges. In: A. Lukin, ed., *The "Roads" and "Belts" of Eurasia*, 1st ed. Singapore: Palgrave Macmillan, 129–146.

Nadir, P. et al. (2019). China: Challenges and prospects from an industrial and innovation powerhouse. Joint Research Centre of European Commission, February. Available at: https://ec.europa.eu/jrc/en/publication/china-challenges-and-prospects-industrial-and-innovation-powerhouse (Accessed 13 March 2020).

Renard, T. (2015). The EU's strategic partnership agreements: balancing geoeconomics and geopolitics. 9 June. Available at: http://www.egmontinstitute.be/eu-strategic-partnership-agreement/ (Acessed 12 March 2020).

Šefčovič, M. (2019). Embracing the European way is crucial for the future of China's Belt and Road. 25 April. Available at: https://eeas.europa.eu/delegations/china/61412/node/61412_ko (Accessed 10 March 2020).

Silva, I. (2020). 'Mask diplomacy': EU-China ties tested during coronavirus pandemic Comments. *Euronews*, 2 April. Available at: https://www.euronews.com/2020/04/02/mask-diplomacy-eu-china-ties-tested-during-coronavirus-pandemic (Accessed 5 Apri 2020).

Valero, J. (2019). European bloc not considering joining China's Belt and Road plans. *EurActiv*, 26 April. Available at: https://www.euractiv.com/section/eu-china/news/european-bloc-not-considering-joining-chinas-belt-and-road-plans/ (Accessed 10 March 2020).

van der Putten, F. et al. (2016). Europe and China's new silk roads: A report by the European Think-tank Network on China (ETNC), December. Available at: https://www.clingendael.org/sites/default/files/pdfs/Europe_and_Chinas_New_Silk_Roads_0.pdf (Accessed 1 April 2020).

von der Burchard, H. (2019). EU slams China as 'systemic rival' as trade tension rises. POLITICO, 3 December. Available at: https://www.politico.eu/article/eu-slams-china-as-systemic-rival-as-trade-tension-rises/ (Accessed 2 April 2020).

Xinhuanet (2017). CPC Q&A: What are China's two centennial goals and why do they matter?, 17 October. Available at: http://www.xinhuanet.com/english/2017-10/17/c_136686770.htm (Accessed 2 April 2020).

4 The BRI Kaleidoscope: European Legal Pluralism and BRI Soft Law

Francis Snyder

Introduction

This chapter[i] deals with the legal or other normative aspects of relations between Europe and China's Belt and Road Initiative (BRI; in Chinese, *yi dai yi lu* 一带一路: One Belt One Road: see Rolland 2019). It makes two assumptions. First, Europe is a *locus classicus* of legal pluralism, and European legal pluralism is embedded in several overlapping social and legal fields. Second, from a normative standpoint, the BRI includes mainly policy documents, memoranda of understanding (MoUs), and business contracts or other agreements.

We can envisage the BRI as the centre of a kaleidoscope and Europe as being comprised of several perspectives on the centre: the European Union (EU), the Member States, and the 17+1 grouping. Part I of the chapter deals with the perspective of the EU, Part II with that of the Member States, and Part III with that of the grouping known as 17+1. For the sake of convenience, each perspective is treated as discrete and relatively unified, even though in practice they overlap and are more diverse than can be discussed here. A brief conclusion summarises the discussion and addresses several of the themes of this book.

Part I: The EU perspective

The EU is a regional integration organization. It does not have a generally agreed-upon policy towards BRI, first because its policy space is limited by the basic EU legal principle of conferral, and second because of disagreements among Member States. The overall bilateral agreement between the EU (then EEC) and China remains the 1985 Agreement on Trade and Economic Cooperation (TECA), which in Article 14 recognized Member States' 'powers…to undertake bilateral activities with the People's Republic of China in the field of economic cooperation and conclude, where appropriate, new economic cooperation agreements with the People's Republic of China' (Snyder 2009: 65–66). TECA 1985 is long out of date, and the normative gap has been filled by subject-specific bilateral agreements and a host of soft law dialogues.

EU policy space is delimited (and limited) by the principle of conferral. Three policy fields illustrate the legal and political issues involved: trade, foreign direct investment, and transport. The EU has exclusive competence for trade as part of the common commercial policy (Article 206–207 TFEU). Following the Lisbon Treaty, the EU also has exclusive competence concerning foreign direct investment (FDI) into the EU.

In Opinion 2/15 the Court of Justice of the European Union (CJEU) (2017) confirmed that FDI falls within the EU's Common Commercial Policy and therefore under the EU's exclusive competence according to Article 3(1)(e) TFEU and Article 207(1) TFEU 'if it relates specifically to such trade in that it is essentially intended to promote, facilitate or govern such trade and has direct and immediate effects on it' (para 36). Portfolio investment (paras 225–228) does not result in a participation 'such as to have direct and immediate effects on trade between that third State and the European Union' (para 84), and certain categories of real-estate investment or the use of loans are outside FDI and inside non-direct investment (para 228). According to the CJEU, Article 207(1) does not distinguish between acts concerning admission or protection of investments (para 87). The EU's FDI screening regulation came into force only on 11 October 2020;[ii] until that time FDI from China into the EU was governed by national law and the EU transition regulation.[iii] Nevertheless, the TFEU free movement of capital provisions apply to China, just as to EU Member States (Article 63 TFEU), so that China can 'claim a right of market access without the need for a specific treaty commitment of the EU vis-à-vis the investor's home State' (Schill 2020: 760), although freedom of establishment applies only to nationals of a Member State and 'the setting-up of agencies, branches or subsidiaries by nationals of any Member State established in the territory of any Member State' (Article 49 TFEU).

Concerning transport, the EU shares competence with the Member States. In Opinion 2/15 the CJEU pointed out that transport is 'excluded from the common commercial policy by Article 207(5) TFEU, according to which the negotiation and conclusion of "international agreements in the field of transport" are to be subject to "Title VI of Part Three [of the FEU Treaty] ..."' on the common transport policy (para 57). According to the CJEU (paras 168–217), transport of different types must be approved according to the division of competences within the field of the common transport policy (para 168), which is governed by Articles 90–100 TFEU. This includes 'transport by rail, road and inland waterway' (Article 100(1) TFEU). Within these fields, as provided in Article 216(1) TFEU, the EU has competence to include any international agreement which 'is likely to affect common rules or alter their scope' (CJEU Opinion, para 171). Consequently, according to the CJEU, competence regarding maritime transport is shared between the EU and the Member States (paras 175–188). Concerning rail transport, however, which is governed by EU Directive 2012/34 on rules of the single European railway area, based on Article 91 TFEU, the EU has exclusive competence because the EU has many common rules and their scope may be affected or altered by commitments such as those in the Singapore FTA Agreement (CJEU para 202). The same applies to road transport (CJEU para 211). The CJEU did not deal with inland waterways transport (para 213 et seq), because this is not mentioned in the Singapore FTA.

Some EU–China subject-specific bilateral agreements directly affect the BRI: scientific and technical cooperation, maritime transport, and customs cooperation, including the Smart-and-Secure Trade Lanes pilot project beginning in 2006 (European Commission 2006).[iv] Outside these areas, most EU–China 'legal' relations have taken the form of hortatory policy documents and bilateral soft law. EU policy documents are not soft law, but they underpin EU soft law sectoral dialogues and soft institutions involving China (Snyder 2009). There are numerous soft law dialogues between the European Commission and Chinese ministries or ministerial-level organisations, sometimes in the form of a memorandum of understanding (MoU). Leaving aside annual summit meetings, the High-Level Trade and Economic Dialogue and the Human Rights Dialogue, sectoral dialogues include (but are not limited to) agriculture, civil aviation, customs cooperation, energy, environment, food safety, government procurement, intellectual property rights, maritime transport, regulatory and industrial policy science and technology, trade policy and transport in general. These dialogues and any related MoU are not legally binding, but they form part of the dense network of norms that are integrated into EU policies and in which Europe–China BRI relations take place.

In 2013, shortly after President Xi Jinping unveiled the BRI initiative (State Council of the People's Republic of China 2018), the EU and China jointly adopted the EU–China 2020 Strategic Agenda for Cooperation (European Commission 2013). The Agenda did not mention the BRI explicitly but regarded China's two centenary goals (lian ge yi bai nian) (Xinhua 2017; Ding 2016) and the 12th Five Year Plan as presenting 'potential for synergies to enhance cooperation for win-win results' (European Commission 2020a: 2). In 2015 the European Commission and the Chinese National Reform and Development Commission (NDRC) established the EU–China Connectivity Platform (Liu and Wei 2019, see also Su, Chapter 8).

In 2016, the Commission recognized the BRI initiative as 'good reason' for China to engage in more 'active participation in global governance, security and defense' (European Commission 2016). Meanwhile, the Commission emphasized that China should make the BRI 'an open platform which adheres to market rules and international norms in order to deliver benefits for all and to encourage responsible economic behavior in' (European Commission 2016: 10). In sum, the 2016 EU Strategy on China was built around the premise that the EU expected their bilateral relationship to be of 'reciprocal benefit in both political and economic terms' (European Commission 2016: 4). By then, however, the BRI already had an impact on the EU, especially through strategic Chinese investments (CIRSD 2019; also see below). This led to EU concerns about divergences between the principled positions of the EU and the practical actions of some Member States, which were expressed explicitly in an April 2018 report by 27 of the national EU ambassadors in China that criticized the BRI as being 'designed to hamper free trade and put Chinese companies at an advantage' (Handelsblatt 2018); the Hungarian ambassador boycotted the document (Heide et al. 2018). Recently, the latest EU-China Strategic Outlook indicates a hardening of EU views: China is described not only as a 'co-operation partner' and 'negotiating partner' but also as a 'strategic competitor in the pursuit of technological leadership, and a systemic rival promoting alternative models of governance' (see Men, Chapter 3).

Within this framework, including dealing with the EU's large trade deficit with China (European Commission 2020b), the importance of continuing links between the EU and China has been recognized in annual soft law EU–China Summit policy statements and joint financial arrangements. The 2018 Summit Joint Statement recognized that the EU and China would continue to develop synergies, including through the EU Investment Plan and the extended Trans-European Transport Networks (European Union External Action Service 2018). This was reaffirmed at the April 2019 EU–China Summit.

Part II: The EU Member States' perspective

What do EU Member States see in the BRI kaleidoscope? This section focuses on Member States other than those in the 17+1 group that are discussed in the next section. Thirteen EU Member States, including Germany, France, Italy, and the Netherlands (as well as the UK) have signed and ratified the Articles of Agreement of the Asian Infrastructure Investment Bank (AIIB) (Asian Infrastructure Investment Bank 2020). Germany was the fourth largest shareholder after China, India, and Russia, having subscribed 4.6% (about 4.5 billion USD) of total AIIB capital. Bulgaria, Greece, Hungary, Poland, and Portugal have individual agreements with China to join the BRI.

Various EU Member States, as well as several non-EU European states (mainly Central and Eastern European countries), have signed an MoU with China within the framework of the BRI; some do not mention the BRI explicitly. Most MoUs have been signed during a visit by Chinese leaders to Europe,[v] at a summit meeting of the 17+1 grouping[vi], or most recently at a Belt and Road forum in Beijing. There seems to be no official list of the BRI MoUs between European parties and China. However, one source reported as of 2019 a total of 17 government-to-government MoUs between China and European countries, including EU Member States and other European countries (Belt and Road Initiative 2019). Another source reported that China has signed 38 MoUs or other BRI cooperation agreements with European partners (Bauschard 2019); this may include both government-to-government agreements and company-to-company agreements. EU Member State governments usually are involved in promoting agreements between companies; the same is true of the Chinese government in relation to the state-owned enterprises (SOEs) that are the leaders of the key Chinese industries in the BRI (The Economist Intelligence Unit 2017; Wübbeke et al. 2016).

The agreements share a similar basic structure. Silk Road Briefing (https://www.silkroadbriefing.com/, Devonshire-Ellis 2018) provides a model MoU, based on several available examples. It states that 'The two Participants will promote cooperation on customs, border entry and exit management, inspection and quarantine and quality standards, especially international standardization. The two Participants will explore [the] possibility to carry out investment and trade cooperation with third countries and facilitate easier access of Chinese exports to the (trade bloc) market'. Priority areas of cooperation are transport, logistics, and infrastructure; trade and investment promotion; cooperation in science and technology; financial cooperation; and cultural and people-to-people exchange.

The MoUs are soft law, with all their advantages and disadvantages. They use mainly hortatory language and in principle are not legally binding, but they are flexible and more open to interpretation and change. For example, the model MoU provided by Silk Road Briefing (Devonshire-Ellis 2018) states: 'This MOU does not constitute legally binding obligations for the two Participants. It is only an expression of their common will to jointly advance the Belt and Road Initiative' (Part V). The 23 March 2019 MoU between Italy and China on BRI is more precise (see Amighini, Chapter 13).[vii] Concerning applicable law, its Paragraph VI states

> This Memorandum of Understanding does not constitute an international agreement which may lead to rights and obligations under international law. No provision of this Memorandum is to be understood and performed as a legal or financial obligation or commitment of the Parties. This Memorandum of Understanding will be interpreted in accordance with the legislations of the Parties and as well as applicable international law and, as for the Italian Party, with the obligations arising from its membership of the European Union.

Despite the cautionary language concerning rights and obligations, it thus provides clearly that the parties agree that the MoU will be *interpreted* in accordance with national legislation, international law, and for Italy, with its obligations under EU law. This leaves open the question as to whether interpretation is necessary for implementation. The MoU does not affect Italy's rights and obligations under EU law. Nevertheless, some commentators suggest that the MoUs 'contain the seeds of what could, in future, be used as diplomatic tools in terms of insisting that agreements have been reached over certain areas' (Devonshire-Ellis 2018; also Bauschard 2019).

A look at several of the larger EU Member States reveals three different situations from the standpoint of governmental policy: use of a governmental soft law agreement to join the BRI, together with numerous agreements or contracts between companies (Italy); expression of a preference for EU-level policy, together with the use of industry associations as a possible platform for small- and -medium-sized enterprises, coupled with individual initiatives by large companies (Germany); and exclusive reliance on business contracts (France).

Italy's MoU with China includes logistics, infrastructure, transportation, trade, environment protection, and finance. Cagliari, the capital of the Italian island of Sardinia, is to be Italy's first 5G smart city based entirely on Chinese technology, linking Huawei and the Italian company Fastweb (Tomás 2019). Italy also hopes to increase its exports to Asia.

Following the MoU,[viii] numerous agreements were signed between China and Italian ministries, public bodies, and companies. They build upon earlier transactions; for example, in 2015 the Silk Road Fund financed ChemChina's acquisition of a controlling share in the international tyre company Pirelli, in which as of September 2019 ChemChina held a 49% share through the intermediate holding company Marco Polo International Italy.[ix] China's group Suning, which is the main shareholder in Inter Milan football club, agreed with the Italian Trade Agency to help increase Made-in-Italy exports to China. Italy's state lender, Cassa Depositi et Prestiti (CDP), signed an agreement with the Bank of China for CDP to sell 'Panda' bonds (debt sold by foreign entities to mainland China investors) and for CDP and BOC to co-finance Italian companies. CDP and Italian gas company Snam signed an MoU with the Chinese Silk Road Fund (SRF) to cooperate on international investments in China and in the numerous countries that had already signed up for BRI and for possible cooperation in the natural gas sector. Daniela, an Italian metals company, has agreed to build part of a steel plant in China that then will be transferred to Azerbaijan. China Communication Construction Company (CCCC) signed cooperation agreements with Trieste port authorities and with the commissioner supervising the reconstruction of the Morandi bridge in Genova that collapsed in July 2019. Ansaldo Energia agreed on technological co-operation with China United Gas Turbine Company (UCTGC) regarding heavy-duty gas turbines and also received a contract to supply a gas turbine and syngas compressor train for a power plant in northeast China. The Italian banking group Intesa Sanpaolo signed an MoU with the city of Qingdao to develop wealth management services for Chinese clients and eventually to sell its own financial products in Qingdao. ENI, a large Italian energy company, signed an MoU with the Bank of China for a credit line. China's largest online travel agency, Ctrip, signed an agreement with the Italian railway group Ferrovie dello Stato, the airport operator Aeroporti di

Roma, and the museums of Ferrari sports cars to develop Chinese tourism in Italy.

Italian policy has been criticised by the European Commission for lack of consistency with the EU's Strategic Agenda, giving preference to bilateral links over EU-wide links with BRI, accepting non-reciprocal arrangements lacking in transparency, and neglecting basic EU trade-policy values such as rule of law, fair trade or a so-called 'level playing field'.[x] The Netherlands, however, considers that bilateral MoUs between a Member State and China 'do not necessarily undermine EU unity, as long as Member States remain committed to EU agreements'.[xi] It is difficult, however, to avoid the conclusion that in pursuing its own bilateral agreements, a Member State is trying to tread the thin and inevitably negotiable line traced in the 1985 TECA between 'trade agreements' and 'economic cooperation agreements'. Is there really any other option, however, in a context of a lack of real EU BRI policy? This leaves aside any question about which if any of these agreements have been implemented.

In contrast, Germany has proposed that the major EU Member States should sign an MoU with China as a bloc.[xii] Pending such a development, German companies have taken the lead. The Bremen-based Federal Association of the German Silk Road Initiative (BVDSI) is a platform for establishing project-related contracts for small- and medium-sized enterprises along the BRI route.[xiii] 2016 saw the establishment of the railway between Chongqing and Duisberg, whose port now is central Europe's logistics hub (EuropeanCEO 2017). Large companies such as Siemens, which long have been in China, and German auto manufacturers, with strong China links, develop their own strategies (Skala-Kuhmann 2019). In 2018, Siemens opened a Belt and Road office in Beijing and held a BRI international summit in the city. It signed nearly a dozen cooperation agreements with leading Chinese enterprises including China Gezhouba Group, Corporation International Engineering Co., China Railway Construction Corporation (International) Ltd., and China Civil Engineering Construction Corporation (CCECC). The German Engineering Federation (VDMA), Europe's largest industry federation, which has offices in Beijing and Shanghai, reported that 49% of VDMA member companies doing business in China have already benefited directly or indirectly, or see opportunities to join BRI.

France has not signed an MoU on BRI (Nicolas 2019, and Chapter 10 in this book), though even as early as 2015 the French government took a generally positive view of BRI.[xiv] In January 2018, China and France signed an MoU on cooperation in the silver economy.[xv] Generally, however, France is reported to prefer to promote EU-level policy (Perring 2019) and French business contracts instead of government agreements. Lyon and Wuhan were connected by rail in 2016.[xvi] Marseille similarly expressed interest in maritime connections (OBOR Europe 2017) due mainly to companies such as CMA CGM LOG, the logistic arm of the CMA CGM Group that hopes to play a key role in BRI relations between France and China.[xvii] In addition, several large contracts were signed during President Xi's visit to Paris in March 2019.[xviii]

Other Member States fall along this triangle. Major Austrian banks, such as Raiffeisen International, have signed an MoU on finance and banking cooperation with China Development Bank and Industrial and Commercial Bank of China (May 2017). Belgium has signed an MoU on strengthening cooperation in the peaceful use of nuclear energy. Cyprus and China have an agreement on education cooperation (May 2017). In June 2014 Finland and China signed an MoU on transport planning, intelligent transport, and environmentally friendly transport, [xix] and other agreements between businesses and public sector organisations were signed in 2017. [xx] In May 2017 Greece signed the '2017–2019 Plan on Key Areas of Cooperation between Greece and China', together with an MoU on 'Strengthening Standards Cooperation and Building the Belt and Road'. Its port of Piraeus is a large investment project, in which China Ocean Shipping Company (COSCO) owns a majority share (for a more in-depth look, see Chapter 12 in this book). Ireland signed a cooperation agreement on inspection and quarantine (May 2017). The Netherlands signed an MoU on customs cooperation at the BRI Forum in May 2017, and COSCO has a 35% stake in the Euromax terminal in Rotterdam, its 'main base for shipping operations' in northwestern Europe (Zhong 2016). Portugal does not have a BRI agreement with China, but its Port of Sines is recognized as ideal for cargo-handling infrastructure as a link between China, western Europe, and Africa. Sweden and China signed an MoU on corporate social responsibility in September 2015. The UK and China have numerous links, including infrastructure project financing and agreement on the Belt and Road Financing Guiding Principle (Embassy of the People's Republic of China in the United Kingdom of Great Britain and Northern Ireland 2017), with the UK especially interested in infrastructure financing, participation in project investment, and financial good governance (Johnson 2019; Flint 2020).

Part III. 17+1

In European relations with China, the EU is challenged by the grouping known as 17+1, described by the European Parliament Think Tank as 'a loose sectoral coordination mechanism, including higher frequency of 17+1 summits and lower-level gatherings'.[xxi] 17+1 today includes 12 EU Member States (Bulgaria, Croatia, Czech Republic, Estonia, Greece [most recent joiner], Hungary, Latvia, Lithuania, Poland, Romania, Slovakia, Slovenia) and five countries that today are outside the EU, including four candidates for EU membership (Albania, Montenegro, Republic of North Macedonia, Serbia) and one potential candidate country (Bosnia and Herzegovina) (see also Xiao 2019). 17+1 has a secretariat in Beijing, and in fact, President Xi Jinping replaced Premier Li Keqiang as host of the 17+1 summit in 2020

(Zhou 2020), but it lacks other common institutions except for three mechanisms hosted by Poland: a Contact Mechanism for the Investment Promotion Agencies, the Business Council and the Coordinating Secretariat for Maritime Issues. It does not have a common policy towards BRI, partly because of differences between members[xxii] and partly because of competition for the benefits of BRI (Szczudlik 2016).

A report from the European Parliament Research Service summarized the grouping's relation to BRI as follows (quoted verbatim):

- 'a Chinese normative basis consisting of principles such as consensus-based decision-making, inclusiveness, non-conditionality, voluntarism, and win-win results,'
- 'context-dependent flexible shifts between multilateral venues for dialogues on the regional agenda and, usually, bilateral project-based implementation, with multilateralism not seen as an aim, but rather as a tool to enhance bilateral ties, which remain instrumental,'
- 'a loose, incrementally expanding institutionalisation pattern, including multi-level gatherings and sectoral coordination mechanisms,'
- 'a China-centred agenda-setting, which, despite the inherent power asymmetry in favour of China, may be challenged by China's counterparts based on the Chinese normative basis of equality, consensus and mutual agreement, and'
- 'Chinese "no strings attached" financing tools that usually take the form of concessional loans from Chinese policy banks (such as the Chinese Development Bank (CDB) or China Export-Import Bank (Exim Bank) or more recently funding derived from Chinese or joint investment funds' (Grieger 2018).

These features are described as consistent with those of similar regional groupings initiated by China (Jakóbowski 2018).

Legally, the grouping's relation to the EU is complex, because of the grouping's lack of a common BRI policy, lack of strong institutional structure, and composition of EU Member States and third countries acting within the framework of public international law but with the EU Member States also bound by certain EU legal obligations such as the duty of loyalty (Article 4 TEU; recall Article 14 TECA) yet often with difficult political relations with the EU as a whole. Recent guidelines for cooperation between China and the CEECs affirm the consistency of 17+1 with EU integration, the 2020 Agenda, and the EU-China Comprehensive Strategic Partnership, and EU law.[xxiii] Nevertheless, in 2019 the EU Commission stated that 'all Member States, individually and within sub-regional cooperation frameworks, such as the 17+1 format, have a responsibility to ensure consistency with EU law, rules, and policies."[xxiv]

Table 4.1 Cooperation Intensity in the 16 [now 17 including Greece]

Cooperation intensity in the 16+1 format	*Country*	*Position towards the EU*
Active participants ('champions', 'leaders')	Czech Republic, Hungary, Poland and Serbia	All are euro-sceptic and all are China's strategic partners
Ambitious partners	Bulgaria, Latvia, North Macedonia, Romania and Slovenia	Most are euro-optimists/ euro-moderates (Bulgaria is euro-sceptic)
Followers	Croatia, Estonia, Lithuania and Slovakia	Euro-optimists/euro-moderates
Laggards	Albania, Bosnia-Herzegovina and Montenegro	Euro-optimists/euro-moderates

The European 17+1 countries do not have equally strong relations with the EU or with China. One study (Oehler-Şincai 2018) classified them, except for Greece, into four groups (see Table 4.1):

It concluded that, even though the 17+1 mechanism had a mobilizing effect on all participants, closer cooperation with China was correlated generally with negative attitudes toward the EU, greater emphasis on national interest and recognition of a need to develop balanced relations with other significant international actors, while less cooperation with China was associated with more Euro-optimism, more dependence on the EU internal market or political inertia. This was consistent with the distribution of BRI benefits so far: As of 2018, Hungary, Poland and the Czech Republic reportedly received over two-thirds of Chinese FDI; and Romania, Bulgaria and Slovakia together accounted for a further 30% (Ma 2018). Only a neo-realist view of international relations would consider this to be consistent with the facts that Poland and Hungary fail to meet EU conceptions of rule of law and benefit most from EU cohesion funding.

All 17+1 countries have signed an MoU with China under BRI, for example about general BRI cooperation (Bulgaria, Croatia, Czech Republic, Hungary, Latvia, Poland, Romania, Slovakia, Bosnia and Herzegovina), port and harbour industrial park cooperation (Bulgaria, Croatia, Latvia, Lithuania), financial, industrial, and health cooperation (Czech Republic), trade in dairy products (Estonia), education (Estonia, Bosnia and Herzogovina, North Macedonia), SMEs (Hungary), research and development (Hungary, Slovenia), forestry cooperation (Slovenia), motorway construction (Albania, Montenegro), and standards cooperation (Slovenia), transport and infrastructure (Slovenia), civil aviation (Slovenia) and container block trains (Poland). Hungarian State Railways is part of a consortium with China Railway Group and China Railway Corporation to link central Europe to the

Greek port of Piraeus, of which COSCO held a 51% share as of August 2016.[xxv] Almost all of the MoUs between these non-EU countries and China were signed during the Belt and Road Forum in May 2017.[xxvi]

Poland is a leading member of 17+1 (Choroś-Mrozowska 2019). It first engaged in the BRI in 2013. Polskie Linie Kolejowe (Polish State Railways, PKP) and China Railways signed an MoU on Further Cooperation on China-Europe Container Block Trains at the Belt and Road Forum. This was followed by the Łódź-Chengdu railway connection, now extended to Xiamen, and the opening of the first container connection (Warsaw-Suzhou) (Choroś-Mrozowska 2019: 42). In 2015 the Polish state development bank, Bank Gospodarstwa Krajowego (BGK) signed an MoU with the Industrial and Commercial Bank of China (ICBC) to define methods of cooperation, including 'sharing experience and know-how in the co-financing of large initiative infrastructure projects, the development of industrial parks or issuing guarantees for large enterprises' (Choroś-Mrozowska 2019: 42). Other MoUs concern communication, environmental resources, and tourism. President Xi Jinping visited Warsaw in June 2016, strengthening the Polish-Chinese strategic partnership, and leading to an agreement for 'the joint formulation of a bilateral cooperation plan' encompassing many areas, including IT, environmental protection standards and certification, and agricultural trade (Choroś-Mrozowska 2019; Snyder and Ni 2017). In 2017, Poland and China signed MoUs on investment cooperation in logistics infrastructure and on facilitating customs clearance. In addition to its strategic location and its primary institutional role, Poland provides opportunities for Chinese companies to participate in public tenders.[xxvii] It also enables Chinese companies to 'launch their products with their own logo on the European market' and issues EU shares, 'which enable companies to expand in Europe'. After Hungary, Poland was the second-largest recipient of Chinese FDI in the CEECs between 2000 and 2016 (Thilo and Mikko 2017: 10), amounting in 2016 to 123.3 million EUR (Choroś-Mrozowska 2019: 49). Poland has a large trade deficit with China (ratio of 11.7 to 1) but since 2014 has ranked second to Germany in EU Member States' exports to China.

Conclusion

This chapter aimed to provide a survey of the interaction between European legal pluralism and BRI soft law and contractual arrangements. It showed that the BRI kaleidoscope is seen in overlapping but distinctly different ways by the actors in three semi-autonomous European social fields: the EU, EU Member States, and the 17+1 grouping. Each party sees somewhat different things in the BRI or interprets them in different ways. We can conclude with several points.

First, the EU has played a marginal role in China's BRI narrative (Zeng 2017). The chapter discussed the impact on the EU of the BRI, the most active EU institutions, incentives for cooperation and cooperation between the different actors, the role of law and regulation in managing EU-China relations concerning the BRI, and engagements of the EU, the Member States, and the 17+1 grouping with the BRI. The kaleidoscope metaphor reveals the weakness of the EU in the BRI, the fragmentation of legitimacy, authority and policymaking within Europe, and the profound differences of view among European countries. The political, economic, social, and cultural consequences of these differences lie outside the scope of the chapter. Clearly, however, to play a more important role, the EU must appreciate simultaneously the numerous roots and branches of BRI.

Second, legal pluralism should be regarded as a European strength vis-à-vis BRI. The EU should aim for greater unity and coherence in its position, despite the differences among Member States in their policies toward China (Fox and Godemont 2009; Godemont and Vasselier 2017). Instead of seeking to export European values to China, the EU should focus on improving procedures. It should take Chinese BRI language seriously. While recognizing that much of BRI is bound up with and determined by Chinese domestic arrangements, the EU should promote the adoption of basic concepts of global administrative law, such as participation, consultation, accountability, and transparency (Cassese 2016). EU Member States, including 17+1 participants, can draw on European legal pluralism, with its conjunction of EU law, national law, and soft law from many sources, to pursue their own interests. Companies, whether European, Chinese, mixed, or other, are more powerful than European governments in the BRI. They are the drivers of much policymaking and normative links in the BRI context, in other words of European legal pluralism. European capitalism differs from Chinese state capitalism (Zheng, Liebman, and Milhaupt 2016), of course, but the BRI testifies to the interdependence between business and government on all sides of the BRI. The nature and consequences of such interdependence need to be explored in more detail.

Third, one is reminded almost inevitably of Richard Nisbett's (2003) distinction between holistic and analytical modes of thought. The BRI, as aggregated by the Chinese government, stems mainly from a holistic mode, which is oriented toward providing a framework, envisaging the long term, and allowing for change and revision; at first it may appear 'overloaded', in the sense of becoming 'far too broad to be meaningful'' (Zeng 2017: 12). In contrast, the analytic mode used mainly on the European side focuses on the normative status (legally binding or not) of an agreement, deadlines for FDI or construction, or other specific details. But BRI is both a 'strategic plan' and a 'systematic project' (Ekman 2019: 26). It reflects and expresses both holistic and analytical modes of thought, as may be seen in comparing MoUs with policy documents concerning the policies previously labelled Made in China 2025 (Wübbeke et al. 2016; United States Chamber of Commerce 2017; Zenglein and Holzmann 2019). Most MoUs, in contrast to specific FDI, are not yet translated into legally binding documents or even implemented in soft law form, but they provide guidance for the future. In principle, most BRI rules between governments remain 'soft', but in many circumstances, soft law may be more effective than hard law or may even become hard law. We need to combine the three perspectives on the kaleidoscope to understand European legal pluralism faced with the BRI.

Notes

i The author is grateful to Wu Yanbin, Yuan Ye, Zhang Hui, and Zhu Mengting for excellent research assistance. This chapter draws freely on our numerous discussions. The author also thanks Stephen Minas, Phil McConnaughay, and Anne-Lise Strahtmann for their help. He is grateful to Peking University School of Transnational Law (STL) and Peking University Shenzhen Graduate School for their support.

ii Regulation (EU) 2019/452 of the European Parliament and of the Council of 19 March 2019, Article 17, OJ:L:2019:0791:TOC.

iii Regulation (EU)1219/2012, OJ 2012 L351/40.

iv European Commission, 'Smart and Secure Trade Lanes Pilot', https://ec.europa.eu/taxation_customs/general-information-customs/customs-security/smart-secure-trade-lanes-pilot-sstl_en.

v Italy's MoU to join the BRI was signed during Xi's state visit to Italy. See https://www.bbc.com/news/world-europe-47679760.

vi As during the fifth summit of "17+1" in 2017, China and Croatia signed the Memorandum of Understanding on Cooperation Involving Seaports and Industrial Zones, which creates a foundation for major projects cooperation. See https://www.fmprc.gov.cn/mfa_eng/wjb_663304/zwjg_665342/zwbd_665378/t1420122.shtml.

vii Memorandum of Understanding Between The Government Of The Italian Republic And The Government Of The People's Republic Of China On Cooperation Within The Framework Of The Silk Road Economic Belt And The 21st Century Maritime Silk Road Initiative, http://www.governo.it/sites/governo.it/files/Memorandum_Italia-Cina_EN.pdf, visited 8 May 2020.

viii https://www.reuters.com/article/us-italy-china-deals-factbox/factbox-italy-signs-deals-worth-2–5-billion-euros-with-china-idUSKCN1R40KN.

ix Wikipedia, Pirelli, https://en.wikipedia.org/wiki/Pirelli, visited 5 May 2020.

x COMM/DG/UNIT (2020): EU-China 2020 Strategic Agenda for Cooperation, p. 2. Available online at https://eeas.europa.eu/delegations/china_bs/15398/EU-China%202020%20Strategic%20Agenda%20for%20Cooperation, updated on 1/27/2020, checked on 1/27/2020.

xi Ministry of Foreign Affairs of the Netherlands, Answers to questions by members Amhaouch, Van den Berg, and Van Helvert about Italy's intention to join China's Belt and Road investment programme, April 2019 (in Dutch), available at https://www.tweedekamer.nl/kamerstukken/kamervragen/detail?id=2019Z04566&did=2019D14342.

xii German Minister: EU Nations Should Join Silk Road as Bloc. Available online at https://www.telesurenglish.net/news/German-Minister-EU-Nations-Should-Join-Silk-Road-as-Bloc--20190427-0011.html, checked on 1/31/2020.

xiii Global Times (2019): German business enthusiasm for Belt and Road Initiative to prompt pragmatism from Berlin - Global Times. Available online at http://www.globaltimes.cn/content/1144461.shtml, updated on 4/4/2019, checked on 1/31/2020.

xiv Speech delivered by Laurent Fabius on June 12, 2015, in Rouen for the opening ceremony of the China-Normandy Forum.

xv https://en.wikipedia.org/wiki/Silver_economy; https://ec.europa.eu/digital-single-market/en/news/silver-economy-study-how-stimulate-economy-hundreds-millions-euros-yea.

xvi Wuhan-Lyon train heralds trade boom - China.org.cn. Available online at http://www.china.org.cn/business/2019-04/15/content_74682011.htm, checked on 1/30/2020.

xvii http://www.cma-cgm.fr/.

xviii https://www.reuters.com/article/us-france-china/france-seals-multi-billion-dollar-deals-with-china-but-questions-belt-and-road-project-idUSKCN1R61NF.

xix https://www.lvm.fi/en/-/china-and-finland-sign-a-mou-on-transport-sector-795325.

xx https://tem.fi/en/article/-/asset_publisher/yrityssopimuksilla-lisaa-vientia-ja-investointeja-kiinan-ja-suomen-valille.

xxi Past yearly annual summits were held in Warsaw (2012), Bucharest (2013), Belgrade (2014), Suzhou (2015), Riga (2016), Budapest (2017), Sofia (2018), and Dubrovnik (2019). See also The 2018 Sofia summit took place shortly before the 20th EU-China summit in July 2018. See GRIEGER, G. (2018). China, the 16+1 format, and the Eu.European Parliamentary Research Service. Retrieved from https://www.europarl.europa.eu/thinktank/en/document.html?reference=EPRS_BRI(2018)625173.

xxii See the articles in Comparative Economic Research. Central and Eastern Europe Volume 22, Number 2, 2019, https://content.sciendo.com/view/journals/cer/22/2/cer.22.issue-2.xml, visited 7 May 2020.

xxiii See eg; Ministry of Foreign Affairs of the People's Republic of China, The Budapest Guidelines for Cooperation between China and Central and Eastern European Countries2017/11/28, https://www.fmprc.gov.cn/mfa_eng/wjdt_665385/2649_665393/t1514534.shtml, visited 5 May 2020, and The Dubrovnik Guidelines for Cooperation between China and Central and Eastern European Countries, 2019/04/17, https://www.fmprc.gov.cn/mfa_eng/wjdt_665385/2649_665393/t1655224.shtml, visited 5 May 2020. This affirmation was not included in The Riga Guidelines for Cooperation between China and Central and Eastern European Countries, 2016/11/08, http://www.china-ceec.org/eng/zdogjhz_1/t1413786.htm, visited 5 May 2020.

xxiv European Union: European Commission, Joint Communication to the European Parliament, the European Council, and the Council - EU-China – A strategic outlook, 3 December 2019, JOIN(2019) 5 final, p. 2, available at: https://op.europa.eu/en/publication-detail/-/publication/3a5bf913-45af-11e9-a8ed 01aa75ed71a1/language-en/format-PDF/source-106825514, visited 25 January 2020.

xxv Wikipedia, Port of Piraeus, https://en.wikipedia.org/wiki/Port_of_Piraeus#Under_COSCO_ownership, visited 5 May 2020.

xxvi https://www.chinadaily.com.cn/china/2017-05/16/content_29359366.htm, accessed 20200208.

xxvii Bachulska, A. (2017), Polska, [in:] Iwanek, K., Pietrewicz, O. (ed.) Chiński projek„ Nowego Jedwabnego Szlaku". Retoryka a rzeczywistość, Raport Ośrodka Badań Azji, Centrum Badań nad Bezpieczeństwem ASW, Warszawa, p. 169.

Bibliography

Asian Infrastructure Investment Bank (2020). Members and prospective members of the bank. https://www.aiib.org/en/index.html; https://www.aiib.org/en/about-aiib/governance/members-of-bank/index.html, visited 7 May 2020.

Bauschard, S. (2019). What does it mean for Europe to "join" the BRI? – Public Forum: DebateUS! (2020). https://pf.debateus.org/blog/2019/08/08/what-does-it-mean-for-europe-to-join-the-bri/, visited on 12 March 2020.

Belt and Road Initiative (2019). Cooperation agreements and MoUs under the Belt and Road Initiative. https://www.beltroad-initiative.com/memorundum-of-understanding-belt-and-road-initiative/, visited 6 May 2020.

Cassese, S. (ed.) (2016). Research Handbook on Global Administrative Law. Edward Elgar Publishing, Cheltenham, UK.

CIRSD (2019). European responses to BRI - An overdue assessment - CIRSD. https://www.cirsd.org/en/horizons/horizons-summer-2019-issue-no-14/european-responses-to-bri-an-overdue-assessment, visited 31 January 2020.

Court of Justice of the European Union (CJEU) (2017). Opinion 1/2015 on the free-trade agreement between the European Union and the Republic of Singapore, ECLI:EU:C:2017:376. https://curia.europa.eu

Ciurtin, H. (2019). The "16+1" becomes the "17+1": Greece joins China's dwindling cooperation framework in Central and Eastern Europe. China Brief, 19, 10. https://jamestown.org/program/the-161-becomes-the-171-greece-joins-chinas-dwindling-co-operation-framework-in-central-and-eastern-europe/, visited 6 May 2020.

Choroś-Mrozowska, D. (2019). The Chinese Belt and Road Initiative from the Polish perspective. Comparative Economic Research. Central and Eastern Europe, 22(2), 39–53. http://doi.org/10.2478/cer-2019-0011.

Devonshire-Ellis, C. (2018). Vassal States: Understanding China's Belt and Road MOU. Op-Ed Commentary, Silk Road Briefing, 8 February. https://www.silkroadbriefing.com/news/2018/02/08/vassal-states-understanding-chinas-belt-road-mou/, visited 6 May 2020.

Ding, L. (2016). China's 'Two Century Goals': Progress and Challenge. East Asian Policy, 8(2), 79–93. https://www.researchgate.net/publication/304669725_China's_Two_Centenary_Goals_Progress_and_Challenge/stats.

Ekman, A. (ed.). (2019). China's Belt & Road and the World: Competing Forms of Globalization. Etudes de l'Ifri, April, Ifri, Paris.

Embassy of the People's Republic of China in the United Kingdom of Great Britain and Northern Ireland (2017). Policy outcomes of the 9th China-UK economic and financial dialogue. http://www.chinese-embassy.org.uk/eng/zywl/t1520081.htm, visited 5 May 2020.

EuropeanCEO (2017). Duisburg is the key link between China and Europe, Digital Editions, 19 July. https://www.europeanceo.com/finance/duisburg-is-the-key-link-between-china-and-europe/, visited 7 May 2020.

European Commission (2006). European Commission, 'Smart and Secure Trade Lanes Pilot'. https://ec.europa.eu/taxation_customs/general-information-customs/customs-security/smart-secure-trade-lanes-pilot-sstl_en https://ec.europa.eu/taxation_customs/general-information-customs/customs-security/smart-secure-trade-lanes-pilot-sstl_en.

European Commission (2013). EU-China strategic agenda for cooperation. European External Action Service. http://eeas.europa.eu/archives/docs/china/docs/eu-china_2020_strategic_agenda_en.pdf, visited 5 May 2020.

European Commission (2016). Joint Communication to the European Parliament and the Council: Elements for a new EU strategy on China, JOIN/2016/030 final,

p. 10. https://op.europa.eu/en/publication-detail/-/publication/c3aa6b64–3919-11e6-a825-01aa75ed71a1, updated 22 June 2016, visited 27 January 2020.

European Commission (2020a). EU-China 2020 strategic agenda for cooperation. https://eeas.europa.eu/delegations/china_bs/15398/EU-China%202020%20Strategic%20Agenda%20for%20Cooperation, updated 27 January 2020, visited 27 January 2020.

European Commission (2020b). Statistics – Trade. https://webgate.ec.europa.eu/isdb_results/factsheets/country/overview_china_en.pdf, visited 7 May 2020.

European Union External Action Service (2018). Joint statement of the 20th EU-China Summit, Brussels, Press Release, 17 July. https://eeas.europa.eu/delegations/china_en/48424/Joint%20statement%20of%20the%2020th%20EU-China%20Summit, visited 7 May 2020.

Flint, Sir D. (2020). The UK's Belt and Road Strategy after Brexit: Keynote address by Sir Douglas Flint. Asia House, 20 February. https://www.youtube.com/watch?v=1wGvfYNMA90, visited 13 August 2020.

Fox, J. and Godemont, F. (2009). A Power Audit of EU-China Relations. European Council of Foreign Relations, London.

Godemont, F. and Vasselier, A. (2017). China at the Gates: A New Power Audit of EU-China Relations. European Council of Foreign Relations, London.

Grieger, G. (2018). China, the 16+1 format and the EU, European Parliament Research Service, Briefing. https://www.europarl.europa.eu/RegData/etudes/BRIE/2018/625173/EPRS_BRI(2018)625173_EN.pdf, visited 7 May 2020.

Handelsblatt (2018). China First: EU ambassadors band together against Silk Road. https://www.handelsblatt.com/english/politics/china-first-eu-ambassadors-band-together-against-silk-road/23581860.html?ticket=ST-7845492-ugEHbVik3fABDOIynwD1-ap2.

Heide, D., Hoppe, T., Scheuer, S. and Stratmann, K. (2018). EU ambassadors band together against Silk Road, Handelsblatt Today, 17 April. https://www.handelsblatt.com/today/politics/china-first-eu-ambassadors-band-together-against-silk-road/23581860.html?ticket=ST-3163734-4t7PZkJQdqhVwsKTAVWm-ap2, visited 15 May 2020.

Jakóbowski, J. (2018). Chinese-led Regional Multilateralism in Central and Eastern Europe, Africa and Latin America: 16 + 1, FOCAC, and CCF. Central and Eastern Europe as a New Frontier of China's Multilateral Diplomacy (Guest Editor: Dragan Pavlićević), Journal of Contemporary China, 7(113), 659–673, visited 7 May 2020. https://doi.org/10.1080/10670564.2018.1458055

Johnson, K. (2019). China gets a British Bedfellow. Foreign Policy, 26 April. https://foreignpolicy.com/2019/04/26/china-gets-a-british-bedfellow-belt-and-road-hammond-xi/, visited 13 August 2020.

Liu, W. and Wei, S. 2019. China-EU Connectivity Platform (Juncker Plan) with the Belt and Road Initiative. In: Cai Fang and Peter Nolan (eds.), Routledge Handbook of the Belt and Road. Routledge, London, 462–466.

Ma, J. (2018). China investment in CEEC surpasses $9b, Global Times, 5 June. http://lv2.mofcom.gov.cn/article/headnews/201806/20180602752361.shtml, visited 7 May 2020.

Nicolas, F. (2019). France and China's Belt and Road Initiative: Commentary in ISPI Dossier: EU-China relations: Challenges and opportunities, 8 April. https://

www.ifri.org/en/publications/publications-ifri/articles-ifri/france-and-chinas-belt-and-road-initiative, visited 7 May 2020.

Nisbett, R.E. (2003). The Geography of Thought. Nicholas Brealey Publishing, London.

OBOR Europe (2017). Marseille, a new destination on the Silk Sea route. https://www.oboreurope.com/en/marseille-silk-sea-route/, visited 7 May 2020.

Oehler-Şincai, I.M. (2018). 16+1: A new issue in EU-China relations? Munich PeREc Archive, MPRA Paper No. 88003, Working paper series of the China-CEE Institute Budapest (2018): pp. 1–11. Institute of the World Economy, Romanian Academy. https://mpra.ub.uni-muenchen.de/88003/, visited 7 May 2020.

Perring, R. (2019). Merkel and Macron meet Juncker today to build a STRONGER EU against China threat, Express, 26 March, visited 7 May 2020.

Rolland, N. (2019). A concise guide to the Belt and Road Initiative. National Bureau of Asian Research (NBR), 11 April. https://www.nbr.org/publication/a-guide-to-the-belt-and-road-initiative/, visited 8 May 2020.

Skala-Kuhmann, A. (2019). European responses to BRI - An overdue assessment, Center for International Relations and Sustainable Development (CIRSD). https://www.cirsd.org/en/horizons/horizons-summer-2019-issue-no-14/european-responses-to-bri-an-overdue-assessment, visited 7 May 2020.

The Economist Intelligence Unit (2017). Cultivating 'Made in China' champions, 2 October. http://www.eiu.com/industry/article/695926453/cultivating-made-in-china-champions/2017-10-02, visited 13 August 2020.

Tomás, J.P. (2019). Italian government approves 5G trial in Cagliari, RCRWireless News, 8 January. https://www.rcrwireless.com/20190108/5g/italian-government-approves-5g-trial-cagliari, 1 April 2020.

Schill, S. (2020). Foreign Direct Investment Control in the European Union: Rising Protectionism or Instrument for Further Investment Liberalization? In: J.H.J. Bourgeois (ed.), EU Framework for Foreign Investment Control. Alphen an den Rijn: Wolters Kluwer, 57–75.

Snyder, F. (ed.) (2009). The European Union and China, 1949-2008: Basic Documents and Commentary. Hart Publishing, Oxford.

Snyder, F. and Ni, L. (2017). Chinese Apples and the Emerging World Food Trade Order. The Chinese Journal of Comparative Law, 5(2), October, 253–307. https://doi.org/10.1093/cjcl/cxx014.

State Council of the People's Republic of China (2018). Chronology of China's Belt and Road Initiative. Archived from the original on 23 September 2018. Retrieved 23 September 2018.

Szczudlik, J. (2016). Perspektywy formatu Chiny – Europa Środkowo-Wschodnia (16+1), Polski Instytut Spraw Międzynarodowych (The Polish Institute of International Affairs), Biuletyn No. 78, 18 November. https://pism.pl/publikacje/Perspektywy_formatu_Chiny___Europa__rodkowo_Wschodnia__16_1_, visited 7 May 2020.

Thilo, H. and Mikko, H. (2017). Record flows and growing imbalances. Chinese investment in Europe in 2016, Joint Report by Rhodium Group and Mercator Institute for China Studies (MERICS), MERICS, Berlin, Papers on China No. 3, January.

United States Chamber of Commerce (2017). Made in China 2025: Global Ambitions Built on Local Protections. U.S. Chamber of Commerce, Washington,

D,C. https://www.uschamber.com/sites/default/files/final_made_in_china_2025_report_full.pdf, visited 7 May 2020.

Wübbeke, J., Meissner, M., Zenglein, M.J., Ives, J. and Conrad, B. (2016). Made in China 2025: The making of a high-tech superpower and consequences for industrial countries. Mercator Institute for China Studies, MERICS Papers on China No. 2, December, MERICS, Berlin. https://www.merics.org/sites/default/files/2017-09/MPOC_No.2_MadeinChina2025.pdf, visited 7 May 2020.

Xiao, H. (2019). West Balkan 6 Connectivity Agenda with the Belt and Road Initiative. In: Cai Fang and Peter Nolan (eds.), Routledge Handbook of the Belt and Road. Routledge, London, 492–496.

Xinhua (2017). CPC Q&A: What are China's two centennial goals and why do they matter?, New China, 17 October. http://www.xinhuanet.com/english/2017-10/17/c_136686770.htm, visited 5 May 2020.

Zeng, J. (2017). Does Europe Matter? The Role of Europe in Chinese Narratives of 'One Belt One Road' and 'New Type of Great Power Relations'. Journal of Common Market Studies, February, 1–15.

Zenglein, M.J. and Holzmann, A. (2019). Evolving made in China 2025: China's industrial policy in the quest for global tech leadership, Mercator Institute for China Studies (MERICS), MERICS Papers on China No. 8, July. https://www.merics.org/sites/default/files/2019-07/MPOC_8_MadeinChina_2025_final_3.pdf, visited 7 May 2020.

Zheng, L., Liebman, B.L. and Milhaupt, C.J. (2016). SOEs and State Governance: How State-Owned Enterprises Influence China's Legal System. In: B.L. Liebman and C.J. Milhaupt (eds.), Regulating the Visible Hand? The Institutional Implications of Chinese State Capitalism. Oxford University Press, Oxford, 203–223.

Zhong, N. (2016). COSCO Pacific takes 35% stake in terminal of Rotterdam. China Daily, 13 May. https://www.chinadaily.com.cn/business/2016-05/13/content_25246994.htm, visited 7 May 2020.

Zhou, L. (2020). Xi to take over as host of '17+1' summit with European leaders, South China Morning Post, Friday, 3 January, p. 1.

5 The Belt and Road in the single market: Towards an EU legal infrastructure to address the regulatory implications[i]

Steven Blockmans and Weinian Hu

1 Introduction

When the European Commission approved the Hungarian government's €45 million investment aid to the Chinese state-owned enterprise (SOE) BorsodChem in September 2018 (Bryant 2011), the legal obstacles that the Belt and Road Initiative (BRI) had encountered in the single market of the EU were removed to serve the "community interest". While the Commission concluded that the investment in BorsodChem was not economically sound (European Commission 2018), it found that the aid would not unduly distort competition in the single market but rather help job creation, regional development and the attainment of environmental objectives.

The BorsodChem case exemplifies a dissonance in perceptions about the BRI as a shared opportunity between the EU and China. For China, the BorsodChem aniline project embodies the motto of the BRI, i.e. "win-win cooperation" that promotes common development and prosperity between China and a BRI hosting country (National Development and Reform Commission 2018). Seen in this light, BorsodChem is a concrete deliverable, a milestone in implementing the BRI.

Launched in a speech by Xi Jinping in 2013, the BRI is the most ambitious project since the 2001 creation of the Shanghai Cooperation Organisation. Given the scale, political drive and financial means committed by China to the BRI, much of the cash-strapped world was initially starstruck, but now increasingly sees it as a challenge. In several European capitals, frustrations about how China has pushed its domestic growth agenda are compounded by worries about Beijing's "imperialist" tendencies and worries that China is throwing its economic weight and political clout around along the new Silk Road (Rachman 2019).

Weakened by years of economic crisis and alarmed at reports about the "debt traps" that China has been laying along the Belt and Road, the EU has flagged its intention to get tougher on foreign direct investment (FDI) inflows into Europe. Other concerns about industrial espionage, national security and public order have led several EU Member States to reject Chinese investments or acquisitions in strategic sectors such as 5G network roll-out (cf. the role of Huawei) (European Council 2019), nuclear energy (cf. the modernisation of two nuclear reactors at Dukovany in the Czech Republic), robotics (cf. the successful takeover of German firm Kuka) and semi-conductors with dual-use potential (cf. the failed attempt to buy German chipmaker Aixtron) (Blockmans and Hu 2019).

The majority of European governments are aware of the risk that China is upsetting the Western-led governance mechanisms by using the BRI as an instrument to export its own development model. In so doing it is eroding the principles of international trade and investment such as national treatment, reciprocity, transparency, environment-friendly rules and social sustainability. "On which standards are we operating?" has become an apparent question in European policy circles.

Rather than debunking the BRI outright, the European Commission and High Representative stated the EU's terms of engagement with China in a "Strategic Outlook", which was welcomed by the Foreign Affairs Council on 18 March 2019. The EU strategy adopts a multifaceted approach and defines the Middle Kingdom simultaneously, in different policy areas, as a partner, competitor and rival (see Bastian, Chapter 6). The EU's ten-point action plan aims to fill the current gaps in EU law on competition and state aid, investment and procurement.

Based on trends of decreasing BRI investments in Europe and of Member States' increasing concerns about economic and national security (Section 2), this chapter provides an analysis of the EU-wide legal bulwarks and regulatory responses to address those concerns (Section 3). It collects ideas on how to increase transparency and convergence between the EU and China, in the spirit of the EU's connectivity strategy with Asia (European Commission and HR/VP 2018) (Section 4). It concludes that, while a more realistic and assertive EU approach toward Chinese market behaviour is welcome, the EU should take China up on its pledge to embolden the BRI with "soft connectivity", i.e. a legal infrastructure, to truly achieve win-win cooperation (Xu 2018), rather than risk mutual harm by adopting too protectionist a stance (Section 5).

2 Why Chinese SOEs' investments challenge single market order

In the 2010s, after an initial surge in Chinese investment in the EU, a decline set in as a result of, *inter alia,* tightened investment-screening regimes erected by a few EU Member States at the end of the decade. One characteristic of China's overall FDI is the investment in "hardware" (ports and utilities, for example) which are along the many branches of the BRI into Eurasia, the Middle East and parts of Africa, for land, maritime, digital and space connectivity. Much of China's investment in southern and eastern parts of Europe has been in utilities and energy, or involves upgrading existing infrastructure, such as the Port of Piraeus in Greece, where the SOE China

Ocean Shipping (Group) Company (COSCO) has acquired a 51% stake in the port authority. As an integral part of the BRI, and in addition to its stake in Rotterdam and Antwerp, which amounts to 35% (143.3 million euro) and 25% (133.9 million euro) respectively, COSCO's expansion in the Belgian port of Zeebrugge has significantly increased the company's presence in the North Sea (Grieger 2018b). Such acquisitions of EU port infrastructure, though they produce economic benefits to the ports concerned, advance China's state interests in the EU, with access to strategic logistics platforms enabling further opportunities to expand business interests and, inevitably, political influence. The latter touches on the core motive of the EU's foreign investment screening instrument, i.e. the unprecedented concerns about the risks to national security or public order that such investments by Chinese SOEs entail (Hanemann and Huotari 2018; Hanemann, Huotari and Kratz 2019).

The risks to public order have to do with certain investment practices of Chinese SOEs that do not follow market principles, and the substantial industrial subsidies which fuel such practices potentially undermining the effectiveness of the WTO Agreement on Subsidies and Countervailing Measures (ASCM). Although SOEs from European and other countries also invest around the globe in strategic sectors, their conduct is expected to be based on commercial considerations and to be non-discriminatory vis-à-vis other market players.[ii] Similarly, many SOEs around the globe receive subsidies. But the ways in which the Chinese government intervenes in SOEs' operations and the manner with which funds are provided by the Chinese authorities could cause injuries to other market players. Coupled with often delayed, incomplete and missing subsidies notifications, it will be very difficult to detect actionable and prohibited subsidies. This leaves injured market players unable to remedy damages. As a result, there have been calls to reform disciplinary action under the ASCM (Hu 2019).

China-specific concerns about unfair competition are to a large extent related to the particularities of the Chinese political economy, where state interference prevails over market forces. In strategic industries such as chemicals, petroleum and telecoms, the government acts as regulator, investor and business operator, thus blurring the lines between what is public and what is private. The initial SOE reforms that China undertook in the run-up to its WTO accession in 2001 were successful but incomplete (Pelkmans et al. 2018). Neither has China fully complied with its WTO accession commitments in, for example, separating the government from SOEs (Hu 2019). Granted favourable policies to operate in home markets and easy access to government funds to compete with ordinary market players abroad, a Chinese SOE has a doubly advantageous position. This constitutes unfair competition and distorts the market order.

As some SOEs act as the Chinese government's agent to roll out national industrial policies, such as the Made in China 2025 Strategy, and because SOEs are the main investors overseas, Chinese FDI flowing into the EU tends to arouse more suspicion about a hidden political agenda than FDI from the US, Japan or South Korea. China's one-party state is an outlier with significant economic leverage, which promotes principles and norms that are frequently at odds with those of law-abiding democracies: the rule of law, transparency and fair competition.

It is against this background that Europe has gradually been erecting its legal defences. Security and public order concerns linked to FDI are addressed at either the EU or Member State levels through competition law, rules on state aid and public procurement. We discuss these sets of rules in turn.

3 European regulatory response mechanisms

3.1 EU competition law

Competition law's most salient tool is the EU Merger Regulation.[iii] Its enforcement is shared between the European Commission and the Member States' anti-trust authorities. This principle may be illustrated by the Alstom-Siemens rail merger proposal, which was blocked by the Commission in February 2019, in spite of reservations by the French and German governments (European Commission 2019).

So far, Chinese investors have not established dominant positions in relevant European markets which warranted an investigation. Whereas EU merger control also caters to the screening of acquisitions of European companies, it does—as of yet,—not allow the Commission to intervene against takeovers solely on the grounds that the buyer benefitted from foreign subsidies. Arguably, trade defence instruments should be able to address unfair foreign subsidies. In view of the finding that the BRI is primarily explored and exploited by state-owned and government-controlled companies and banks from China (European Union Chamber of Commerce 2020), it makes sense to consider EU rules on state aid and public procurement more closely and then look into investment-screening mechanisms.

3.2 EU rules on state aid and public procurement

State aid

The EU places stringent restrictions on state aid to investment projects involving private parties. Article 107 TFEU denounces any aid that may distort competition or affect trade between Member States. Article 108(3) TFEU therefore obliges Member States to notify the Commission of any plan to grant such aid. Note that within the context of the internal market, state aid means any aid, regardless of its form, granted to certain undertakings by national public authorities. By virtue of Article107(3)(a) and (c) TFEU, certain state aid may be found compatible with the internal market if it is granted for the purpose of supporting economic development in disadvantaged regions and for creating economic activities and jobs.

In light of the above, Chinese state funding pouring into the EU is regarded with suspicion, especially when the investor is an SOE and the investment comes in the form of a loan that is granted to a BRI project through an inter-bank on-lending facility between, for example, the China Development Bank and a national bank of a Member State (China Development Bank 2018). Such funds are qualified as aid from a Member State rather than from a third country government. Within this context, the Commission's investigation and clearance of the BosodChem project is a case in point (cf. Section 1).

Public procurement

As indicated above, Chinese companies participating in EU public procurement activities are bound by EU public procurement rules, which are based on the principles of transparency, non-discrimination and competitiveness.

Within the remit of the EU public procurement directives,[iv] all undertakings, either public or private, are guaranteed participation in procurement tendering, as long as a public undertaking tenderer's participation does not cause any distortion to competition vis-à-vis private undertaking tenderers. With regard to the eligibility of public undertaking tenderers, directly or indirectly subsidised undertakings by a state (or other contracting authorities or even by the contracting authority itself) may legitimately take part in a tender.[v] The criterion that may disqualify a tenderer includes "abnormally low tenders",[vi] or if a tenderer violates relevant labour and environmental legislation.

Projects with third countries are implemented through international agreements, under which the parties can agree on specific procurement rules. In this case, the EU procurement instruments are not applicable, but such specific procurement rules must comply with basic treaty principles of transparency and equal treatment.

It is acknowledged that Chinese investors possess certain qualities, such as technical expertise, efficiency and a can-do attitude, which are highly valuable, especially for large infrastructure projects. But due to the massive state funds that they are provided in connection with Chinese contractors, a chief legal obstacle that Chinese investors face in public procurement tenders in Europe is "low price" (Grieger 2018a). And this may disqualify their bids since an abnormally low bid, amounting to dumping, is not seen as being compatible with the "best value for money" approach adopted by the EU public procurement rules, and principles such as fair competition may also be brought to question the legitimacy of a Chinese SOE's bid. The saga of the Pelješac bridge in Croatia illustrates this misgiving (Blockmans and Hu 2019). The EU's Strategic Outlook for China states that, "a more strategic approach to the EU's procurement framework could help to identify and address obstacles and loopholes that impede a level playing field in [global markets]. For instance, the rules could be revised or their application strengthened in order to ensure that procurement procedures conducted in the EU on the basis of international agreements comply with the [EU legal] principles [such as] transparency and equal treatment" (European Commission and HR/VP 2019).

By way of sub-conclusion, EU rules on state aid and public procurement suffer from two major deficiencies: they only cover aid granted by Member States and do not fully address the effects within the single market of subsidies granted by foreign governments; nor was there a systematic and centralised FDI screening on security grounds at the EU level. Among the 27 EU Member States, a majority of them have no screening mechanism. In the Member States that do there are significant differences. We will discuss these issues in turn, first by focusing on what scope for FDI screening exists at the level of the Member States, and then by analysing the new regulation on the EU-wide FDI screening mechanism.

3.3 FDI screening mechanisms

National level

By virtue of Article 21 of the EU Merger Regulation Member States have the exclusive competence to scrutinise, and therefore to take proper measures with regard to acquisitions in order to protect national interests on the grounds of public security, a plurality of the media and prudential rules, also known as "recognised interests", in the defence, media and financial services sectors. At present, among the EU27 14 Member States[vii] have a legal framework for scrutiny in place or have performed case-by-case reviews for reasons of national security or restrictions on qualifications of expatriates and reciprocity. The 14 FDI scrutiny mechanisms differ in design and scope, for example in terms of prior authorisation and *ex post* screening (European Commission 2020a).

Those Member States embracing a narrow interpretation of national security (limited to the weapons industry), such as Denmark, Sweden, and Slovenia, have introduced restrictions under a specific legal basis. The prevailing approach uses case-by-case scrutiny, while automatic scrutiny is mostly linked to the requirement to hold a licence for commercial activity. Ireland has no formal screening mechanism but prohibits foreign (and domestic) investment in the armaments sector. Denmark has both a formal scrutiny procedure for the weapons industry and excludes FDI from its gas and electricity infrastructure, which must remain public property. In Spain and Sweden, screening is mandatory for the defence sector, while it is run case-by-case for other sectors.

In recent years, several Member States, including Finland, France, Germany, Italy, Poland and Portugal have revised their FDI screening procedures to determine whether essential security interests or public order are endangered by impending acquisitions. In the case of Germany, the country's Federal Ministry for Economic Affairs and Energy in July 2017 tightened the Foreign Trade Ordinance (Blockmans and Hu 2019) and introduced obligations to report foreign takeovers of German companies in various areas of critical infrastructure, including defence and IT security (and cryptographic equipment). Also, cross-sector scrutiny may be triggered by the acquisition of more than 25% of voting rights in the company to be acquired, although the latter is only applied to investments from non-EU and non-European Free Trade Association countries.

The existence of a patchwork of FDI screening mechanisms in nearly half of the Member States has sparked a debate whether Union-level tools should be developed to adequately tackle the perceived challenges posed by the BRI to all Member States.

Concerns about unfair competition from China through bids that cross between private investment and state-orchestrated takeovers (see the failed Aixtron takeover) have added to longstanding worries about the persistent lack of reciprocal access for EU companies to the Chinese market, though China, based on its Foreign Investment Law, has made an attempt to address some of the biggest challenges faced by foreign businesses such as national treatment, unfair technology transfers, IPR protection and equal opportunities in public procurement. Nonetheless, China still has one of the most restrictive FDI regimes in the world. In 2018, China was the sixth most FDI-restrictive among 69 countries surveyed by the OECD, though the country was equally ranked as one of the top reformers between 1997 and 2018 having nearly halved FDI restrictiveness (Organisation for Economic Co-operation and Development 2020).

This asymmetrical situation and the perceived regulatory gap on the side of Member States and EU competition law triggered a debate in Brussels about the need for legislative action to create a new EU-wide FDI screening mechanism (European Commission 2017; Elysée 2018). Of course, such a mechanism is only a defence measure against external risks aimed at addressing distortive effects caused by foreign industrial subsidies in the single market and to tackle foreign access to EU public procurement and EU funding. To strengthen the functioning of the single market from within, promote a global level playing field and maintain the EU's economic competitiveness in the world, the Commission published in March 2020 a new Industry Policy Strategy (European Commission 2020e). We will discuss these measures in turn.

EU-level

AN FDI SCREENING MECHANISM

The underlying philosophy of an EU-wide screening mechanism is that better coordination of national policies is contingent on a common legal framework to protect essential strategic interests, increase legal certainty and ensure transparency, while sustaining one of the most open investment regimes in the world. Although some experts have stressed that positive reciprocity rather than return harm should be privileged,[viii] a transparent EU-wide mechanism would provide certainty for investors and eliminate the inconsistencies of the current patchwork system. Insisting on transparency should also ensure fair competition within the remit of public procurement rules, not least because it is clear who buys in Europe and how purchases are financed. A common review system would allow the identification of sectors that are vital for EU security, and where the concentration of economic power by non-EU investors risks being abused.

The new instrument, which entered into force on 10 April 2019 (with full application from 11 October 2020 onwards),[ix] is expected to detect foreign investment in critical assets, technologies and infrastructure. Pre-emptive measures against circumvention are equally included in the legislation, in which case, for example, European-domiciled companies that are owned or controlled by a foreign investor could be scrutinised. The framework prioritises multi-level cooperation: it enables the Commission to issue non-binding opinions on investment concerning several Member States or when an investment could affect the "Union interest" (e.g. Galileo[x]), but leaves untouched the Member States' competence to decide whether a particular investment threatens national security interests or public order.[xi]

By way of further clarification, the FDI screening instrument provides that in determining whether foreign investment is likely to affect security or the public order, Member States may take into account whether the foreign investor is controlled by the government of a third country, including through significant and opaque subsidy programmes.

In view of the outbreak of the COVID-19 pandemic, the Commission called on Member States to be vigilant against attempts to acquire strategic industrial capacities (e.g. for the production of medical or protective equipment) or research centres (e.g. those developing vaccines) through foreign direct investment (European Commission 2020d).

A NEW INDUSTRIAL STRATEGY

To deliver the three key priorities set out by the new industrial strategy of March 2020 (see above), the Commission has started to review the competition rules (e.g. merger control and state aid guidelines) and trade defence mechanisms. On 17 June 2020, the Commission published a white paper to kickstart the public consultation process on how to address distortive effects caused by foreign subsidies in the single market and to tackle foreign access to EU public procurement and EU funding.[xii] A proposal for a legal instrument will be released in 2021, which should complement the ongoing efforts to strengthen the disciplines of industrial subsidies in the WTO and actions to address the lack of reciprocal access for public procurement in third countries (European Commission 2020e).

The present efforts to strengthen the discipline of industrial subsidies within the remit of the ASCM in the WTO are four-fold, encompassing provider and recipient of a subsidy, the manner in which a subsidy is provided, and the obligation of notification and transparency. The ultimate purpose of ascertaining these four elements is to detect specific subsidies which may be prohibited or actionable, so that if they cause injuries to a business, remedies could be sought either in the WTO or as countervailing duties. China is not the only WTO member whose industrial practices could undermine the effectiveness of the ASCM. For example, many members neglect their obligation for subsidy notification prescribed by Article 25 of the ASCM. But given its economic weight, the increasingly large scale of its industrial programmes, the state's growing intervention in the economy, which could see the government act as both a subsidy provider (i.e. as a public body) and a recipient (i.e. SOE), it is China and its practice in industrial subsidies that can be considered as the main target of the ASCM reform. The BRI may be seen as an embodiment of this practice.

However, the present initiatives to reform the ASCM have a few drawbacks. Efforts at the multilateral level in the WTO will be drawn out and most likely futile. The plurilateral approach might produce changes more quickly, but if China remains absent from, for example, the EU-Japan-USA trilateral meeting of trade ministers (United States Trade Representative 2017), such initiatives would miss the target. Given China's development-based WTO reform philosophy, it is almost certain that the country will not join such initiatives (Hu 2019). As part of its industrial strategy, the EU's new legal instrument might therefore provide a solution at the bilateral level.

We will now turn to issues of regulatory convergence from a multilateral, regional and bilateral perspective.

4 Increasing regulatory convergence?

In an effort to circle the wagons as Beijing makes political and economic inroads into the wider European regulatory space, the European Commission and the High Representative have since March 2019, pushed the Member States into endorsing a consistent posture to deepen cooperation with China on trade and investment while dealing with strategic and security tensions around Chinese technology (European Commission and HR/VP 2018). As one of the ten actions set out in the Strategic Outlook, the EU also wanted to seal an ambitious Comprehensive Agreement on Investment (CAI) with China by the end of 2020 (European Commission and HR/VP 2018). While progress was slowed down by a combination of different approaches to investment negotiations (Pelkmans et al. 2018) and the COVID-19 crisis, the ambition to close the many regulatory gaps nevertheless revealed a new level of activism in bilateral ties. During the

May 2020 round, negotiations continued on market access, including sector-specific market access asks, and on disciplines related to investment liberalisation and a level playing field, notably, the rules for SOEs and reinforced disciplines tackling forced technology transfers (European Commission 2020c). A few hard-core market access issues have been solved since, chiefly by the introduction of China's Foreign Investment Law, and reinforced by the US-China Economic and Trade Agreement, also known as the "Phase One Agreement". The areas that China has committed to structurally reform encompass IP protection (including pharmaceutical-related patent protection), technology transfers, financial services and macroeconomic policies. Whereas China's efforts look credible, a track record of deliverables is required to convince an increasingly sceptical EU that a level playing field will be achieved. Gaps remain, for example, on issues such as subsidies transparency.

To address the issue, the Commission already back in 2016 adopted an amended proposal for an International Procurement Instrument (IPI): a regulation "on the access of third-country goods and services to the Union's internal market in public procurement and procedures supporting negotiations on access of Union goods and services to the public procurement markets of third countries" (European Commission 2016). Once implemented, the IPI would help to guarantee reciprocity of access to public procurement markets in the EU and China by European and Chinese businesses. However, the file seems to be stuck in the legislative process and is unlikely to be adopted any time soon, even if the Commission's industrial strategy of March 2020 revived an earlier ambition to adopt the IPI before the end of 2019 (European Commission and HR/VP 2018). But the issue of "abnormally low" bids that Chinese SOEs are able to offer in order to succeed in acquiring procurement contracts along the Belt and Road is expected to be addressed in the Commission's legal instrument on foreign subsidies, scheduled for 2021.

China's accession to the Government Procurement Agreement (GPA) would be another avenue through which the EU could achieve a level playing field on public procurement. In negotiations on a revised GPA in the context of the WTO, the European Commission has advocated an ambitious opening of international public procurement markets (European Union Internal Market 2020). As to its GPA accession commitment, China has since December 2007 submitted seven offers, each with more entities and activities covered, as well as lowered thresholds. In its last offer, submitted in October 2019, China proposed a list of new government entities (at the level of China's autonomous regions and 16 SOEs) to be covered. These would be required to open their public tenders to foreign competition. Apparently, all construction services are now covered by the offers, as well as postal and transportation services, including railways and highways. But offers still fell short of expectations of GPA parties and remained deficient because in a number of critical areas (including thresholds, entity coverage and offsets), the professed openness is still not commensurate with what GPA parties offered (United States Trade Representative 2020).

In the wake of the EU–China Summit of 16 July 2018, the EU and China also set up a joint working group geared towards WTO reform. The precise mandate of the Working Group is not known, however. In March 2020, the EU, China and 17 other WTO members established a contingency multi-party interim appeal arbitration arrangement, i.e. a separate appeal system to settle trade disputes to compensate for the shutdown of the Appellate Body in December 2019. On structural reform issues, such as strengthening the WTO rule-making capacity in a number of disciplines, including industrial subsidies, there seemed to be no progress.

Convergence would be more forthcoming if China were to faithfully deliver on the commitments pledged on the occasion of its accession to the WTO, in particular those concerning the above-mentioned four aspects that industry subsidy reform aims to remedy within the remit of the ASCM. For example, China pledged that SOEs would be reformed by "a separation of government from enterprise", and that the growth of the state-owned sector would occur through independent operation and competitive market discipline, with banks, too, being responsible for their own profits and losses. The government also committed to notifying about any subsidy programme at all administrative levels and pledged that the information provided in notifications should be as specific as possible, and that it would progressively work towards full notification of subsidies as required by Article 25 of the ASCM and Annexes 5A and 5B of its Accession Protocol (World Trade Organisation 2001).

If, as its leadership proclaims, China is committed to uphold and modernise the multilateral trade system (Zhang 2018), then it should (continue to) deliver on its WTO commitments and also mobilise the broad international buy-in for its connectivity and growth strategy to fit the BRI with a legal architecture and dispute settlement mechanism that spurs international solutions rather than imposes Chinese legal constructs. Given the magnitude of EU–China trade and investment links, the Union has stressed the importance of developing a more balanced and reciprocal economic relationship by working together with China in international fora to upgrade the rules (European Commission and HR/VP 2018). Whereas the EU's 2019 Strategic Outlook on China focuses on the WTO, one could easily include the BRI as well.

5 Concluding remarks

Chinese policymakers like to brand the BRI as a "win-win cooperation". There is, however, a marked disconnect between that rhetoric, the realities on the ground, and increasingly negative perceptions in the EU about this cooperation. Europeans have woken up to the fact that all roads no longer lead to Rome but to Beijing, and that they are lagging behind China and the

US in preparing for the fourth industrial revolution—an international economy based on telecommunications infrastructure, artificial intelligence and space technologies (Renda 2019). Member State governments have been updating their respective FDI screening laws to respond to aggressive overtures from China towards their economies and protect their strategic sectors from being taken over by SOEs with opaque operational modes. But in spite of the 2018 EU Strategy on Connecting Europe and Asia, Europe's response overall has been rather incoherent. The strategic course correction of March 2019 aimed to change this but the follow-up by Member States remains inconsistent.

Our own empirical research has exposed the need to plug the gaps in the intersection between EU competition law, rules on state aid and public procurement—with links to the relevant WTO disciplines, and the regulatory patchwork of Member States' FDI review mechanisms (Blockmans and Hu 2019). In the political sphere, Member States would do better to coordinate their actions at 27 and to prevent the Union from falling prey to the imperial doctrine of "divide and rule". Even if its relative global weight is waning, the European Union is still the world's largest economic collective and a regulatory powerhouse to be reckoned with. Existing EU legislation (for example on public procurement) already has a deterrent effect on malpractices (cf. delayed investments, derailed proposals). The new EU-level FDI screening mechanism will help to reinforce these legal defences against external risks while the industrial policy strategy of March 2020 is expected to optimise the functioning of the single market and strengthen the EU's global competitiveness from within.

Europe must not fall into the trap of protectionism. It should not ignore the fact that, over the past four decades, China has accrued considerable economic strength and know-how. Beijing can be a constructive partner, especially in view of an unpredictable trading partner across the Atlantic. The EU needs to perform a delicate balancing act to convince China of the need for a level playing field and to turn the BRI into a two-way street for economic growth. This is not only in Western Europe's interest—the main trading and investment destination for China—but also in that of the 17 countries of Central and Eastern Europe, as well as the Caucasian and Central Asian countries along the new Silk Road. Reciprocal benefits beat mutual harm.

The assertiveness expressed by the EU's Strategic Outlook on China should alert policymakers in Beijing to the fact that Europe's common legal defences will bar Chinese investors from the single market if, in spite of a change of official rhetoric in favour of free and fair trade a few years ago, the BRI continues to lack inclusiveness, fails to invite foreign participants, and does not observe best practices of commercial and legal governance. For the sake of the BRI's success and mutual economic benefit, Chinese policymakers would be well advised to address European concerns in a fair-minded and constructive manner, rather than stonewall the EU with ever-louder empty messages that the Belt and Road Initiative is a panacea for all. In view of the West's negative perceptions of the way Beijing handled the outbreak and spread of the coronavirus and the introduction of the national security law in Hong Kong in the first half of 2020, a more balanced and reciprocal approach to relations with the EU is key in toning down calls for a much more aggressive stance on relations with China.

Notes

i This contribution is an updated and shortened version of Blockmans and Hu (2019).

ii Article XVII, GATT.

iii Council Regulation (EC) No 139/2004.

iv Directive 2014/24/EU on public procurement, and Directive 2014/25/EU on procurement by entities operating in the water, energy, transport and postal services sectors.

v Case C-94/99, ARGE Gewässerschutzt v. Bundesministerium für Land und Forstwirtschaft [2000] ECR I-11037.

vi Case 76/81, SA Transporoute et Travaux v. Minister of Public Works [1982] ECR I-457.

vii Austria, Denmark, Finland, France, Germany, Hungary, Italy, Latvia, Lithuania, Poland, Portugal, Spain, the Netherlands and Romania.

viii This would imply that FDI screening must be limited to national security considerations and that it must exclude economic security issues.

ix Regulation (EU) 2019/452 of the European Parliament and of the Council of 19 March 2019 establishing a framework for the screening of foreign direct investments into the Union, OJ L 79I/1, 21.03.2019.

x Galileo is the EU's Global Satellite Navigation System (GNSS). Sometimes called the "European GPS", Galileo provides accurate positioning and timing information. Galileo is a programme under civilian control and its data can be used for a broad range of applications. Further information is available at: https://ec.europa.eu/growth/sectors/space/galileo_en.

xi In reviewing FDI, a Member State may consider the potential effect of the investment on areas including, critical infrastructure (e.g. energy, transport, communications), critical technologies (e.g. artificial intelligence, robotics), security of supply of critical inputs, access to sensitive information or the ability to control sensitive information.

xii The White Paper proposed a number of options to tackle the negative impact of competition in the Single Market, but fall outside EU state aid control, including a notification requirement for acquisitions of companies based in the EU, as in European Commission (2020b).

Bibliography

Blockmans, S. and Hu, W., 2019. *Systemic Rivalry and Balancing Interests: Chinese Investment Meets EU Law on the Belt and Road* [online]. Brussels: CEPS Policy Insights, No.4. [viewed 20 July 2020]. Available from https://www.ceps.eu/ceps-publications/systemic-rivalry-and-balancing-interests-chinese-investment-meets-eu-law-belt-and-road/

Bryant, C., 2011. *Wanhua Takes Full Control of BorsodChem* [online]. Budapest: Financial Times. [viewed 22 July 2019]. Available from https://www.ft.com/content/1aadca66-2e2e-11e0-8733-00144feabdc0

China Development Bank, 2018. *Annual Report 2018* [online]. Beijing: China Development Bank. [viewed 22 July 2020]. Available from http://www.cdb.com.cn/English/gykh_512/ndbg_jx/2018_jx/

Elysée, 2018. *Speech by Emmanuel Macron, President of the Republic at European Parliament* [online]. Elysée [viewed 22 July 2020]. Available from https://www.elysee.fr/emmanuel-macron/2018/04/17/speech-by-emmanuel-macron-president-of-the-republic-at-european-parliament.en

European Commission, 2016. *Amended Proposal for a REGULATION OF THE EUROPEAN PARLIAMENT AND OF THE COUNCIL on the Access of Third-Country Goods and Services to the Union's Internal Market in Public Procurement and Procedures Supporting Negotiations on Access of Union Goods and Services to the Public Procurement Markets of Third Countries, Brussels, 29 January 2016 COM (2016) 34 final* [online]. Brussels: European Commission. [viewed 22 July 2020]. Available from http://trade.ec.europa.eu/doclib/docs/2016/january/tradoc_154187.pdf

European Commission, 2017. *Commission Decision of 29.11.2017 Setting Up the Group of Experts on the Screening of Foreign Direct Investments in the European Union, Brussels, 29.11.2017 C(2017) 7866 final* [online]. Brussels: European Commission. [viewed 22 July 2020]. Available from https://ec.europa.eu/transparency/regexpert/index.cfm?do=groupDetail.groupDetailDoc&id=36097&no=1

European Commission, 2018. *State Aid: Commission Approves Hungary's €45 Million Investment Aid to Chemical Company BorsodChem Zrt to be in Line with EU State Aid Rules, Press release, Brussels, 28 September 2018* [online]. Brussels: European Commission. [viewed 22 July 2020]. Available from https://ec.europa.eu/commission/presscorner/detail/en/IP_18_5941

European Commission, 2019. *Mergers: Commission Prohibits Siemens' Proposed Acquisition of Alstom, Press Release, Brussels, 6 February 2019* [online]. Brussels: European Commission. [viewed 22 July 2020]. Available from https://ec.europa.eu/commission/presscorner/detail/en/IP_19_881

European Commission, 2020a. *List of Screening Mechanisms Notified by Member States* [online]. Brussels: European Commission. [viewed 20 July 2020]. Available from https://trade.ec.europa.eu/doclib/docs/2019/june/tradoc_157946.pdf

European Commission, 2020b. *White Paper on Levelling the Playing Field as Regards Foreign Subsidies, Brussels, 17.6.2020 COM(2020) 253 final* [online]. Brussels: European Commission. [viewed 22 July 2020]. Available from https://ec.europa.eu/competition/international/overview/foreign_subsidies_white_paper.pdf

European Commission, 2020c. *Report of the 29th Round of Negotiations on the EU-China Comprehensive Agreement on Investment, Brussels, 29 May 2020 TRADE.B2/* [online]. Brussels: European Commission. [viewed 22 July 2020]. Available from https://trade.ec.europa.eu/doclib/docs/2020/may/tradoc_158765.pdf

European Commission, 2020d. *Guidance to the Member States Concerning Foreign Direct Investment and Free Movement of Capital From Third Countries, and the Protection of Europe's Strategic Assets, Ahead of the Application Of Regulation (EU) 2019/452 (FDI Screening Regulation), Brussels, 25.3.2020 C(2020) 1981 final* [online]. Brussels: European Commission. [viewed 22 July 2020]. Available from https://trade.ec.europa.eu/doclib/docs/2020/march/tradoc_158676.pdf

European Commission, 2020e. *A New Industrial Strategy for Europe, Brussels, 10.3.2020 COM (2020) 102 final* [online]. Brussels: European Commission. [viewed 22 July 2020]. Available from https://ec.europa.eu/info/sites/info/files/communication-eu-industrial-strategy-march-2020_en.pdf

European Commission and HR/VP, 2018. *Connecting Europe and Asia – Building Blocks for an EU Strategy, Brussels, JOIN(2018) 31 final, 19 September 2018* [online]. Brussels: European Commission and HR/VP. [viewed 22 July 2020]. Available from https://eeas.europa.eu/sites/eeas/files/joint_communication_-_connecting_europe_and_asia_-_building_blocks_for_an_eu_strategy_2018-09-19.pdf

European Commission and HR/VP, 2019. *EU-China – A Strategic Outlook, Strasbourg, 12.3.2019 JOIN(2019) 5 final* [online]. Strasbourg: European Commission and HR/VP. [viewed 22 July 2020]. Available from https://ec.europa.eu/commission/sites/beta-political/files/communication-eu-china-a-strategic-outlook.pdf

European Council, 2019. *Conclusions on the Significance of 5G to the European Economy and the Need to Mitigate Security Risks Linked to 5G, 3 December 2019, doc. 14517/19* [online]. Brussels: European Council. [viewed 22 July 2020]. Available from https://www.consilium.europa.eu/media/41595/st14517-en19.pdf

European Union Chamber of Commerce in China, 2020. *The Road Less Travelled: European Involvement in China's Belt and Road Initiative* [online]. Beijing: European Union Chamber of Commerce in China. [viewed 22 July 2020]. Available from https://static.europeanchamber.com.cn/upload/documents/documents/The_Road_Less_Travelled[762].pdf

European Union Internal Market, 2020. *Public Procurement*. [viewed 23 July 2020]. Available from https://ec.europa.eu/growth/single-market/public-procurement_en

Grieger, G., 2018a. *China, the 16+1 Format and the EU* [online]. European Parliamentary Research Service. [viewed 20 July 2020]. Available from: https://www.europarl.europa.eu/thinktank/en/document.html?reference=EPRS_BRI(2018)625173

Grieger, G., 2018b. *China's Maritime Silk Road Initiative Increasingly Touches the EU* [online]. European Parliamentary Research Service. [viewed 20 July 2020]. Available from: https://www.europarl.europa.eu/thinktank/en/document.html?reference=EPRS_BRI(2018)614767

Hanemann, T. and Huotari, M., 2018. *EU-China FDI: Working Towards Reciprocity in Investment Relations* [online]. Berlin: Rhodium Group and the Mercator Institute for China Studies. [viewed 22 July 2020]. Available from https://merics.org/en/report/eu-china-fdi-working-towards-more-reciprocity-investment-relations

Hanemann, T., Huotari, M. and Kratz, A., 2019. *Chinese FDI in Europe: 2018 Trends and Impact of New Screening Policies* [online]. Berlin: Rhodium Group and the Mercator Institute for China Studies. [viewed 22 July 2020]. Available from https://rhg.com/research/chinese-fdi-in-europe-2018-trends-and-impact-of-new-screening-policies/

Hu, W., 2019. *Industrial Subsidies, State-Owned Enterprises and Market Distortions: Problems, Proposals and a Path Forward* [online]. Adelaide: Institute for International Trade, University of Adelaide. [viewed 22 July 2020]. Available from https://iit.adelaide.edu.au/system/files/media/documents/2019-12/IIT%20PB05%20Industrial%20Subsidies.pdf

National Development and Reform Commission, 2018. *Vision and Actions on Jointly Building Silk Road Economic Belt and 21st Century Maritime Silk Road.* [viewed 22 July 2020]. Available from https://en.ndrc.gov.cn/newsrelease_8232/201503/t20150330_1193900.html

Organisation for Economic Co-operation and Development, 2020. *FDI Regulatory Restrictiveness Index* [online]. Paris: Organisation for Economic Co-operation and Development. [viewed 22 July 2020]. Available from http://www.oecd.org/investment/fdiindex.htm.

Pelkmans, J., Hu, W. et al., 2018. *Tomorrow's Silk Road: Assessing an EU-China Free Trade Agreement.* 2nd ed. Brussels and London: CEPS and Rowman and Littlefield International.

Rachman, G., 2019. *The US, China and the Return of a Two-Bloc World* [online]. Financial Times. [viewed 22 July 2019]. Available from https://www.ft.com/content/35accdc0–43de-11e9-a965-23d669740bfb

Renda, A., 2019. Digital Economy, Industry and Innovation. In S. Blockmans, ed. *What Comes After the Last Chance Commission? Policy Priorities for 2019-2024.* Brussels: Ceps, p. 92.

United States Trade Representative, 2017. *Joint Statement by the United States, European Union and Japan at MC11* [online]. Washington DC: United States Trade Representative. [viewed 22 July 2020]. Available from https://ustr.gov/about-us/policy-offices/press-office/press-releases/2017/december/joint-statement-united-states

United States Trade Representative, 2020. *2019 Report to Congress on China's WTO Compliance* [online]. Washington DC: United States Trade Representative. [viewed 22 July 2020]. Available from https://ustr.gov/sites/default/files/2019_Report_on_China%E2%80%99s_WTO_Compliance.pdf

World Trade Organisation, 2001. *Report of the Working Party on the Accession of China, WT/MIN(01)/3, 10 November 2001.* Geneva: World Trade Organisation.

Xu, W., 2018. *Beijing Will Work to Ensure Belt, Road Transparent* [online]. China: China Daily. [viewed 22 July 2020]. Available from http://usa.chinadaily.com.cn/a/201807/04/WS5b3c2f47a3103349141e0943.html

Zhang, M., 2018. *China Supports and Upholds Multilateral Trading System* [online]. Brussels: EU Observer. [viewed 22 July 2020]. Available from https://euobserver.com/stakeholders/142470

Part III

Belt and Road Factors in EU law and policy

6 Sino-European financial linkages underpinning BRI projects in Europe

Jens Bastian

Introduction

This contribution focuses on financial linkages underpinning the implementation of China's Belt and Road Initiative in Europe with a specific emphasis on the region of Southeast Europe.[i] An emboldened China is becoming more assertive on the global political economy stage, inviting and challenging individual countries to redefine their strategic policy priorities vis-à-vis Beijing. For EU member states from Central, Eastern and Southeast Europe and EU candidate countries from the Western Balkans China's investment and overseas lending outreach raise profound questions about political standards and rules of engagement for infrastructure project financing.

Since its official launch in 2013 by President Xi Jinping China's flagship foreign policy project — the Belt and Road Initiative (BRI)[ii] — invests on a global scale in land-based and maritime projects, primarily through transport connectivity and trade-enhancing infrastructure. Under the aegis of the BRI, promises of "shared prosperity" are promoted to participating countries. China's BRI combines unprecedented amounts of investment and loan funding for ambitious infrastructure projects across continents, regions and individual countries. Beijing-based policy banks are the primary providers of funding arrangements for these projects.

For the European Commission in Brussels and individual EU member states, the BRI raises profound questions concerning their political relationship and investment arrangements with China. While the Commission seeks to develop a coherent strategy vis-à-vis China's BRI ambitions, Beijing is busy offering loan facilities, Chinese labour and services for the construction of bridges, highways and the modernization of ports and railways across Europe.

In what follows, the contribution will first discuss the political economy dynamics behind the expanding financial interlinkages. The incentives for cooperation with China's BRI are challenging to reject for countries in Southeast Europe, all the more when Chinese financing institutions leverage concessional lending opportunities for large-scale infrastructure. The multiplication of BRI projects and participating countries has advanced institutional innovation in areas such as dispute resolution and mediation with "Chinese characteristics". This policy area illustrates how China is also engaged in setting new rules and standards while creating institutions for legal redress in BRI-related cases. Section 2 discusses these aspects.

Section 3 turns the reader's attention to individual country cases, namely Hungary, Serbia and Montenegro. What emerges from these country cases are different patterns of financial interlinkages. The impact of the BRI on the EU is discussed in Section 4. The need for consistency and unity of purpose vis-à-vis China represents the biggest challenge for the EU. Various initiatives seek to address this challenge and provide policy guidance through recent Commission communications and regulatory interventions. The concluding section provides a twofold perspective. For one, an outlook on Sino-European relations and secondly, a brief discussion regarding the consequences of the coronavirus pandemic for Sino-Southeast European cooperation.

I Goals, tools and actors of China's policy in Southeast Europe

How do Chinese political authorities frame the BRI in Southeast Europe? When Chinese representatives visit countries in the region they regularly emphasize how "to dovetail" the Belt and Road Initiative with the development strategies of participating countries in the region. When the Chinese Premier Li Keqiang visited Dubrovnik in April 2019 to attend the ninth China-Central and Eastern European Countries (CEEC) Business Forum, he underlined the momentum of economic and commercial cooperation, including tourist arrivals from China, the flow of Chinese bank credit for major infrastructure projects and corporate acquisitions in Southeast Europe (China.org.cn 2019).

These economic, commercial and financial sector developments highlight an emerging reality in Southeast Europe: China matters to the region. Greece, Serbia and Turkey stand out as the flag bearers of Chinese foreign direct *investment*, while concessionary *lending* to governments for infrastructure projects has targeted Montenegro, Bosnia and Hercegovina as well as North Macedonia. The outlier in this "expeditionary capital" process[iii] is Kosovo. China has steadfastly refused to recognize the sovereignty of Kosovo, thus siding with Serbia. The flip side of this argument also holds. The region of Southeast Europe is of growing economic, commercial and strategic importance for China. Apart from the numerous infrastructure projects, the most visible sign of this importance is the political effort China has put into establishing and subsequently enlarging an institutional architecture for bilateral cooperation under the heading of the "17+1 Network" (which was "16+1" before the participation of Greece in 2019).

II Shifting arbitration and mediation to China

The role of legal redress and mediation in managing China's BRI projects abroad is increasingly gaining traction in Beijing. Arbitration procedures and the legal dispute resolution of contracts based on the BRI are gradually being relocated to China and administered according to Chinese law. China's expanding footprint in BRI dispute resolution is illustrated by establishing two new international commercial courts (Yang 2018; see also Chapter 2 in this publication). In June 2018, China's *Supreme Peoples' Court* established these new legal institutions:

- In Xi'an (the capital city in the province of Shaanxi) for the land-based Silk Road Economic Belt
- In Shenzhen (in the province of Guangdong) for the Maritime Silk Road

China argues that both courts are necessary to address the growing number of legal cases that have arisen in the context of the BRI's expansion. These novel courts provide litigation, arbitration and mediation services. The objective for China is to have all BRI-related disputes resolved in these two courts and based on Chinese jurisprudence. The courts will only deal with legal cases between businesses and investors. BRI-related disputes between states or between investors and states are *not* [yet] part of the new courts' jurisdiction. The judges assigned to both courts are nominated by the Supreme Peoples' Court. This arrangement integrates the new courts into China's legal and judicial system. However, this system cannot be viewed as independent from the political authorities in Beijing.

Given the fact that most BRI projects are internationally intertwined, the courts in Xi'an and Shenzhen have the discretion to process mediation and arbitration cases with the assistance of existing international dispute resolution institutions. This includes the *London Court of International Arbitration* and the *Hong Kong International Arbitration Centre*. Furthermore, international commercial cases are administered by the *Singapore International Commercial Court* and the *International Finance Centre Courts* in Dubai. Depending on the specifics of dispute resolution, foreign litigants may still reserve the right to choose between the international or the Chinese location for dispute resolution.

But this option faces the following constraint: Chinese companies involved in any BRI-related legal complaint prefer the newly created courts in China. This preference can already be included in the contractual arrangements stipulating the financial, operational and legal details of any bilateral BRI project. In a word, China is gradually developing its own cross-border system of BRI jurisdiction. This development will present major legal, operational and administrative challenges for EU member states in Southeast Europe, and even more so for EU candidate and accession countries in the Western Balkans. The country case of Montenegro discusses these challenges with regard to a controversial highway infrastructure project.

III Country cases

Hungary: The perils of railway modernization

The flagship project along the BRI *rail route* in Southeast Europe concerns the modernisation of a China-financed cross-border high-speed railway connection between Budapest and Belgrade. The trilateral profile of the project involves the EU member state Hungary, the EU candidate country Serbia, and in the middle, China as a non-EU external actor. There is also a larger political economy dimension in this flagship infrastructure development project. Hungary's Prime Minister Viktor Orbán highlighted this dimension at the opening of the China—Central and Eastern Europe Summit in Budapest in 2017:

> Globalization's new world order has also brought new configurations. We look upon the President of China's One Belt One Road Initiative as one of globalisation's new configurations: one which will no longer divide the world into teachers and students, but which will provide the basis for mutual respect and mutual advantage (The Hungarian Government 2017).

The initial Memorandum of Understanding (MoU) between Hungary, China and Serbia was signed in December 2014. The construction contract for the Hungarian part of the project was then awarded in a non-competitive bid to the *China Railway International Corp.*, the state-owned Chinese rail company. Hungarian law permits no-bid contracting when public land is involved, and if the investment is projected to result in wider economic benefits for the country.

In November 2016, China's *Exim Ban*k agreed to fund 85% of the Hungarian route of the railway project. The construction of the Hungarian stretch is budgeted at approximately 550 billion forints (USD 2.1 billion). The duration of the credit line is for 20 years and the annual interest rate fixed at 2.5%. Prime Minister Orbán asserted the need for the Belgrade-Budapest railway project, and for Chinese investment in general, as follows:

> We need to carry out numerous investments for which *there is not enough capital* in the Hungarian economy or *in the European Union*…That is why *we are financing the Budapest-Belgrade railway line with Chinese assistance* (GCR 2017, emphasis added).[iv]

In January 2017, the European Commission launched a preliminary investigation into the landmark railway project against Hungary. The infringement proceedings focused on procurement procedures and financial arrangements on the Hungarian side of the rail project. The probe contended that Hungary was in breach of EU procurement laws by not initiating a proper public tender. The allegation of having violated EU procurement rules is a serious matter, both for the political authorities in Budapest as much as for the reputational capital that Chinese companies are seeking to build vis-à-vis EU institutions.

It is instructive to see what happened next. In reaction to the Commission's inquiry, the Hungarian authorities relaunched the tender for the 152-kilometer route from Budapest to the border crossing with Serbia in November 2017. Two years later the public tender was won by a Hungarian-Chinese joint venture. The new contract was awarded to the *CRE Consortium*, half of which is owned by a unit of the Hungarian holding company *Opus Global* (RM International Zrt.). The Chinese half of the joint venture is owned by *China Tiejiuju Engineering & Construction Kft.* and *China Railway Electrification Engineering Group Kft.*, representing the Chinese state-owned railway company. Following the finalization of financing arrangements with *Exim Bank* in the third quarter of 2019, the five-year construction period was to start in the fourth quarter. But due to the coronavirus pandemic work has been delayed.

Despite this increase in externally mandated transparency from Brussels, the Hungarian government continued to shield critical parts of the project from public scrutiny. The emergency powers given to prime minister Orbán in April 2020 by parliament during the coronavirus outbreak enabled the government to keep critical details of a feasibility study and the construction contracts classified for ten years. The government argues that their publication could "threaten Hungary's ability to pursue its foreign policy and trade interests without undue external influence" (Financial Times 2020).

What can we learn from this series of events in a flagship infrastructure project that involves an EU member state, an EU candidate country negotiating accession chapters with the Commission in Brussels and China linking both countries as an intermediary finance provider and construction contractor? For one, as Hungary faced an infringement procedure by the Commission against EU law it agreed to compromise and proceed in compliance with public procurement regulations defined in and monitored by Brussels. Apart from considerable financial risks, reputational capital was at stake for China. It was in the joint interest of Budapest *and* Beijing to engage in railway diplomacy and seek a fast-track resolution instead of drawn-out legal proceedings with the authorities in Brussels.

Secondly, the case illustrates that the regulatory arm of the Commission is constrained. The outcome of the revised tender yielded similar results, i.e. the inclusion of the Chinese companies based on the lowest bid submitted and shortened construction time. Put otherwise, both Hungary and China formally applied greater transparency regarding adherence to the rules of engagement in EU procurement standards. But in substance, it did not change the end result. Moreover, the continued secrecy surrounding certain details of the project by the Hungarian authorities underscores that Budapest is willing to play by its own rules. Awarding the tender to the lowest bidder begs the question if subsidized Chinese state-owned enterprises (SOEs) should have been disqualified in the first place?

Serbia: A gateway between East and West?

Serbia is increasingly becoming the principal investment gateway for China in the Western Balkans. Seven years ago, the Serbian president Aleksandar Vučić characterized his country as "well placed to become the gateway between East and West" (Financial Times 2014). As a land-locked country, the establishment of such a gateway architecture requires considerable investments which Serbia cannot mobilize, let alone finance itself. Since 2015, China has invested in and provided loan facilities to Belgrade for the construction and financing of major infrastructure projects.[v] To illustrate this dynamic, consider the following examples between 2017 and 2019:

- In May 2017, Serbia agreed to borrow USD 298 million from China's *Exim Bank* to finance the first components of the construction works of the Belgrade—Budapest railway project (Garcevic 2018). The ceremonial start of the Serbian stretch took place in November 2017 in Belgrade's Zemun neighborhood. It includes the construction of a 34 km new line to the northern town of Stara-Pazova by *China Railway International*. Seen in conjunction with the credit line provided by *Exim Bank* of China, both the contractor and the financier of the project are from China.
- A characteristic of China's expanding equity footprint in Serbia concerns the energy sector. The Chinese *Zijin Mining Company*—third-largest copper and gold producer in China based in Fujian—was chosen by the Serbian government in August 2018 in an open tender process to acquire the *Rudarsko Topionicarski Basen Bor* (RTB Bor) copper mining and smelting complex. Zijin acquired a 63% stake in the complex located in eastern Serbia for USD 1.26 billion. According to Serbia's Minister of Energy and Mining Aleksandar Antic, Zijin promised to cover RTB Bor's USD 200 million debt and keep 5,000 jobs at the mine.
- With this acquisition, the Chinese Zijin Mining company is investing almost USD 3 billion to stake major claims in the Serbian copper industry. The RTB Bor equity investment represents back-to-back mining transactions by Zijin in Serbia. In October 2018, Zijin acquired the Canadian base metals producer *Nevsun Resources* for USD 1.4 billion. The acquisition included the *Timok* copper-gold mining exploration in Cukar Peki near Bor.
- Finally, in November 2019 Zijin bought Freeport McMoran Inc's copper and gold assets in Serbia for an additional USD 390 million. The unprecedented element in Zijin's RTB Bor acquisition is the fact that it submitted the winning bid in the final stage of the tender process

against a Russian competitor, *U Gold.* Despite strong political economy ties with Russia, the government in Belgrade opted for the Chinese company, as it pledged more follow-up investment.

- In the Belgrade suburb of Borca the *China Road and Bridge Corporation* (CRBC) has agreed to build the first industrial park in Serbia. CRBC's total investment of 220 million euros in the *Mihajlo Pupin Industrial Park* is financed by a consortium of three Chinese banks, namely *Export-Import Bank*, *China Development Bank* (CDB) and *China Construction Bank* (CCB).

Why is China investing such large amounts in the Serbian mining sector? One answer can be found in industrial policy-making priorities in China. Zijin Mining is focusing on the resource-abundant area in eastern Serbia. It is doing so because of the growing demand from China's *New Energy Vehicle* sector (NEV). This sector includes vehicles that are powered by electricity.

The production of batteries for NEV cars, buses and trucks requires copper and zinc. Seen in this context, Chinese companies are establishing supply chain networks in Serbia in order to advance the execution of industrial policy objectives in China. RTB Bor and Timok are the second and third mining companies Chinese firms bought in Serbia. Already in 2016, China's *Hebei Iron and Steel Group* (HBIS) acquired *Zelezara Smederevo*, a loss-making steel plant that is being extensively restructured through technology transfers from China to Serbia.

A further reason for Serbia's openness towards China is the willingness of the government in Beijing to emphasize that its bilateral cooperation is less cumbersome in administrative terms and transparency requirements than the EU process of accessing project financing. This interpretation is reflected in the following statement from Serbia's minister responsible for innovation and technology, Nenad Popovic, who underlines: "*Western countries' investment in Serbia usually has strings attached, but China's investment never does*" (China Daily 2019). This widening Sino-Serbian economic engagement is also visible at the political level. Since 2017, both countries have established a visa-free regime, and in 2018 the bilateral relationship was elevated to a "comprehensive strategic partnership".

The depth of this partnership is also reflected in bilateral cooperation during the outbreak of the Covid-19 coronavirus crisis. The EU initially set limits on exports of medical equipment to non-EU countries, including for accession countries currently negotiating membership. As Serbia faced acute shortages of medical supplies and protective gear to fight Covid-19, it was China that quickly filled the void (Die Zeit, 18th March 2020). In March 2020, Beijing flew six doctors, medical masks, test kits and ventilators to Belgrade. These supplies were partly donated while others were sold at discounted market prices. President Vučić made his vocal disavowal of the EU's policies loud and clear when stating that "*I believe in Chinese help. The only country that can help us is China. To the others, thanks a lot for nothing*" (Seghier 2020).

This statement stands in stark contrast to the following development: In April 2020, the European Commission announced a package of coronavirus support measures for the Western Balkans, including over 93 million euros of financial resources for Serbia (European Commission 2020). Despite such tangible solidarity, shaping the narrative of corona virus-related health diplomacy appears to have been won by Beijing and not Brussels. In Belgrade, various large-scale billboards could be seen in March and April 2020 praising Chinese President Xi Jinping for his country's efforts to assist Serbia in its measures to fight the Covid-19 pandemic. No such advertisement was visible regarding the European Commission's package of support schemes.

Montenegro: Entrapped in debt?

The Sino-Montenegrin highway project is the flagship cooperation initiative between Beijing and Podgorica. The 165 km flagship project links the Port of Bar on Montenegro's Adriatic coast to the border of landlocked neighboring Serbia. Anybody familiar with the mountainous terrain, viaducts and canyons of Montenegro will immediately understand what a complex undertaking it is to build a highway that requires a number of imposing bridges and deep-cut tunnels. The first phase of the project started in 2014. The contract was awarded without an open tender process to a consortium including the *China Road and Bridge Corp.* (CRBC) as well as Montenegro's *Bemax* (Hopkins and Kynge 2019).

The remaining three parts are planned to be completed by CRBC in a public-private partnership (PPP, Barkin 2018). China's *Exim Bank* is providing a USD 944 million (809-million-euro) loan to finance the project's first section.[vi] This represents 85% of the total loan, at a 2% interest rate. The repayment is structured over a 20-year duration with a six-year grace period. The government in Podgorica has provided Exim Bank with a sovereign guarantee on the loan. A closer look at the financing and construction agreements also yields the following:

- The Chinese company chosen to construct the priority section of the Bar-Boljare highway will not have to pay any taxes in Montenegro or customs duties for the import of construction materials.
- More specifically, Podgorica is exempting Chinese contractors and subcontractors working on the new highway from paying VAT, customs duties, taxes and fees for engaging foreign workers and corporate income tax.
- The Chinese will also pay three times less in excise taxes on fuel imports.
- Significantly, in case of disputes over the construction and financing contracts, the competent courts will be situated in Beijing and arbitration efforts are undertaken according to Chinese law. Montenegro is the

first country in the Western Balkans to include such arbitration provisions in the terms of reference for a high-profile infrastructure development project.

Two elements of this Sino-Montenegrin highway project have given rise to specific concerns: For one, the lending standards Chinese companies demand from the host country in concession contracts. This includes the exemption from taxation, customs duties but also demanding sovereign guarantees for projects whose economic viability is in question. The insertion of flexible funding arrangements if and when host countries use Chinese workers and equipment is particularly contentious.

The other issue concerns the potential for debt-sustainability challenges. Other international lenders such as the *World Bank*, the *IMF* and the *European Investment Bank* (EIB) have raised red flags, i.e. that the infrastructure project puts Montenegro at risk of debt distress, thereby shrinking the government's fiscal space in the future. The label "debt-trap diplomacy" has become a recurring criticism of Chinese banks' funding arrangements vis-à-vis countries that are rather inexperienced in the complexities of project financing in infrastructure lending. The highway project in Montenegro is thus a cautionary tale in its own right:

- In 2018, Montenegro's public debt (general government gross debt) reached USD 3,891 million, increasing by USD 671 million compared to 2017. The debt-to-GDP ratio in 2018 reached 72.07%, a 5.77 percentage point rise from 2017, when it registered at 66.3% of GDP (Countryeconomy.com 2019).
- China's loan substantially increased Montenegro's debt-to-GDP ratio, and there are convincing reasons to be critical about the loan and the highway project. When considering that Exim Bank's loan totaled USD 944 million, then China's share of Montenegro's total public debt reached 24.26% in 2018. If we consider the data for 2014—when the loan was made (Montenegro's public debt stood at USD 2,911 million)—then China's share is even higher, reaching 32.42% (author's calculations based on data from Countryeconomy.com 2019).

This debt exposure to a single country, based on a single, multi-year infrastructure project is exceptionally high and raises questions of sustainability. However, in budgetary terms, an important caveat is in order. Since it is a multi-decade loan, including a grace period and maturities of 20 years, the debt indeed remains a repayment challenge, but its details are not insurmountable. The problems rather arise from other indicators, e.g. when the projected toll revenue does not materialize, if the PPP model is not bankable, when additional debt is necessary to complete other sections of the highway, or when currency fluctuations adversely impact the repayment modalities.

It remains to be seen if Montenegro may require a restructuring of its debt exposure to China in the future. If the government in Podgorica were to default within the specified timeframe on the concession agreement, "the terms of its contract for the loans … give China [i.e. Exim Bank] *the right to access Montenegrin land as collateral*" (Hopkins and Kynge 2019, emphasis added). The option for a transfer of accumulated and non-repayable external debt into land rights is significant. Johannes Hahn, the former EU Commissioner for European Neighborhood Policy and Enlargement Negotiations critically remarked in March 2019: "China never cares how and if a country is able to pay its loans. And if they cannot pay, there is some pressure that things are transferred into their ownership" (Financial Times 2019).

As a member of the 17+1 cooperation network, Montenegro has engaged with China in various online meetings focusing on health policies during the Covid-19 pandemic. The greatest economic and employment concern in Podgorica is the effects of the pandemic on the tourism season. Over the course of the past decade Montenegro has increasingly recalibrated its tourism policies to accommodate Chinese citizens visiting the Adriatic coast. Given existing travel restrictions and freedom of movement limitations, receipts from tourism arrivals will adversely impact airports, cruise ships, restaurants, hotels, museums, etc. in Montenegro.

IV The EU's reaction to China's growing footprint in Southeast Europe?

China's financial and infrastructure footprints have quickly evolved in the Western Balkans (Bastian 2017). In some countries, it is more visible and articulated than in others. But with the exception of Kosovo, China is in play and intends to stay in the region. In doing so, there are lessons to be learned for subsidized Chinese companies, the political authorities in Beijing and governments in Southeast Europe. The Budapest-Belgrade railway project controversy illustrates that as a non-EU external actor, China is learning the rules of engagement with EU member states and candidate countries. This experience includes the (belated) adherence to EU procurement standards.

But the amount of railway diplomacy necessary for the Budapest-Belgrade project to continue illustrates that China is starting to face a much more proactive European Commission in Brussels. This assertiveness is not only confined to the enforcement of transparent financing arrangements, adherence to EU procurement standards and open tender procedures. The Commission in Brussels is also recalibrating its strategic outlook vis-à-vis China. In its March 2019 communication, the Commission labeled China

> *simultaneously*, in different policy areas, a *cooperation partner* with whom the EU has closely aligned objectives, a *negotiating partner* with

> whom the EU needs to find a balance of interests, an *economic competitor* in the pursuit of technological leadership, and a *systemic rival* promoting alternative models of governance (European Commission 2019, emphasis added).

For those familiar with the diplomatic wording and rhetorical compromises necessary in Commission communications, the March 2019 EU–China strategic outlook represented a robust and, in many respects, new departure of describing the current relationship between the EU and China. But the Communication also allows China to interpret its wording by focusing more on the "partner" characterizations than on the "rival" terminology. Beijing can argue that the EU does not exclusively consider China as a systemic rival. However, the Commission emphasizes that

> Neither the EU nor any of its Member States can effectively achieve their aims with China without **full unity**. In cooperating with China, **all Member States, individually and within sub-regional cooperation frameworks**, such as the 16+1 format, have a responsibility to ensure consistency with EU law, rules and policies (ibid, emphasis in the original).

It is precisely this need for consistency and unity of purpose vis-à-vis China that represents the biggest challenge for the EU, its member states and the accession countries in the Western Balkans. According to a joint op-ed published by Josep Borell, High Representative of the European Union for Foreign Affairs and Security Policy, as well as Vice-President of the European Commission and the Commissioner for the Internal Market, responsible for the defense industry, Thierry Breton, the EU's reaction to the coronavirus crisis and the lessons learned therefrom call for "a united, resilient and sovereign Europe" (Borrell and Breton 2020).

One central policy field where such unity is increasingly relevant concerns investment screening regulations in Europe. Former Commission President Jean-Claude Juncker first tabled the idea of EU-wide screening regulations in September 2017. On the occasion of his yearly *State of The Union* address before the European Parliament, he did not explicitly identify China by name. But Mr. Juncker focused his remarks on the need for new investment screening rules on precisely those European sectors in which China had invested heavily in the preceding years.

> Let me say once and for all: we are not naïve free traders. Europe must always defend its strategic interests. This is why today we are proposing a new EU framework for investment screening. If a foreign, state-owned, company wants to purchase a *European harbor*, part of our *energy infrastructure* or a *defense technology firm*, this should only happen in transparency, with scrutiny and debate. It is a political

> responsibility to know what is going on in our own backyard so that we can protect our collective security if needed (European Commission 2017, emphasis added).

To back up its rhetoric and strategic recalibration vis-à-vis China, the European Commission adopted new regulations that established such a framework for screening non-EU foreign direct investment (for a more in-depth look at this, see Chapter 5 in this book). The regulation entered into force in April 2019 and fully applies across member states 18 months later, i.e. from October 2020 onwards. The 27 EU member states, including the 12 EU countries that are part of the 17+1 platform, will have to adapt their national legislation to reflect the Commission's investment screening regulations. While the EU regulation provides a framework, the right of each EU member state to decide whether or not to screen a particular non-EU foreign direct investment cannot be curtailed by the Commission in Brussels (Mayerbrown 2018).

For countries in the Western Balkans the debate over the need for investment screening procedures, in particular with regard to non-EU external actors such as China, Russia or Turkey, is non-existent. Neither Serbia and Montenegro nor Northern Macedonia and Albania have adopted such regulatory screening procedures. Bosnia and Herzegovina has various energy infrastructure projects that are loan-financed by Chinese policy banks. Kosovo is not being recognized by China as a sovereign state, thereby China is publicly siding with Serbia's irredentist position.

It will be telling to observe to what degree the Commission can insist on such screening mechanisms in the accession negotiations with the two countries—Serbia and Montenegro—that are most advanced in the process. Serbia has the most diverse range of cooperation with China in the region while Montenegro has the highest lending exposure (in percent of annual GDP) to China in 2018. The open question is if political authorities in Belgrade or Podgorica will push back against such screening measures when Commission negotiators address them? Alternatively, they could slow-walk their implementation because the mechanism formally does not (yet) apply to non-EU countries in the Western Balkans.

Conclusions and outlook

China's activities in Southeast Europe are not exclusively BRI-driven. Some of its investments, lending and infrastructure development activities took place *before* the launch of the BRI in 2013. Furthermore, China is learning from its engagement with countries in Southeast Europe. During the past decade, Beijing has formed a better understanding of the operational environment and political challenges it faces in the region, particularly in the Western Balkans. This body of experience translates into gradual and persistent policy adjustments on the ground.

- Project finance is being diversified to include multi-lateral European institutions such as the *European Bank for Reconstruction and Development* (EBRD) or the *European Investment Bank* (EIB). In the case of the Pelješac Bridge project in Croatia, Chinese construction companies are benefiting from co-financing arrangements provided by structural funding programs of the European Union. The Commission is in a challenging position here. Authority for EU Structural Funds rests with national ministries and regulatory bodies. Time will inform us if Chinese firms participating in EU co-financed projects could import European financing standards, e.g. regarding transparency and reporting requirements. This outreach to European funding institutions and programs is also a reflection of Chinese policy banks becoming more restrictive in their lending policies.
- There is a greater awareness among Chinese authorities that large-scale infrastructure projects in the region need to support the local economy, thus presenting additionality to SMEs and domestic sub-contractors. The initial approach of Chinese companies to provide the financing, human capital and construction materials for such projects is increasingly challenged by civil society representatives and media outlets and is being acknowledged as obsolete by ministries in host countries.
- The tripartite Sino-Hungarian-Serbian railway project has been a lesson learned for Chinese authorities in the complexities of European Union *Realpolitik*. This experience includes demands for increased transparency in BRI-related infrastructure projects, an open procurement process according to EU rules and regulations with competitive bidding and better risk assessment in project selection between all parties concerned.
- As Chinese financed and constructed infrastructure projects materialize across the Western Balkans, the debate over its environmental impact has grown in volume. Particularly in Bosnia and Hercegovina the construction and modernization of coal-fired thermal power plants has put China on the spot. The contradiction of policy-making is evident. President Xi Jinping has strongly advocated support for the Paris Climate Accord. But simultaneously Chinese banks are financing and Chinese firms constructing coal-fired power plants in Tuzla and have completed work on another thermal power plant in Stanari, Republika Srpska.[vii]
- This apparent contradiction has impacted the reputational capital of China's BRI. In order to address the public debate about the BRI's environmental impact, the Chinese authorities launched a green investment principle for Belt and Road projects at the second Belt and Road Forum in April 2019, emphasizing that future BRI-related investments will strive to be low-carbon and climate resilient.

Seen from the perspective of countries in the region we can argue that initially, their interactions with China lacked policy coherence. The formulation of comprehensive country strategies vis-à-vis China is only gradually taking place.[viii] Its definition is also the result of lessons learned in the course of the past decade when engaging with China.

What we can observe is the transformation of ad hoc initiatives with China towards the emergence of a set of strategic priorities, a better understanding of the legal implications of infrastructure project finance with Chinese interlocutors, the preparation of independent feasibility studies and the acknowledgement of the urgency of capacity building in administrative expertise. This is a work in progress for most countries dealing with Chinese counterparties, particularly those in the Western Balkans. In short, countries in the region are in the process of developing agency and competence vis-à-vis China.

What makes China's activities in Southeast Europe such a challenge for European policymakers is the observation that through the BRI, countries in the region are putting themselves in a position to implement large-scale infrastructure projects *without* the need for EU (financial) assistance. Initially, the EU did too little to publicly challenge China's deepening engagement in Southeast Europe. With the official launch of the BRI in 2013, China signaled its intention to expand investments and trade. As more countries from Southeast Europe signed up to the BRI, their political leadership saw an unprecedented opening: the dire need for infrastructure upgrades could be achieved through initiatives with Chinese characteristics.

As countries in Southeast Europe seek to cope with the consequences of the Covid-19 pandemic in their health sectors, across society and from the emerging economic fallout, they are also having to reconsider their bilateral relations with China. The same holds for China, which is seeking to rewrite the narrative of the coronavirus. Beijing's focus rests on switching perceptions from the incubation of a pandemic in Wuhan, Hubei Province, to its promoted role as a responsible and proactive global leader helping other countries in times of urgent need. Chinese assistance in delivering medical supplies to Albania, Serbia, Bosnia-Hercegovina and Slovenia during the pandemic in March and April 2020 underscores Beijing's efforts at repositioning itself diplomatically and with practical, on the ground support. But it has to be emphasized that in practical terms Beijing's assistance does *not* match the amount of financial resources that the European Commission is providing to countries in the Western Balkans.

The institutional capacity-building work China has undertaken in the course of the past decade in the region helps in these endeavors. China has used the 17+1 network to organize video conferencing meetings on Covid-19 with participating countries from Central, Eastern and Southeast Europe. But the signature event for China and its relations to countries in Central, Eastern and Southeast Europe in 2020 had to be postponed. The ninth annual summit of the 17+1 Network was scheduled to take place in mid-April 2020 in Beijing. With its postponement, participating countries in the 17+1 network will have an opportunity to re-evaluate their future cooperation priorities with China. The mantra of business as usual will not be an option, given the consequences of the Covid-19 pandemic. This recalibration option will equally provide an opportunity for participating countries to formulate strategic roadmaps stipulating what they expect to achieve in cooperation with China and where the limits of this cooperation rest.

Notes

i The region of Southeast Europe comprises 16 countries: Albania, Bosnia and Herzegovina, Bulgaria, Croatia, Cyprus, Greece, Hungary, Kosovo, North Macedonia, Moldova, Montenegro, Romania, Serbia, Slovakia, Slovenia and Turkey.

ii A word about terminology needs to be clarified from the outset. Since its inception by President Xi Jinping in 2013, China's representatives use the term *One Belt – One Road* (OBOR). The term *Belt and Road Initiative* (BRI) introduced in 2016 is a linguistic compromise to the English language. For our analysis, we shall use the BRI terminology.

iii I am grateful to Kurt Bassuener and Tim Zajontz for alerting me to this terminology.

iv Hungary has positioned itself as the financial hub for Chinese banks. The *Bank of China* has its regional headquarters in Budapest. China has also opened a European clearing center for its currency, the renminbi. In 2016, Hungary became the first country in the region to issue a renminbi-denominated sovereign bond.

v To lend symbolic credence to this "gateway" rhetoric, China financed and built the *Pupin Bridge*, named after the Serbian scientist Mihajlo Pupin. The bridge over the Danube River in Belgrade is also called the "Friendship Bridge" between Serbia and China. It was inaugurated in December 2014. The Pupin Bridge was the first bridge project that China completed in Southeast Europe.

vi It is important to underline that the loan repayment is denominated in USD currency. This implies the risk of currency fluctuations between USD and the euro, thus potentially making the loan more expensive (or cheaper) over time. However, the contract does not include any financial hedging arrangements from the Montenegrin side to account for such potential currency fluctuations.

vii The Stanari power plant was constructed by China's *Dongfang* and financed by the *China Development Bank*. The plant officially started commercial operations in September 2016. By that time Stanari was already out of date in terms of environmental standards. Its environmental permit stipulates compliance with the older EU Large Combustion Plants (LCP) Directive, not with the newer Industrial Emissions Directive (CEE Bankwatch Network 2019).

viii In 2017, Slovakia's government was the first country in the 17+1 network to develop an extensive "*Strategy for the Development of Economic Relations with China 2017–2020*" (Turcsanyi 2017).

Bibliography

Barkin, Noah (2018): "Chinese 'highway to nowhere' haunts Montenegro", 16 July 2018, [Online available]: https://www.reuters.com/article/us-china-silkroad-europe-montenegro-insi-idUSKBN1K60QX, accessed 14 October 2019.

Bastian, Jens (2017): "The potential for growth through Chinese infrastructure investments in Central and South-Eastern Europe along the "Balkan Silk Road", independent report commissioned by the *EBRD*", September 2017, [Online available]: https://www.ebrd.com/news/2017/what-chinas-belt-and-road-initiative-means-for-the-western-balkans.html, accessed 09 October 2019.

Borrell, Josep and Thierry Breton (2020): "For a united, resilient and sovereign Europe", 09 June 2020, [Online available]: https://eeas.europa.eu/headquarters/headquarters-homepage/80567/united-resilient-and-sovereign-europe_en, accessed 13 July 2019.

CEE Bankwatch Network (2019): "Stanari lignite power plant, Bosnia and Herzegovina", [Online available]: https://bankwatch.org/project/stanari-lignite-power-plant-bosnia-and-herzegovina, accessed 11 October 2019.

China.org.cn (2019): "Full text of Chinese Premier Li Keqiang's speech at 9th China-CEEC Business Forum", 13 April 2019, [Online available]: http://www.china.org.cn/china/Off_the_Wire/2019-04/13/content_74677826.htm, accessed 08 October 2019.

China Daily (2019): "Serbia's first industrial park to break ground", 26 April 2019, [Online available]: http://global.chinadaily.com.cn/a/201904/26/WS5cc25deca3104842260b87a9.html, accessed 16 October 2019.

Countryeconomy.com (2019): "Montenegro national debt 2018", [Online available]: https://countryeconomy.com/national-debt/montenegro, accessed 14 October 2019.

European Commission (2017): "State of the Union 2017 - Trade Package: European Commission proposes framework for screening of foreign direct investments", 14 September 2017, [Online available]: http://europa.eu/rapid/press-release_IP-17–3183_en.htm, accessed 05 April 2019.

Ibid. (2020): "EU response to the coronavirus pandemic in the Western Balkans", April 2020, [Online available]: https://ec.europa.eu/neighbourhood-enlargement/sites/near/files/coronavirus_support_wb.pdf.

Ibid. (2019): "Joint Communication [with the High Representative of the Union for Foreign Affairs and Security Policy] to the European Parliament, the European Council and the Council, EU-China – A Strategic Outlook", 12 March 2019, JOIN (2019) 5 final, [Online available]: https://ec.europa.eu/info/publications/eu-china-strategic-outlook-commission-contribution-european-council-21-22-march-2019_en, accessed 14 April 2019.

Financial Times (2014): "Blog post", 15 December 2014: https://www.ft.com/content/97c3ee47–63cf-3966–9122-c653fc6cb4f3.

Ibid. (2019): "Brussels says EU has 'underestimated' China's reach in Balkans", *Financial Times*, 05 March 2019, [Online available]: https://www.ft.com/content/4ba18efa-377b-11e9-b72b-2c7f526ca5d0, accessed 22 May 2019.

Ibid. (2020): "Hungary to keep details of Beijing-funded rail link secret", *Financial Times*, 03 April 2020, [Online available]: https://www.ft.com/content/251314b5-8d6a-4665-a14b-0110dd88754c, accessed 17 April 2020.

Garcevic, Vesko (2018): "China's stealthy advance in Balkans should worry EU", BIRN, 11 January 2018, [Online available]: https://balkaninsight.com/2018/01/11/china-s-stealthy-advance-in-balkans-should-worry-eu-01-11-2018/, accessed 15 October 2019.

GCR (2017): "China starts building Serbia-Hungary Railway", *Global Construction Review*, 04 December 2017, [Online available]: http://www.globalconstructionreview.com/news/china-starts-building-serbia-hungary-railway/, accessed 10 October 2019.

Hopkins, Valerie and James Kynge (2019): "Montenegro fears China-backed highway will put it on road to ruin", *Financial Times*, 12 April 2019, [Online available]: https://www.ft.com/content/d3d56d20-5a8d-11e9-9dde-7aedca0a081a, accessed 17 May 2019.

Mayerbrown (2018): "EU agrees on FDI screening framework", 18 December 2018, [Online available]: https://www.mayerbrown.com/en/perspectives-events/publications/2018/12/eu-agrees-on-fdi-screening-framework, accessed 02 April 2019.

Seghier, Milan (2020): "The Coronavirus pandemic lets China score a win in Serbia", *Transatlantic Take*, 23 March 2020, [Online available]: https://www.europarl.europa.eu/RegData/etudes/BRIE/2020/649349/EPRS_BRI(2020)649349_EN.pdf, accessed 26 April 2020.

The Hungarian Government (2017): "Prime Minister Viktor Orbán's speech at the opening of the China – Central and Eastern Europe Summit in Budapest", 27 November 2017, [Online Available]: http://www.kormany.hu/en/the-prime-minister/the-prime-minister-s-speeches/prime-minister-viktor-orban-s-speech-at-the-opening-of-the-china-central-and-eastern-europe-summit-in-budapest, accessed 10 October 2019.

Turcsanyi, Q. Richard (2017): "Slovakia's overdue China strategy", *The Diplomat*, 03 November 2017, [Online available]: https://thediplomat.com/2017/11/slovakias-overdue-china-strategy/, accessed 17 October 2019.

Yang, Sheng (2018): "China to set up international courts to settle belt and road disputes", *Global Times*, 28 June 2018, [Online available]: https://www.globaltimes.cn/content/1108794.shtml, accessed 16 August 2018.

7 The Belt and Road Initiative and state-owned enterprises: Is it time for reform of the EU merger control?

Alexandr Svetlicinii

I Introduction: East meets West on the New Silk Road

> *The government should encourage enterprises and other social forces to participate in the [Belt and Road] initiative, with a view to forming a cooperation model that features guidance by the government, participation of enterprises and support of people's organizations.* (Xi Jinping, pp. 547–548)[i]

On 7 September 2013, Chinese President Xi Jinping delivered a speech entitled "Promote Friendship between Our People and Work Together to Build a Bright Future" at the Nazarbayev University in Nur-Sultan (formerly Astana), Kazakhstan.[ii] According to Xi Jinping, the Belt and Road Initiative (BRI) was launched in order "to forge closer economic ties, deepen cooperation and expand development space in the Eurasian region; we should take an innovative approach and jointly build an 'economic belt along the Silk Road'".[iii] In 2015, the Chinese authorities published a more detailed Action Plan on the BRI.[iv] In the same year, China unveiled its industrial policy "Made in China 2025" (see Mair and Schaff, Chapter 11).[v] While the former called for "policy coordination, connectivity of infrastructure and facilities, unimpeded trade, financial integration, and closer people-to-people ties",[vi] the latter aimed at "securing China's position as a global powerhouse in high-tech industries such as robotics, aviation, and new energy vehicles such as electric and biogas".[vii]

The parallel implementation of the above-mentioned high-profile policies has resulted in the rise of Chinese investments in the European Union (EU). For example, the year 2016 saw a 77% increase in the investment volumes of Chinese enterprises in Europe (Hanemann and Huotari 2017, 4). This surge largely coincided with the sovereign debt crisis in a number of EU Member States, which presented Chinese investors with depressed prices, a greater number of assets for sale and reduced political resistance to foreign acquisitions (Meunier 2014).

Unlike the EU and its Member States, which embraced a capitalist free-market economy, China adheres to the state-directed economic model, where the state plays a triple role of planner-competitor-regulator in relation to economic processes. First, the state makes general and long-term strategies for economic development. Second, the state participates in the market directly through state-owned enterprises (SOEs). Third, the state shapes markets through its regulatory powers in the form of legislative and administrative interventions (Che, 2019, 29). As a result, it came as no surprise that primary economic actors involved in the outward investment activities under the BRI and the "Made in China 2025" policy were the SOEs that benefited from the preferential access to financing while being subjected to state guidance of their overseas investments (Bath 2015).

The current international economic order, which was designed in the aftermath of World War II primarily by Western powers, gradually embedded the model of free-market capitalism into the international regulatory framework (He and Ye, 2017Fan Remler 2017). For example, international trade law based on WTO agreements approaches subsidies and other forms of state support as unfair competition and allows the affected countries to apply countervailing duties.[viii] The mode of operations of the Chinese SOEs prompted the question of whether SOEs should be viewed as "public bodies" for the purpose of imposing the respective countervailing measures (Ding 2014; Du 2014a; Liao 2013). Similarly, in the field of competition law, the state's interference with market forces through the exercise of regulatory powers or directly through SOEs can be viewed as an anti-competitive restraint that should be prevented (Drexl and Bagnoli 2015).

One of the illustrative encounters of the Chinese economic statecraft and European protection of free-market competition occurred when the Chinese SOE acquisitions reached the "community dimension" under the EU Merger Regulation (EUMR)[ix] and were notified for competitive assessment to the EU Commission. The assessment of these acquisitions raised a number of questions concerning the application of the traditional competition law concepts such as "concentration", "single economic unit", "control" and "decisive influence" to the Chinese "national champions" (Svetlicinii 2017). It was also noted that the "spirit of mistrust toward competition combined with pervasive state-ownership and guidance lends itself to unusually high levels of coordination among Chinese players, with noncommercial considerations as a focus" (Huotari and Kratz 2019, 14). Nevertheless, the application of the current EU merger control rules based on the principle of competitive neutrality, or non-discrimination between companies based on their ownership or nationality, led to the unconditional clearance of the notified concentrations.[x] The continuous growth of Chinese investments after launching the Made in China 2025 initiative in 2015, especially in high-tech sectors, prompted the industrialized EU Member States to fear for their own global leadership in these sectors (Hooijmaaijers 2019). As a result, the increased scrutiny of Chinese investments by several national regulators led to a sharp decline by 18% worldwide of Chinese overseas investments in 2018 (Huang et al. 2019, 1).

On the other hand, the same EU merger control rules did not allow the establishment of European "national champions": on 6 February 2019, the EU Commission prohibited the proposed acquisition of Alstom (France) by Siemens (Germany) due to the concern that the merger would lead to price increases on the market for signaling systems for high-speed trains.[xi] These developments have prompted numerous calls from the industry and policymakers for the reform of the EU merger control in order to address the competitive challenges coming from the Chinese SOE acquisitions in Europe (Heim 2019b). China, on the other hand, continued to push ahead with the reform of its SOEs, which would make them more competitive on the global markets and at the same time more efficient conductors of industrial policies such as BRI and "Made in China 2025" (Che 2019). The current phase of the SOE reform commenced in 2015 under the Guiding Opinions of the CPC Central Committee and the State Council.[xii] On one hand, it entails further separation between the government and SOEs by promoting mixed ownership (private investment in SOEs) and establishing state asset management companies. On the other hand, it tightens the political control over the SOEs through personnel appointments and CPC organizations within the SOEs.

The present chapter addresses the regulatory challenges that Chinese SOE investments faced through EU competition law enforcement, and by regulatory reform proposals for tackling the above-mentioned regulatory gap. The discussion commences with a brief review of the specifics of corporate governance and state control over Chinese SOEs in order to highlight the aspects that will be relevant for the competitive assessment under the EU merger control regime. The discussion then proceeds with the identification of the regulatory challenges encountered by the EU merger control when applied to Chinese SOE acquisitions in Europe. Finally, the chapter concludes with a discussion of the regulatory reform proposals currently being debated in the EU.

II State-owned enterprises: China's "National Champions" going global

> *The same veil of secrecy the Party threw over its own affairs at home obscured the government's role in state companies as they went abroad. As a consequence, working out where the state ended in government companies and the commercial enterprise began was often nigh impossible for foreigners* (McGregor 2010, 56–57).

The SOEs represent a pillar of "socialism with Chinese characteristics for a new era"[xiii] and an important tool of Chinese economic statecraft. The Constitution of the Communist Party of China (CPC) reiterates the dominant role of public/state ownership in the national economy: "the Party must uphold and improve the basic economic system whereby public ownership plays a dominant role and economic entities under diverse forms of ownership develop side by side."[xiv]

One of the primary objectives of the ongoing reform of the Chinese SOEs is to make them more efficient and thus to "turn Chinese enterprises into world-class, globally competitive firms".[xv] With these objectives in mind, Western scholars have frequently argued that the success of the SOE reform in China will depend to a large degree on decoupling SOE management from political control of the ruling party and making the SOE executives accountable to their corporate boards and shareholders (Li and Brødsgaard 2013, 75). However, Chinese political leadership has been continuously moving in the opposite direction by strengthening its political control over SOEs.

In 2015, in parallel with the "go global" policy for Chinese SOEs, the central government released guiding opinions on the reform of the SOEs (Leutert 2016). These opinions, issued jointly by the CPC Central Committee and the State Council, emphasized that the party organizations within the SOEs should be given a statutory position along with other company bodies.[xvi] Furthermore, the detailed party regulations, as amended in 2019, required that the status of the party organizations within the SOEs should be included in the corporate charters and all major decisions of the boards of directors and management should be submitted for prior discussion within the SOE's party organization.[xvii] Consequently, party members who hold the positions of directors or managers must implement the party organization's decisions.[xviii] A recent study on the remuneration incentives for the management of Chinese state-owned commercial banks (SOCBs) concluded that the managers' incentive mechanisms within these banks follow the principles applied to civil servants while political promotion remains the most important incentive for the top management of the SOCBs (Lu 2019, 489). An earlier study of Chinese national oil companies (NOCs) concludes that while the government may not interfere in the daily commercial activities of the NOCs, there are instances where such interventions are made in the name of broadly defined national interests (Taylor 2012, 75).

The corporatization of the SOEs allowed the state to centralize its control by establishing the State-owned Assets Supervision and Administration Commission (SASAC) and to shield the SOEs from regulatory interventions or judicial oversight (Guo 2013). For example, an analysis of the corporate governance of the China Investment Corporation (CIC) suggested that the similarities between the CIC's corporate structures and supervisory boards of continental Europe were motivated primarily by the intention to maintain the CIC's legitimacy through the use of well-recognized institutional forms (Clark et al. 2013, 115). In his speech at the National Conference on Party Development in SOEs on 10 October 2016, Xi Jinping explained the specifics of SOE corporate governance in the following way: "SOEs' modern corporate system with Chinese features is unique because it incorporates the Party's leadership into all aspects of their corporate governance and Party organizations into the corporate governance structure. It also clarifies and ensures the legal status of Party organizations in the legal person corporate governance system, with Party organizations and personnel being in place, clear responsibilities, and strict supervision".[xix]

Although often portrayed as China's grand strategy to become the world's dominant economic power, the BRI has been to a large degree a response to the growing economic challenges that China has faced in its current stage of development: overcapacity and excess of foreign exchange reserves (Wang 2016; Clarke 2017). The EU, with its developed markets and advanced technologies, presents an attractive destination for Chinese investments. As specified in China's 2018 policy paper on the EU: "China hopes that the EU will keep its investment market open, reduce and eliminate investment hurdles and discriminatory barriers, and provide Chinese companies investing in Europe a fair, transparent and predictable policy environment and protect their legitimate rights and interests".[xx]

In order to ensure that overseas investments of Chinese companies correspond to the objectives of the country's foreign policy and in particular, with the aims of the BRI, Chinese authorities issued the 2017 Guidance of Further Directing and Regulating Overseas Investment Direction.[xxi] The Guidance instructs Chinese companies when going overseas to direct their investment into sectors that have been prioritized under the BRI as well as to refrain from investments in sectors and countries that would run contrary to the nation's foreign policies. In parallel, the Ministry of Finance issued the Regulation on State-owned Enterprises' Overseas Investment Financial Management to prevent financial risks and improve the efficiency of the SOEs' overseas investments.[xxii] A study analyzing motivations for Chinese SOEs' overseas investments in the light of the ongoing market-oriented reforms of Chinese SOEs concluded that many of those investments are commercially motivated (Du 2014b). Other scholars cautioned that the government is continuously using its SOEs to achieve certain policy objectives (Liao and Zhang 2014). This combination of market-oriented commercial conduct under the managerial autonomy and implementation of the industrial policy objectives under political supervision and control presented a number of challenges for the application of the EU merger control rules that require a forward-looking assessment of the commercial conduct of the merging parties.

III China's SOE acquisitions under the EU merger control

> *Europe will always fight for a level playing field and be strong against those who compete by dumping, deregulating or subsidizing.*[xxiii]

The capitalist market economy model departs from the presumption that SOEs should appear on the markets only for the purpose of remedying the market failures (Putniņš 2015). According to the Organisation for Economic Co-operation and Development (OECD), competition policy tools such as antitrust and merger control can be used in order to level the playing field for SOEs and private companies (Organisation for Economic Co-operation and Development 2016, 8). In order to adhere to the principle of competitive neutrality, the OECD calls its members to apply competition laws in an origin-, ownership- and nationality-neutral manner (Organisation for Economic Co-operation and Development 2015, 12). The EU Merger Regulation adheres to the principle of competitive neutrality and applies to acquisitions by the SOEs in the same way as it applies to private takeovers.[xxiv] For example, a merger of two SOEs can qualify as an economic concentration if the two SOEs are effectively controlled by different state entities because in that case, the two SOEs were formerly part of different economic entities with autonomous decision-making.[xxv] In other words, the EU merger control regime does not regard all SOEs owned by the same state as part of the same economic entity unless there is clear evidence that the state coordinates the conduct of these SOEs on the market.[xxvi] Therefore, the decision on whether such coordination exists will determine whether a concentration has to be notified under the EU merger-control regime and will affect the EU Commission's competitive assessment of the notified concentration.

A string of acquisitions notified by the Chinese SOEs in recent years demonstrated that the answer to the above questions is far from straightforward (Svetlicinii 2019, 5–11). In 2011, the subsidiary of the wholly owned Chinese SOE China National Chemical Corporation (ChemChina) notified its acquisition of the Norwegian company Elkem.[xxvii] In its assessment, the EU Commission had to determine whether ChemChina is an independent economic entity or whether it belongs to a wider economic group including other Chinese SOEs. The merging parties submitted that SASAC, which holds the shares of all major Chinese SOEs, acts as a non-managerial trustee and does not interfere in the decision-making of the companies, so they cannot be regarded as belonging to the same economic group.[xxviii] In another case, the EU Commission with reference to an OECD study acknowledged that the Chinese state can influence the decisions of its SOEs in a number of ways, both formal and less formal, and testing a "worst-case" scenario considered the cumulative market share of all Chinese SOEs active on the relevant market.[xxix]

In 2016, the EU Commission assessed a joint acquisition of control by Electricite de France SA and China General Nuclear Power Corporation (CGN) over NNB Holding Company operating three nuclear power plants in the United Kingdom.[xxx] There, the Commission concluded that the SASAC can influence the CGN's decisions on major issues such as strategy, business plans and budget.[xxxi] As a result, the Commission considered that all Chinese SOEs in the energy sector controlled by the SASAC form a single economic entity, which meant that their market share and commercial conduct had to be considered cumulatively (Svetlicinii 2019, 9). The Commission's assessment has set an "antitrust time bomb" because if all Chinese SOEs are regarded as a part of a single economic entity, then their mergers and agreements would be exempt from the merger control and competition scrutiny in the EU (Zhang 2012).

Nevertheless, due to the currently low market shares of Chinese companies in the EU markets, all of around 40 Chinese SOE acquisitions notified at the time of writing have been cleared under the EUMR. Only the acquisition of the Swiss agro-chemical company Syngenta by the Chinese SOE ChemChina has been allowed with conditions.[xxxii] At the same time, several mergers of the Chinese SOEs fell outside the reach of the EU merger control because, due to the low turnovers of the merging parties within the EU, these concentrations were not subject to review under the EUMR. For example, in 2015, China merged two of its state-owned rolling stock manufacturers, China CNR Corporation Limited (CNR) and China South Locomotive & Rolling Stock Corporation Limited (CSR), to create the "world's largest train builder" - China Railway Stock Corp. (CRRC).[xxxiii] When two European corporations, Alstom and Siemens, attempted to consolidate their railway manufacturing capacities, their concentration was blocked by the EU Commission under the EUMR.[xxxiv] One of the arguments advanced by the merging parties was their intention to become more competitive against CRRC on the global markets.[xxxv] However, under the EUMR, the Commission has focused its assessment on the potential anti-competitive effects on the EU markets. EU Commissioner Vestager explained that based on the previous market data, Chinese suppliers never participated in the European tenders for railway signaling equipment and no market entry by a Chinese competitor was foreseeable in the near future.[xxxvi]

It should be noted that out of 4,680 transactions notified to the Commission under the EUMR in 2005-2019, only 11 concentrations were prohibited, with 17 notifications withdrawn before a final decision was taken, which made the accusation that the Commission used merger control to prevent the emergence of 'European Champions' unfounded (Heim and Midoes 2019). Also, despite the occasional calls to the contrary, the empirical studies analyzing the application of the EU merger control rules in relation to foreign acquisitions reveal no signs of protectionism (Bradford et al. 2018). Nevertheless, blocking the *Siemens/Alstom* merger on the background of unopposed acquisitions of the Chinese SOEs, prompted numerous calls for the reform of the EU merger control regime, which will be addressed in the following section.

IV EU merger control and beyond: Regulatory responses

One of the most prominent proposals for regulatory reform was embedded in the "Franco-German Manifesto for a European industrial policy fit for the 21st Century", which questioned whether the existing regulatory framework allows European companies to compete effectively with foreign, heavily subsidized companies and called for a fairer and more effective level playing field at the global level.[xxxvii] France and Germany put forward several directions for the reform of the EU regulatory framework that would counteract the competitive disadvantage of European companies, which compete on the global markets with the Chinese SOEs that receive state subsidies and are shielded from competition law enforcement in the domestic markets. The manifesto contains the following options: (1) reforming EU merger control rules in a way that would allow consideration of state support received by the merging companies; (2) updating the current merger control guidelines to allow the EU Commission to consider competition on the global markets; (3) granting the Council of the EU the right to hear appeals against the EU Commission's merger decisions (Svetlicinii 2019, 17).

The German Industrial Strategy 2030 called for a broader reform of EU competition law to account for international competition from foreign companies.[xxxviii] It also addressed the issue of foreign acquisitions in strategic sectors, which should be assessed in terms of risk to national security.[xxxix] The German proposal echoed an earlier call for reforming the EU competition policy advanced by 18 Member States. This earlier intervention argued that European competition policy should give more consideration to the global competitive environment.[xl]

A group of European academics led by Motta and Peitz voiced strong opposition to the Franco-German proposal and argued that competition policy should be independent from political interference and continue to focus on economic efficiency and protection of the competitive process.[xli] A similar position was supported by the Austrian competition authority, arguing that the establishment of the European champions may be subjected to arbitrary regulatory interventions, which in the long run would harm the interests of European companies and consumers.[xlii]

In 2019, France, Germany and Poland in their joint statement entitled "Modernising EU Competition Policy" urged the EU Commission to consider changes in the EU merger control so that the merger review of foreign acquisitions would include the consideration of the financial power of state-controlled and state-subsidized companies.[xliii] In order to cater to the global competitiveness of European companies, the merger assessment should take into account competition on the global level as well as consideration of the trade and industrial policy of third countries. More specifically, the three Member States urged the Commission to consider that for subsidized SOEs, the low profitability may not present a market barrier as the foreign state would compensate for any losses sustained as a result of the strategic decisions taken by its SOEs.[xliv] In relation to mergers of the European companies that should be able to compete on the global markets, France, Germany and Poland suggested taking into account the competitiveness of EU industries and European value chains by using more flexibility in adopting merger remedies that should take the form of behavioural conditions rather than structural divestitures.[xlv]

The above-mentioned proposals for the reform of the EU merger control rules can be summarized as follows: (1) relaxing merger review conditions to allow for greater European market concentration; (2) tolerating more expansive "legitimate interest" exceptions in merger control; (3) promoting a more expansive single-economic-entity approach beyond formal aspects of state control (Huotari and Kratz 2019, 24). While the majority of these proposals were voiced during the term of the Juncker Commission, it will be for the new team of commissioners led by Ursula von der Leyen to formulate the regulatory responses that would address the "anti-competitive distortions" caused by the Chinese SOEs. One of the first actions of the newly elected President of the EU Commission was the mission letter addressed to Margrethe Vestager, calling upon "the Executive Vice-President for a Europe fit for the Digital Age" to develop tools and policies that would address the market distortions caused by the foreign state ownership and subsidization.[xlvi]

The Commission's call for the new regulatory tools has been answered by the Dutch government, which proposed adding a sixth branch to the EU competition law—a level-playing-field mechanism.[xlvii] The analysis of the Dutch government essentially highlights the fact that without an effective state aid control and antitrust enforcement at the global level, foreign companies benefiting from subsidies and unchecked market power in their home jurisdictions will be able to leverage that market power into the European market at the expense of their European competitors.[xlviii] The Dutch proposal then identifies two possible options for action: (1) first-best option would be to harmonize the regulation of state aid and market power on the global level; (2) second-best solution would be to harmonize the regulation of state aid and market power between EU and third countries through bilateral trade agreements.[xlix] While none of the above solutions have been achieved vis-à-vis China, the third-best option, in line with the Dutch proposal, would be to introduce stricter EU supervision over economic operators with discriminatory state aid benefits and unregulated market power.

According to the Dutch proposal, if a company threatens to distort competition in the internal market because it (1) receives government support or (2) has an unregulated dominant position in a third-country market, it can be subjected to the following prohibitions imposed after an investigation by the EU Commission: (1) supply constraints that are not in line with market conditions; (2) price and product differentiation between different market operators on comparable transactions; (3) tied selling, whereby additional conditions are imposed with no (apparent) relationship to the transaction; (4) wholesale/retail pricing that is not a reflection of market prices and/or production costs; (5) investments in assets with no apparent business case, i.e. that are insufficiently profitable.[l] Hence, the Dutch proposal introduces a "sixth branch of EU competition law" that would target potential distortionary behavior on the internal market. It would combine some features of antitrust such as prohibition of certain anti-competitive conduct as well as merger control since the said prohibitions would be based on the *ex ante* assessment concerning the state support enjoyed by the economic operator in question.[li] The proposal has been already praised by Commissioner Vestager: "It is very ambitious and it is also quite worked through. So I think it's an important contribution to the debate".[lii] This statement indicates the Commission's preference for finding alternative regulatory solutions as opposed to politicizing or modifying the existing merger control rules.

The Commission's preference for addressing SOE-related market distortions through a trade remedy instrument rather than through reforming the EU competition law and merger control has been reflected in the new Industrial Strategy unveiled on 10 March 2020.[liii] The policy document contains an acknowledgment of protectionism, market distortions, trade wars and other competitive challenges on the global markets. However, it emphasizes that "Europe's response cannot be to erect more barriers, shield uncompetitive industries or mimic the protectionist or distortive policies of others".[liv] Instead, the Commission decided that the level playing field within the EU internal market should be protected by limiting the ability of foreign companies to obtain foreign state subsidies in a similar way that European companies are subjected to EU state aid law when receiving economic benefits from the EU Member States. The Commission's vision was crystalized in the White Paper on foreign subsidies published on 17 June 2020 for public consultation until 23 September 2020.[lv]

The White Paper proposes to close an alleged gap existing within the current regulatory frameworks that are deemed insufficient when addressing market-distorting effects of foreign subsidies. In particular, the Commission noted that the EU merger control rules do not specifically consider whether an acquiring undertaking has benefited from foreign subsidies.[lvi] To close this alleged gap, the White Paper introduces an *ex ante* review of the planned acquisitions involving foreign subsidies.[lvii] Here, the term acquisition is defined in broader terms than concentrations under the EUMR and covers the acquisition of control and acquisition of a certain percentage of the shares or voting rights that would enable the acquirer to exercise "material influence" in an undertaking.[lviii] If the acquirer received a financial contribution from any third country in the past three years or expects to receive such contribution in the coming year, the acquisition will be subject to notification and review by the competent authority.[lix] If it is established that the proposed acquisition benefited from foreign subsidies in relation to the size of the subsidy, situation of the beneficiary, market conditions, level of activity in the EU internal market or other factors that would distort the internal market, the competent authority would prohibit the acquisition or subject it to a set of remedies, mainly of structural nature.[lx] It is also presumed that foreign subsidies below EUR 200,000 over a period of three years would not create distortions in the internal market.[lxi] The White Paper suggests that the Commission should be exclusively competent to carry out the aforementioned review in order to ensure a one-stop-shop control across the EU for acquisitions reaching certain quantitative thresholds. The Commission would also be responsible for applying the so-called "EU interest test" that would allow it to balance between the potentially distortive effects of the proposed acquisition and other EU public policy objectives such as creating jobs, digital transformation, security, public order and public safety, etc.[lxii] The proposed foreign subsidy screening mechanism will apply in parallel to the EU and national merger control regimes based on a competitive assessment of the notified concentrations.[lxiii]

Conclusion

> *The EU has awakened to the challenge but it has not yet defined its response. It needs to shape a strategy for its foreign policy, its technology and investment policy and its policy on China in third markets and multilateral institutions.* (Leonard et al. 2019, 4)

The preceding discussion has shown that the ongoing reform of the Chinese SOEs and their "going global" in pursuit of the objectives enshrined in the BRI, "Made in China 2025" and other industrial policies have resulted in an increase of their corporate acquisitions in the EU. The conceptual differences in approaches towards the role of SOEs in the economy between China and the EU have resulted in practical difficulties of applying the EU merger control rules based on the principle of competitive neutrality to the acquisitions of Chinese SOEs in Europe. Increasingly focused on the corporate channels for exercising control over companies, the EU merger assessment encountered difficulties in discovering and evaluating the exercise of political control, an important tool in China's economic statecraft. The calls for acknowledging political control over SOEs in merger assessment remain largely academic (Petit 2016; Riley 2016).

Although Chinese SOEs have not yet featured in the antitrust investigations of the EU Commission, it should be expected that the aforementioned conceptual differences will also present certain challenges in applying EU competition rules to the commercial practices of these SOEs. For example, market dominance in EU competition law is defined "as a position to behave to an appreciable extent independently of its competitors, customers and ultimately of its consumers";[lxiv] when applied to the SOEs, it may require an assessment of the state support and control instead of merely profit-maximizing incentives of a company. The same issue will be relevant in the investigation of predatory pricing instances where the comparison between the cost structures of an SOE and its private competitors may not be adequate for establishing an "equally efficient competitor" (Heim 2019a, 5).

It should be noted that antitrust enforcement against SOEs at the EU level is scarce (Schrepel 2019) and the lack of guidance in relation to the application of antitrust and merger control rules vis-à-vis SOEs led to inconsistent enforcement at the level of individual Member States. An earlier survey of the national merger control legislation of the Member States identified three broad groups of jurisdictions: (1) jurisdictions with specific rules or guidelines addressing application of merger control to SOE-related concentrations; (2) jurisdictions with no specific SOE-related rules or guidelines; (3) jurisdictions with sector-specific merger rules concerning the SOEs (Svetlicinii 2018). The enforcement of the merger control rules in relation to the acquisition of Chinese SOEs at the level of Member States also portrayed a heterogeneous landscape: while some national competition authorities (NCAs) explicitly address the SOE status of the merging parties, the majority of the NCAs do not provide any assessment of the state control in their merger decisions. That is why it was argued that that the EU Commission should consider issuing analytical guidelines on how to address the specific characteristics of SOEs in merger and antitrust investigations (Heim 2019a, 7).

Despite the earlier calls of individual Member States and other stakeholders for the reform of the existing merger control and antitrust rules in the EU in order to block foreign acquisitions and promote European "national champions", the EU Commission has been continuously opposed to the politicizing of the competition policy and using it for the purposes of economic protectionism. Instead, the Commission is currently considering a number of alternative regulatory tools that could address the "market distortions" that can be caused by Chinese SOEs. The recent publication of the White Paper on foreign subsidies was among the first steps in this direction.

Notes

i Xi Jinping, *The Governance of China II* (Foreign Languages Press, 2017), pp. 547–548.

ii See Ministry of Foreign Affairs of the People's Republic of China, *Promote Friendship between Our People and Work Together to Build a Bright Future* (8 September 2013), <https://www.fmprc.gov.cn/mfa_eng/wjdt_665385/zyjh_665391/t1078088.shtml> accessed 20 May 2021.

iii Ibid.

iv See full text: Action Plan on the Belt and Road Initiative (30 March 2015), <http://english.www.gov.cn/archive/publications/2015/03/30/content_281475080249035.htm> accessed 20 May 2021.

v The full text is available in Chinese at http://www.gov.cn/zhengce/content/2015-05/19/content_9784.htm.

vi Office of the Leading Group for the Belt and Road Initiative, *Building the Belt and Road: Concept, Practice and China's Contribution* (Foreign Languages Press, 2017), p. 18.

vii Institute for Security and Development Policy, *Made in China 2025* (June 2018), <https://isdp.eu/content/uploads/2018/06/Made-in-China-Backgrounder.pdf> accessed 20 May 2021, p. 1.

viii See World Trade Organization, Subsidies and countervailing measures, <https://www.wto.org/english/tratop_e/scm_e/scm_e.htm> accessed 20 May 2021.

ix Council Regulation (EC) No 139/2004 of 20 January 2004 on the control of concentrations between undertakings (the EU Merger Regulation), OJ L 24,

29.1.2004, p. 1–22, recital 10: "A concentration with a Community dimension should be deemed to exist where the aggregate turnover of the undertakings concerned exceeds given thresholds; that is the case irrespective of whether or not the undertakings effecting the concentration have their seat or their principal fields of activity in the Community, provided they have substantial operations there".

x A notable exception was the conditional clearance of the acquisition of Swiss agro-chemical company Syngenta by Chinese SOE ChemChina. Case No. COMP/M.7962 *ChemChina/Syngenta*, decision of 5 April 2017. See EU Commission, press release IP/17/882 *Mergers: Commission clears ChemChina acquisition of Syngenta, subject to conditions* (5 April 2017), <https://ec.europa.eu/commission/presscorner/detail/en/IP_17_882> accessed 20 May 2021.

xi See EU Commission, press release IP/19/881 Mergers: Commission prohibits Siemens' proposed acquisition of Alstom (6 February 2019), <https://ec.europa.eu/commission/presscorner/detail/en/IP_19_881> accessed 20 May 2021.

xii Guiding Opinions of the Central Committee of the Communist Party of China and the State Council on Deepening the Reform of State-owned Enterprises (24 August 2015).

xiii See Backgrounder: Xi Jinping Thought on Socialism with Chinese Characteristics for a New Era (Xinhua, 17 March 2018), <http://www.xinhuanet.com/english/2018-03/17/c_137046261.htm> accessed 20 May 2021.

xiv Constitution of the Communist Party of China, revised and adopted at the 19th National Congress of the Communist Party of China on 24 October 2017.

xv Xi Jinping, *Secure a Decisive Victory in Building a Moderately Prosperous Society in All Respects and Strive for the Great Success of Socialism with Chinese Characteristics for a New Era*, speech Delivered at the 19th National Congress of the Communist Party of China (18 October 2017), <http://www.xinhuanet.com/english/download/Xi_Jinping's_report_at_19th_CPC_National_Congress.pdf> accessed 20 May 2021, p. 29.

xvi See Guiding Opinions of the Central Committee of the Communist Party of China and the State Council on Deepening the Reform of State-owned Enterprises (24 August 2015).

xvii See Regulations of the Communist Party of China on the Work of Primary Organizations of State-owned Enterprises (29 November 2019), Article 13.

xviii Ibid., Article 14.

xix Xi Jinping, *The Governance of China II* (Beijing: Foreign Languages Press), 2017, p. 193.

xx China's Policy Paper on the European Union (19 December 2018), <https://eng.yidaiyilu.gov.cn/zchj/zcfg/75172.htm> accessed 20 May 2021.

xxi National Development and Reform Commission, Ministry of Commerce, Ministry of Foreign Affairs and the People's Bank of China, Guidance on Further Directing and Regulating Overseas Investment Direction (August 2017), <https://eng.yidaiyilu.gov.cn/zchj/zcfg/35989.htm> accessed 20 May 2021.

xxii Ministry of Finance, Regulation on State-owned Enterprises' Overseas Investment Financial Management (12 June 2017), <https://eng.yidaiyilu.gov.cn/zchj/zcfg/35991.htm> accessed 20 May 2021.

xxiii Ursula von der Leyen, *A Union that strives for more: My agenda for Europe*, <https://ec.europa.eu/info/sites/default/files/political-guidelines-next-commission_en.pdf> accessed 20 May 2021, p. 17.

xxiv EU Merger Regulation, recital 22: "In the public sector, calculation of the turnover of an undertaking concerned in a concentration needs, therefore, to take account of undertakings making up an economic unit with an independent power of decision, irrespective of the way in which their capital is held or of the rules of administrative supervision applicable to them".

xxv Commission Consolidated Jurisdictional Notice under Council Regulation (EC) No 139/2004 on the control of concentrations between undertakings (2008/C 95/01), para. 153.

xxvi Ibid., para. 194.

xxvii Case No. COMP/M.6082 *China National Bluestar/Elkem*, decision of 31 March 2011.

xxviii Ibid., paras 18–21.

xxix Case No. COMP/M.6113 *DSM/Sinochem/JV*, decision of 19 May 2011.

xxx Case No. COMP/M.7850 *EDF/CGN/NNB*, decision of 10 March 2016.

xxxi Ibid., para. 37.

xxxii Case No. COMP/M.7962 *ChemChina/Syngenta*, decision of 5 April 2017.

xxxiii See David Briginshaw, *CNR and CSR finalise merger to become CRRC* (International Railway Journal, 2 June 2015), <https://www.railjournal.com/financial/cnr-and-csr-finalise-merger-to-become-crrc/> accessed 20 May 2021.

xxxiv Case COMP/M.8677 *Siemens/Alstom*, decision of 6 February 2019.

xxxv See David Fickling, *Alstom and Siemens Show How Not to Deal with China* (Bloomberg, 6 February 2019), <https://www.bloomberg.com/opinion/articles/2019-02-06/alstom-and-siemens-show-how-not-to-deal-with-china-and-vestager> accessed 20 May 2021.

xxxvi See EU Commission, press release 19/889 Statement by Commissioner Vestager on the proposed acquisition of Alstom by Siemens and the proposed acquisition of Aurubis rolled Products and Schwermetall by Wieland (6 February 2019), <https://ec.europa.eu/commission/presscorner/detail/en/STATEMENT_19_889> accessed 20 May 2021.

xxxvii A Franco-German Manifesto for a European industrial policy fit for the 21st Century (19 February 2019), <https://www.gouvernement.fr/en/a-franco-german-manifesto-for-a-european-industrial-policy-fit-for-the-21st-century> accessed 20 May 2021.

xxxviii See Federal Ministry for Economic Affairs and Energy, National Industrial Strategy 2030: Strategic guidelines for a German and European industrial policy (5 February 2019), <https://www.bmwi.de/Redaktion/EN/Publikationen/Industry/national-industry-strategy-2030.html> accessed 20 May 2021, p. 14.

xxxix Ibid, p. 15.

xl See Joint statement by France, Austria, Croatia, Czech Republic, Estonia, Finland, Germany, Greece, Hungary, Italy, Latvia, Luxembourg, Malta, Netherlands, Poland, Romania, Slovakia, Spain (18 December 2018), <https://www.bmwi.de/Redaktion/DE/Downloads/F/friends-of-industry-6th-ministerial-meeting-declaration.pdf?__blob=publicationFile&v = 6> accessed 20 May 2021, p. 4.

xli Open letter: More, not less, competition is needed in Europe (10 February 2019), <https://www.competitionpolicyinternational.com/more-not-less-competition-is-needed-in-europe/> accessed 20 May 2021.

xlii See Federal Competition Authority, *Position Paper on National and European Champions in Merger Control* (November 2019), <https://www.bwb.gv.at/fileadmin/user_upload/PDFs/Positionspapier_European_Champions_EN.pdf> accessed 4 August 2020, p. 25.

xliii See Modernising EU Competition Policy, <https://www.bmwi.de/Redaktion/DE/Downloads/M-O/modernising-eu-competition-policy.pdf?__blob=publicationFile&v = 4> accessed 20 May 2021, p. 1

xliv Ibid., p. 2.

xlv Ibid., p. 3.

xlvi Ursula von der Leyen, President-elect of the European Commission, *Mission letter to Margrethe Vestager, Executive Vice-President-designate for a Europe fit for the Digital Age* (10 September 2019), <https://ec.europa.eu/commission/commissioners/sites/default/files/commissioner_mission_letters/mission-letter-margrethe-vestager_2019_en.pdf> accessed 20 May 2021, p. 6.

xlvii The current five branches of EU competition law address collusive behaviour (Article 101 TFEU), abuse of dominant position (Article 102 TFEU), merger control (EUMR), state aid (Article 107 TFEU) and public undertakings (Article 106 TFEU).

xlviii Non-paper strengthening the level playing field on the internal market (9 December 2019), <https://www.permanentrepresentations.nl/documents/publications/2019/12/09/non-paper-on-level-playing-field> accessed 20 May 2021.

xlix Ibid., p. 1.

l Ibid., p. 2.

li See Thorsten Kaeseberg, *A new EU-level playing field instrument: Potential goals and design* (CEPR Policy Portal, 15 January 2020), <https://voxeu.org/article/new-eu-level-playing-field-instrument> accessed 20 May 2021.

lii Javier Espinoza and Sam Fleming, *Margrethe Vestager examines curbs on non-EU state-backed companies* (Financial Times, 16 December 2019), <https://www.ft.com/content/452d2c7a-1f0e-11ea-92da-f0c92e957a96> accessed 20 May 2021.

liii EU Commission, press release IP/20/416 Making Europe's Businesses Future-Ready: A New Industrial Strategy For a Globally Competitive, Green and Digital Europe (10 March 2020), <https://ec.europa.eu/commission/presscorner/detail/en/ip_20_416> accessed 20 May 2021.

liv EU Commission, A New Industrial Strategy for Europe, COM(2020) 102 final (10 March 2020), p. 3.

lv EU Commission, White Paper on leveling the playing field as regards foreign subsidies, COM(2020) 253 final (17 June 2020), <https://ec.europa.eu/competition/international/overview/foreign_subsidies_white_paper.pdf> accessed 20 May 2021.

lvi Ibid., p. 9.

lvii Ibid., p. 23.

lviii Ibid., p. 23.

lix Ibid., p. 24.

lx Ibid., p. 28.

lxi Ibid., p. 46.

lxii Ibid., p. 17.

lxiii Ibid., p. 40.

lxiv Commission Notice on the definition of relevant market for the purposes of Community competition law, 97 C/ 372/03, para 10.

Bibliography

Bath, Vivienne, 2015 "Chinese Companies and Outbound Investment: The Balance between Domestic and International Concerns". In Lisa Toohey, Colin B. Picker and Jonathan Greenacre (eds.), *China in the International Economic Order: New Directions and Changing Paradigms* (Cambridge), 227–244.

Bradford, Anu, Robert J. Jackson, Jr. and Jonathon Zytnick, 2018 "Is E.U. Merger Control Used for Protectionism? An Empirical Analysis". *Journal of Empirical Legal Studies* 15(1): 165–191.

Clark, Gordon L., Adam D. Dixon and Ashby H.B. Monk, 2013 *Sovereign Welfare Funds: Legitimacy, Governance, and Global Power* (Princeton University Press).

Clarke, Michael, 2017 "The Belt and Road Initiative: China's New Grand Strategy?" *Asia Policy* 24: 71–79.

Ding, Ru, 2014 "'Public Body' or Not: Chinese State-Owned Enterprise". *Journal of World Trade* 48(1): 167–190.

Drexl, Josef and Vicente Bagnoli, 2015 *State-Initiated Restraints of Competition* (Edward Elgar).

Du, Ming, 2014a "China's State Capitalism and World Trade Law". *International & Comparative Law Quarterly* 63(2): 409–448.

Du, Ming, 2014b "When China's National Champions 'Go Global': Nothing to Fear but Fear Itself?" *Journal of World Trade* 48(6): 1127–1166.

Guo, Rui, 2013 "The Creation of Modern State Ownership: Legal Transplantation and the Rise of the Modern State-Owned Big Businesses in China". *Peking University Journal of Legal Studies* 69–91.

He Fan and Ye Qianlin, 2017 "World Economic Order: Present and Future". In Daniel Remler and Ye Yu (eds.), *Parallel Perspectives on the Global Economic Order: A U.S.-China Essay Collection* (Center for Strategic and International Studies), 9–11, https://www.csis.org/world-economic-order-present-and-future

Hanemann, Thilo and Mikko Huotari, 2017 *Record Flows and Growing Imbalances: Chinese Investment in Europe in 2016* (Mercator Institute for China Studies), https://merics.org/en/report/record-flows-and-growing-imbalances-chinese-investment-europe-2016.

Heim, Mathew, 2019a *How Can European Competition Law Address Market Distortions Caused by State-Owned Enterprises?* (Bruegel), https://bruegel.org/2019/12/how-can-european-competition-law-address-market-distortions-caused-by-state-controlled-enterprises/.

Heim, Mathew, 2019b *Modernising European Competition Policy: A Brief Review of Member States' Proposals* (Bruegel, 24 July), https://bruegel.org/2019/07/modernising-european-competition-policy-a-brief-review-of-member-states-proposals/.

Heim, Mathew and Catarina Midoes, 2019 *European Championships: Industrial Champions and Competition Policy* (Bruegel, 26 July), https://bruegel.org/2019/07/european-champion-ships-industrial-champions-and-competition-policy/.

Hooijmaaijers, Bas, 2019 "Blackening Skies for Chinese Investments in the EU?" *Journal of Chinese Political Science* 24: 451–470.

Huang, Betty, Alvaro Ortiz, Tomasa Rodrigo and Le Xia, 2019 *China: Five Facts About Outward Direct Investment and Their Implication for Future Trend* (BBVA Research), https://www.bbvaresearch.com/en/publicaciones/china-five-facts-about-outward-direct-investment-and-their-implication-for-future-trend/.

Huotari, Mikko and Agatha Kratz, 2019 *Beyond Investment Screening: Expanding Europe's Toolbox to Address Economic Risks from Chinese State Capitalism* (Bertelsmann Stiftung), https://www.bertelsmann-stiftung.de/en/publications/publication/did/beyond-investment-screening/.

Leonard, Mark, Jean Pisani-Ferry, Elina Ribakova, Jeremy Shapiro and Guntram Wolff, 2019 *Redefining Europe's Economic Sovereignty* (European Council on Foreign Relations), https://www.ecfr.eu/publications/summary/redefining_europes_economic_sovereignty.

Leutert, Wendy, 2016 "Challenges Ahead in China's Reform of State-Owned Enterprises". *Asia Policy* 21: 83–99.

Li, Xin and Kjeld Erik Brødsgaard, "SOE Reform in China: Past, Present and Future". *Copenhagen Journal of Asian Studies* 31(2): 54–78.

Liao, Yi, 2013 "Whether China's State-Owned Commercial Banks Constitute "Public Bodies" within the Meaning of Article 1.1 (a) (1) of the Agreement on Subsidies and Countervailing Measures: Analysis of US-Definitive Anti-Dumping and Countervailing Duties on Certain Products from China". *Beijing Law Review* 4(4): 198–218.

Lu, Longjie, 2019 "Bankers' Remuneration and Political Incentives in Chinese State-Owned Commercial Banks: Regulation and Practice". *Journal of Corporate Law Studies* 19(2): 451–503.

Luyao, Che, 2019 *China's State-Directed Economy and the International Order* (Springer).

McGregor, Richard, 2010 *The Party: The Secret World of China's Communist Rulers* (Penguin Books).

Meunier, Sophie, 2014 "'Beggars Can't Be Choosers': The European Crisis and Chinese Direct Investment in the European Union". *Journal of European Integration* 36(3): 283–302.

Organisation for Economic Co-operation and Development, 2015 *Roundtable on Competition Neutrality: Issues Paper by the Secretariat* (Organisation for Economic Co-operation and Development), http://www.oecd.org/officialdocuments/publicdisplaydocumentpdf/?cote=DAF/COMP(2015)5&docLanguage=En.

Organisation for Economic Co-operation and Development, 2016 *Governments as Competitors in the Global Marketplace: Options for Ensuring a Level Playing Field* (Organisation for Economic Co-operation and Development), http://e15initiative.org/publications/governments-as-competitors-in-the-global-marketplace-options-for-ensuring-a-level-playing-field/.

Petit, Nicolas, 2016 *Chinese State Capitalism and Western Antitrust Policy* (SSRN, 20 June), https://papers.ssrn.com/sol3/papers.cfm?abstract_id=2798162.

Putniņš, Tālis J., 2015 "Economics of State-Owned Enterprises". *International Journal of Public Administration* 38(11): 815–832.

Riley, Alan, 2016 "Nuking Misconceptions: Hinkley Point, Chinese SOEs and EU Merger Law". *European Competition Law Review* 37(8): 301–324.

Schrepel, Thibault, 2019 *Antitrust Without Romance* (SSRN, 30 May), https://papers.ssrn.com/sol3/papers.cfm?abstract_id=3395001.

Shuping, Liao and Yongsheng Zhang, 2014 "A New Context for Managing Overseas Direct Investment by Chinese State-Owned Enterprises". *China Economic Journal* 7(1): 126–140.

Svetlicinii, Alexandr, 2017 "The Acquisitions of the Chinese State-Owned Enterprises under the EU Merger Control Regime: Time for Reflection?" *Revue Lamy de la concurrence* 67: 30–36.

Svetlicinii, Alexandr, 2018 "The Acquisitions of the Chinese State-Owned Enterprises under the National Merger Control Regimes of the EU Member States: Searching for a Coherent Approach" *Market and Competition Law Review* 2(1): 99–120.

Svetlicinii, Alexandr, 2019 "The Interactions of Competition Law and Investment Law: The Case of Chinese State-Owned Enterprises and EU Merger Control

Regime". In Julien Chaisse, Leïla Choukroune and Sufian Jusoh (eds.), *Handbook of International Investment Law and Policy* (Springer), 1–21.

Taylor, Monique, 2012 "China's Oil Industry: 'Corporate Governance with Chinese Characteristics'". In Xu Yi-chong (ed.), *The Political Economy of State-Owned Enterprises in China and India* (Palgrave).

Wang, Yong, 2016 "Offensive for Defensive: The Belt and Road Initiative and China's New Grand Strategy". *The Pacific Review* 29(3): 455–463.

Zhang, Angela Huyue, 2012 "The Single-Entity Theory: An Antitrust Time Bomb for Chinese State-Owned Enterprises?" *Journal of Competition Law and Economics* 8(4): 805–830.

8 EU-China cooperation on promoting sustainable development under the Belt and Road Initiative—Consensus built on divergence

Su Xueji

1 Introduction

Ever since the launch of the Belt and Road Initiative (BRI), the EU has been grappling with forming a unified and coherent response to this China-led economic development and inter-regional connectivity proposal (Vangeli 2018). Tension between the willingness to cooperate on the basis of pragmatic interests and disparities between approaches and normative foundation of two sides characterizes almost every respect of current EU–China relations. Their cooperation on the BRI and sustainable development is no exception.

In September 2018, the EU launched a new strategy on "Connecting Europe and Asia" (see Zhao and Chen, Chapter 2). The key objective of this new strategy was to strengthen "sustainable connectivity" between Europe and Asia, which encapsulates "the European way" (Broer 2018). This new strategy commits to high standards of transparency, environmental protection and ensuring a level playing field for enterprises (Elmer 2018). In effect, the aspect of "sustainable development" is rather ubiquitous in EU–China cooperation. It is presented in several EU–China joint announcements, covering a broad range of themes, including urbanization, investment, energy, connectivity, environmental protection, agriculture and peace (Joint statement of the 21st EU–China summit 2020). The idea "sustainable connectivity" is best demonstrated in the EU–China flagship cooperation program, the Connectivity Platform (Terms of References of the Joint Study on Sustainable Railway-based Transport Corridors between Europe and China 2019).

On the surface, this trend seems to indicate that the pursuits of sustainable development in the regions of two sides have dovetailed. However, it still remains murky how far this joint commitment will bring EU–China cooperation on the BRI and its impact on bolstering regional sustainable development, on which this chapter focuses.

To begin with, a brief introduction of sustainable development seems to be indispensable. Derived from debates in the 1960s among conservationists, the concept of sustainable development was initially expounded by the

World Commission on Environment and Development (WCED) in 1987 in the report "Our Common Future", widely known as the Brundtland Report. The report defined sustainable development as "development that meets the needs of the present without compromising the ability of future generations to meet their own needs" (Brundtland Commission 1987). The significance yet ambiguity of this definition has spurred consequent efforts to explicate and substantiate this concept. Among all, the "triple-bottom-line" structure or "three pillars" emerged. This structure refers to the three main aspects that constitute sustainable development—first economic development, secondly social development and thirdly environmental protection.

Despite being endorsed by a number of international organizations including the UN itself, the concept of sustainable development is still elusive and nebulous (Pope et al. 2004, 595). A plethora of theoretical formulations and applications of sustainability have mushroomed, founded upon common concerns and principles yet with varying emphases. When the term "sustainability" is in usage as political discourse, international actors could be intentionally equivocal about its meaning in order to justify manifold diplomatic and political goals (Pope et al. 2004). Therefore, instead of semantic or conceptual analyses, this chapter appraises the objectives and behaviors of the actors — the EU and China. However, owing to the broad and obscure contours of sustainable development, this chapter might not be able to delve into details on each aspect. Rather, it hopes to provide a holistic review.

To this end, this chapter is structured as follows: Section 2 introduces the BRI and its performance in regional sustainable development, which is in line with the principles of China's foreign policy. Following that, Section 3 sketches out the EU's approach built upon its basic values to the promotion of sustainable development, with a reference to the pragmatic transition of the EU's foreign aid and development policies. Section 4 examines cooperative modes of the EU–China partnership for regional sustainable development, through examples of two selected BRI-related projects—the Connectivity Platform and the Asian Infrastructure Investment Bank (AIIB).

2 BRI and China's approach to sustainable development promotion

2.1 A China-led developmental initiative

Notwithstanding its controversial and often misconstrued definition, the rationale underneath the BRI seems to be more intelligible to many. Under the pressure of a domestic economic downturn, China maintains that nurturing foreign markets, coupled with comprehensive connectivity and trading networks, could engender new economic stimulus. The initiative is deeply rooted in this idea (Solmecke 2016, 9; Song 2018). In this sense, the BRI is a development-oriented endeavor in essence with its primary stage centered on connectivity and other infrastructure projects—the so-called "hard" connectivity, while paving the way to a more integrated, prosperous and free-flowing regional market. To this end, an unprecedented amount of capital has been channeled into this initiative and more will follow (OECD 2018; Solmecke 2016; Song 2018). The initiative is endowed with remarkable developmental potential, paired with political and economic implications for the regions covered and for the globe.

2.2 Sustainable development in the construction of the BRI and the Chinese approach

Although China has singled out "ecological civilization" (Minister of Ecology and Environment of the People's Republic of China 2017a,b) as one of the primary goals of the BRI, the scenario it may create for regional sustainability is ambivalent (UNEP). On the one hand, it is widely acknowledged that sustainability must be pursued in a world of linkages and interdependencies (see Sala et al. 2015, 314; Shah 2016; Jin 2018, 278), which is a scenario the BRI is presumably dedicated to. On the other hand, precisely because of its magnitude, if executed poorly, ramifications of the initiative for regional and global sustainable development will be too sizeable to be overlooked (WWF 2017).

Suspicions and criticisms abound about the formation of sustainable BRI at its outset. In 2018, 65 civil society organizations raised concerns against the Chinese Development Bank supporting Ghana's bauxite development because of the possible repercussions for Ghana's forest reserves and overall biodiversity (Rao and Baruah 2018). Following that, another wave of intensive denunciation was triggered by the BRI's funding of several coal plants (Watts 2019). Controversy around BRI-related projects is associated with not only social and environmental aspects but also economic ones. Central to the debate are claims regarding detrimental consequences of the loans granted by China without condition. The argument is that in absence of good governance and well-designed national infrastructure schemes, loans might eventually result in unbearable indebtedness and wasted resources, and undermine the benefits of infrastructure investment for local communities. It might also afflict the environment of the recipient countries. Such an argument culminated in the suspension of the Malaysia East Coast rail project at the initiative of the new Malaysian government (Pham 2018).

These events have undoubtedly captured the attention of the international community, including the Chinese government itself. As a result, in the second BRI Forum, China pledged to put a new debt sustainability framework on its agenda for the purpose of objectively assessing local financing ability—an action welcomed by other participants, including the EU (Wong 2019; see also Šefčovič 2019). Besides, in collaboration with the United Nations Development Programme, China Development Bank has been working on "a new study reviewing the actual practice of applying financing and investment standards for sustainable development within China and the rest of the world". The study "aims to identify a core set of practices that could (...) serve as building blocks for harmonized BRI standards that could be applied in diverse partner countries" (Xu 2019; see also UNDP 2019). Overall, the second BRI Forum put forward a series of arrangements for sustainable development, including the formulation of Green Investment Principles for BRI, *inter alia*, aiming to assemble environmental expertise for the purpose of forging long-term green and sustainable development in all concerned countries in support of the 2030 Agenda for Sustainable Development (UNEP).

In light of these prompt and amicable responses to criticisms, it seems to be unfair to suggest the Chinese government has an absolutely *laissez-faire* attitude towards sustainable development under the BRI. In fact, China has been proactive in participating in the shaping of sustainable development agendas. It has been on the frontline of clean technologies investment for years, with multilateral accords signed for the protection of biodiversity and climate-related cooperation. BRI could be regarded as a continuation of this policy. To understand the less satisfactory results, the guiding principles of China's foreign policy and its idiosyncratic approach to foreign aid and investments should not be ignored.

2.3 The principle of "non-interference"

As Vangeli aptly points out,

> The vision of world as comprised by nation-states that all develop in different, idiosyncratic way, is where China and the BRI diverge, if not contradict the idea of liberal democracy and its universal value and applicability. The political philosophy of the BRI, a consequence of China's exceptionalism is rooted in the objection of the assumed universal values, standards and blueprint rooted in liberal democracy promoted by the Western powers and international organizations (Vangeli 2018).

This philosophy is pronounced in all of China's foreign aid programs and China-led multilateral financial institutions, with the "non-interference" principle as its incarnation (Su forthcoming). During a visit to Indonesia in October 2013, President Xi first mentioned the idea of a new Asian bank, which later became the AIIB. The AIIB works along the lines of the Beijing Consensus (Wissenbach and Wang 2016, 253) that is giving loans with "no strings attached" (Danner 2019). It inherits China's conventional principles of external assistance, including "mutual benefit" and "non-interference" (Peng and Tok 2016, 736). The principles harken back to the 1960s, when China's external assistance commenced (Peng and Tok 2016), enunciated by Zhou Enlai during his first trip to Africa (Wissenbach and Wang 2016, 253).

Five decades later, in China's National Plan on Implementation of the 2030 Agenda for Sustainable Development, two familiar general principles are, among others, listed, the Principle of Sovereignty and Voluntary Action and the Principle of "Common but Differentiated Responsibilities" (China's National Plan on Implementation of the 2030 Agenda, 2016). The former essentially repeats the long-standing norm, referring to the entitlement of countries to formulate their domestic development strategies and take measures independently. The latter underlines the international principle that allows proportionate and diversified responsibility among countries, especially between the groups of developed countries and developing countries (Yan and Torney 2016).

Upholding these principles, China consistently refrains from tying aid, and hence the construction of the BRI to a large degree is subject to and depends on the domestic law and policy of the participant countries on the ground. A very logical result is that in countries devoid of good governance and rigorous rules for sustainable development, BRI-related projects could be "less" sustainable or even detrimental to sustainability. This situation is aided by China's traditional preference for economic development. Akin to its domestic development model, under the BRI, China still prioritizes economic development on the basis of the perception that growth enables positive transformative changes (Vazquez and Chin 2019, 593). On this ground, at the rudimentary stage of the BRI, connectivity plays a critical role while the environmental and social developments are subordinate with few prescriptions. Therefore, in social and environmental aspects, there might be little incentive for China to push forward a regional sustainable development agenda at the cost of its normative image.

3 The traditional and modern EU approach to promoting sustainable development

3.1 "Poverty eradication" as priority in the EU's development policy

To start with, development and cooperation policy was the first pillar of the EU's external policies when the European Community was created six decades ago (Hahlen 2019, vi). European foreign aid programs commenced in the wake of the Second World War, almost in the same epoch when the Chinese external assistance emerged (Beringer 2019, 17; Mah 2015, 44).

Internally, the EU has entrenched a fully fledged framework composed of regulations and guiding principles to support sustainable development. The external dimension of sustainable development "has been factored into EU internal policy-making and through integration of Sustainable Development considerations in EU's external policies" (EU Sustainable Development Strategy). The primary goal of development cooperation, pursuant to Article 208 of the Treaty on the Functioning of the EU (TFEU), is "reduction and, in the long term, the eradication of poverty (Article 208).

Besides, development cooperation shall be guided by a series of principles that informed the EU's own creation—democracy, rule of law, universality, indivisibility of human rights and fundamental freedoms, respect for human dignity, equality and solidarity, as well as respect for principles of the UN Charter and international law.

The policy is also rich in environmental and social dimensions. The EU has long taken the lead in environmental protection, notably framed under the umbrella of climate change. It commits to aligning its own development policies to the priorities of the SDGs (European Parliament 2013) and has since launched several flagship initiatives (Beringer 2019). Additionally, the EU values international public finance and has traditionally followed the Official Development Assistance (ODA) model in its provision of aid (Wissenbach and Wang 2016, 253; see also OECD 2019a,b). So far it is the world's largest donor in international development (Beringer 2019, 18).

3.2 A pragmatic transition of the EU's development policy

However, the genesis of the EU's development policy elicited criticisms in the early 2000s, partly because of the growing presence of non-traditional donors such as BRICS countries and their example of the South-South Cooperation (SSC) approach (Li 2018; European Commission 2018). Skepticism and negative perception abounded among Europeans, questioning the effectiveness of the EU's norm-driven and value-added aid praxis (Beringer 2019, 28). Compared to the traditional ODA approach, which features a donor-recipient relationship, the SSC approach is clearly more commercially constructed, underscoring economic benefits to both recipients and providers (Beringer 2019, 27; Chandy and Kharas 2011, 739–751). This created a background against which concerns as to a lack of benefits to the EU as such in its aid programs have arisen, accentuated by burgeoning global competition for energy and other strategic resources among great powers (Beringer 2019, 27; Rogerson 2004).

In response to criticisms, the EU began to look for alternatives to its traditional donor-recipient relationship and a transformation of its aid agenda. In 2011, the European Commission and the Member States reached an agreement on a new development policy framework that introduced the "Agenda for Change". This Agenda outlines a partnership-like development policy which "deliver[s] clear results (…) and achieve[s] greater effectiveness and accountability for spending" (European Commission 2016a). It is stated in the Agenda that "the EU aimed for a more targeted and coordinated allocation of funds." Whereas the funds "should be selected in accordance with the partner's demand, they also had to be consistent with the EU's (and Member States') expertise, track-record, and preferences" (Beringer 2019, 28). The Agenda also promulgates financing schemes based on the public-private partnerships (PPPs) which are embodied by the composition of public loans and private funds. It called for public contributions from emerging donors (European Parliament 2016). The new aid Agenda signaled that the EU is in a shift towards a self-interest, partnership-like "development effectiveness" approach (European Parliament 2020). This is also notable in the European Consensus on development. The Consensus proposed to work together with other actors and tailor development partnerships to reflect the capabilities and needs of the recipient countries (European Commission 2016c). The EU's turn to pragmatism and the partnership-like method in its development policy render the EU–China cooperation on sustainable development feasible and set the tone for it.

4 The cooperation paradigm of the EU and China on sustainable development under the BRI

4.1 The EU's response to sustainability issues of the BRI

On the surface, both the EU and China have committed to comprehensive sustainable development which encompasses economic, environmental and social dimensions. Seemingly, this lays a foundation for their cooperation towards a more sustainable, resilient Eurasian region. However, when it comes to the specific goals, practical standards and approaches to sustainability, the two sides diverge substantially. From the economic perspective, a major disagreement lies in the fiscal sustainability concerning the way in which China invests and grants its loans. Environmentally, China's promotion of a "green belt and road" so far appears to be a compound of political rhetoric, general guidelines and pilot projects, eliciting suspicions from EU officials. Last but not least, the social dimension seems to be mostly contentious, particularly with the possible inclusion of human rights issues.

Theoretically, all facets of human rights protection could be regarded as preconditions to development (e.g. gender equality; labor standards; protection of vulnerable groups). Therefore, they could be formalized under the term of either "human rights protection" or "sustainable development" (Novitz 2018, 113–134). Although generally speaking, the EU's external policies and actions must comply with its fundamental values, it shows an intention to separate and lift out the traditional human rights issues from its sustainable development cooperation with China. It is also noticeable that the social aspect of sustainable development is diluted or tacitly removed in their collaboration agendas.[i]

This chapter is of the view that normative conflicts do not necessarily hamper cooperation. In the case when two sides are prone to cooperate, driven perhaps by pragmatic and material interests, they tend to seek common ground and tactically avoid touching upon disparities (Crooks 2013, 639–63). The following two case studies will further elaborate how pragmatic interests enable and navigate the cooperation projects between the EU and China under the BRI.

4.2 The connectivity platform—An EU–China joint commitment to sustainable corridors

Although the EU and Member States have been involved in the BRI in various forms, few formalized BRI-wide cooperation processes between the EU and China could be identified. The Connectivity Platform stands out. The Connectivity Platform was established in 2015 as a mutual commitment by the EU and China to maintaining and developing robust and fruitful relations in the area of transport. It is led by the European Commission's directorate-general for mobility and transport (DG MOVE) on the EU side and the National Development and Reform Commission (NDRC) on the Chinese side. Its main objective is "to explore opportunities for further cooperation in the area of transport with a view to enhancing synergies between the EU's approach to connectivity, including the Trans-European Transport Network (TEN-T), and China's BRI" (Memorandum of understanding on establishing a Connectivity Platform between the EU and China, 2015). The platform embraces four specific functions: information sharing, identifying cooperation opportunities, exploring business and investment opportunities, and creating a favorable environment for sustainable and interoperable cross-border infrastructure networks (NDRC and European Commission 2018). The EU indicated it as the main vehicle for working with China to connect the Eurasian continent (European Commission 2016b).

The fourth meeting of the Chairs of the EU–China Connectivity Platform, held in April 2019, unveiled a joint study on sustainable railway-based transport corridors. The primary purpose of this study was to "identify the most appropriate railway corridors, identify bottlenecks, identify and prioritize the missing links to improve the capacity and efficiency of rail corridors" (Terms of References of the Joint Study on Sustainable Railway-based Transport Corridors between Europe and China 2019). This joint study had been assigned to examine the merits and shortcomings of different corridors, taking into account socio-economic factors (economic efficiency, costs, construction feasibility, construction risks); environmental impacts, decarbonization benefits, climate and weather conditions; geographical factors; financial sustainability of corridor projects and fiscal impact on recipient countries. At least ostensibly, this joint study could be deemed as a mutual and consensual commitment made by the two sides to regional sustainability. Although traces of environmental and social consideration are discernible, the joint study should not be easily taken as any kind of sustainable impact assessment, but rather a general feasibility study of sorts.

In correspondence with its partnership-like development policy, this platform allows the EU and its Member States to mandate projects that suit their interests. To generalize, the establishment of the Connectivity Platform is designed to address at least three pressing concerns of the EU. First, the EU longs for the economic potential that the BRI entails to alter the unbalanced regional interconnectivity configuration. The vast majority of land routes linking East Asia and Europe are within the territory of Russia (Huijskens et al. 2017). This *status quo* has long concerned the EU. It needs to pool investments and other resources to the TEN-T priority projects, "that otherwise might not have happened or would have taken longer to build" (Pardo 2018, 237–250). In this way, BRI connectivity projects could generate transport flows that benefit the EU (European Commission 2018). Secondly, the Platform is expected to secure business opportunities for EU private companies and financial institutions and consequently improve the level playing field. Through the Platform, European enterprises would have a greater chance to partake in BRI projects. This could, to a certain extent, counteract their competitive disadvantage *vis-à-vis* Chinese enterprises in the regions. Lastly, the EU lamented the sole focus of the BRI on infrastructure and doubted the reasonableness of debt-fuelled investment for most countries on the Asian continent, especially for countries neighboring the EU (Leijen 2018). The platform may help direct financial resources to projects favorable to sustainability, provided that in the cooperation the EU would see to its stringent rules and standards on sustainable development.

The BRI is characterized by the participation of a substantial number of private actors. Creating an enabling environment for profound sustainability-relevant changes requires the adaptation of well-tested business practices of private participants (Solmecke 2016, 9). This requires prescriptive rules. The Connectivity Platform, however, was created as a non-institutionalized platform for liaison, and thus would not be able to yield more stringent standards or mandatory requirements for all. In the end, the extent to which these EU–China joint projects are sustainable still hinges on the varying national policies and rules where projects are to be carried out. Hence, judging from the sustainable development perspective, the participation of the EU might not make the scenario much better off. However, the Platform could facilitate regional development by optimizing the configuration of financial resources.

Nevertheless, the aforementioned incentives of the EU behind the establishment of the Connectivity Platform determine that the focus is likely on the economic sectors, whereas the environmental aspect is substandard and the social one is virtually sidelined. But as the Connectivity Platform is still in its infancy, more remains to be seen.

4.3 AIIB and its sustainable standard—Credit to the European members?

The last method is the project-specific approach exemplified by the AIIB. Unlike the Connectivity Platform, the AIIB is a highly institutionalized organization that could engender far-reaching normative implications by ascertaining concrete rules and standards. Prior to substantive analysis, two caveats should be added. First, although the AIIB management has posited that the AIIB is not a Chinese policy bank or part of the BRI (Umuhumuza 2019), the BRI and the AIIB were both ushered in by China for a rather similar mandate—enhancing regional infrastructure and, by extension, connectivity and interoperability (Ujvari 2016). As a result, many of the countries that have so far received funding from the AIIB are along the BRI (Shepard 2017). Secondly, while it is not the EU itself but rather 19 Member States[ii] that have joined the AIIB, the fact that the majority of Member States have joined would unavoidably bring to bear the normative influence of the EU. For these reasons, the AIIB is included as a case study for EU–China cooperation in the BRI context. These Member States joined the AIIB without Brussels' imprimatur or coordination in advance (Callaghan and Hubbard 2016; EPSC 2015).

European countries have grouped themselves into two constituencies in the AIIB.[iii] In order to coordinate and forge a common ground and concerted actions, the Economic and Financial Committee of the EU held several discussions in preparation for AIIB participation and interactions (Parliamentary Questions 2019). Therefore, despite an initial discrepancy in incentives among European countries when they decided to enter into the institution (Gabusi 2019; Nicolas and Meglio 2015), a well-coordinated common position soon followed. This position arguably embodies the EU's new engagement strategy. This is a strategy that enables the EU to reinvigorate established international practices and global systems by engaging with emerging regimes from within (Gabusi 2019; Zhao 2015). Accordingly, in the context of the AIIB, an overriding interest of the EU as a bloc is to uphold and embed in the AIIB the labor, social, environmental and procurement standards currently employed in other major multilateral development banks (MDBs), the so-called "best practice" (Ujvari 2016; Zhao 2015). As non-regional members of the AIIB, accounting for nearly 14% of the voting power,[iv] the EU Member States who are in the game have great bearing on the decision-making and standard-setting of the AIIB. In view of the AIIB's financial weight, as with the launch of the Connectivity Platform, the EU is also prone to use its leverage power within the bank to gain projects consistent with its geopolitical goals (Huijskens et al. 2017). Nevertheless, the rationale behind the EU's position on the AIIB (akin to that of the Connectivity Platform) is a hybrid of inextricably knitted pragmatic and normative interests.

But the participation of the EU seems to be more assertive and its normative impact more laudable than in the case of the Connectivity Platform. Some European sensibilities such as transparency and environmental and social standards are well manifested in the AIIB (Danner 2019). The bank's president Jin Liqun has proclaimed the bank to be "clean, lean and green" (Editorial Office 2018, 1), and the AIIB abides by these standards to an ample extent (Huijskens et al. 2017; Brombal 2018). Over a half-decade, it is widely acknowledged across Western capitals that the bank has brought its standards and policies on a par with other MDBs (Huijskens et al. 2017), vindicating early speculation. Some observers believe this success should be attributable to the endeavors of European members, or to all Western countries involved in general (Danner 2019; Gabusi 2019; Chin 2019). On different occasions, the AIIB's European Members have reiterated their insistence on higher institutional, social and environmental standards for the AIIB (Gabusi 2019). In practice, they play a pivotal role in pairing the AIIB and other MDBs, including the European Investment Bank (EIB). As a result, the AIIB co-financed the majority of early projects with other established MDBs. This situation has accelerated and influenced the formation of the AIIB's own Environmental and Social Framework.

Due to space limits, we will not elaborate on how sustainable the AIIB is or how it approaches sustainability differently. But two highly relevant points are worth referring to, one of which is the role China plays in the AIIB. Compared to China's domestic investment banks (Vazquez and Chin 2019), the AIIB has more comprehensive and stricter rules and standards on sustainable development, which in some aspects deviate from China's own developmental and aid experience (Gransow and Price 2019). On this account, accepting European sensibility and "best practices" into the AIIB has often been depicted as a trade-off made by China for international credibility and managerial skills. Here it should be useful to recall that although the AIIB is by and large characterized by multilateralism (Callaghan and Hubbard 2016; Gu 2017; Scott 2013), China is still a leading force in the institution. In line with the AIIB's three-pronged voting mechanism, China by virtue of its shares has *de facto* veto power over decisions requiring a special majority (Gu 2017). This means that to a great extent the *modus operandi* of the AIIB reflects China's own reformist shift towards "ecological civilization" (Nassiry and Nakhooda 2016; Solmecke 2016; Hanson 2019). This is by no means to suggest that the AIIB is a China-dominated institution. Rather, it should be regarded as a tentative effort to test and contextualize the multilateral governance model China envisions, which is still founded upon the "non-interference" principle. Likewise, equivalent general commitments made to sustainable development are also traceable in other China-initiated international financial institutions, for instance, the New Development Bank (NDB) (Ujvari 2016), albeit the NDB has failed to flesh out details on its sustainable development framework (Svetlicinii 2019). But suffice it to say, so far the achievements of the AIIB in terms of social and environmental standards are still in line with China's own interests and principles. In a practical sense, the inclusion of European allies assists China in solving the dilemma between its "non-interference" commitment and the demand for resilient and functional local governments which would benefit its "go-global" investments (Su forthcoming).

Frustration arises, however, when it comes to some fundamental diversions of the AIIB from the traditional MDBs. Quite a number of researchers and civil society groups, even the AIIB's European members, have voiced their concerns over the implementation of the bank's environmental and social commitments (Summers 2017; Kjell 2018). They have accused the AIIB of merely paying lip service to their sustainable pledges and being less efficient in information disclosure than other MDBs (Mendel and Summers 2016). The fact that the AIIB does not in principle and in practice phase out oil and coal-fired power plants financing have borne the brunt of criticisms.

This scenario has less to do with how green the AIIB is designed to be, and more with how it approaches sustainability. The bank follows gradualist, incremental steps towards its sustainable development goals. This means although the bank prioritizes investments in renewable energy, it does not immediately rule out the possibility of funding fossil fuels, especially when there is no viable or affordable substitute (Vazquez and Chin 2019). Another prominent difference between the AIIB and other MDBs lies in its criteria of "commercial viability", which requires AIIB projects to be profitable. A comparison between the performance indicators of AIIB and the EIB may well show the difference. The current performance indicators of the AIIB mainly focus on annual lending volume ambitions and the expected contribution of AIIB-financed projects to the GDP growth of beneficiary countries. In this respect, the EIB is bound to dedicate a minimum of 25% of its annual lending to climate action (Huijskens et al. 2017), and is committed to increasing the share to 50% in 2025 (European Investment Bank 2019). Instead of viewing itself as a traditional development "aid" agency that might provide grants or interest-free loans, the bank considers itself as "an instrument for our clients to achieve their commitments to the Paris goals" (Vazquez and Chin 2019). Moreover, the AIIB is more deferential than other MDBs, at least as it alleged, to the national political reality of their recipients (Saldinger 2019). But why would this approach lead to the AIIB's lenient stance on non-green energy? The primary focus of the AIIB on Asia and the crucial role oil and gas play in the development of Asian countries may provide the answer. Asia has half of the world's oil and gas reserves, which prompts some AIIB members to lobby intensively for non-green projects (Vazquez and Chin 2019; Ujvari 2016).

This scenario, therefore, cannot be properly dealt with at once. Clearly, the identity and attitude of the AIIB mirror very much the normative foundation of China's foreign aid policy. But in the meantime, they are somewhat in line with the new aid strategy of the EU, which equally embarks on a "development effectiveness" and partnership-based path. Above all, the governance modality of the AIIB has so far presented an auspicious start for EU–China cooperation on sustainable development, contributing not only to regional sustainability transformation financially but also to paradigmatic innovation of sustainable investments and aid.

5 Conclusion

Domestically, the EU and China alike have made their commitments to sustainability goals and actively integrate them into their own development objectives. At an international level, both the EU and China are supportive of the SDGs and the significance of "development effectiveness" (General Assembly Resolution 69/313 2015). In a normative sense, representing themselves as a "good force" (Kavalski 2013), both ought to act as responsible, proactive players in regional sustainable development. On a material basis, the EU and China would mutually benefit from common prosperity, stabilized and advanced regional markets in the Eurasian region.

However, the two sides have traditionally differed in their approaches to define, employ and implement their sustainable agendas. For China, sustainable development comprises economic growth, infrastructure and efforts in environmental protection, combined with incremental and practical solutions to problems in partner countries, in line with its guiding external principles of non-interference and un-conditionality. The EU's sustainable development agenda was traditionally associated with ODA and trade preferences, in parallel with robust environmental and social protections and policy prescriptions based on the values of democracy, human rights and universality (Wissenbach and Wang 2016, 253). However, as the term "sustainability" is theoretically open to interpretation and barely legalized, the two sides could carefully eschew their divergences in specific sub-goals, preferable approaches and latent norm contestation. Pragmatic interests, be they geopolitical or economic, propelled the launch of the Connectivity Platform and the EU Member States' decisions on joining the AIIB. It is testified that the collective efforts of the EU and China could transcend norm contestation and conceptual gaps, contributing to regional sustainability.

Owing to the wide contours of sustainable development studies, this chapter can go as far as to provide an overview of the EU–China cooperation on sustainable development in the context of the BRI. However, it hopes to invite further research in this respect, especially in empirical and comparative terms. For instance, in comparison with the Connectivity Platform, the AIIB is high-profile and more institutionalized, which submits to well-structured standards. Would institutionalized cooperation between the two sides find better consonance with the sustainable development agenda? Is multilateral cooperation better than bilateral? These questions merit further study.

Notes

i See for instance Joint statement of the 20th EU–China summit and Joint statement of the 21st EU–China summit. In the text of both announcements, sustainable development has been associated with a wide range of economic and environmental issues, such as forest management, fisheries, energy, Railway-based Corridors, with little reference to social dimensions.

ii Austria, Belgium, Denmark, Finland, France, Germany, Greece, Hungary, Ireland, Italy, Luxemburg, Malta, Netherlands, Poland, Portugal, Romania, Spain, Sweden, Cyprus.

iii The first one comprises exclusively eurozone countries (France, Italy, Portugal, Spain, Belgium, Ireland, Austria, Finland, Germany, Luxembourg, Malta, Cyprus and the Netherlands). The second consists of some non-eurozone EU members (Denmark, Poland, Sweden and Romania) and non-EU European countries (Iceland, Norway, Switzerland and United Kingdom). See the AIIB website. AIIB Board of directors, <https://www.aiib.org/en/about-aiib/governance/board-directors/board-members/index.html>.

iv See the AIIB website. Members and Prospective Members of the Bank, <https://www.aiib.org/en/about-aiib/governance/members-of-bank/index.html>.

Bibliography

Beringer, S. L. (2019). Energy, Climate Change and EU Development Policy. In S. L. Beringer, M. Sylvia, & T. Markus (Eds.), *EU Development Policies: Between Norms and Geopolitics*. (pp. 17–34). Palgrave Macmillan.

BIC-Europe and IDI (2018). *Moving Beyond Rhetoric: How the AIIB Can Close the Loophole on Fossil Fuels*. Bank Information Center-Europe and Inclusive Development International.

Broer, B. (2018, September 19). *The EU's Connectivity Strategy: An Answer to China's Belt and Road Initiative? EU-Asia Center*.

Brombal, D. (2018). Planning for a Sustainable Belt and Road Initiative (BRI): An Appraisal of the Asian Infrastructure Investment Bank (AIIB) Environmental and Social Safeguards. In W. Shan, K. Nuotio, & K. Zhang (Eds.), *Normative Readings of the Belt and Road Initiative*. (pp. 129–146). Springer.

Brundtland Commission (1987). *Report of the World Commission on Environment and Development: Our Common Future*. Oxford University Press.

Callaghan, M., & Hubbard, P. (2016). The Asian Infrastructure Investment Bank: Multilateralism on the Silk Road. *China Economic Journal 9*(2), 116–139.

Chaisse, J., & Matsushita, M. (2018). China's "belt and road" Initiative: Mapping the World Trade Normative and Strategic Implications. *Journal of World Trade 52*(1), 163–185.

Chandy, L., & Kharas, H. (2011). Why Can't We All Just Get Along? The Practical Limits to International Development Cooperation. *Journal of International Development 23*, 739–751.

Chin, G.T. (2019). The Asian Infrastructure Investment Bank - New Multilateralism: Early Development, Innovation, and Future Agendas. *Global Policy 10*(4), 569–581.

Crooks, P. I. (2013). Resetting EU–China Relations From a Values-Based to an Interests-Based Engagement. *International Politics 50*(5), 639–663.

Danner, L. K. (2019). European Involvement in China's Asian Infrastructure Investment Bank: Geopolitical Pragmatism or Normative Engagement? In S. L. Beringer, M. Sylvia, & T. Markus (Eds.), *EU Development Policies: Between Norms and Geopolitics*. (pp. 79–94). Palgrave Macmillan.

Editorial Office (2018). Lean, Clean and Green: A New Model of Multilateral Development Bank for Building Infrastructure in Asia and Beyond - An Interview with AIIB President Jin Liqun. *Journal of Infrastructure, Policy and Development 2*(1).

Elmer, K. (2018, September 20). *European Union Has a Plan for Asian Infrastructure but Will It Collide with China's Belt And Road? South China Morning Post*.

EPSC (2015, April 24). *The Asian Infrastructure and Investment Bank: A New Multilateral Financial Institution or a Vehicle for China's Geostrategic Goals. EPSC Strategic Notes.*

European Commission (2018, July). EU–China Connectivity Platform Short-Term Action Plan. Brussels: European Union, Retrieved from https://ec.europa.eu/transport/sites/transport/files/2018-07-13-eu-china-connectivity-platform-action--plan.pdf

European Commission (2016a). *EU Communication on the Agenda for Change.* European Commission.

European Commission (2016b). *Joint Communication to the European Parliament and the Council, Elements for a new EU-Strategy on China.* European Commission.

European Commission (2016c). *Communication from the Commission to the European Parliament, the Council, The European Economic and Social Committee and the Committee of Regions.* Proposal for a new European consensus on development our World, our dignity, our future. COM/2016/0740 final.

European Commission (2018, April 23). *Investing in Sustainable Development -The EU at the Forefront in Implementing the Addis Ababa Action Agenda.* Staff Working Document.

European Investment Bank (2019, November 14). *EU Bank Launches Ambitious New Climate Strategy and Energy Lending Policy.* Retrieved from https://www.eib.org/en/press/all/2019-313-eu-bank-launches-ambitious-new-climate-strategy-and-energy-lending-policy#.

European Parliament (2013, January 29). *The European Year for Development. Europe in the World.* European Parliament Briefing.

European Parliament, (2019, May 27). 'Parliamentary Questions, Answer Given by Mr Moscovici on Behalf of the European Commission', Retrieved from https://www.europarl.europa.eu/doceo/document/P-8-2019- 001855-ASW_EN.html

European Parliament (2020, January). *Understanding Development Effectiveness Concepts, Players and Tools.* European Parliament Briefing.

European Parliament, Directorate-General for External Policies (2016). *Good Governance in EU External Relations: What Role for Development Policy in a Changing International Context?* Brussels: European Parliament.

European Union (2016). *Consolidated Versions of the Treaty on European Union and the Treaty on the Functioning of the European Union.* European Union.

Gabusi, G. (2019). Global Standards in the Asian Infrastructure Investment Bank: The Contribution of the European Members. *Global Policy 10*(4), 631–638.

General Assembly Resolution 69/313 (2015, July 27). *Addis Ababa Action Agenda of the Third International Conference on Financing for Development (Addis Ababa Action Agenda)*, A/RES/69/313.

Government of the People's Republic of China (2016). *China's National Plan on Implementation of the 2030 Agenda for Sustainable Development.* Government of the People's Republic of China.

Gransow, B., & Price, S. (2019). Social Risk Management at AIIB – Chinese or International Characteristics? *Journal of Chinese Political Science 24*, 289–311.

Gu, B. (2017). Chinese Multilateralism in the AIIB. *Journal of International Economic Law 20*, 137–158.

Hahlen, R. (2019). Foreword. In S. L. Beringer, M. Sylvia, & T. Markus (Eds.), *EU Development Policies: Between Norms and Geopolitics.* (pp. v–ix). Palgrave Macmillan.

Hall, I. (2017, October 16). Belt and Road: The Case for "wait and see". *The Interpreter*. Retrieved from https://www.lowyinstitute.org/the-interpreter/belt-and-road-case-wait-and-see.

Hanson, A. (2019, December). *Ecological Civilization in the People's Republic of China: Values, Action, and Future Needs*. ADB East Asia Working Paper Series 21.

Huang, Y. (2018, January 14). Why China's Good Environmental Policies Have Gone Wrong. *The New York Times*. Retrieved from https://www.nytimes.com/2018/01/14/opinion/china-environmental-policies-wrong.html.

Huijskens, F., Turcsanyi, R., & Ujvari, B. (2017, May). The EU in the AIIB: Taming China's Influence from Within. Security Policy Brief 86.

Jin, L. (2018). Synergies Between the Belt and Road Initiative and the 2030 SDGs: From the Perspective of Development. *Economic and Political Studies 6*(3), 278–292.

European Comission (2018, July 16). Joint statement of the 20st EU–China summit.

European Comission (2019, April 9). Joint statement of the 21st EU–China summit: Rebalancing the strategic partnership, Press release.

Kavalski, E. (2013). The Struggle for Recognition of Normative Powers: Normative Power Europe and Normative Power China in context. *Cooperation and Conflict 48*(2), 247–267.

Kjell, P. (2018, June 21). Why Is the World's Newest Development Bank Investing Coal Despite Its Green Promise? *Climate Home News*. Retrieved from https://www.climatechangenews.com/2018/06/21/worlds-newest-development-bank-invests-coal-despite-green-promise/.

Leijen, M. V. (2018, September 18). EU Commission: The Belt and Road Initiative Is a Chinese project. *RailFreight.com*. Retrieved from https://www.railfreight.com/specials/2018/09/18/eu-commission-the-belt-and-road-initiative-is-a-chinese-project/.

Li, Y. (2018, November). *Assessment of South-South Cooperation and the Global Narrative on the Eve Of Bapa+40*. South Centre Research Paper.

Loke, B. (2018). China's Economic Slowdown: Implications for Beijing's Institutional Power and Global Governance Role. *The Pacific Review 31*(5), 673–691.

Mah, L. (2015). *Reshaping EU Development Policy: Collective Choices and the New Global Order*. CEsA Working Papers 130.

Manners, I. (2009). The EU's Normative Power in Changing World Politics. In A. Gerrits (Ed.), *Normative Power Europe in a Changing World: A Discussion.* (pp. 9–24). Netherlands Institute of International Relations.

Mendel, T., & E. Summers. (2016, December). *Comments on the Public Information Interim Policy of the Asian Infrastructure Investment Bank*. The Centre for Law and Democracy and the Bank Information Center.

Minister of Ecology and Environment of the People's Republic of China (2017a). The Belt and Road Ecological and Environmental Cooperation Plan. Minister of Ecology and Environment of the People's Republic of China.

Ministry of Foreign Affairs of the People's Republic of China (2017b). China's Progress Report on Implementation of the 2030 Agenda for Sustainable Development. Ministry of Foreign Affairs of the People's Republic of China.

ModernDiplomacy (2018, October 19). *ASEM Summit: Europe and Asia: Global Partners for Global Challenges. ModernDiplomacy.*

Nassiry, D., & Nakhooda, S. (2016, March). *The AIIB and Investment in Action on Climate Change*. Overseas Development Institute Working Paper 433.

Nicolas, F., & Meglio, J. F. D. (2015, March 18). Les raisons du ralliement européen à la banque chinoise concurrente de la Banque mondiale. *Atlantico*. Retrieved from https://www.atlantico.fr/decryptage/2045013/les-raisons-du-ralliement-europeen-a-la-banque-chinoise-concurrente-de-la-banque-mondiale-francoise-nicolas-jean-francois-di-meglio.

Novitz, T. (2018). Labour Standards and Trade: Need We Choose Between "Human Rights" and "Sustainable Development"? In H. Gött (Ed.), *Labour Standards in International Economic Law*. (pp. 113–134). Springer.

OECD (2018). China's Belt and Road Initiative in the Global Trade, Investment and Finance Landscape. *OECD Business and Finance Outlook 2018*.

OECD (2019a). *A Fairer, Greener, Safer Tomorrow*. OECD Development Cooperation Report 2019.

OECD (2019b). *Official Development Assistance (ODA)*. OECD.

Office of the Leading Group for Promoting the Belt and Road Initiative (2019, April). The Belt and Road Initiative Progress, Contributions and Prospects. Retrieved from https://eng.yidaiyilu.gov.cn/zchj/qwfb/86739.htm.

Pan, Z. Q. (2012). Introduction: Exploring the Conceptual Gaps in China-EU Relations. In Z. Pan (Ed.), *Conceptual Gaps in China-EU Relations*. Palgrave Macmillan.

Pardo, R. P. (2018). Europe's Financial Security and Chinese Economic Statecraft: The Case of the Belt and Road Initiative. *Asia Europe Journal 16*(2), 237–250.

Peel, M. (2018, September 20). Europe Unveils Its Answer to China's Belt and Road Plan. *Financial Times*. Retrieved from https://www.ft.com/content/bbcda96a-bc1b-11e8-8274-55b72926558f.

Peng, Z. Z., & Tok, S. K. (2016). The AIIB and China's Normative Power in International Financial Governance Structure. *Chinese Political Science Review 1*(4), 736–753.

Pham, S. (2018, July 5). Malaysia Halts a big China-Backed Infrastructure Project. *CNN*. Retrieved from https://money.cnn.com/2018/07/05/news/economy/malaysia-china-rail-project-suspended/index.html.

Pope, J., Annandale, D., & Saunders, A. M. (2004). Conceptualising Sustainability Assessment. *Environmental Impact Assessment Review 24*(6), 595–616.

PwC's Growth Markets Centre (2016, February). China's New Silk Route: The Long and Winding Road. *PwC.*

Rao, D. N., & Baruah, A. G. (2018, September 25). Is China Going Green by Dumping Brown on its BRI Partners? *East Asia Forum*. Retrieved from https://www.eastasiaforum.org/2018/09/25/is-china-going-green-by-dumping-brown-on-its-bri-partners/.

Rogerson, A. (2004). *The International Aid System 2005–2010: Forces For and Against Change*. Overseas Development Institute Working Paper 235.

Sala, S., Ciuffo, B., & Nijkamp, Peter. (2015). A Systemic Framework for Sustainability Assessment. *Ecological Economics 119*, 314–325.

Saldinger, A. (2019, October 25). What's New with the AIIB. *DEVEX*. Retrieved from https://www.devex.com/news/what-s-new-with-the-asian-infrastructure-investment-bank-95885.

Scott, D. A. (2013). Multipolarity, Multilateralism And Beyond …? EU–China Understandings of the International System. *International Relations 27*(1), 30–51.

Šefčovič, M. (2019, April 25). Connecting Europe and Asia: seeking synergies with China's Belt and Road. *Delegation of the European Union to China*. Retrieved from https://eeas.europa.eu/delegations/china/61412/node/61412_hy.

Shah, A. (2016). Building a Sustainable 'Belt and Road'. *Horizons7*(1), 212–222.

Shepard, W. (2017, January 16). The AIIB One Year In: Not as Scary as Washington Thought. *Forbes*. Retrieved from https://www.forbes.com/sites/wadeshepard/2017/01/16/the-aiib-one-year-in-not-as-scary-as-washington-thought/#7518f2f25e83.

Solmecke, U. (2016). Multinational Enterprises and the "one belt, one road" Initiative: Sustainable Development and Innovation in a Postcrisis Global Environment. *The Copenhagen Journal of Asian Studies 34*(2), 9–27.

Song, S. (2018, April 26). Here's How China Is Going Green. *World Economic Forum*. Retrieved from https://www.weforum.org/agenda/2018/04/china-is-going-green-here-s-how/.

Su, X. (forthcoming). Normative Power Europe in the Belt and Road Initiative: Challenge for Constructing the Self or an Opportunity for Changing Others? In J. Wouters, M. Egan, K. Raube, & J. Chaisse (Eds.), *At the Crossroads of World Order: Contestation, Global Governance and Europe*. Palgrave Macmillan.

Summers, E. (2017, June). *AIIB Must Do More to Meet Its Environmental and Social Commitments*. Business and Human Rights Resource Centre's Chinese Responsible Investment Overseas Newsletter Issue 2.

Svetlicinii, A. (2019). Sustainable Development and the New Development (BRICS) Bank: The Contribution of the BRICS Countries. In J. A. Puppim de Oliveira & Y. J. Jing (Eds.), *International Development Assistance and the BRICS, Governing China in the 21st Century*. (pp. 119–147). Palgrave Macmillan.

European Commission (2019, April 8). Terms of References of the Joint Study on Sustainable Railway-Based Transport Corridors Between Europe and China, Annex of the Minutes to the 4th Chair's Meeting, The EU-China Connectivity Platform, Retrieved from https://ec.europa.eu/transport/sites/transport/files/4th_chairs_meeting_minutes_en.pdf

The National Development and Reform Commission of the People's Republic of China and the European Commission (2015, September). *Memorandum of Understanding on Establishing a Connectivity Platform between the EU and China*. The National Development and Reform Commission of the People's Republic of China and the European Commission.

The National Development and Reform Commission, Ministry of Foreign Affairs, and Ministry of Commerce of the People's Republic of China, with State Council authorization (2015, March). *Vision and Actions on Jointly Building Silk Road Economic Belt and 21st-Century Maritime Silk Road*. National Development and Reform Commission.

Ujvari, B. (2016, June). *The European Union and the China-Led Transformation of Global Economic Governance*. EGMONT Paper 85.

Umuhumuza, C. (2019, April 23). On Message: Aid in China, Interview with AIIB Communications Lead. *DEVEX*.

United Nations Department of Economic and Social Affairs. Jointly building belt and road towards SDGs. Retrieved from https://www.brisdgs.org/

United Nations Environment Programme (2019). The Belt and Road Initiative International Green Development Coalition. *UNDP*. Retrieved from https://www.unenvironment.org/regions/asia-and-pacific/regional-initiatives/belt-and-road-initiative-international-green.

Vangeli, A. (2018). The Normative Foundations of the Belt and Road Initiative. In W. Shan, K. Nuotio, & K. Zhang (Eds.), *Normative Readings of the Belt and Road Initiative*. (pp. 59–83). Springer.

Vazquez, K. C., & Chin, G. T. (2019). The AIIB and Sustainable Infrastructure: A Hybrid Layered Approach. *Global Policy 10*(4), 593–603.

Watts, J. (2019, April 25). Belt and Road Summit Puts Spotlight on Chinese Coal Funding. *The Guardian*. Retrieved from https://www.theguardian.com/world/2019/apr/25/belt-and-road-summit-puts-spotlight-on-chinese-coal-funding.

Wissenbach, U., & Wang, Y. (2016). Development Policy: Alternatives, Challenges, and Opportunities. In J. Wang & W. Song (Eds.), *China, the European Union, and the International Politics of Global Governance*. (pp. 251–269). Palgrave Macmillan.

Wong, C. (2019, April 25). China Aims to Address 'Debt Trap' Criticism at Second Belt and Road Forum. *Sounth China Morning Post*.

WWF (2017, May). *The Belt and Road Initiative: WWF Recommendations and Spatial Analysis*. WWF Briefing Paper.

Xu, H. (2019, April 27). Harmonized Standards Can Make Belt and Road a Driver to Attain SDGs. *ChinaDaily*. Retrieved from http://www.chinadaily.com.cn/a/201904/27/WS5cc3b24aa3104842260b8b32.html?from=singlemessage&isappinstalled=0.

Yan, B., & Torney, D. (2016). Confronting the Climate Challenge: Convergence and Divergence Between the EU and China. In J. Wang & W. Song (Eds.), *China, the European Union, and the International Politics of Global Governance* (pp. 213–232). Palgrave Macmillan.

Zhao, K. (2015). 欧盟亚太政策转向新接触主义 - 理解欧盟国家加入亚投行的行为逻辑 (EU's Asia-Pacific Policy: A New Engagement? How to Understand the Behavior Logic in the EU's Member States Entry into the AIIB).欧洲研究 *Chinese Journal of European Studies*, *33*(2), 16–30.

9 COVID-19 and EU-China relations

Mario Esteban and Ugo Armanini

1 Introduction

There is a lively debate in policymaking, business, and academic circles throughout the world about the implications of the COVID-19 pandemic in international affairs. Three main positions can be identified: those who argue that we will forget about this crisis sooner rather than later as it will have no lasting effect once we have a vaccine; those who interpret it as an accelerator of previous trends; and those who discern a momentous breakthrough for a new world order. It might be too early to give a definitive verdict. However, the central role played by China in both the spread and the management of a crisis with such dramatic effects on the safety and welfare of the European population indicates that this issue most likely will have had some impact on EU–China relations. This looks even more plausible when considering the extensive coverage and discussion that European media have provided both at EU and Member State levels, which is quite natural given that public health is a competence of Member States, and considering the active public diplomacy campaign conducted by Chinese diplomatic missions throughout the EU.

More specifically, it will be argued that COVID-19 is intensifying some emerging tendencies in Europe regarding EU–China relations, including increased contestation and polarization on links with China; securitization of a relationship traditionally analysed from a business perspective; and pressure from the China-US strategic rivalry. This growing complexity, controversy, and salience of EU–China relations were already evident at the time of the publication of the European Commission strategic outlook in March 2019, which depicted China simultaneously as partner, competitor, and systemic rival (European Commission 2019; see Bastian, Chapter 6). This perception of a variety of roles played by China in its engagement with the EU is even stronger today. China has been a key partner for EU national governments in their fight against COVID-19, while that experience has also made more apparent some of the limitations and challenges of depending on China for such strategic issues.

This chapter is structured as follows. The next section addresses Chinese health cooperation with EU Member States regarding COVID-19. Section 3 analyses China's public diplomacy campaign on COVID-19 throughout the EU. Section 4 presents the impact of COVID-19 on perceptions of China by EU citizens. Section 5 discusses the pandemic's impact on recent developments on EU–China relations. Section 6 analyses the implications of COVID-19 for the engagement of EU institutions and Member States in the BRI. Section 7 concludes.

2 Necessary cooperation for battling COVID-19

COVID-19 has had dramatic health and socioeconomic impacts on the EU. This pandemic has focused attention on China, first when the virus was spreading there and, later, as a major supplier of medical equipment to EU countries.

The EU and some Member States provided material assistance and political support to China as the country managed the crisis when COVID-19 first appeared (Esteban and Armanini 2020b; European Commission 2020d). Once the centre of the pandemic shifted to Europe, China reciprocated at several levels, through the mobilization of central and local governments, companies, and Chinese society at home and abroad (Busse et al. 2020). Assistance provided by the Chinese business sector has far exceeded that from public authorities. Several Chinese private actors have stood out, like the Jack Ma Foundation and several firms with high visibility and commercial interests in the EU, including Huawei, China Three Gorges, Cosco Shipping Corporation, and Xiaomi.

While it did not go unnoticed that, despite the emphasis on cooperation and assistance, the bulk of Chinese supplies have been shipped on a commercial basis, this significant Chinese engagement was very welcome, particularly as the EU's reaction to the virus was slower and the US took a passive stance. Since China has been an essential provider of medical equipment and supplies during the pandemic, national and local authorities throughout the EU have levered political and business contacts and networks in the country to secure and facilitate the supply of much-needed health materials. These flows of health supplies were complemented by information and knowledge on how to deal with COVID-19 and provided opportunities to underline close bilateral relations and promote bilateral agreements such as the strategic partnership with Portugal or the Memorandum of Understanding (MoU) on the BRI signed by Italy (Bei 2020; Ministry of Foreign Affairs of the People's Republic of China [MOFA] 2020f; see also Chapter 13 in this publication).

Even if a significant volume of equipment did not meet quality standards and was rejected by several EU countries like Belgium (RTBF 2020), Finland (Teivainen 2020) or the Netherlands, where more than half a million masks failed to meet expected results despite Chinese KN95 certification

(NIS Cooperation Group 2020; Van den Brink 2020), China was consistently regarded in the EU as a necessary partner for overcoming the crisis. This has been the case not only regarding logistics but also from a political perspective, as there was widespread consensus among EU institutions and countries about the need to resort to multilateralism in articulating an effective pandemic response. Despite some criticism and difficulties, EU countries have maintained a non-confrontational approach towards China and focused on international cooperation. As High Representative Josep Borrell wrote:

> It must be clear that Europe still has an enduring interest to work together with China, even if difficult, on a number of global issues on which it plays a crucial role. China has necessarily to be part of global solutions to planet-size problems like tackling the Covid-19 pandemic or mitigating climate change (Borrell 2020a).

3 China's controversial public diplomacy

Chinese authorities are well aware that the COVID-19 crisis may have a significant impact on the country's position within the international community. The scale of the threat and its apparent origin in Wuhan led multiple actors inside and outside China to question the role of Chinese authorities in the management of the crisis, stressing governance shortcomings like ineffective regulation of wild animal consumption and lack of transparency. In this context, Chinese public diplomacy has been very proactive in sharing a narrative that defends and improves China's international image.

Almost all EU countries have witnessed a significant increase in Chinese public diplomacy activities. Chinese embassies and diplomatic officials have been exceptionally proactive in traditional and social media (Seaman 2020; Esteban and Armanini 2020a). Chinese public diplomacy has been quite consistent throughout Europe in highlighting international solidarity and cooperation, promoting China's measures and experience to fight the epidemic, and seeking to counter negative narratives. Chinese diplomats publicised and praised assistance provided by Chinese public and private stakeholders, including Chinese communities in Europe. They also stressed the speed and effectiveness of sanitary and economic measures adopted in China to face the crisis, quoting support received from various international institutions like the World Health Organization (WHO) and International Monetary Fund.

However, there are significant differences in the communication strategies of Chinese missions in Europe ranging from low key (Latvia and Romania) to provocative or aggressive (Sweden, Germany, and France) to charm offensives (see Italy, Poland, Portugal, and Spain) (Seaman 2020, 8). Some of these communication practices have been much more controversial than

Chinese health cooperation itself; in particular, when Chinese officials resorted to disinformation techniques for countering critical narratives; for example, through criticising European authorities for their poor management of the pandemic to the point of blaming them for the spread of COVID-19, or pointing to Western democracies in order to sow doubt about the pandemic's origins. This aggressive communication strategy triggered some pushback from EU institutions and some influential members like France and Germany (Verma 2020).

The European External Action Service has monitored narratives and disinformation promoted by non-EU media and officials and has published some reports on this issue, underlining that part of China's official narrative on COVID-19 has mimicked Russia's confrontational tone and disinformation practices and that both countries are helping each other to spread misleading narratives (European External Action Service [EEAS] 2020a, 2020b, 2020c; Verma 2020). In addition, Borrell questioned the lack of rigour of some of the narratives spread by Chinese actors on COVID-19 and complained that in the battle of narratives 'we have also seen attempts to discredit the EU as such and some instances where Europeans have been stigmatised as if all were carriers of the virus'. Borrell also noted that 'there is a geo-political component including a struggle for influence through spinning and the "politics of generosity"' (Borrell 2020b).

Official declarations by the French government on China and COVID-19 had a positive tone until mid-April, when they soured in response to a series of articles posted on the webpage of the Chinese embassy in Paris. These articles spread the theory that COVID-19 originated in the US, scorned French parliamentarians for supporting racist remarks against the WHO Director, and claimed that European retirement home workers were deserting collectively, 'leaving their residents to die of hunger and disease' (Julienne 2020). On April 14, Foreign Minister Jean-Yves Le Drian summoned the Chinese ambassador to complain. Two days later, President Macron made a veiled criticism of the pandemic management of Chinese authorities (Mallet and Khalaf 2020).

Conversely, national authorities of the mainly southern and eastern EU countries where Chinese diplomacy followed a friendlier narrative, such as Czechia, Italy, Poland, Portugal, and Spain, tended to reciprocate with more praise for Chinese domestic handling of the pandemic and gratitude for Chinese cooperation with their countries (CGTN 2020; MOFA 2020b, 2020c, 2020d, 2020e).

This assessment of Chinese public diplomacy in different EU countries does not imply a static communication strategy by Chinese officials. Taking Spain as an example, Chinese public diplomacy had a prominent defensive orientation until March when referring to COVID-19. This was evidenced by the Chinese embassy's website and social media and by interviews of Chinese diplomats during this period. The Embassy's communications during the first two months of 2020 sought to avoid stigmatization of the

Chinese community in Spain, any restrictions on transport and communications with China, and criticism of Chinese authorities for their role in the origin and spread of COVID-19. On the last point, the official Chinese narrative tried to avoid association between wild animal consumption without adequate sanitary controls and the origin of COVID-19, as well as downplaying any lack of transparency regarding the disease's spread.

Once the pandemic's epicentre moved to Europe, Chinese diplomacy turned more assertive. From March, Chinese official discourse started to emphasize China's contribution to stop the spread, both through domestic measures and through assistance it could provide to other countries in terms of medical material and good practices. China presented itself as a top scientific and medical power capable of developing and producing state-of-the-art vaccines, medicines, health protocols, and medical equipment (Embassy of China in Spain 2020b, 2020c, 2020d). Additionally, some limited use of disinformation strategies by Chinese diplomats in Spain occurred in the second half of March, e.g. the retweet by the Chinese embassy's Twitter account of a message from Hua Chunying, spokeswoman of the Chinese Foreign Ministry, which generated confusion by linking the origin of COVID-19 to the United States (Embassy of China in Spain 2020a).

There is no definitive answer yet on the reasons for the above-mentioned inter-state differences in Chinese public diplomacy across the EU: whether they reflect a plurality of ways of thinking within the Chinese diplomatic apparatus or a unified strategy that adapts to diverse audiences or bilateral relations. This section has illustrated how those variations in communication strategy triggered different reactions by various EU and national authorities. The next section will show how varying Chinese public diplomacy also had a diverse impact on public opinion in different EU countries.

4 Evolving perceptions of EU citizens on China

COVID-19 has had a clear and significant impact on EU public perceptions of China. Early surveys like the Elcano Royal Institute Barometer (conducted 2-19 March 2020) showed no relevant change in China's image in Spain while others even provided slight evidence that China might have benefited from COVID-19 to improve its image in other EU countries. A survey conducted in Italy, 1–3 April 2020, showed a significant increase of respondents—from 10 to 52%—acknowledging China as a 'friend' of Italy. 36% of respondents identified China as the 'preferred ally outside the EU', ahead of the US (30%) (De Palo 2020). However, the long-term picture appears different, as revealed by a European Council on Foreign Relations (ECFR) poll (23 April–5 May 2020). This survey (Dennison and Zerka 2020) captures the widespread deterioration of China's image across nine EU countries comprising more than 73% of the EU's population. Almost half of respondents acknowledged that their view of China worsened as a result of COVID-19, with only 12% declaring it had improved.

It is very likely that this deterioration is linked with the emergence of COVID-19 in Wuhan, its connection with poorly regulated wildlife consumption, and China's initial epidemic management, involving censorship which facilitated COVID-19's spread. A qualitative study by the Swedish Institute of International Affairs shows that Swedish media portrayed a negative image of China, with a focus on the initial cover-up and later Chinese disinformation (Jerdén 2020). An ongoing analysis of the two main Spanish newspapers —*El Mundo* and *El País*—conducted by Elcano Royal Institute for the European Think-tank Network, reveals that from April to May 2020, 120 (of 319) articles on China referred to the pandemic's origin and that more than one third of these occurrences were critical of Chinese authorities and linked COVID-19 with Chinese censorship or lack of adequate sanitary regulation.

Chinese cooperation contributed to some extent towards mitigating these negative perceptions. Inter-state variations in Figure 9.1 suggest that countries—Denmark, Germany, France, Sweden— which received the lowest amount of donations from China, both total and *per capita*, registered a higher share of negative perceptions than those —Bulgaria, Italy, Portugal, Spain—which received more assistance from China (Table 9.1)

The communication strategy adopted by China in each country is also likely to have influenced its image. The groups of countries mentioned above mostly intersect with two categories of China's public diplomacy: 'aggressive' and 'charm offensive'. The former mainly applies to France and Sweden, where China's public diplomacy has been particularly assertive

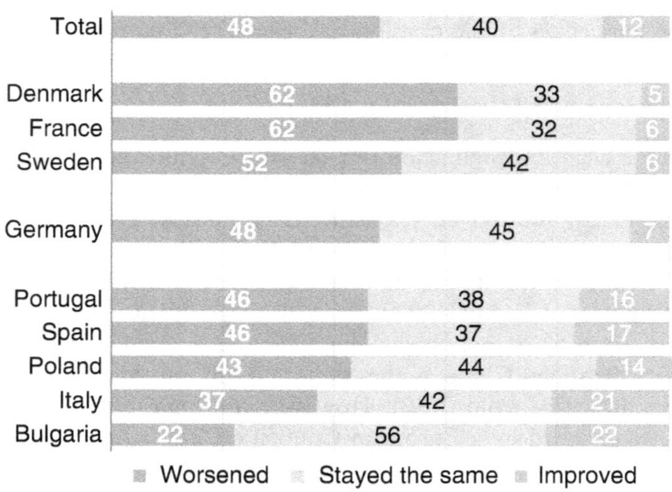

Figure 9.1 Evolution of China's image across EU member states, (%), May 2020. Source: ECFR.

Table 9.1 Chinese donations to EU member states[i], March–April 2020

Country	*Amount (millions of units)*	*Amount (units per 100,000 inhabitants)*
Bulgaria	182	2600
Denmark	571	9.8
France	40	60
Germany	391	471
Italy	3726	6173
Poland	68	177
Portugal	1414	13,755
Spain	2427	5170
Sweden	0	0

Source: ECFR, European Solidarity Tracker.

(Baker and Emmott 2020; Julienne 2020). This resulted in negative media coverage and strong political reactions from French and Swedish officials, which may have further damaged China's image. Germany is a particular case within this category. Despite (unsuccessful) Chinese propaganda efforts that have attracted harsh criticism in the media and from the political opposition, there have been no assertive statements from Chinese diplomats and no public confrontation between Chinese and German officials (Pongratz 2020; Reuters 2020). Attempts to frame public opinion and German official discourse surely constitute elements of assertive public diplomacy, but they also appear more 'low-profile' and less publicized. This may be another explanation why the country has a slightly better perception of China. On the other hand, Poland is a noticeable example of the positive impact of China's public diplomacy. Poland has received relatively low volumes of assistance from China, but variation of China's image in Poland is closer to the surveyed Southern and Central and Eastern Europe countries which were also on the receiving end of China's charm offensive.

A comparison between the degradation of China's image and the assistance citizens believe they have received from China illustrates the divide between these two groups of countries. Arguably, the *perceived* assistance from China encompasses both volume of donations and their visibility, which may have been increased by China's proactive charm diplomacy, or decreased by negative reactions to aggressive communications (Figure 9.2).

In contrast to all the other cases, Bulgaria registers the lowest share of respondents whose view of China has worsened, equalled by the share of respondents whose view of China has improved. Bulgaria received significant amounts of donations *per capita* and has been a target of China's charm offensive. Bulgaria's case also shows that worsening perceptions build on pre-existing negative impressions. When comparing with the results of the Spring 2019 Global Attitudes Survey conducted by the Pew Research Institute (2020), it appears that the sharpest degradation of China's image

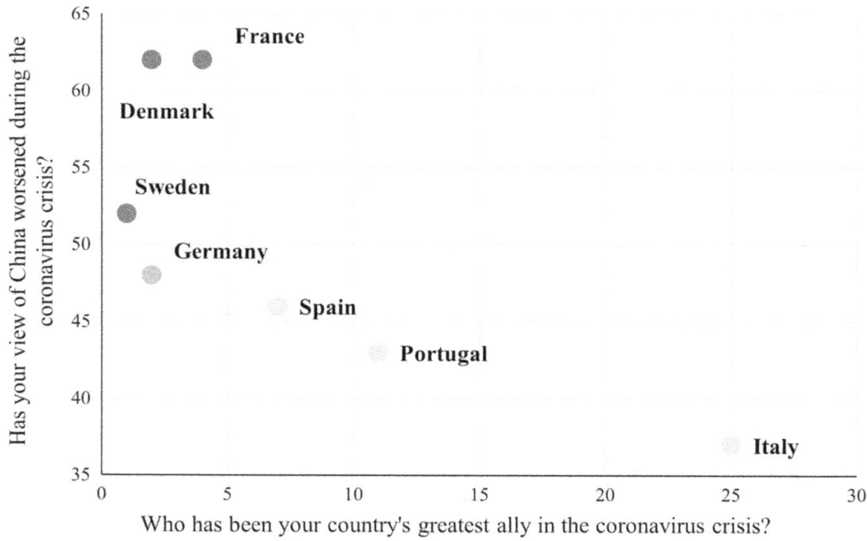

Figure 9.2 Impact of China's actions on China's image across EU member states, (% of respondents to the survey questions), May 2020. Source: ECFR.

happened in countries which already had the highest negative perceptions of China before the pandemic, i.e. Sweden (62%) and France (62%). In contrast, Bulgaria, with the lowest share of negative perceptions in 2019 (20%), registered the lowest drop. Overall, it is apparent that COVID-19 has resulted in widespread deterioration of China's image inside the EU.

5 Recent developments on EU–China relations: During or because of COVID-19?

2020 was expected to be a momentous year in EU–China relations, full of milestones such as the adoption of a new comprehensive agenda for bilateral cooperation, the decision on a comprehensive agreement on investment, and the celebration of an EU–China summit with the participation, for the first time, of heads of state or government of all 27 Member States. In addition, there were other key issues at the national level such as the role of Chinese companies in the development of 5G networks.

COVID-19 also revealed the convenience of having smooth relations with China, as China is the main external provider of health supplies needed for fighting the pandemic, especially personal protective equipment (see Figure 9.3). Hence, even EU countries whose bilateral relationships with Beijing were not optimal, such as Czechia and Sweden, resorted to China to purchase equipment (Seaman 2020, 9). In addition, the global and

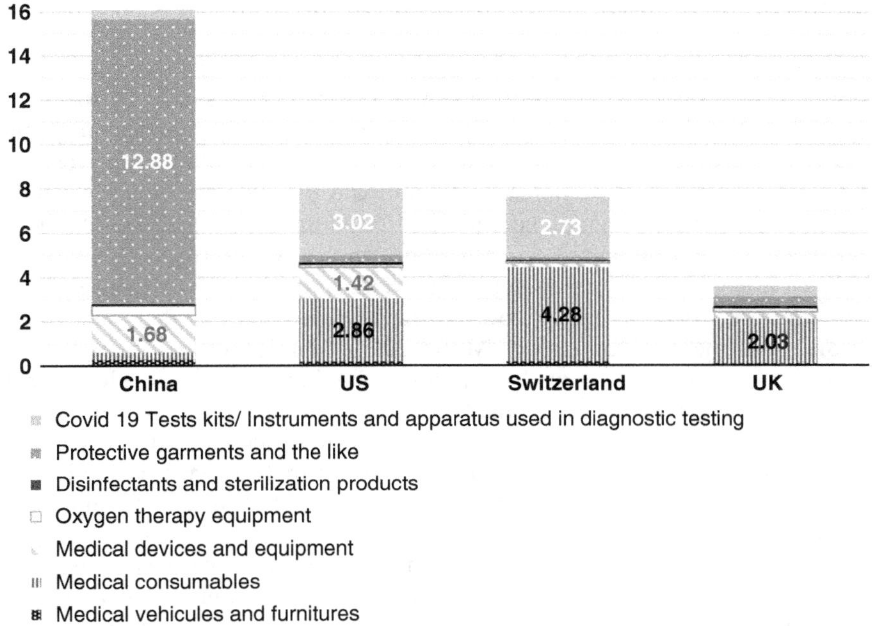

Figure 9.3 EU imports of COVID-19 medical supplies from main extra-EU partners, EUR billion, March–May 2020[ii]. Source: Eurostat (2020).

transnational nature of the pandemic evidenced the advantages in the eyes of European authorities of articulating a multilateral response. However, there was also a recognition that the pandemic aggravated worrisome developments in Chinese foreign policy. As China becomes more powerful and relevant for tackling global challenges, it has become also 'more assertive' and 'friendless', 'as it uses economic coercion' and 'did not hesitate to leave aside international commitments' (Borrell 2020a). This perception has also accentuated a trend in the China policy of the EU and many Member States: a more demanding position for engagement. Deepening relations with China is not regarded as a goal in itself anymore by many EU stakeholders, with balancing the relationship through reciprocity and a level playing field taking precedence. This has led to a stalemate in bilateral relations between the EU and China, as Chinese leaders do not want to accommodate requests that would weaken their control over the economy. This gridlock was reflected in the lack of joint statements after the 10th EU–China strategic dialogue on 9 June 2020 and the EU–China summit of 22 June, and in the postponement of the much-anticipated summit between Xi and the leaders of all Member States (Walker 2020).

This firmer negotiating position of EU actors with China, coupled with some lessons extracted from their engagement with Beijing during the pandemic, may influence issues such as diversification of supply chains, stricter conditions for Chinese FDI, ideological competition, and restrictions on Chinese providers of 5G equipment (Le Corre 2020; Small 2020). There have been signs, if not explicit declarations, in many EU countries that have acknowledged national vulnerabilities to (over)concentrated supply chains and outlined better diversification to mitigate (over)dependence on single suppliers (AFP 2020; Lourenço and Sílvo 2020; Szczudlik 2020). COVID-19 has been a harsh reminder that public health is a top strategic sector to be closely monitored. Across the EU, national and regional industries have already retrofitted or highly boosted production to respond to the initial shortage of medical equipment (Moret 2020). This is not to say that there will be a European push for 'decoupling' with China, but possible long-term supply chain restructuring in *some* strategically important sectors should not be ignored. In that sense, Borrell (2020d) has envisioned a post-coronavirus world with reformed supply chains through diversification, a reduction of EU dependence on essential products, and partial relocation of some strategic market segments.

Unlike the eurozone crisis, when Chinese investment was welcomed as a much-needed stimulus by some cash-strapped EU economies, now there is much more concern inside the EU about implications of Chinese investments for the welfare and security of the EU population. The European Commission introduced in March 2019 legislation to develop an FDI screening mechanism, which was strengthened a year later in response to potential vulnerability to external takeover of critical European assets and technology during the pandemic (European Commission 2020b). Some countries like Germany (also driven by Donald Trump's attempt to acquire CureVac for the sole benefit of the US market), Sweden, and Spain have recently strengthened—or planned to strengthen—their investment screening mechanisms to protect critical infrastructure and domestic firms from foreign investors (Caballero 2020; Fischer 2020).

Concerns about dependency on Chinese actors in strategic sectors are also present regarding the role of Chinese providers in developing 5G networks in the EU. This is reflected in the tougher tone against high-risk suppliers of the *Report on Member State's progress in implementing the EU toolbox on 5G Cybersecurity* published in July 2020 (NIS Cooperation Group 2020)—compared to the toolbox released by the EU Commission (2020a, 2020e) in late January 2020—and in decisions in some EU countries that will limit or exclude Chinese companies from the development of their 5G networks (Cerulus 2020; Lee 2020). In France, most authorisations to use Huawei's equipment have been granted for three-year periods—less than the five years granted to Nokia and Erikson's equipment—and are not expected to be renewed afterward, leading to a *de facto* ban (Gehrke 2020).

Romania's future legislation of 5G providers is also likely to prevent Huawei's participation in national networks (Gascón Barbera 2020).

This more demanding attitude from EU stakeholders regarding engagement with China will more likely hinder the development of the BRI in the EU, unless China is willing to abide by norms and standards followed by the EU.

6 Implications for European BRI engagement

Chinese authorities have tried to take advantage of COVID-19 to promote the BRI in the EU, e.g. through the revitalisation of the so-called Health Silk Road, which was established by China and the WHO in January 2017 with the objective to improve the health of people in BRI countries (Baijie 2017). Contrary to the expectations of some European leaders and many analysts (Beg 2020; Shepard 2020; Wu and Wong 2020), these efforts do not seem to have succeeded.

Take the example of Italy, the first EU country severely struck by COVID-19 and the biggest EU economy that has signed a BRI MoU. Both Xi Jinping and Foreign Minister Wang Yi linked the Health Silk Road, in conversations with Italian counterparts, with practical bilateral and multilateral COVID-19 cooperation (MOFA 2020g; Xinhua 2020a). Moreover, Foreign Minister Luigi Di Maio claimed that the Silk Road 'has allowed us to save lives in Italy' (Bei 2020). Nevertheless, when China organized in June 2020 a ministerial-level video conference with the WHO Director-General and the Administrator of the United Nations Development Programme under the theme of *Belt and Road International Cooperation: Combating COVID-19 with Solidarity*, only Greece and Hungary participated from the EU (MOFA 2020a).

Having subscribed to a BRI MoU does not imply endorsement of the Health Silk Road even at a time when health cooperation is a central issue for all involved countries. That kind of political support is the fruit of closer political alignment with Beijing. In addition to having BRI MoUs, both Greece and Hungary are members of the 17+1 initiative, have close political relations with Beijing to the point of having broken EU unanimity on China-related issues (Cottey 2019; Emmott and Koutantou 2017), and participate in key projects for the Chinese connectivity blueprint for Europe (Esteban and Li 2019). The signing of a financing agreement with the Hungarian government for building the Hungarian section of the Belgrade-Budapest railway is so far probably the most significant result of the BRI in Europe during the pandemic (Than and Komuves 2020).

Nevertheless, this project is far from being the showcase for boosting the BRI in Europe that the Chinese authorities expected when they started to discuss it with interested EU Member States in November 2013. There are many reasons that will not allow this project to have a promotional effect for the BRI in Europe, including delays in implementation, normative and governance deficiencies, growing US diplomatic pressure on European allies, and deterioration of EU–China relations (Brînză 2020, Keller-Alánt 2019). Other BRI-related projects also suffered significant setbacks in the EU after the COVID-19 outbreak, e.g. cancellation by state-owned company Nuclearelectrica of its contract with China General Nuclear Power Corporation to expand the Cernavoda nuclear power plant in Romania; and the expected rejection of a China-funded project for building an underwater tunnel linking Helsinki and Tallinn in favour of a project backed by Estonian and Finnish public authorities (Abdel-Aziz et al. 2020; Posaner 2020).

Chinese leaders seemed to be aware not only of these obstacles for promoting the BRI in Europe but also of how these difficulties were aggravated by COVID-19. Publications of the China Institute of International Studies (affiliated with the Chinese Ministry of Foreign Affairs) have underlined two negative effects of COVID-19 on the development of the BRI in Europe (Hongjian 2020; Hongjian et al. 2020). One is increased visibility of some of the risks associated with globalisation with the ensuing challenge to the integrated supply chains between China and the EU. The other is the *parochialisation* of political agendas of political leaders both in China and the EU. In the severe socioeconomic context of the pandemic, they will feel domestic pressure to devote national resources to national recovery. In the case of China, Chinese leaders would be expected to prioritize domestic stability over controversial foreign policy initiatives and to reduce financing resources available for BRI projects, as many Chinese citizens are quite critical of financial transfers that they see as a waste of national capital overseas. The effect of such funding cuts could be particularly severe for projects hosted in Europe, as this region is not a priority for the BRI (Esteban and Li 2020; Kavalski 2020).

It therefore should not be surprising that when it comes to the post-pandemic development of the BRI in the EU, Chinese authorities are following a conservative strategy, oriented to avoid deterioration of the BRI's standing in this region, instead of a growth strategy. An indicative example of this approach concerns conversations between Chinese authorities and their Spanish counterparts during the pandemic.

Spain is the only country of the southern EU member and the biggest EU economy after Germany and France that has not signed a BRI MoU. As Spain was severely hit by COVID-19 and Spanish authorities recognized the instrumental role played by Chinese cooperation in overcoming this emergency, Madrid would have been a very likely target for a BRI expansion strategy (Esteban and Armanini 2020b). However, unlike in their conversations with Italian and Portuguese authorities (MOFA 2020g; Xi-Conte phone talk significant for coronavirus fight: Italian analysts 2020), neither Xi Jinping nor Wang Yi mentioned the BRI in calls with Spanish counterparts in March 2020 (MOFA 2020c; MOFA 2020h; Xinhua 2020c).

This conservative strategy was also evident in China's dealings with EU institutions. The coverage of Wang Yi's participation in the 10th EU–China Strategic Dialogue in June 2020 by Chinese media did not include any of the typical references to the BRI and nor did High Representative Borrell, in the press conference, mention the BRI. He only made one reference to connectivity as a cooperation area where the EU 'seeks to have a balanced and reciprocal approach' (Borrell 2020c; Xinhua 2020b; Mo 2020).

7. Conclusion

In conclusion, the pandemic has not strengthened EU–China relations, but reduced the appetite in the EU for increasing interdependency with China and hence undermined the BRI's appeal in Europe. More scrutiny can be expected by the EU and most Member States when dealing with BRI projects, with less interest in participating in projects that do not share the principles on Europe-Asia connectivity presented by the European Commission (European Commission 2020c), since less EU stakeholders regard increasing relations with China as an objective in itself anymore.

Notes

i Amounts based on the data compiled by the ECFR European Solidarity Tracker on Chinese donations of personal protective equipment and medical material (Busse et al. 2020).

ii The period covers the outbreak of the pandemic in the EU until the latest available data as of 13 September 2020.

Bibliography

Abdel-Aziz, A., Van Soelen, L., & Hanebach, M. (2020). 'Romania's Cernavodă nuclear power plant looking for new investors as partnership with China General Nuclear Power Corporation terminated'. *Gowling WLG.* https://gowlingwlg.com/en/insights-resources/articles/2020/romania-cernavoda-nuclear-looking-for-new-investor/.

AFP. (2020). 'Coronavirus: pour Bruno Le Maire, l'épidémie change la donne de la mondialisation'. *La Tribune*, 25 February.

Baijie, A. (2017). 'WHO, China sign pact establishing "health Silk Road"'. *China Daily*, 19 January.

Baker, L., & Emmott, R. (2020). 'As China pushes back on virus, Europe wakes to "Wolf Warrior" diplomacy'. *Reuters*, 14 May.

Beg, Z. (2020). '"The Health Silk Road": Implications for the EU under Covid-19'. *European Institute for Asian Studies.*

Bei, F. (2020). 'Il Pd attacca Di Maio: Troppo "filo-cinese"'. *La Stampa*, 24 March.

Borrell, J. (2020a). 'China, the United States and us'. *European External Action Service.*

Borrell, J. (2020b). EU HRVP Josep Borrell: The Coronavirus pandemic and the new world it is creating [Press statement]. Delegation of the European Union to China.

Borrell, J. (2020c). EU–China strategic dialogue: Remarks by High Representative/ Vice-President Josep Borrell at the press conference [Press conference].

Borrell, J. (2020d). 'The post-coronavirus world is already here'. *European Council on Foreign Relations.*

Brînză, A. (2020). 'China and the Budapest-Belgrade railway saga'. *The Diplomat*, 28 April.

Busse, C., Esther Franke, U., Loss, R., Puglierin, J., Riedel, M., & Zerka, P. (2020). *European Solidarity Tracker*. London: European Council on Foreign Relations. https://www.ecfr.eu/solidaritytracker.

Caballero, D. (2020). 'La doble moral del Gobierno con China: Sí al comercio y veto a las inversiones'. *ABC*, 11 April.

Cerulus, L. (2020). 'UK ban on Huawei prompts calls for tougher EU approach'. *Politico*, 15 July.

CGTN. (2020). 'Czech President Milos Zeman thanks China for support amid Covid-19'. *Youtube*. https://www.youtube.com/watch?v=IcqbL6JS1OE.

Cottey, A. (2019). 'Europe and China's sea disputes: Between normative politics, power balancing and acquiescence'. *European Security* 28(4), pp. 473–492. DOI: 10.1080/09662839.2019.1636784.

De Palo, F. (2020). 'W la Cina! Il sondaggio Swg che non ti aspetti. Parla pier Ferdinando Casini'. *Formiche*, 7 April.

Dennison, S., & Zerka, P. (ed.) 2020. *Together in Trauma: Europeans and the World After Covid-19*. London: European Council on Foreign Relations.

Elcano Royal Institute. (2020). Barómetro del Real Instituto Elcano: Resultados marzo de 2020, 41ª oleada. Madrid: Elcano Royal Institute.

Embassy of China in Spain. (2020a). 20 March. https://twitter.com/ChinaEmbEsp/status/1241052218935128068.

Embassy of China in Spain. (2020b). 31 March. https://twitter.com/ChinaEmbEsp/status/1244949854272524288.

Embassy of China in Spain. (2020c). 2 April. https://twitter.com/ChinaEmbEsp/status/1245655528593707008.

Embassy of China in Spain. (2020d). 5 April. https://twitter.com/ChinaEmbEsp/status/1246726939982868481.

Emmott, R., & Koutantou, A. (2017). 'Greece blocks EU statement on China human rights at U.N.'. *Reuters*, 18 June.

Esteban, M., & Armanini, U. (2020a). *China-Spain Relations Amid Covid-19 in a Comparative Perspective: An Enduring Partnership Facing Potential Uncertainties* [Online]. Working Paper 2020 n°18. Budapest: China-CEE Institute.

Esteban, M., & Armanini, U. (2020b). *Spain-China Relations and Covid-19: The Bright and Dark Sides of a Necessary Partnership for Spain* [Online]. ARI n°62/ 2020. Madrid: Elcano Royal Institute.

Esteban, M., & Li, Y. (2019). 'Motivations, Actors, and Implications for the New Silk Road trains'. In Li, Y., & Taube, M. (eds.). *How China's Silk Road Initiative Is Changing the Global Economic Landscape*. New York, Abingdon: Routledge.

Esteban, M., & Li, Y. (2020). *Demystifying the Belt and Road Initiative: Scope, Actors and Repercussion for Europe* [Online]. Working Papers on East Asian

Studies, n°117/2017. Duisburg: University of Duisburg-Essen, Institute of East Asian Studies.

European Commission. (2019). *EU–China-A Strategic Outlook*. Strasbourg: European Commission.

European Commission. (2020a). 5G security: Member states report on progress on implementing the EU toolbox and strengthening safety measures [Press Release].

European Commission. (2020b). Coronavirus: Commission issues guidelines to protect critical European assets and technology in current crisis [Press Release].

European Commission. (2020c). *Connecting Europe and Asia -Building Blocks for an EU Strategy*. Brussels: European Commission.

European Commission. (2020d). *Crisis Management and Solidarity*. Brussels: European Commission. https://ec.europa.eu/info/live-work-travel-eu/health/coronavirus-response/crisis-management-and-solidarity_en#assistance-outside-the-eu.

European Commission. (2020e). Cybersecurity of 5G networks - EU Toolbox of risk mitigating measures [Press Release].

European External Action Service (EEAS). (2020a). 'EEAS Special Report Update: Short Assessment of Narratives and Disinformation Around the Covid-19 Pandemic'. Update 20–27 March 2020.

European External Action Service (EEAS). (2020b). 'EEAS Special Report Update: Short Assessment of Narratives and Disinformation Around the Covid-19/ Coronavirus Pandemic'. Updated 2–22 April.

European External Action Service (EEAS). (2020c). 'EEAS Special Report Update: Short Assessment of Narratives and Disinformation Around the Covid-19 Pandemic'. Update 23 April–18 May.

Eurostat. (2020). EU trade since 2015 of COVID-19 medical supplies [Online]. *Eurostat*. https://ec.europa.eu/eurostat/en/web/products-eurostat-news/-/ddn-20200618-2 Link to dataset: https://appsso.eurostat.ec.europa.eu/nui/show.do?query=BOOKMARK_DS-1180622_QID_-B1BCB1E_UID_-3F171EB0&layout=PERIOD,L,X,0;REPORTER,L,Y,0;PARTNER,C,Z,0;PRODUCT,L,Z,1;FLOW,L,Z,2;INDICATORS,C,Z,3;&zSelection=DS-1180622PARTNER,EU27_2020_EXTRA;DS-1180622FLOW,1;DS-1180622PRODUCT,A;DS-1180622INDICATORS,VALUE_IN_EUROS;&rankName1=PARTNER_1_2_-1_2&rankName2=INDICATORS_1_2_-1_2&rankName3=FLOW_1_2_-1_2&rankName4=PRODUCT_1_2_-1_2&rankName5=PERIOD_1_0_0_0&rankName6=REPORTER_1_2_0_1&sortC=ASC_-1_FIRST&rStp=&cStp=&rDCh=&cDCh=&rDM=true&cDM=true&footnes=false&empty=false&wai=false&time_mode=NONE&time_most_recent=false&lang=EN&cfo=%23%23%23,%23%23%23.%23%23%23

Fischer, S.-C. (2020). 'EU foreign direct investment screening: Protecting strategic assets and technology during the corona crisis'. *Center for Security Studies*.

Fratelli d'Italia. (2020). 'Coronavirus, Fidanza: M5s vuole svendere l'Italia alla Cina'. Fratelli d'Italia. 23 April. https://www.fratelli-italia.it/2020/04/23/coronavirus-fidanza-m5s-vuole-svendere-litalia-alla-cina/.

Gascón Barberá, M. (2020). 'Romanian conditions for 5G race would rule out Huawei'. *Balkan Insight*, 5 August.

Gehrke, L. (2020). 'France introduces de facto ban on Huawei 5G equipment by 2028'. *Politico*, 23 July.

Granlund, J. (2020). 'Riksdagen överens om M-förslag: Främmande uppköp ska stoppas'. *Aftonbladet*, 20 April.

Hongjian, C. (2020). 'China-EU at crossroads'. *China-US Focus.*

Hongjian, C., Yan, S., Bei, Z., Zili, Y., Hong, H., & Zhengjie, F. (2020). *China-Europe Solidarity in Fighting Covid-19 with a Shared Commitment to Safeguard Human Health* [Online]. 'China and the World' Report Series, n°8. Beijing:China Institute of International Studies.

Jerdén, B. (2020). 'Sweden: Not Quite Friends in Need with China Amid the Covid-19 Crisis'. In Seaman, J. (ed.). *Covid-19 and Europe-China Relations: A Country-Level Analysis.* Paris: French Institute of International Relations, pp. 68–70.

Julienne, M. (2020). 'France: Between Health Care Cooperation and Political Tensions with China amid Covid-19'. In Seaman, J. (ed.). *Covid-19 and Europe-China Relations: A Country-Level Analysis.* Paris: French Institute of International Relations, pp. 21–24.

Kavalski, E. (2020). 'How China lost central and eastern Europe'. *The Conversation*, 27 July.

Keller-Alánt, A. (2019). 'Whose line is it anyway?' *Echowall*, 8 August.

Le Corre, P. (2020). 'The EU's new defensive approach to a rising China'. *Carnegie Endowment for International Peace.*

Lee, J. (2020). 'The global war for 5G heats up'. *The Diplomat*, 31 July.

Lequesne, C., & Wang, E. (2020). 'Covid-19: Lessons from China's public diplomacy in the EU'. *The Conversation*, 24 June.

Lourenço, E., & Vieira, S. (2020). 'António Costa. "Portugal terá de voltar a produzir o que se habituou a importar da China"'. *Renascença*, 3 April.

Mallet, V., & Khalaf, R. (2020). 'FT interview: Emmanuel Macron says it is time to think the unthinkable'. *Financial Times*, 16 April.

Ministry of Foreign Affairs of the People's Republic of China (MOFA). (2020a). 'Joint statement of the high-level video conference on Belt and Road International Cooperation: Combating Covid-19 with solidarity'. *MOFA.*

Ministry of Foreign Affairs of the People's Republic of China (MOFA). (2020b). 'President Xi Jinping speaks by phone with Polish President Andrzej Duda'. *MOFA.*

Ministry of Foreign Affairs of the People's Republic of China (MOFA). (2020c). 'President Xi Jinping speaks with Portuguese President Marcelo Rebelo de Sousa on the phone'. *MOFA.*

Ministry of Foreign Affairs of the People's Republic of China (MOFA). (2020d). 'President Xi speaks with Spanish PM on the phone'. *MOFA.*

Ministry of Foreign Affairs of the People's Republic of China (MOFA). (2020e). 'President Xi Jinping talked with Italian Prime Minister Giuseppe Conte over the phone'. *MOFA.*

Ministry of Foreign Affairs of the People's Republic of China (MOFA). (2020f). 'State Councilor and Foreign Minister Wang Yi spoke with Portuguese and Luxembourg Foreign Ministers over the phone'. *MOFA.*

Ministry of Foreign Affairs of the People's Republic of China (MOFA). (2020g). 'Wang Yi had a phone call with Italian Foreign Minister to express sympathy' *MOFA.*

Ministry of Foreign Affairs of the People's Republic of China (MOFA). (2020h). 'Xi Jinping mantiene una conversación telefónica con Primer Ministro Español Pedro Sánchez Pérez-Castejón'. *MOFA.*

Mo, J. (2020). 'China, EU are long-term strategic partners: Wang Yi'. *China Daily*, 10 June.

Moret, X. (2020). 'El Covid-19 ha aflorado capacidades desconocidas de la industria y ahora el reto es saber explotarlas'. *Valencia Plaza*, 14 April. https://valenciaplaza.com/el-covid-19-ha-aflorado-capacidades-desconocidas-de-la-industria-y-ahora-el-reto-es-saber-explotarlas.

NIS Cooperation Group. (2020). 'Netherlands recalls hundreds of thousands of defective Chinese face masks'. *Euronews*, 29 March. https://ec.europa.eu/newsroom/dae/document.cfm?doc_id=68510.

'Nouveau coup dur pour la Belgique: Les 3 millions de masques FFP2 livrés la semaine dernière sont inutilisables' (2020). *RTBF*, 10 April.

Oertel, J. (2020). 'China, Europe, and covid-19 headwinds'. European Council on Foreign Relations.

Pew Research Institute. (2020). 'Global indicators database'. Pew Research Institute. https://www.pewresearch.org/global/database/indicator/24/.

Pongratz, B. (2020). 'Sino-German relations in the Corona crisis: It's time to make decisions'. Mercator Institute for China Studies [MERICS].

Posaner, J. (2020). 'Estonia to reject China-backed Baltic tunnel plan over security fears'. *Politico*, 31 July.

Reuters. (2020). 'Germany says China sought to encourage positive COVID-19 comments'. *Reuters*. 26 April.

Seaman, J. (ed.) (2020). *Covid-19 and Europe-China Relations: A Country-Level Analysis*. Paris: French Institute of International Relations.

Shepard, W. (2020). 'China's "Health Silk Road" gets a boost from Covid-19'. *Forbes*, 27 March.

Simons & Simons. (2020). 'Germany intends to tighten the rules for foreign direct investments.' Simons & Simons. https://www.simmons-simmons.com/en/publications/ck8zy54il0t470a65h4tewry5/germany-intends-to-tighten-the-rules-for-foreign-direct-investments.

Small, A. (2020). 'The meaning of systemic rivalry: Europe and China beyond the pandemic'. European Council on Foreign Relations.

Szczudlik, J. (2020). 'Poland: Mutual "Charm Offensive" with China Amid Covid-19'. In Seaman, J. (ed.). *Covid-19 and Europe-China Relations: A Country-Level Analysis*, pp. 50–53. Paris: French Institute of International Relations.

Teivainen, A. (2020). 'Masks ordered from China prove unfit for hospital use - Finland disappointed.' *Helsinki Times*, 9 April.

Than, K., & Komuves, A. (2020). 'Hungary, China sign loan deal for Budapest-Belgrade Chinese rail project'. *Reuters*, 24 April.

Van den Brink, R. (2020). 'Honderdduizenden Chinese mondmaskers teruggeroepen uit Nederlandse ziekenhuizen'. *NOS*, 28 March.

Verma, R. (2020). 'China's 'mask diplomacy' to change the Covid-19 narrative in Europe'. *Asia Europe Journal* 18, pp. 205–209. DOI:10.1007/s10308-020-00576-1.

Walker, R. (2020). 'EU–China summit: What really happened?'. *Deutsche Welle*, 4 June.

Wu, W., & Wong, C. (2020). 'How China's coronavirus response may shape the future of its flagship Belt and Road Initiative'. *South China Morning Post*, 21 March.

Xinhua. (2020a). 'Xi-Conte phone talk significant for coronavirus fight: Italian analysts'. *Xinhua*, 18 March.

Xinhua. (2020b). 'China to take actions to help Spain fight Covid-19 epidemic: Chinese FM'. *China Internet Information Center*, 16 March.

Xinhua. (2020c). 'China, EU agree to improve ties at 10th high-level strategic dialogue'. *Xinhua*, 10 June.

Part IV

EU Member State experiences and debates

10 France, China and the BRI: The challenge of conditional engagement

Françoise Nicolas

Introduction

Moving away from its traditional low-profile attitude (described as 'hiding capabilities and biding time'[i]), China has gradually shifted to a muscular foreign policy in the wake of the 2008 global financial crisis and the resulting change in the global balance of power. The Belt and Road Initiative (BRI) is the latest expression of China's rising assertiveness and willingness to play a more central role on the global stage.

These new developments are particularly challenging for the European Union as a whole and for its Member States individually at a time of turbulence and uncertainty for the European project. A major difficulty has arisen, as all EU member states are not necessarily on the same page in their approach to China, which is skillfully taking advantage of these divergences. While France may be tempted to take the lead, it is probably not in the best position to do so, due to its highly asymmetrical relationship with China concerning trade in particular. Since the mid-1960s, France has maintained what is often described as a privileged relationship with China, but beyond this general description, the reality has been—and still is—more nuanced. The new direction taken by China under President Xi's leadership adds further complexity to the Sino-French relationship.

Before exploring the French position on BRI—President Xi's signature project—it is worth providing some background and analyzing how this relationship has evolved over time. As a second step, this chapter examines the French response to the BRI, which can be described as a strategy of conditional engagement. While France is reluctant to endorse the Chinese initiative in its entirety, it is fully aware that it cannot afford to antagonize China. As a result, the favored option is to stress the need for sustainability (both environmentally and financially) and to favor punctual cooperation through projects in third countries. Whether this strategy succeeds in turning the BRI into a genuinely "win-win" scheme remains, however, an open question.

A new French China strategy in the making

The myth of a privileged political relationship

Official relations between France and the People's Republic of China (PRC) date back to 1964, when Paris, under President De Gaulle, was the first major Western capital to officially recognize and establish full diplomatic relations with the PRC[ii] on January 27 that year. Although France continued at first to maintain diplomatic ties with the Republic of China (RoC) in Taiwan,[iii] even after having recognized the Communist government, the initial ambiguity of its position could not last for long. Taipei announced a breach of diplomatic relations with France shortly afterwards.

President De Gaulle's bold decision was based on his conviction that China was a country with great potential, destined to be a global player with the transformative power to shape the world's future, due to its size, civilization and population. This was undoubtedly further compounded by his attraction to countries that could counterbalance the domination of the US in world affairs and his strategy of not siding systematically with Washington (Cabestan 2001). In his own words: "It is somewhat odd that France does not have relations with the most populated country in the world, just because the United States does not like its regime and would not like us to engage with it" (Peyrefitte 1997, 318; author's translation).

This "early" recognition is now part of a common narrative in China, which stresses the special (or even privileged) relationship between the two countries. On the occasion of the 50th anniversary of the establishment of diplomatic relations in 2014, this audacious historical move was widely celebrated. Other factors explaining the close relationship between the two countries include the special ties created due to former Chinese Communist Party (CCP) leaders like Zhou Enlai and Deng Xiaoping studying in France in the early 20th century.

The 1964 episode is often opportunistically mentioned by the two capitals, but Chinese diplomacy is particularly skillful at keeping alive the French hope for a privileged relationship with Beijing. Nonetheless, the symbolism projected by this discourse conceals a very different reality on the ground, as the exceptionalism of the bilateral relationship is clearly a myth (Mengin 2002).

To be fair, France is indeed in a special position compared to other EU Member States (and in particular compared to Germany) because of its international status as a permanent member of the United Nations Security Council and nuclear power. France is also the only EU country with a military presence in Asia—both in the Pacific and the Indian Ocean—and it is therefore still viewed as an important and special diplomatic partner.

However, the two countries do not see eye to eye on many issues and have clashed very often over several of them, ranging from the "one-China policy" to human rights. Since the early 1980s, and especially in the post-Mao era, politically, the bilateral relationship has varied over time from tense, under French Presidents Mitterrand and later Sarkozy, to warm, under Chirac, and neutral, under Hollande (Le Corre 2018). In the last two decades, the two countries have engaged in a "strategic dialogue" (2001), which was later elevated (2004) to a "global strategic dialogue". In the context of the latter, they discussed all sorts of issues, including global governance. They have also engaged in a high-level economic and financial dialogue, which is a key platform for bilateral communication and policy coordination on overarching strategic and long-term issues in the economic and financial fields. Despite this, this supposedly close relationship has never translated into privileged economic treatment, as reflected in their persistently unbalanced trade.

An unbalanced economic relationship

Economically, the bilateral relationship has been long unbalanced in China's favor. In this respect, France is in a different position vis-à-vis China, as compared in particular to Germany. According to a report published in 2019 by the French government (Direction Générale du Trésor 2019), France imported an estimated €50 billion (US$56 billion) in goods and services from China in 2018, representing 9.1% of the country's total imports. Going the other way, France exported an estimated €21 billion (US $23 billion) in goods and services to China, making up 4.2% of France's total exports and leaving it with a €29 billion (US$32.8 billion) trade deficit. In contrast, Germany has the smallest trade deficit with China among the large European economies, about €13 billion in 2018. France's share of the Chinese market amounts to about 1.4%, while China holds approximately 9% of the French market. Rebalancing the relationship has thus ranked high on France's priority list at least for the past decade.

French exports are mainly in the aeronautics sector, which were up 33% in 2018 compared to 2017; agro-food products (up 21%); cosmetics (up 33%); and pharmaceuticals (up 15%). France is also the top European tourist market for Chinese travelers, attracting more than two million visitors from China in 2018. The goods imported from China were mostly low-value-added products, such as textiles, mechanical and household equipment and furniture.

In terms of investment, France has been active in China for a long time, with more than 1000 French companies present on Chinese territory, but as in the case of trade, it lags behind Germany. In addition, a number of big French companies have recently pulled out of the Chinese market or reduced their business presence (Carrefour, Alstom, Auchan) as a result of rising constraints and restrictions being imposed on foreign companies operating in China (Shoulberg 2019).

For all these reasons, France is in a position of economic weakness vis-à-vis China, and, more importantly, France's and Germany's interests are not fully aligned as a result of their very different economic positions. The absence of sufficient alignment in the Franco-German axis makes co-operation on a common China strategy between them and at a European level a challenging task.

A less naive but constructive approach

The last few years have seen a clear shift in France's approach to China away from what may have been called naivete and towards more firmness. For France, China is an economic partner, but it is at the same time a competitor and even a rival, in particular in high-tech activities such as aeronautics, artificial intelligence and the like, and also in promoting alternative models of governance. As such, China has to be treated fairly but without naivete so as to ensure conditions for fair competition and preserve the existing liberal rules-based order. France's new stance can be summarized as open when possible and protective where necessary.[iv]

The first reason for this shift has to do with France's frustration with the failure of China to reform its economy in line with the commitments made when entering the World Trade Organization (WTO) in 2001. It was hoped at that time that China would gradually "normalize", but these hopes have been dashed. The persistence of state support to Chinese companies is an undeniable source of distortion that is now openly criticized, as exemplified by the statements and reports of the EU or the French chamber of commerce in China. Similarly, restrictions to market access still remain, hampering free competition. On this specific point, Paris broadly shares the Trump Administration's assessment that China has failed to live up to its commitments but draws different conclusions in terms of policy responses. While the US administration has opted for a confrontational and unilateral approach, relying on threats and sanctions, France is more inclined to maintain an open dialogue with Beijing in the hope of encouraging reform.

The French government has been calling for years for a rebalancing of bilateral trade, but more than balanced trade (which might not be achieved through the imposition of voluntary exports restraints or of prohibitive tariffs), what it is actually seeking is ensuring reciprocity in market access and achieving a level playing field. To be more specific, France perceives it as completely unfair that Chinese companies have free access to the French market in almost all sectors while the Chinese market remains closed to foreign firms in sectors as diverse as insurance and construction. Moreover, Chinese companies are still heavily subsidized while state aid is prohibited in the EU.[v] In a nutshell, French and Chinese companies cannot compete on equal footing in China. It is with the objective of correcting this unfair treatment that Paris has been pushing for more openness and reciprocity from China on several fronts, such as public procurement.

The second reason for taking a tougher stance vis-à-vis China has to do with France's (and most European countries') rising wariness of Beijing's economic and political ambitions. The acquisitions by Chinese (often state-related) companies of critical infrastructure or strategic assets in EU member states[vi] are perceived as particularly challenging by a number of national capitals. As a result, these moves call for protective measures. This is what lies behind France's support for the establishment of an EU-wide screening mechanism targeting foreign direct investments when these investments pose a threat to host countries' national security.

Despite this tougher stance, France is fully aware that antagonizing China may not be the best option and may even be counterproductive. Given the asymmetry between the two partners, China is indeed in a much better position to exert influence or even coercion. Moreover, the French government is fully aware that China's cooperation is needed in order to effectively respond to a broad range of key global issues close to Paris' heart. In particular, taking President Xi Jinping at his word, it is seeking China's support to defend the multilateral rules-based order and to fight against climate change.

France and a "whole of EU" approach to China

Another tenet of France's China strategy is to push for a "whole of EU" approach vis-à-vis China. First, on some policies such as trade, the exclusive competence lies with the EU, and not with the individual Member States. Secondly, on other issues, given the differences in size between France and China, a better approach is for France to team up with the other EU Member States to have more weight in negotiations with China.

Under President Macron, France has sought to forge a more united European front to deal with China and confront its advances in trade and technology. "For many years we had an uncoordinated approach and China took advantage of our divisions. An awakening was necessary, and Europe must be united and have a coherent message", Macron said a couple of days before Xi's visit to Paris in March 2019. Following this logic, in an attempt to move away from pure bilateralism (which tends to be China's favored approach)[vii], Macron invited the then president of the European Commission Jean-Claude Juncker and German Chancellor Angela Merkel to join him on the second day of this visit, to show a "united front".

Beyond symbolism, the perception in Paris of the necessity of a coherent China approach on the part of the EU is based on a double conviction: first, that France is in a position of weakness vis-à-vis China and thus needs to be backed by its EU partners, and, second, that none of the EU Member States can afford to act alone. This approach, which had been already developed under Sarkozy (2002–2007) and Hollande (2007–2012) is also clearly favored, even more forcefully, by Macron. At the same time, his intention is to reposition France at the center of Europe.

The Europeanization of France's China strategy starts with closer cooperation with Germany. Interestingly, despite the lack of alignment, the two countries' interests have been converging over the past few years. While in the past Berlin tended to be more engaged with China as German industry was able to keep a competitive edge, it recently realized that China's rise as a technological power carries significant security risks challenging Germany in sectors where it used to have an upper hand, such as heavy machinery. The acquisition in 2016 of German robotics company Kuka by China's Midea was a major shock that triggered this change in Berlin's position.

France and Germany have been instrumental in pushing for the adoption of an EU-wide FDI screening mechanism. The proposal tabled by the Commission was adopted by the European Parliament and by the Council in March 2019 and the EU FDI screening regulation entered into force on 10 April 2019. As also discussed by Blockmans and Hu (Chapter 5) and Svetlicinii (Chapter 7), its objective is to coordinate at the EU level the screening of foreign investments likely to affect the security and public order of the Union and of its Member States.

From the two countries' perspective, what has been done on strategic investments could and should be done in other domains like industrial policy. Their aim is to protect their industrial base from what they regard as predatory competition from China. To that end, they would be ready to enable EU "champions" to emerge in manufacturing, and in new industries such as electric cars and artificial intelligence. With this objective in mind, in February 2019, France and Germany issued a joint manifesto for a European industrial policy fit for the 21st century (French Government 2019), calling for a more ambitious European industrial strategy with clear objectives for 2030 and pooling Europe's strengths in order to face global competition. This call is reflected in the EU industrial strategy released in March 2020 by the new European Commission.

France and China's BRI: Positive but principled

A late awakening

When China's President Xi Jinping launched his flagship project on the "Silk Road Economic Belt" in Astana in the fall of 2013, followed by the "21st Century Maritime Silk Road" in Jakarta a few weeks later, these developments mostly passed unnoticed in France, except perhaps for a few experts in academic circles or research institutions focusing on China.

There is no denying that it took a long time both for the French government and other French economic actors from the private sector, such as business associations, to take the issue seriously and start thinking of a possible response to the Chinese project. A flurry of analyses has been published since then, however, with the French Senate issuing a report on the New Silk Road in May 2018 (Allizard et al. 2018), the French Ministry of Finance releasing a note in October of the same year (Direction Générale du Trésor 2018) and the Paris Chamber of Commerce and Industry publishing a position paper in June 2019 (Chambre de Commerce et d'Industrie de Paris 2019b).

While this relatively belated reaction may be perceived as reflecting a lack of foresight at the time, there were many good reasons for France to overlook the project and underestimate its potential impact, at least in the first couple of years following its launch.

The primary reason is that France was initially not considered as a potential target, and no single project was envisaged on its territory. Furthermore, the Chinese project was initially so unclear that it was extremely difficult to fully grasp its scope and objectives. What eventually came to be known as the "One Belt, One Road" (OBOR) and later as the "Belt and Road Initiative" (BRI) was at the time a relatively fuzzy concept. The institution in charge of implementing the initiative (China's National Development and Reform Commission—NDRC) never released a map or a list of projects. Also, while it was clear that the project involved infrastructure development and investments with a view to enhancing connectivity between China and Europe through a multiplicity of economic corridors, the exact way of achieving the objective remained to be defined, and the geographical location of such corridors remained extremely vague.

Actually, what made the project unique and unprecedented (hence difficult to assess) was precisely the fact that the concept was launched even before its exact content was defined. Interestingly, China's partners were frequently encouraged to provide ideas on how to give more substance to the scheme and how to achieve its outcomes. Never in recent history has a project been launched by a government with so much determination, so much investment in terms of its national and international promotion, but with so much ambiguity.[viii] As a result, the concept itself has been subject to continuous adjustments by the Chinese authorities over time, leaving China's partners unsettled.

As time went by, however, the project became increasingly concrete (with the first trains connecting Wuhan and Lyon in April 2016) and some EU countries were directly targeted (the acquisition of 51% of Greece's Piraeus Port Authority by China's COSCO Shipping in 2016 as part of the "maritime" portion of BRI, and the planned construction of a high-speed rail line between Budapest and Belgrade being two of the most illustrative examples of this). At the same time, beyond the physical (hard) infrastructure, the intangible (soft) dimension of the project became increasingly conspicuous, suggesting that China's objectives were more far-reaching than initially anticipated and encompassed the promotion of new standards, courts, customs, police co-operation mechanisms, etc. (Ekman 2019).

To top it all, the positive response given to the project in the following years by some EU Member States —in particular with one of the founding fathers, Italy, agreeing to sign a BRI Memorandum of Understanding (MoU)—made the need to develop a strategic response at the national as well as at the EU level compelling.[ix]

A diversity of perspectives

Different players (private or public) may be affected in different ways by the implementation of BRI, leading to a wide array of possible reactions.

Although the reactions range from skepticism to enthusiasm on the part of the French business community (depending on the sector), the perception has been on the whole rather positive, as explained in the position paper issued by the Paris Chamber of Commerce and Industry (Chambre de Commerce et d'Industrie de Paris 2019b). Considering that the BRI can be an opportunity for the French economy and business sector, the CCIP suggested opting for "a conquering and constructive attitude which would make it possible to move from being a receiver of proposals to a promoter of initiatives". In this perspective, it was therefore deemed necessary to combine cooperation and competition, i.e. "to be in co-opetition" (Chambre de Commerce et d'Industrie de Paris 2019b).

A number of companies have shared this positive stance. This is particularly prevalent among logistics companies, such as Forwardis, a rail and multimodal freight forwarder, or CMA CGM LOG, the logistics arm of the CMA CGM Group, which aims to become a key player in the international supply chain management market and a model for services connecting China, Russia, central Asia and Europe in both directions. Similarly, other companies such as Bolloré Logistics have engaged in trade and logistics within the context of BRI and have therefore played a key role in Sino-European trade, working in partnership with Chinese port operators and shipping companies. Also, companies like the oil giant Total have already participated directly in major infrastructure development initiatives in the energy sector, such as the Yamal liquefied natural gas (LNG) project.

Interestingly, the private sector's position is somehow disconnected from that of the public sector and does not seem to have a major impact on it. On the public sector side, a distinction needs to be made between the local and central level, with more enthusiasm shown by the former than the latter. For instance, as indicated earlier, the second-largest city in the country, Lyon, welcomed the arrival of the first Belt and Road train connecting it with Wuhan in April 2016; the city of Le Havre is seeking to attract Chinese investors in its deep-water port connected to the inland ports of Rouen and Paris (the so-called Haropa complex); and the city of Marseille also tends to look at the BRI more as an opportunity than as a threat, with the hope of participating in the digital aspects of the initiative through the establishment of data centers (Chambre de Commerce et d'Industrie de Paris 2019a).

At the central government level, by contrast, the position has been more nuanced, translating into an approach that can be more accurately described as conditional engagement. The reason is that the Chinese initiative is not exclusively perceived as an economic project but as a potentially geopolitical endeavor. Although the BRI did not initially top the list of priorities, the French approach was overall vaguely favorable to the project, at least to its objective of connectivity enhancement. As early as June 2015, then Minister of European and Foreign Affairs, Laurent Fabius, was quoted as saying: "We welcome the New Silk Road Initiative",[x] but he remained evasive as to the way this could materialize and simply referred to possible cooperation opportunities in third-party markets. Macron echoed a similar view when he reasserted France's support for the Chinese initiative during his first trip to China in early 2018. However, he defined the conditions for his support more explicitly, calling in particular for reciprocity and stressing that, "By definition, these roads [the New Silk Roads] can only be shared. If they are roads, they cannot be one-way" (Rose 2018).

In concrete terms, and unlike Italy, French authorities have not signed an MoU on BRI and do not plan to do so in the near future. Although they refuse to endorse the Chinese initiative in its entirety, they do not reject it either. Instead, they are seeking cooperation on a project-by-project basis with a view to raising the growth potential in host countries. To that end, emphasis is placed first and foremost on economic cooperation, primarily between French and Chinese companies in third countries.[xi] In this context, the French authorities insist on the benefits that French (and European) businesses should be able to reap from such joint projects. The fact that the vast majority of Chinese financing has in the past gone to Chinese companies is clearly perceived as highly problematic and not in line with the supposed "win-win" logic often stressed by Chinese counterparts. This latter realization serves to reinforce the cautious stance favored by France.

As an indirect response to the BRI, France has developed its own Indo-Pacific (IP) strategy, which is a way of engaging with a number of countries targeted by the Chinese initiative. What triggered this move is undoubtedly the rise of China and its increasing assertiveness, which Paris perceives as posing a threat to multilateralism and the international rules-based order. The BRI is seen as an instrument to position China at the center of a new international order. From a French perspective, the objective of its IP strategy is not to antagonize or contain China, but to protect both the country's interests in the region and global common goods and values through cooperation with like-minded countries. In other words, France's IP strategy seeks to propose a stable, multipolar order, based on the rule of law and the free movement of people and goods, and fair and efficient multilateralism, with the Indo-Pacific region at the heart of this strategy.

France's public strategy of conditional engagement on BRI

France is favorable to the BRI's overall objective of connectivity enhancement but under certain conditions, and primarily through punctual co-operation in third markets.

France's official position reflects the "EU common messages" set out in 2017[xii] during the first Belt and Road Forum held in Beijing: pushing for transparency, interoperability and economic, financial, social and environmental sustainability (Direction Générale du Trésor 2018). These conditions are considered essential to achieving balanced cooperation, but they are also a way of pushing China to conform to multilaterally agreed-upon high-level rules and standards.

The first condition refers to environmental sustainability, and France insists in particular on compliance of connectivity projects with the provisions of the Paris Agreement on Climate Change. Another major concern expressed by the French government relates to the risk for countries receiving financing from China to be dragged into a "debt trap", as was the case in Sri Lanka, for instance.[xiii] As a result, the French government places a heavy emphasis on the need to follow the "G20 Operational Guidelines for Sustainable Financing" agreed upon in 2017 (Bundesmisterium für Finanzen 2017), the objective of which is to ensure that creditor and debtor countries' lending and borrowing practices facilitate sustainable public debt levels. This position is in line with the French Senate's report on BRI, which emphasizes the need for transparency and reciprocity, and argues in favor of ensuring local country benefits and the prevention of debt distress.

By pushing for these high-level standards, France is seeking to influence the Chinese project. France's decision to join the Asian Infrastructure Investment Bank (AIIB) was similarly motivated by the conviction that it would provide a way of exerting pressure on the institution so that it would abide by the rules in terms of social and environmental standards. This is an excellent example of active but conditional engagement with a view to influencing China's behavior.

Interestingly, the French approach to China is rather similar to the Japanese one. At first, Japan was unresponsive, expressing neither interest nor hostility towards the BRI; later on, Tokyo started showing signs of openness to the initiative (in July 2017), when it announced that it would consider the possibility of becoming involved in BRI-related projects. But for Japan to accept collaborating with BRI projects, they must be characterized by, "(1) openness; (2) transparency; (3) economic sustainability; and (4) the ability of the developing countries involved to claim financial ownership over the projects in question" (Umirdinov 2019). Japan, therefore, made it clear that any official support would be limited and conditional, dependent on the projects satisfying the "quality infrastructure" principles.

The pressure exerted by Japan is apparently bearing fruit, as China officially announced a move towards a "higher quality" BRI during the second Belt and Road Forum held in Beijing in April 2019. Beyond this specific example, exerting pressure on China seems indeed to be working: in terms of financing, China's approach has proven to be "adaptive",[xiv] in particular with an increasing recognition of the debt risks caused by BRI financing, for instance (Bertuzzi et al. 2019).

The focus on third-party market cooperation

In order to show support without endorsing the whole logic of the BRI, France has chosen to favor cooperation in third countries.

The mechanism of *third-party market cooperation* (3PMC), which was first used by China and France in June 2015,[xv] is an innovative international cooperation model initiated by China. It mainly refers to partnerships between Chinese companies and their counterparts in developed countries with the objective of doing business in markets in the developing world, that is, the third parties in these processes. These partnerships are thought to effectively link the leading production capacity of China, the advanced technologies of developed countries and the development needs of developing countries. In the context of the BRI, Xi is strongly encouraging the use of such 3PMC agreements (3PMCAs). In his own words: "We welcome the participation of multilateral and national financial institutions in BRI investment and financing and encourage third-party market cooperation. With the involvement of multiple stakeholders, we can surely deliver benefits to all" (Xi 2019).

From China's perspective, the 3PMCAs may also fit another purpose, which is to counter an oft-heard criticism of Chinese projects and help demonstrate that the BRI is open for everyone rather than exclusively driven by China (Mhtembu 2020).

In the wake of Chinese Premier Li Keqiang's visit to France (June 2015), China and France agreed in November 2016 to set up the Sino-French Third-Party Investment Fund, which is jointly funded and managed by the Chinese sovereign fund CIC Capital (a subsidiary of China Investment Corporation) and the French CDC International Capital[xvi]—a subsidiary of the French Caisse des Dépôts et Consignations (CDC)—which has now become the Public Investment Bank - BPI. The fund was initially endowed with € 300 million, equally split between France and China, but could be increased to up to €2 billion. Its objective is to channel capital into investment projects in such third-party markets and its activities are supposed to be evenly distributed among Africa, Asia and the rest of the world (Allizard et al. 2018).

Pushing for this form of cooperation is a sign of goodwill on the part of France, suggesting that caution does not mean obstruction. But it is also probably the best way to implement the strategy of conditional engagement highlighted above. Through these mechanisms, France indeed seeks to level up the behavior of Chinese companies and the Chinese economy as a whole so that they converge with Western best practices in terms of corporate social responsibility norms, environmental standards, labor practices and debt sustainability (Duchâtel 2019). This clearly dovetails with the objectives of conditional engagement.

To be more specific, from a French perspective the 3PMC agreements (3PMCAs) can be used to push climate-related objectives, as they can effectively leverage the BRI to support the aims of the Paris Agreement and those of the 2030 Agenda for Sustainable Development. The France-China 2015 3PMCA places a clear emphasis on a green agenda, which is a priority for the French government. During Xi's visit to France in March 2019, a quadripartite cooperation agreement was signed between BPI, CIC, Shanghai SUS Environment Co. Ltd and Quadran International to direct funds to solar, wind and waste-to-energy projects in third markets.

In addition, 3PMCAs could also be a tactical option for France and Europe to further the dialogue with China on sustainable international finance.

The normative contents in the 3PMCA with China are noteworthy, with the two countries referring to compliance with "established international norms and standards, international obligations, and relevant commercial principles", and committing to "abide by the shared principles of market rules, transparency, sustainable economic development, open procurement and a level playing field for all investors".[xvii]

However, the implementation of the 3PMCAs is proving more complicated than anticipated. An initial list of a dozen projects was submitted by France to Beijing, but this did not fit Beijing's purposes, leading to the submission of an alternative list by China. At the end of the negotiation, four projects in third countries were identified, in particular in the energy sector. The two countries have come to an agreement on the principle, but no specific projects have started yet. In the joint communiqué issued in the wake of the 7th High Level Economic and Financial Dialogue held on July 21, 2020, the two parties reiterated their commitment and "expect the China-France Third Market Cooperation Fund to develop viable projects in line with sustainable development approaches. The Chinese side welcomes more proposals from the French side for such cooperation in Africa and in Asia" (Ministère de l'Economie, des Finances et de la Relance 2020). Until now, the Sino-French collaboration at the government level has focused on potential cooperation only in a developed country, Hinkley Point—the first in a new generation of nuclear power stations in the United Kingdom.

For the time being, the only existing cases of Sino-French third market cooperation have been commercially based (Wang 2018). Indeed, French companies are involved as subcontractors in several Chinese infrastructure projects, as in the case of the Suez-CMEC (China Machinery and Engineering Corporation) water dam and treatment plant project in the Sanaga River in Cameroon; Bolloré-China Harbor Engineering Corporation joint investment in the Kribi port; and NOX-China Railway Construction Corporation partnership on the O Tower in Rabat.

While France is in favor of cooperation in third countries, if the actual projects are business-to-business, they may not serve the government's purposes. In particular, there is a risk of mismatch between companies' and governments' objectives, as the former may be ready to seize an opportunity by engaging in a project that does not fit the latter's standards. For instance, the objectives of sustainability may not necessarily be a priority (Duchâtel 2019).

Another snag is that from China's perspective, the objectives of 3PMCAs are primarily about access to technology and management skills, which is not in line with France's objectives (Duchâtel 2019). The mismatch in interests and objectives is also a source of difficulties in the implementation of 3PMCAs and a clear limitation to their effectiveness.

Conclusion: Combining openness and firmness may be paying off

As China becomes increasingly assertive on the global stage, France has developed a new China strategy that combines openness and firmness. The current French government under President Macron is pushing for a principled approach towards China, defending the preservation of a rules–based multilateral world order. Although France would like to be able to rely on a coherent and single-voiced EU, this cannot be easily achieved. As mentioned above, the interests and positions of EU member states are not always aligned, and, while on a converging path, the Franco-German motor may not be strong enough to set the tone for the rest of the EU. As Germany is weakened by domestic political difficulties, France has been trying to take the lead in the EU, but it is faced with EU-wide interest divergence as well as with the reluctance by some to accept French leadership.

Although President Macron's ambitions to unify Europe's position on economic and political relations with China may prove difficult to turn into reality, Sino-French bilateral relations continue to move forward. With regard to China's BRI, Paris seeks to push its own singular voice and position. In contrast to what is often claimed, there is no systematic opposition to the project on the part of France, but there is no blind endorsement either. Taking Xi at his word, Macron is placing the emphasis on the conditions to be met for the cooperation to be fruitful and really of a "win-win" nature. Interestingly, this tougher French stance has not led to any pushback from Beijing so far; far to the contrary, there are even signs that mild pressure has paid off, with China gradually integrating some widely agreed-upon principles. However, whether these commitments will become reality remains to be seen.

In this respect, the signals sent by China during the recent Covid-19 pandemic do not bode well for the future of the relationship. The Covid-19 crisis has so far simultaneously brought Europe and China into closer cooperation, pushed them further apart, and seemingly amplified many of the fractures that exist within Europe on how to approach an increasingly powerful and influential China (Seaman 2020). As for France and China, while the Covid-19 crisis has pushed the two partners to demonstrate mutual assistance and express their solidarity with each other, their bilateral relationship has also been tested, particularly as the Chinese embassy in Paris has published articles on its website aggressively denigrating Western democracies' (including France's) management of the health crisis.[xviii] This aggressive attitude (dubbed "Wolf Warrior" diplomacy, after the patriotic Chinese blockbuster movie) risks undermining the views of China in France, be it within the wider public or within official circles, which could affect bilateral relations. In particular, President Macron is likely to feel vindicated in his tough approach to China as well as in his defense of multilateralism and his quest for "strategic autonomy".

Notes

i This ancient Chinese proverb "Tao guang yang hui" (hide your brightness, bide your time) was often quoted by Deng Xiaoping to describe the strategy that China should follow: to keep its capabilities secret until the moment is right to reveal them.

ii A number of other countries (Denmark, Finland, Norway, the Netherlands, the United Kingdom, Sweden and Switzerland) had established diplomatic representations in Beijing as early as 1950 but without exchanging ambassadors.

iii The January 27 communiqué included neither an allusion to Taiwan nor to the future of France-ROC relations.

iv On this point France shares the Dutch position for instance (Esteban and Otero-Iglesias 2020), but this is also the position defined in the 2019 EU China Strategic Outlook (European Commission 2019).

v The Treaty on the Functioning of the European Union generally prohibits state aid, unless it is justified by reasons of general economic development.

vi One example is the acquisition by China Three Gorges (CTG), a state-owned firm, of a stake in Energias de Portugal (EDP), Portugal's primary energy utility.

vii Indeed, China often seeks to exploit the differences in EU Member States' interests and prefers to engage in bilateral negotiations, in which it can easily take advantage of the asymmetrical relation.

viii For more details on the methodology of BRI, see Ekman et al. (2018).

ix As a result, a number of reports were issued in 2018 by the French Treasury, the Banque de France, as well as by the French Senate in particular.

x Speech delivered by Laurent Fabius on June 12, 2015, in Rouen for the opening ceremony of the China-Normandy Forum.

xi Again, this position has been held by the French government right from the start; cooperation in third-party markets was already stressed in Fabius's speech at the China-Normandy forum in June 2015.

xii These messages were adopted by the EU Member States in a joint-position statement issued during the first Belt and Road Forum held in Beijing in March 2017. Ever since, the EU has adopted a flexible approach towards BRI, emphasizing the need for the initiative to comply with European standards and principles.

xiii But this needs to be qualified, as it would be erroneous to argue that China actively and deliberately pushed Sri Lanka into a debt trap: Sri Lanka was already heavily indebted when China stepped in. Another major issue is that a rising share of Sri Lanka's debt has been contracted on commercial and not on concessional terms (Moramudali 2019). However, over 60% of the debt owed to China was contracted on concessional terms. Sri Lanka's problem is thus a much wider current account problem. (Weerakoon and Jayasuriya 2019).

xiv Allowing or even instructing those involved to make practical adjustments as they implement the initiative, in order to respond to criticisms by participating states (Bertuzzi et al. 2019).

xv France was the first developed country with which China engaged in such a cooperative mechanism. It was soon followed by Canada (2016), New Zealand

(2017), Belgium (2018), Portugal (2018), Singapore (2018), Japan (2018), Germany (2019), Italy (2019), Luxembourg (2019) and finally, the Netherlands (2019) (Zhang 2019).

xvi This is the financial subsidiary of the French Caisse des Dépôts et Consignations (CDC), whose objective is to partner with foreign sovereign wealth funds.

xvii Gradually the normative content has been enriched and step-by-step international organizations and Western developed nations succeeded in inserting powerful principles such as "transparency", "open procurement" and "level playing field" (Umirdinov 2019).

xviii The behavior of the Chinese embassy in France resulted in the summoning of the ambassador by the French Minister of Foreign Affairs.

Bibliography

Allizard, P. et al. (2018), Pour la France, les nouvelles routes de la soie: simple label économique ou nouvel ordre mondial? *Rapport d'information* No 520 Paris Commission des Affaires Etrangères, de la Défense et des Forces Armées, Sénat.

Bertuzzi, M., T. Melonio, A. Pornet and L. Tremel (2019), Vers de « Nouvelles routes de la soie » durables? Pistes de réflexion pour un référentiel commun de développement durable *Policy Paper AFD* No 2, November [online]. Viewed 15 June 2020. Available at: https://www.afd.fr/fr/nouvelles-routes-soie-durables.

Bundesmisterium für Finanzen (2017), *G20 operational guidelines for sustainable financing* [online]. Viewed 22 September 2020. Available at: https://www.bundesfinanzministerium.de/Content/EN/Standardartikel/Topics/world/G7-G20/G20-Documents/g20-operational-guidelines-for-sustainable-financing.pdf?__blob=publicationFile&v=1.

Cabestan, J.-P. (2001), France's Taiwan policy: A case of shopkeeper diplomacy, *unpublished mimeograph* July.

Chambre de Commerce et d'Industrie de Paris (2019a), *Les nouvelles routes de la soie – Enjeux et opportunités économiques*, Paris. Viewed 15 June 2020. Available at: http://www.cci-paris-idf.fr/sites/default/files/etudes/pdf/documents/routes-de-la-soie.pdf.

Chambre de Commerce et d'Industrie de Paris (2019b), *New Silk Roads and French businesses - Enter into a logic of 'coopetition'*, Position paper Paris. Viewed 15 June 2020. Available at: http://www.cci-paris-idf.fr/sites/default/files/etudes/pdf/documents/position_paper_silk_roads_paris_chamber_of_commerce_and_industry.pdf.

Direction Générale du Trésor (2018), *Les Nouvelles Routes de la Soie*, *Trésor-éco*, No 229, October.

Direction Générale du Trésor (2019), *Les relations commerciales de la France et la Chine en 2018*, 4 April [online]. Viewed 22 September 2020. Available at: https://www.tresor.economie.gouv.fr/Articles/16671c85-d180–452d-8078-ae555409b06e/files/750f4203-2af0–4cca-a1f3–34256e36c1cf.

Duchâtel, M. (2019), Triple win? – China and Third Market Cooperation *Blog post* Institut Montaigne, July 10. [online]. Viewed 15 June 2020. Available at: https://www.institutmontaigne.org/en/blog/triple-win-china-and-third-market-cooperation.

Ekman, A. (ed.) (2018), La France face aux Nouvelles routes de la soie chinoises, *Etudes de l'Ifri,* October. [online]. Viewed 15 June 2020. Available at: https://

www.ifri.org/fr/publications/etudes-de-lifri/france-face-aux-nouvelles-routes-de-soie-chinoises-0.

Ekman, A. (ed.) (2019), China's Belt and Road and the World: Competing forms of globalization, *Etudes de l'ifri*, April. [online]. Viewed 15 June 2020. Available at: https://www.ifri.org/en/publications/etudes-de-lifri/chinas-belt-road-and-world-competing-forms-globalization.

Esteban, M. and M. Otero-Iglesias (2020). *Europe in the Face of US-China Rivalry*. A Report by the European Think-tank Network on China. Elcano Royal Institute, Madrid.

European Commission (2019), *EU-China – A strategic outlook*, March 12. Available at: https://ec.europa.eu/commission/news/eu-china-strategic-outlook-2019-mar-12_en.

French Government (2019), A Franco-German Manifesto for a European industrial policy fit for the 21st century, 19 February. [online]. Viewed 22 September 2020. Available at: https://www.gouvernement.fr/en/a-franco-german-manifesto-for-a-european-industrial-policy-fit-for-the-21st-century.

Le Corre, P. (2018), Macron's Travel Diaries – First Step: China, Blog post, Institut Montaigne, January 8. [online]. Viewed 15 June 2020. Available at: https://www.institutmontaigne.org/en/blog/macrons-travel-diaries-first-step-china.

Mengin, F. (2002). France's China Policy: From the Myth of a Privileged Relationship to a Normalization Syndrome, in Cabestan, J.-P. and W. Meissner (eds.), *The Role of France and Germany in Sino-European Relations*, East-West Dialogue, vol. VII, No 2, June, 99–125.

Mhtembu, P. (2020). China's Belt and Road Initiative – How Can Africa advance its Strategic Priorities?, in Kornegay, F. and P. Mthembu (eds. 2020), *Africa and the World: Navigating Shifting Geopolitics*, Mistra, Johannesburg, 134–159.

Ministère de l'Economie des Finances et de la Relance (2020), *China-France Joint Fact Sheet on the 7th High Level Economic and Financial Dialogue*, 21 July. [online]. Viewed 23 September 2020. Available at: https://www.economie.gouv.fr/files/files/2020/communique-conjoint-dialogue-franc-chinois.pdf.

Moramudali, U. (2019), Is Sri Lanka Really a Victim of China's 'Debt Trap'. *The Diplomat*, May 14.

Nicolas, F. (2017). The Economics of OBOR: Putting Chinese Interests First, in Ekman, A. et al., *Three Years of New Silk Roads: From Words to (Re)Action?*, Etudes de l'ifri, Ifri, Paris, February [online]. Viewed 15 June 2020. Available at: https://www.ifri.org/sites/default/files/atoms/files/ekman_et_al_china_new_silk_roads_2017.pdf.

Nicolas, F. (2019), France and the Belt and Road: A Positive Yet Principled Position, in Amighini, A. and G. Sciorati, *EU-China Relations: Challenges and Opportunities*, ISPI, 8 April. [online]. Viewed 15 June 2020. Available at: https://www.ispionline.it/en/pubblicazione/france-and-chinas-belt-and-road-initiative-22787.

Peyrefitte, A. (1997). *C'était de Gaulle (volume 1)*, Editions de Fallois, Paris.

Rose, Michel (2018), China's new Silk Road cannot be one-way, France's Macron says, *Reuters, Business News*, January 8. [online]. Viewed 22 September 2020. Available at: https://www.reuters.com/article/us-china-france/chinas-new-silk-road-cannot-be-one-wayfrances-macron-says-idUSKBN1EX0FU.

Seaman, J. (ed.) (2020), Covid-19 and Europe-China Relations – A Country-level Analysis, *ETNC Special Report*, Ifri, 29 April. Available at: https://www.ifri.org/sites/default/files/atoms/files/etnc_special_report_covid-19_china_europe_2020.pdf.

Shoulberg, W. (2019), Carrefour Is the Latest Victim of the China Retail Syndrome, *Forbes*, June 24. [online]. Viewed 22 September 2020. Available at: https://www.forbes.com/sites/warrenshoulberg/2019/06/24/carrefour-is-the-latest-victim-of-the-china-retail-syndrome/#896e6b52037b.

Skala-Kuhmann, A. (2019), European Responses to BRI – An Overdue Assessment, *Horizons/Journal of International relations and Sustainable Development*, No 14, Summer, 144–155.

Thomala, Lai Lin (2020), International Tourism Spending of Chinese Tourists 2008–2018. *Statista.com*. https://www.statista.com/statistics/249702/international-tourism-expenditure-of-chinese-tourists/.

Umirdinov, A. (2019), Generating a Reform of the BRI from the Inside - Japan's Contribution via Soft Law Diplomacy, *RIETI Discussion Paper Series*, 19-E-076, September. [online]. Viewed 15 June 2020. Available at: https://www.rieti.go.jp/jp/publications/dp/19e076.pdf.

Wang, X. (2018), Third Country Cooperation in the China's Belt and Road Initiative, *IDDRI Blog Post*, July 19. [online]. Viewed 17 June 2020. Available at: https://www.iddri.org/en/publications-and-events/blog-post/third-country-cooperation-chinas-belt-and-road-initiative.

Weerakoon, D. and S. Jayasuriya (2019), Sri Lanka's Debt Problem Is Not Made in China, *East Asia Forum*, February 28. [online]. Viewed 15 June 2020. Available at: https://www.eastasiaforum.org/2019/02/28/sri-lankas-debt-problem-isnt-made-in-china/.

Xi, Jinping (2019), Working Together to Deliver a Brighter Future For Belt and Road Cooperation, *Keynote Speech*, Opening Ceremony of the Second Belt and Road Forum for International Cooperation, 26 April. [online]. Viewed 23 September 2020. Available at: https://www.fmprc.gov.cn/mfa_eng/zxxx_662805/t1658424.shtml.

Zhang, Y. (2019), Third Party Market Cooperation under the Belt and Road Initiative: Progress, Challenges, and Recommendations. *China International Strategy Review*, No 1, 310–329.

11 Between commerce and geopolitics: Is there a German China strategy?

Stefan Mair and Ferdinand Schaff

I Championing engagement with a rising China

The German-Chinese economic partnership

China's economic rise in the past 30 years has been without doubt beneficial for many German companies—especially in the export-oriented automotive, chemical, electronics and tools and machinery sectors. At the same time, the largescale engagement of German companies has aided China's rapid economic development, bringing capital, technology and know-how to the country, forging a mutually beneficial economic partnership.

The first German investors had already started to look for business opportunities in China in the early 1980s, immediately after Deng Xiaoping started to open up the Chinese economy. After the mid-1990s, when China's opening-up accelerated in the run-up to its accession to the World Trade Organisation (WTO) in 2001, both bilateral trade and German investments in China expanded rapidly. The investment spree of German business in China mirrored the 'cluster pattern'—a characteristic feature of German industry: namely the clustering of mid-sized and small firms as suppliers around a few big companies in the same sector.

Between 1991 until 2011, China's annual GPD growth averaged 10.4% (World Bank Group 2020) and its share of global GDP (PPP Basis) more than tripled from 4.4% to 14.7% (reaching 19.3% in 2019) (IMF 2020). As Kroeber (2016, Chapters 3 and 4) shows, China's growth model during this period of rapid development focused heavily on infrastructure building and the expansion of an export-oriented manufacturing sector. Germany, with its relatively industry-heavy and export-oriented economy, was particularly well positioned to benefit from this historically unprecedented economic expansion. The structure of German-Chinese economic relations in this period is often described as 'complementary' (Hauschild et al. 2015, 23; Huotari 2015, 32). Germany supplied high-value investment goods and consumer products, and China supplied consumer products and intermediate goods in the low-technology sector.

This complementary relationship started being increasingly interspersed with fields of direct competition in the early 2010s, as China began to embrace an economy driven by domestic consumption and innovation. Despite this, however, the significance of China for German companies has by no means diminished. New business opportunities have emerged over time in areas such as healthcare, insurance, environmental technology and smart manufacturing, and China also increasingly matters as a location for research and development, as well as digital innovation. For a few larger German firms, China nowadays accounts for an inordinate share of their global turnover. Recently, Germany's close economic ties have raised questions about a German overreliance on China and an unhealthy dependency. However, while some larger companies indeed are very much dependent on the Chinese market, the overall dependency of the German economy on China is only moderate. Germany's most important market by far remains the EU single market.

This close German-Chinese economic partnership is by no means without its problems. Longstanding issues raised by German companies have included restrictions such as joint-venture requirements in several industries (most notably automobile), limited access to public procurement, forced transfer of technology beyond what would be expected under market conditions, inadequate protection of intellectual property rights, non-transparent and discriminative licensing processes and the preferential treatment of Chinese firms—State Owned Enterprises (SOEs) in particular—by regulators. China's piecemeal approach to opening up the market has resulted in a serious 'promise fatigue' among the sections of the German business community that engage with and operate in China, and calls for a more ambitious opening-up agenda have gotten much louder in recent years. With China's influence on global markets expanding rapidly—a development decisively supported by the BRI—there has also been an increasing sense of urgency about asymmetries in market access and distorted competition.

The constants of German China policy

The vast economic opportunities of China's rise have been a major motivating factor for all German governments across party lines since the beginning of China's reform and opening-up in 1978. Nonetheless, it would be oversimplified to place this relationship solely in its economic context. Indeed, two other main constants in German China policy can be identified: the goal of involving and integrating a rising China in world affairs and encouraging its economic and political liberalisation.

Early German engagement with China in the 1970s was largely driven by the political dynamics of the Cold War. Under Helmut Kohl (CDU, Chancellor from 1982 until 1998) economic relations became the primary focus of the country's China policy. The political tensions following the harsh crackdown of the Tiananmen protests in 1989 and the ensuing flare-up of the human rights question in the German China debate did not weigh on economic relations for long. After sanctions were lifted (although a weapons embargo remains in place until today), Kohl visited Beijing in 1993, reigniting economic cooperation (Huang 2019, 60). The Kohl administration's emphasis on economics should be viewed against the backdrop of Germany's wider post-Cold War geostrategic situation. As Kundnani (2015, 83) argues, after reunification, Germany's foreign policy, in general, became increasingly driven by economic considerations, since its two overriding strategic goals during the Cold War, namely, rehabilitation and security, had been largely achieved.

Two concepts that informed Kohl's China policy of centring on economic engagement and that continue to reverberate throughout German policy towards China in the present were: 'Wandel durch Handel' (change through trade) and 'stille Diplomatie' (quiet diplomacy). 'Stille Diplomatie' describes the preference for addressing sensitive political issues in closed-door meetings instead of criticising the Chinese government in public. This approach is a very effective means to separate political differences from economic relations, and it drew inspiration from Willy Brandt's[i] 'Ostpolitik' and its central slogan of 'Wandel durch Annäherung' (change through rapprochement) aimed at German reunification (Kundnani 2015, 82). On the other hand, it was premised on the expectation that China would ultimately become more liberal politically and more open and market-oriented, the more it developed economically. China's accession to the WTO in 2001 and the continued reform rhetoric of most Communist Party leaders would nurture this expectation for years to come.

Gerhard Schröder (SPD, Chancellor from 1998 until 2005) intensified engagement with China. He visited China almost every year during his tenure, usually accompanied by a business delegation—a tradition Angela Merkel (CDU, Chancellor since 2005) would continue. Schröder's administration, a coalition of the SPD and the Green Party, highlighted political issues by setting up annual bilateral dialogues on the rule of law and human rights, but by and large, continued Kohl's emphasis on fostering economic ties. However, his administration also set out the goal of integrating 'China, a country rapidly growing in political and economic significance, into the international community' and of 'convinc[ing] China' to assume its increasing global responsibility, as the 2002 regional concept on East Asia by the foreign office reads (Auswärtiges Amt 2002).

The Merkel administration's approach to China's growing global weight embraced the idea of encouraging Beijing to become a responsible stakeholder in the international system and a partner in dealing with global challenges such as climate change, conflict prevention and resolution and development. This approach to China (and other emerging economies) was explained in the foreign office's 2012 'Gestaltungsmächtekonzept' (transformative powers concept)[ii] which emphasised the need to cooperate with emerging powers on further developing the international system and the rules of globalisation in an increasingly multipolar world (Auswärtiges Amt 2012).

Under Merkel, the 'strategic partnership' with China was transformed from a political label to a broad institutionalised cooperation framework. When Xi Jinping visited Germany in 2014, ties were further elevated to a 'comprehensive strategic partnership', which today encompasses about 80 dialogue formats on a wide range of economic, political, social and cultural issues (Auswärtiges Amt 2020a). As Huotari (2015, 31) notes, compared to other European countries' relations with China, Germany's cooperative arrangements seem to 'exhibit an unusual degree of institutionalization and a notably long-term outlook'. In this sense, Merkel considerably widened the focus of Germany's China policy beyond the economic realm. Climate cooperation and Berlin's efforts to secure the involvement of China in global conflict resolution (e.g. China's joining of the Iran nuclear deal) are often hailed as prime examples.

However, economic interests have continued to be the main driver of the bilateral agenda. In the years leading up to Xi Jinping's rule, the notion of 'Wandel durch Handel' was still regularly invoked by business leaders and politicians, despite continued political repression and the absence of any major market-oriented economic reforms since China's WTO accession. This was based on the widely held assumption that progress might be slow and sometimes even reversed, but eventually unstoppable. Furthermore, while a transformation of China's party state into a liberal democracy might be unrealistic, the perception was that political liberalisation in small steps might not be and will therefore continue to happen in China. A third argument was that even if political liberalisation continues to stall, economic necessities would force Beijing to at least adopt far-reaching economic liberalisation measures, given the inefficiency of China's state sector as well as the persistent challenges in its innovation system.

Waking up to the new China challenge

Soon after Xi had taken over as General Secretary of the CCP in 2012, he deviated more and more from his predecessors' leadership style. He steered China in a more authoritarian and centralised direction and reasserted the party's firm grip on the government, the economy and society at large. Among German foreign policymakers and the business community, three events or developments in China were decisive in dashing any hopes that China's system was on a long-term trajectory towards convergence with their own system.

The first one was the 'Made in China 2025' (MiC25) strategy, published in May 2015. MiC25 is China's flagship industrial policy initiative aimed at transforming the nation into a globally competitive 'manufacturing superpower' largely independent of foreign technology (Wübbeke et al. 2016, 6). The strategy lists 10 key sectors such as information technology, robotics, maritime and railway equipment, aviation, green energy and energy-saving vehicles, machinery or medical devices. These sectors all correspond with sectors that today strongly contribute to economic growth in advanced economies, which is particularly true for Germany with its relatively industry-heavy economic structure (Ibid).

The strategy relies on a number of top-down industrial policy tools: for example, subsidies, government-backed investment funds, local government support measures, state-directed mergers and politicisation of SOEs, restrictions for foreign companies on market access and government procurement or forced technology transfers from foreign companies to name just a few (see European Union Chamber of Commerce in China (EUCCC) 2017, Chapter 5). Most of these policy tools were in common use long before. However, MiC25 represents a 'far more holistic and sophisticated approach to developing China's manufacturing base', and it came with a considerable increase in government funding (Ibid, 15).

While German companies previously understood China's industrial policy mainly as protective and supportive of a nascent domestic industry which would diminish as soon as Chinese companies became more competitive, the first years of MiC25's implementation made it clear that top-down industrial policy would continue to play a central role in China's future development strategy. This view was corroborated by a string of state-coordinated mega-mergers of central SOEs since 2015—most notably the creation of the world's largest rolling stock manufacturer CRRC—with the clear goal of creating national champions able to compete globally (see Leutert and Godement 2016, 2–3).

In the short term, MiC25 is a double-edged sword for German companies. On the one hand, demand for high-tech investment goods such as industrial robots or smart sensors has risen sharply because of the massive government-led push to modernise Chinese industry (see Zenglein and Holzmann 2019, Chapter 4; European Union Chamber of Commerce in China (EUCCC) 2017, 12). German companies offering 'Industry 4.0' solutions are particularly sought-after partners. On the other hand, foreign companies cannot participate in MiC25 as 'equal partners' and suffer from distorting industrial policy measures that favour their Chinese competitors (European Union Chamber of Commerce in China (EUCCC) 2017, 15). This will become more problematic the more those competitors close existing technology gaps.

One important issue in this respect is Chinese industrial overcapacities. In the past, this used to be a problem mostly in less technology-intensive sectors such as steel or solar panel production. In the future, serious overcapacities in high-tech sectors such as robotics with profound negative consequences for global markets are not unlikely (see Zenglein and Holzmann 2019, 23). Another major concern is the more aggressive attitude of Chinese companies in the acquisition of high-tech companies abroad, a factor often seen in connection with MiC25. Studies show that there is a strong overlap between the Chinese acquisition of companies in Germany and the EU and the 10 focus sectors of MiC25 (see for example Hanemann et al. 2019; Jungbluth 2018). The take-over of the leading German industrial robotics company KUKA by the Chinese household appliances maker Midea in 2016 was a particularly controversial case that led to many alarm bells in Germany. The German government reacted to this development by tightening rules on investment screening for national security purposes.

The second game-changing event in terms of the German political and business establishment's perception of China was the 19th party congress of the CCP in October 2017.

It was only after the 19th Party Congress that the idea of a convergence of economic systems aided by 'Wandel durch Handel' was increasingly called into question and instead the idea of a global "systemic competition" between China's model of a state-led hybrid economy and the market economic model began to take root within the German business community. An influential China paper published by the Federation of German Industries (BDI) in January 2019 entitled "Partner and systemic competitor" established the notion of a 'systemic competition' with China in the German business community. The party congress also unveiled China's growing global ambition. For the first time, China was explicitly promoting its own system as a model for other countries seeking to modernize (Tobin 2020). The role of the BRI as Xi's central foreign policy initiative is crucial in this respect and it was underlined during the congress insofar as it was written into the country's constitution (Xinhua 2017).

The BRI, then, represents the third decisive factor that brought about a change in perception regarding China's development under Xi in Germany. Due to the initiative's rather elusive and evolving nature, however, this happened gradually. German businesses were initially mainly concerned about how they would get better and fairer access to BRI projects than about its potential structural and macro-economic impact on third markets. As the following section of this chapter argues, these interpretations fundamentally misunderstand the overarching role of the BRI in China's overall foreign policy strategy and the corresponding geostrategic and geoeconomic challenges.

China's development under Xi has made it clear that all three constants of Germany's China policy—strengthening a mutually beneficial economic relationship, encouraging China's liberalisation and involving China in global problem-solving as a responsible stakeholder in the international system—are facing increased challenges. China's doubling down on its state-led economic model, represented by its flagship industrial policy plan MiC2025 and the profound changes in China's political system under Xi, both have important implications for Germany's overall China policy. The rest of this chapter will concentrate on the implications of the BRI for German China policy.

II The BRI turns 'Wandel durch Handel' on its head

On a basic level, German China policy was and continues to be directed at inducing change in China through engagement, encouragement, cooperation and dialogue—be it on market opening, strengthening the rule of law or climate policy. While this approach did deliver some successes, it seems to neglect the fact that China is less and less shaped by the world around it but is increasingly shaping the world itself—turning the concept of 'Wandel durch Handel' on its head. Xi Jinping has left Deng Xiaoping's foreign policy doctrine that China should 'bide its time and hide its capabilities' and adopted a much more assertive foreign policy. Xi sees China as 'moving closer to the centre of the world stage' (Tobin 2020). The BRI as the administration's central foreign policy initiative draws other countries closer into China's orbit by increasing trade, infrastructure, financial, policy and people-to-people connectivity.

The BRI as China's vehicle for its global vision

The significance of the BRI for China's overall foreign policy can hardly be overestimated. Major foreign policy initiatives are often directly framed as sub-strategies of the BRI (e.g. 'Digital Silk Road', 'Polar Silk Road', 'Space Silk Road'). At the same time, central national strategies for China's domestic development, in particular MiC25, explicitly refer to the BRI as the strategic framework for their external dimension (Corff 2018, 168–170).

Most observers affirm that the BRI represents more than just a massive infrastructure building project and that China also pursues wider geopolitical goals through it. Corff (2018) and others such as Clarke (2017) even argue that the BRI should in fact be regarded as (part of) China's 'grand strategy' that integrates different economic and geopolitical objectives into a long-term global strategy. As Swielande and Vandamme (2020, 4) put it: the BRI is 'Beijing's grand strategy to assert and legitimize its foreign policy objective of becoming world leader by 2049.' In her analysis of China's vision for a new world order, Rolland (2020, 48) concludes that at the core of this vague concept, drawing inspiration from traditional Chinese thought as well as from Marxist ideology, stands a rejection of the established liberal order: '[…] Beijing's vision for a new world order […] is mostly about inveighing against a Western-dominated liberal order that is deemed threatening to the CCP's survival and about altering the world to make it safer for China's unimpeded rise under the party's continuous rule'.

Challenging Germany's cooperation with China on global issues

China's global ambitions run directly counter to the idea of encouraging China to become a responsible stakeholder in the established liberal international system—which as described earlier is a long-standing goal of

German China policy. China does not outright challenge the established international order, as it benefits greatly from being part of it (see Hillmann 2020, 2). China's WTO membership is a prime example, as it assures China's access to global markets.

China instead pursues a double strategy. On the one hand, it sets up new multilateral institutions in parallel to existing ones and on the other hand, China is increasing its influence within existing institutions and trying to reshape liberal norms. China's efforts to set up new multilateral institutions, however, do not always constitute a challenge to the established order but are sometimes complementary to it. The Asian Infrastructure Investment Bank (AIIB), set up by China in 2015, is the most important example of a China-centred institution that replicates existing practices instead of revising them. Germany has joined the AIIB as a founding member and is its largest non-Asian contributor. The AIIB seems to largely adhere to the standards of established multilateral development banks and about half of the AIIB's projects are co-financed by them (Hillmann 2020, 3). However, many other institutions set up by China such as the New Development Bank (informally known as the BRICS Bank) lack a similar adherence to established global standards.

Overall, the current scale and effectiveness of China's efforts to establish new institutions are relatively limited. As Hillmann (2020, 2) notes, 'Beijing's willingness to start new institutions underscores its global ambitions and adds weight to its rhetoric about creating an alternative order. But [...] the more immediate and higher-stakes battle for influence remains within existing institutions'. A case in point is the UN Human Rights Council (HRC) where China is emerging as a pivotal player that assertively pushes its positions. The BRI plays a crucial role in this context, as it ties participating countries closer to China economically and politically. As Piccone (2018, 1) argues, 'states with important economic and political ties to Beijing are more likely to mute any criticism of China's human rights record and/or support its efforts to weaken the international human rights system'. The German government recognises this challenge. After the US left the HRC in 2018, Germany has become an increasingly important actor within the UN, pushing back against China's human rights agenda. The diplomatic efforts within the UN seem to entail relatively low political costs in Germany's relations to China. However, it should be questioned how effective this approach can remain as long as Germany continues to adhere to the approach of 'stille Diplomatie' in its bilateral relationship.

Outside of existing institutions, the BRI plays a central role in China's efforts to spread its own domestic technical standards globally. China, for example, includes cooperation mechanisms between national standardisation agencies in most of its bilateral BRI agreements. However, these cooperation mechanisms alone give countries relatively little incentives to adopt domestic Chinese standards instead of international ones. Much more meaningful is the incorporation of Chinese technical standards into concrete

BRI infrastructure projects (Rühlig 2020, 24). This could have far-reaching consequences for German companies' access to third markets. As Rühlig (2020, 28) argues, '[a]ccepting domestic Chinese standards instead of international ones comes with lock-in effects. Countries building their infrastructure on Chinese technical standards depend on Chinese manufacturers for decades to come'.

An important aspect in this discussion is played by the Digital Silk Road (DSR) component of China's BRI, which was first unveiled in a 2015 white paper. The deployment of telecom infrastructure, data centres and smart cities under the DSR has 'become the focal point of the BRI as controlling the flow of data becomes increasingly important for shifting the balance of geopolitical power in China's favor' (Kitson and Liew 2019). Projects under the DSR largely rely on Chinese technology standards and China's national tech champions, making it difficult for foreign firms 'to compete anywhere along the hardware and software value chain' (European Union Chamber of Commerce in China (EUCCC) 2017, 3).

A major focus of the DSR is 5G mobile networks. In many countries, China's 5G ambitions are increasingly viewed in terms of related national security concerns. Countries such as the US, Australia, Japan and most recently the UK have excluded Chinese suppliers from the build-up of their national 5G networks. For Germany, the question of whether or not to include Huawei (or other Chinese companies) in its 5G network has become a central focus of public debate. The Chinese government has made clear that it sees Huawei's inclusion in national 5G networks as a defining question for bilateral relations. Whatever the decision turns out to be—inclusion, exclusion or something in between—the very fact that the decision-making process is taking so long suggests the lack of strategic clarity in Germany's current China policy.

The BRI also has implications for Germany's climate cooperation agenda with China. Germany is working closely with China on climate policy through the German-Chinese climate dialogue, pushing it to set more ambitious domestic goals. However, China's national climate policy is only part of the issue. Under the BRI, China is exporting its own resource-intensive development model to other developing countries. Despite China's repeated claims to make the BRI 'greener', China is engaging massively in the expansion of fossil-fuelled energy in BRI participating countries. According to a recent report from the World Resources Institute (2018), about 75% of the US$145 billion in international loans from China's major financing institutions in BRI countries was dedicated to fossil fuel energy projects,[iii] including US$10 billion for coal plants.

Germany's evolving response to the BRI

Initially, the German government was cautiously optimistic about the BRI. It welcomed the initiative's stated aims of closing existing infrastructure gaps in Eurasia and its potentially positive effects on trade and regional economic development. A first cautious note was the fact that Chinese investment in many Central and Eastern European countries affected existing EU infrastructure initiatives such as the Trans-European Transport Network. According to Harnisch (2017, 16) it was on Germany's insistence that the EU set up a cooperative mechanism with China to avoid conflicts and realize synergies in infrastructure building. Consequently, the 2015 EU–China Connectivity Platform was created. Germany's joining of the AIIB in the same year was a relatively strong signal of support for the development goals of the BRI and for China's wider efforts to actively contribute to the further development of the multilateral order—in particular when seen in contrast to the US opposition to the AIIB.

Since then, however, the German government has grown more critical of the BRI. At the centre of its criticism is the lack of transparent access for German companies to BRI projects and their undercutting of established international social, environmental and financial standards. Germany has clearly voiced such criticism publicly at both Belt and Road Forums (BRF) in 2017 and 2019 in Beijing. At each BRF, Germany was represented by its Minister of Economic Affairs despite China's lobbying for the participation of the Chancellor—a sign of Germany's reluctance to lend full political support to the BRI. At the first BRF in 2017, Germany, together with all other EU member states, refused to sign the Forum's closing statement, since China was unwilling to include proposed language on the strict adherence of BRI projects to international standards. At the second BRF, Beijing prevented such an outcome by going without a closing statement. Instead, the Chinese Ministry of Foreign Affairs (2019) presented a list of '283 concrete results' consisting of new projects and initiatives within the BRI and a plethora of bi- and plurilateral memorandums of understanding, agreement letters, cooperation documents and declarations of intent.

In addition to objections about the general conditions of BRI projects, the German government was also critical about some of the economic and political ramifications of the BRI in the EU. Germany increasingly realised that China's initiative pursued a comprehensive geo-economic and geopolitical approach. Economically, questions have been raised about BRI projects crowding out European competitors by undermining EU rules for transparent public procurement and environmental and social standards. These issues were brought to wide attention in Germany when the European Commission in February 2017 launched an investigation into the procurement conditions of the Belgrade-Budapest high-speed railway upgrade—one of the largest BRI projects in the EU. China's political influence on EU member states that profit from BRI projects was also increasingly seen as a problem by the German government.

In 2017 the German government increasingly voiced concerns about China's so-called '17+1 initiative'[iv]. Foreign Minister Sigmar Gabriel in 2017 even called on China to adhere to a 'one Europe policy' in the same way the EU respects the one-China policy (Handelsblatt 2017). China's palpable influence on European politics and in particular on the EU's China policy through the 17+1 initiative convinced many German and other European political leaders that BRI poses a fundamental challenge to the EU. It was in this context that Germany together with France pushed the EU to step up its efforts for its own comprehensive strategy for connectivity between the EU and Asia. Consequently, in 2018, the EU adopted its 'Europe Asia Connectivity Strategy', which aims at promoting connectivity in the 'European way: sustainable, comprehensive and rules-based' (European Commission 2018, 2). The strategy is widely regarded as a direct response to the BRI. So far, however, the EU's strategy pales in comparison to China's BRI both in terms of financial muscle and branding.

The response of German companies to the BRI has been mixed. In general, larger companies have been able to leverage their business and political networks within China as well as their experience and established position in emerging markets in order to gain access to BRI projects. However, Siemens CEO Joe Kaeser, while generally quite optimistic about the BRI's economic potential, has also acknowledged that, so far, the BRI has mostly been a 'one-way street' (Süddeutsche Zeitung 2018). This sentiment is shared by many small and medium-size companies, which to a large degree, have not been able to get a foot in the door because BRI projects often lack open and transparent tenders (see European Union Chamber of Commerce in China (EUCCC) 2017, 5).

The frustration over a continued lack of transparency and access has been growing in recent years. In a survey by the German Engineering Federation (VDMA), for example, 49% of German member companies operating in China stated in 2018, that they either benefited directly or indirectly from the BRI or at least saw a potential for doing so. In 2019, this rate had shrunk to under 30% (Stüwe 2019).

Yet, perhaps a bigger problem than the BRI's lack of openness itself are the long-term effects on competition the initiative could have on third markets more broadly. In the past, market distortions arising from China's state-led economic model and its tight market access controls were mainly problems for foreign companies either active in the Chinese market or eager to enter it. With Chinese companies expanding their global economic footprint, these problems have become global as well. 'China's national champions, which emerged in China's restricted sectors, are going abroad after having achieved extraordinary economies of scale. This situation is being compounded by the fact that the BRI is providing them additional support" (European Union Chamber of Commerce in China (EUCCC) 2017, 3). BRI projects often constitute 'package deals' in which Chinese companies (mostly SOEs) in coordination with state agencies and aided by diplomatic support offer 'everything from project management, financing, materials and construction services, all the way to post-completion services' (European Union Chamber of Commerce in China (EUCCC) 2017, 2). This state-coordinated approach results in a lack of competition.

III Leaving the strategic grey zone?

The BRI exposes the geopolitical blind spots and weaknesses of Germany's China policy. As indicated above, in recent years the concepts of China as a 'responsible stakeholder' and 'Wandel durch Handel' have lost their usefulness as the theoretical underpinning of Germany's China policy. Germany seems to have entered what Barkin (2020, 6) called a 'strategic grey zone', 'aware that its largest trading partner is evolving into a bigger and brasher threat, but unwilling to test the relationship in any serious way'. To leave this strategic grey zone requires overcoming two obstacles in the way of strategic clarity vis-à-vis China—a China-specific one and a general one. The China-specific element emerges from the erosion of the old consensus among political and economic leaders about how to assess and deal with China's rise. There is a felt need to replace the vestiges of the old consensus, but a new one has yet to emerge. In this respect, four groups with diverging views about China are identifiable.

First, there are those who still hold onto the notion of 'Wandel durch Handel', believing that China's leadership will eventually return to the reform path. This view often goes hand in hand with an overconfidence in the effectiveness of liberal political and economic systems and results in a certain naivety in dealing with China. It seems to remain particularly strong among some business leaders, many academics in natural science and political leaders of local communities. But even the Minister of Economic Affairs, Peter Altmaier, while certainly not blind to the challenges China poses, displays a continued belief in the concept of 'Wandel durch Handel': 'I have always been convinced and I still believe that change can be achieved through trade' (Karnitschnig and Vela 2020).

The second group presumes a more opportunistic attitude. They are convinced that China's rise is inevitable and that the new superpower will define the terms of future cooperation and the setting of international standards. The faster political and business leaders adapt to this new world, it is assumed, the better it will be. This conviction is often combined with an overgenerous admiration for China's achievements, for the speed and consistency of its decision-making and its assertiveness. This view is supported by very different parts of society such as the business community, the political left—where some relate to China's rhetoric about leading the developing world against the capitalist West—and the populist right—where some admire Xi Jinping's strongman politics. Some even regard the Chinese authoritarian political system as superior to the complex, slow and continuously challenged democracies of the West.

The third group contains those who see China both as a systemic competitor and as an indispensable economic partner at the same time—as BDI titled its respective paper of January 2019. The systemic challenge posed by China would require Germany and the EU to promote their own strengths especially regarding innovation and competitiveness, to shield their political system from unacceptable interference and manipulation, protect their economic system against state-capitalistic influences, to pursue a united and coherent European approach and to find partners in dealing with China multilaterally. Both the European Commission and the European business umbrella group BusinessEurope published strategy papers that are very much in line with this approach. The Commission's 'strategic outlook' published in March 2019 was a particularly important milestone in the European China debate, as it was the first time that the Commission used the label 'systemic rival' to describe China. The Commission, however, also emphasised the need for a balanced and multipronged approach: 'China is, simultaneously, in different policy areas, a cooperation partner with whom the EU has closely aligned objectives, a negotiating partner with whom the EU needs to find a balance of interests, an economic competitor in the pursuit of technological leadership, and a systemic rival promoting alternative models of governance' (European Commission 2019, 1). The view of China as both a systemic rival and an economic partner has gained widespread support among Germany's political and business establishment.

The fourth group still represents a clear minority but is gaining in strength: they share the perception of China as a systemic rival—a rivalry that is fundamentally incompatible with deep economic partnership and cooperation. It can only be dealt with by decoupling China's economy more and more from global value chains in order to slow down its economic and technological rise. This approach seems to increasingly shape American strategic thinking and has been relatively marginal in Germany and Europe until recently. But it is gaining ground in European capitals, especially in the context of debates about the national security implications of technological exchange and integration with China and because of the increasing use of coercive diplomacy by Beijing.

Germany's fractured China debate might explain the lack of an explicit China strategy on the part of its government, but it also follows a decades-long reluctance to develop and submit comprehensive strategy papers. The few which exist deal with issues and regions that, compared to China, have played a less prominent role in German foreign policy: sub-Saharan Africa, Latin America, Central Asia. The 'Policy Guidelines on the Indo-Pacific' published in September 2020 constitute a long overdue deviation from this rule. They delineate Germany's strategic approach to the key region 'shaping the international order in the 21st century', as the document states (Auswärtiges Amt 2020b). However, the guidelines fail to explicitly acknowledge and comprehensively address the systemic challenge posed by China. There is an unwillingness to state openly the objectives of the German government in dealing with its major partners, be they in Europe, the US or China. German foreign policymakers usually refrain from committing and binding themselves to clearly stated objectives for fear of affronting partners, reducing diplomatic flexibility and making the success of their policies measurable. The best indication outside observers might acquire of the German government's China strategy is the latter's tacit support for the BDI's China paper and for the European Commission's strategic outlook on China. The German government has indicated that it generally supports the European Commission's approach to China, but it has so far refrained from publicly embracing the label 'systemic rival'.

Conclusion

The three long-standing goals of Germany's China policy—strengthening a mutually beneficial economic relationship, encouraging China's liberalisation and involving China as a responsible stakeholder in the international order—are being increasingly challenged by a more assertive and outward-looking China. With the BRI, Beijing emerges as a strategic global actor that shapes markets, norms and institutions far beyond its borders. The German business and foreign policy establishment has, by and large, realised the existence of this challenge, but a consensus on a clear strategy of how to deal with it has yet to emerge. German China policy is in need of a strategic rethink.

This is not to argue against engagement, cooperation and dialogue with China. On the contrary, in a highly inter-connected world engaging and cooperating with the second-largest economy that harbours almost one fifth of the global population remains very much in Germany's strategic interest. An aggressive confrontational policy that aims at comprehensive economic and technological decoupling from China entails enormous costs and risks. As Kevin Rudd (Lawler 2019) put it: 'A fully "decoupled world" would be a deeply destabilizing place, undermining the global growth assumptions of the last 40 years, heralding the return of an iron curtain between East and West and the beginning of a new conventional and nuclear arms race with all its attendant strategic instability and risk'. The strategic rethink of Germany's China policy should thus not be about the question of whether or not to engage China, but about the basic mode of engagement. Instead of unconditionally engaging with China, engagement should be conditioned in a way that ensures alignment with Germany's and the EU's values and long-term strategic interests. This might include heeding the principle of reciprocity, drawing clear red lines and assertively standing up for one's values and interests, even if it comes with economic costs and short-term setbacks in the political relationship with China. A more principled stance on values and long-term interests will have to entail a greater tolerance for short-term conflict.

Notes

i Chancellor Willy Brandt, 1969–1973.

ii In the official English translation titled: 'Shaping Globalization – Expanding Partnerships – Sharing Responsibility'.

iii The study does not indicate how many of these projects were officially labelled as BRI projects. However, one can assume that most large-scale Chinese infrastructure projects in countries that participate in the BRI are in fact labelled as BRI projects.
iv The '17+1 initiative' (formerly 16+1) is a cooperation framework China set up in 2012 initially with 16 Central and Eastern European countries among them both EU and non-EU members. In 2019, Greece became the 17th member of the initiative.

Bibliography

Auswärtiges Amt, (2002). *Asia at the Beginning of the 21st Century: Tasks for German Foreign Policy* [online]. May 2002, Berlin. [Accessed 10 July 2020]. Available from: https://www.auswaertiges-amt.de/blob/231800/756f9f7a0ea08ba707759d3b052e6682/konzeptostasien-data.pdf.

Auswärtiges Amt, (2012). *Shaping Globalization – Expanding Partnerships – Sharing Responsibility: A Strategy Paper by the German Government* [online]. Berlin. [Accessed 10 July 2020]. Available from: https://www.auswaertiges-amt.de/blob/610644/49a58b5ecfd5a78862b051d94465afb6/gestaltungsmaechtekonzept-engl-data.pdf.

Auswärtiges Amt, (2020a). *Deutschland und China: Bilaterale Beziehungen* [Germany and China: bilateral relations] [online]. 5 March 2020, Berlin. [Accessed 10 July 2020]. Available from: https://www.auswaertiges-amt.de/de/aussenpolitik/laender/china-node/bilateral/200472.

Auswärtiges Amt, (2020b). Policy Guidelines for the Indo-Pacific [online]. September 2020, Berlin. [Accessed 20 May 2021]. Available from: https://www.auswaertiges-amt.de/blob/2380514/f9784f7e3b3fa1bd7c5446d274a4169e/200901-indo-pazifik-leitlinien--1--data.pdf

Barkin, N., (2020). *Germany's Strategic Gray Zone With China* [online]. March 2020, Carnegie Endowment for International Peace. [Accessed 28 July 2020]. Available from: https://carnegieendowment.org/files/Barkin_Germany_China_Policy.pdf.

Clarke, M., (2017). The Belt and Road Initiative: China's New Grand Strategy? *Asia Policy* [online]. (24) 71–79. [Accessed 14 July 2020]. Available from: doi: 10.1353/asp.2017.0023.

Corff, O., (2018). Chinas Seidenstraßeninitiative: Anatomie einer Leitstrategie [China's Silk Road initiative: anatomy of a guidance strategy]. Clausewitz-Gesellschaft Jahrbuch, 164–176 [online]. Clausewitz-Gesellschaft e.V, Hamburg, [Accessed 14 July 2020]. Available from: https://static.clausewitz-gesellschaft.de/wp-content/uploads/2019/04/Clausewitz-Jahrbuch-2018.pdf.

European Commission, (2018). *Connecting Europe and Asia - Building Blocks for an EU Strategy.* Joint Communication to the European Parliament, the Council, the European Economic and Social Committee, the Committee of the Regions and the European Investment Bank [online]. 19 September 2019. [Accessed 29 July 2020]. Available from: https://eeas.europa.eu/sites/eeas/files/joint_communication_-_connecting_europe_and_asia_-_building_blocks_for_an_eu_strategy_2018-09-19.pdf.

European Commission, (2019). *EU-China – A Strategic Outlook.* Joint Communication to the European Parliament, the European Council and the Council [online]. 12 March 2019. [Accessed 29 July 2020]. Available from: https://

ec.europa.eu/commission/sites/beta-political/files/communication-eu-china-a-strategic-outlook.pdf.

European Union Chamber of Commerce in China (EUCCC), (2017). *The Road Less Travelled: European involvement in China's Belt and Road Initiative* [online]. [Accessed 12 July 2020]. Available from: https://static.europeanchamber.com.cn/upload/documents/documents/The_Road_Less_Travelled[762].pdf.

Handelsblatt, (2017). Gabriel warnt Europäer vor Spaltung durch China [Gabriel warns Europeans about division by China]. *Handelsblatt* [online]. 30 August 2017. [Accessed 7 July 2020]. Available from: https://www.handelsblatt.com/politik/international/europaeische-union-gabriel-warnt-europaeer-vor-spaltung-durch-china/20260368.html?ticket=ST-12086370-zldBNhTWeusIkmW3JIO9-ap1.

Hanemann, T., Huotari, M. and Kratz, A., (2019). *Chinese FDI in Europe: 2018 Trends and Impact of New Screening Policies*. MERICS Papers on China [online]. March 2019, Mercator Institute for China Studies (MERICS), Berlin, [Accessed 12 July 2020]. Available from: https://merics.org/en/report/chinese-fdi-europe-2018-trends-and-impact-new-screening-policies.

Harnisch, S., (2017). *Deutschlands Politik gegenüber der Belt-and-Road-Initiative der Volksrepublik China 2013–2018* [Germany's Policy towards the Belt-and-Road Initiative of the People's Republic of China 2013–2018] [online]. 4 December 2017, Universität Heidelberg. [Accessed 29 July 2020]. Available from: https://www.uni-heidelberg.de/md/politik/harnisch/person/publikationen/harnisch_deutschlands_reaktion_auf_die_seidenstrasseninitiativen_zeitschrift_asien.pdf.

Hauschild, H. et al., (2015). *China – Partner und Konkurrent: Eine Analyse der deutsch-chinesischen Handelsbeziehungen* [China - Partner and Competitor: An Analysis of German-Chinese Trade Relations] [online]. Gütersloh: Bertelsmann Stiftung. [Accessed 7 July 2020]. Available from: https://www.bertelsmann-stiftung.de/de/publikationen/publikation/did/china-partner-und-konkurrent/.

Hillmann, J., (2020). *A 'China Model?' Beijing's Promotion of Alternative Global Norms and Standards*. Statement before the U.S. - China Economic and Security Review Commission [online]. 13 March 2020, Center for Strategic and International Studies (CSIS). [Accessed 28 July 2020]. Available from: https://csis-website-prod.s3.amazonaws.com/s3fs-public/congressional_testimony/ts200413_Jonathan_Hillman.pdf.

Huang, Y., (2019). *Die Chinapolitik der Bundesrepublik Deutschland nach der Wiedervereinigung: ein Balanceakt zwischen Werten und Interessen* [Germany's China policy after reunification: a balancing act between values and interests]. Springer Vs, Springer Fachmedien Wiesbaden, Wiesbaden.

Huotari, M., (2015). Germany's China policy: No honeymoon forever. Mapping Europe-China Relations: A Bottom-Up Approach [online]. pp. 30–35. European Think-tank Network on China (ETNC). [Accessed 7 July 2020]. Available from: https://www.ifri.org/sites/default/files/atoms/files/etnc_web_final_1-1.pdf.

International Monetary Fund (IMF), (2020). *China: Gross Domestic Product Based on Purchasing-Power-Parity (PPP) Share of World Total (Percent)* [online data set]. [Accessed 7 July 2020]. Available from: https://www.imf.org/external/pubs/ft/weo/2019/02/weodata/weorept.aspx?sy=1991&ey=2024&scsm=1&ssd=1&sort=country&ds=.&br=1&c=924&s=PPPSH&grp=0&a=&pr.x=89&pr.y=9.

Jungbluth, C., (2018). *Is China Systematically Buying Up Key Technologies?: Chinese M & A Transactions in Germany in the Context of "Made in China 2025"*. GED

Papers [online]. 2018, Bertelsmann Stiftung, Gütersloh, [Accessed 12 July 2020]. Available from: https://www.bertelsmann-stiftung.de/fileadmin/files/BSt/Publikationen/GrauePublikationen/MT_Is_China_Systematically_Buying_Up_Key_Technologies.pdf.

Karnitschnig, M. and Vela, J., (2020). Germany's economy minister defends Berlin's muted response to China's crackdown in Hong Kong. *Politico* [online]. 15 July 2020. [Accessed 28 July 2020]. Available from: https://www.politico.com/news/2020/07/15/germany-hong-kong-china-365499.

Kitson, A., and Liew, K., (2019). *China Doubles Down on Its Digital Silk Road* [online]. 14 November 2019, Center for Strategic and International Studies (CSIS). [Accessed 28 July 2020]. Available from: https://reconnectingasia.csis.org/analysis/entries/china-doubles-down-its-digital-silk-road/.

Kundnani, H., (2015). *The Paradox of German Power*. 1st ed. Oxford University Press, New York.

Kroeber, A., (2016). China's Economy: What Everyone Needs to Know. Oxford University Press, New York.

Lawler, D., (2019). The great U.S.-China "decoupling" dilemma. *Axios* [online]. 11. November 2019. [Accessed 28 July 2020]. Available from: https://amp.axios.com/kevin-rudd-decoupling-us-china-trump-xi-jinping-d7f6797f-8a94–4450-8447-583a4023bfa8.html.

Leutert, W. and Godement, F., (2016). *Big Is Beautiful? State-Owned Enterprise Mergers Under Xi Jinping*. China Analysis, Special Issue [online]. November 2016, European Council on Foreign Relations (ECFR). [Accessed 12 July 2020]. Available from: https://www.ecfr.eu/page/-/China_Analysis_–_Big_is_Beautiful.pdf.

Martina, M., (2017). Exclusive: In China, the Party's Push for Influence Inside Foreign Firms Stirs Fears. *Reuters* [online]. 24 August 2017. [Accessed 12 July 2020]. Available from: https://www.reuters.com/article/us-china-congress-companies/exclusive-in-china-the-partys-push-for-influence-inside-foreign-firms-stirs-fears-idUSKCN1B40JU.

Ministry of Foreign Affairs of the PRC, (2019). *List of Deliverables of the Second Belt and Road Forum for International Cooperation* [online]. 27 April 2019. [Accessed 29 July 2020]. Available from: https://www.fmprc.gov.cn/mfa_eng/zxxx_662805/t1658767.shtml.

Piccone, T., (2018). *China's Long Game on Human Rights at the United Nations* [online]. Brookings, Washington, [Accessed 28 July 2020]. Available from: https://www.brookings.edu/wp-content/uploads/2018/09/FP_20181009_china_human_rights.pdf.

Rolland, N., (2020). *China's Vision for a New World Order* NBR special report (83) [online]. January 2020, The National Bureau of Asian Research. [Accessed 28 July 2020]. Available from: https://www.nbr.org/wp-content/uploads/pdfs/publications/sr83_chinasvision_jan2020.pdf.

Rühlig, T., (2020). *Technical Standardisation, China and the Future International Order: A European Perspective* [online]. March 2020, Heinrich Böll Stiftung. [Accessed 29 July 2020]. Available from: https://eu.boell.org/sites/default/files/2020-03/HBS-Techn%20Stand-A4%20web-030320-1.pdf.

Stüwe, H., (2019). Offene Märkte stehen in Asien weiter hoch im Kurs [Open markets remain high on the agenda in Asia]. *Germany Trade and Invest (GTAI)* [online]. [Accessed 28 July 2020]. Available from: https://www.gtai.de/gtai-de/

meta/ueber-uns/was-wir-tun/schwerpunkte/offene/offene-maerkte-stehen-in-asien-weiter-hoch-im-kurs-19780.

Süddeutsche Zeitung, (2018). Jenseits der Seidenstraße. *Süddeutsche Zeitung* [Beyond the Silkroad] [online]. 4 November 2018. [Accessed 29 July 2020]. Available from: https://www.sueddeutsche.de/wirtschaft/geschaefte-in-fernost-jenseits-der-seiden-strasse-1.4195961.

Swielande, T. and Vandamme, D., (2020). The new Silk Roads: Defining China's Grand Strategy. In: F. Leandro and P. Duarte, eds. *The Belt and Road Initiative: An Old Archetype of a New Development Model.* Palgrave Macmillan, Singapore. pp. 3–22.

Tobin, D., (2020). *How Xi Jinping's "New Era" Should Have Ended U.S. Debate on Beijing's Ambitions* [online]. Center for Strategic and International Studies (CSIS). [Accessed 12 July 2020]. Available from: https://csis-website-prod.s3.amazonaws.com/s3fs-public/publication/200508_Tobin_NewEra_v4%5B2%5D.pdf.

Wirtschaftswoche, (2017). Deutsche Firmen warnen vor Einfluss von Parteizellen. Wirtschaftswoche [German companies warn against the influence of party cells.], [online]. 27 November 2017. [Accessed 12 July 2020]. Available from: https://www.wiwo.de/politik/ausland/china-deutsche-firmen-warnen-vor-einfluss-von-parteizellen/20635426.html.

World Bank Group, (2020). *GDP growth (annual %) – China* [online data set]. [Accessed 7 July 2020]. Available from: https://data.worldbank.org/indicator/NY.GDP.MKTP.KD.ZG?end=2011&locations=CN&start=1991&view=chart.

World Resources Institute, (2018). *Will China Seize the Biggest Green Opportunity of the Coming Decade?* [online]. 8 November 2018, World Resources Institute [Accessed 29 July 2020]. Available from: https://www.wri.org/blog/2018/11/will-china-seize-biggest-green-opportunity-coming-decade.

Wübbeke, J. et al., (2016). *Made in China 2025: The Making of a High-Tech Superpower and Consequences for Industrial Countries.* MERICS Papers on China [online]. December 2016, Mercator Institute for China Studies, Berlin. [Accessed 12 July 2020]. Available from: https://merics.org/en/report/made-china-2025.

Xinhua, (2017). "Belt and Road" Incorporated into CPC Constitution. *Xinhua* [online]. 24 October 2017. [Accessed 12 July 2020]. Available from: http://www.xinhuanet.com/english/2017-10/24/c_136702025.htm.

Zenglein, M. and Holzmann, A., (2019). *Evolving Made in China 2025: China's Industrial Policy in the Quest for Global Tech Leadership.* MERICS Papers on China [online]. July 2019, Mercator Institute for China Studies, Berlin. [Accessed 12 July 2020]. Available from: https://merics.org/en/report/evolving-made-china-2025.

12 Greece between crisis, opportunity and risk as a key BRI node

Dimitri Kokoromytis and Angelos Chryssogelos

Introduction

By focusing on the case of Greece, this chapter aims to demonstrate a) the impact of the Belt and Road Initiative (BRI) on the European Union (EU), b) the opportunities for cooperation and the challenges of competition of Chinese and EU actors partaking in the BRI, and c) whether the EU is engaging, or should engage, with the BRI at a pan-European level, as Member States, or in other configurations. First, the chapter opens with the background of Sino-Greek relations as established since 1972. Then it assesses Chinese objectives regarding the BRI and how they translate in the Mediterranean and the Balkans. Then it discusses the expectations Greece has from China and explores how economics and politics impact the Chinese presence in Greece. Finally, the chapter places Sino-Greek relations within the EU context.

Background of Greek-Chinese relations

Sino-Greek relations in their current form began in 1972, when the then Greek military dictatorship decided to *de-recognize* the Republic of China (Taiwan) and recognize the People's Republic of China (PRC) as the sole government of China. A Greek embassy was established in Beijing on November 17, 1972 (Ministry of Foreign Affairs: Hellenic Republic n.d.).

After a group of Greek army colonels launched a *coup d'état* in 1967, the Greek junta found itself isolated from Western Europe. The Greek junta started opening to its Balkan neighboring countries (including Albania), the Communist bloc, and African countries, embodying the military leaders' supposedly pro-Third World proclivities and the need for international acceptance (Chourchoulis, Koumas, and Panoutsopoulos 2020, 71–72). The rapprochement with Albania facilitated the warming of relations with China, because the former was a *de facto* ally of the latter (Ibid; Chourchoulis 2019, 64). Nixon's visit to Beijing expedited the normalization of Sino-Greek relations. At the same time, China had reversed course in the wake of the Cultural Revolution and decided to break its isolation from the international system in which Beijing had condemned itself.

The Turkish invasion in Cyprus in 1974 made Greek politicians realize that the threat from the Warsaw Pact was not as imminent as the one from Turkey. The pursuit of a multilateral foreign policy after the restoration of democracy in July 1974, and the inaction of NATO in the Turkish invasion in Cyprus, motivated Greece to further improve relations with the socialist countries in the Balkans, break the impasse with the Soviet Union, strengthen ties to Western Europe, and deepen its relations with China.

Consequently, Sino-Greek relations improved considerably but without delivering what Greece had hoped. Beijing encouraged Greece's application for membership in the European Economic Community. However, due to its underdeveloped economy, China prioritized trade relations with the developed economies of the United States, Western Europe, and Japan at the expense of economies such as that of Greece (Chourchoulis 2019, 74).

The first term of the Panhellenic Socialist Movement (PASOK) government (1981–5) saw a hiatus in the Sino-Greek relationship, as Athens paid lip service to the sensitivities of the Greek Communist Party (KKE) and other leftists who considered China an aggressive power against the Soviet Union. PASOK's second term (1985–9) saw an exchange of visits between political leaders of Greece and China that cleared mutual suspicions. Nonetheless, the events in Tiananmen Square and the crackdown on student protests froze Sino-Greek relations again (Chourchoulis 2019, 76–81). Greece followed the cues from other European Community members whose relations with China thawed by the mid-1990s.

Since the normalization of relations, Sino-Greek relations have mostly focused on trade and economics. Greece's geographic position at the crossroads of southeastern Europe, western Asia, and North Africa, and its proximity to the Suez Canal have made the country a transportation hub over land and sea.

Until recently, this strengthening of Sino-Greek relations did not raise eyebrows among Greeks and non-Greeks alike. However, economic relations have of course not been without challenges. The economic sanctions the West imposed on China after the crackdown in Tiananmen Square and the 2010 Greek debt crisis both dented increasing trade between the two countries (see Figures 12.1 and 12.2).

In the first case, the use of economic statecraft was counterproductive because it hurt international trade without achieving the Western goals of affecting the Chinese government's stance towards dissidents and reformists—an outcome congruent with the literature on economic sanctions (Baldwin 1985; Chan and Drury 2000; Drezner 1999). In the second case, Greek companies had difficulties exporting to the Chinese market because of the dire situation of Greece's banking system that could not meet the need for capital during the debt crisis. Chinese or other foreign banks had to step in to finance Greek commerce. Handing part of Greek exports to

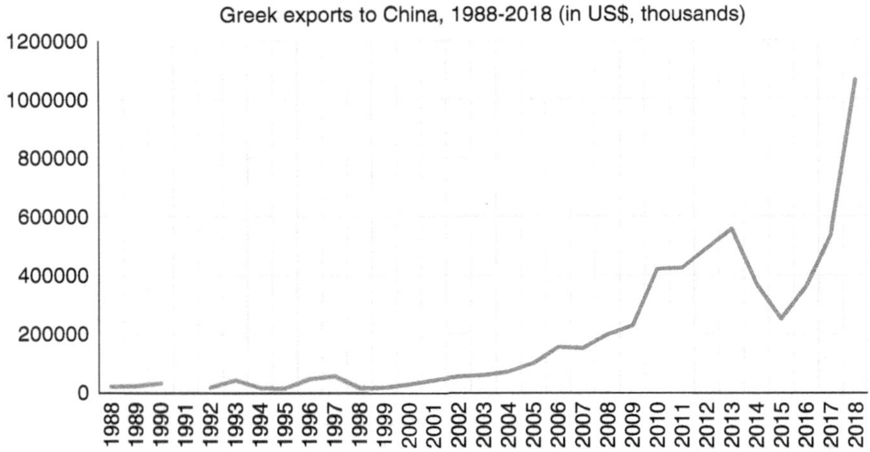

Figure 12.1 Greek exports to China, 1988–2018 (in US$). Source: World Integrated Trade Solution, https://wits.worldbank.org/CountryProfile/en/Country/GRC/StartYear/1988/EndYear/2018/TradeFlow/Export/Partner/CHN/Indicator/XPRT-TRD-VL

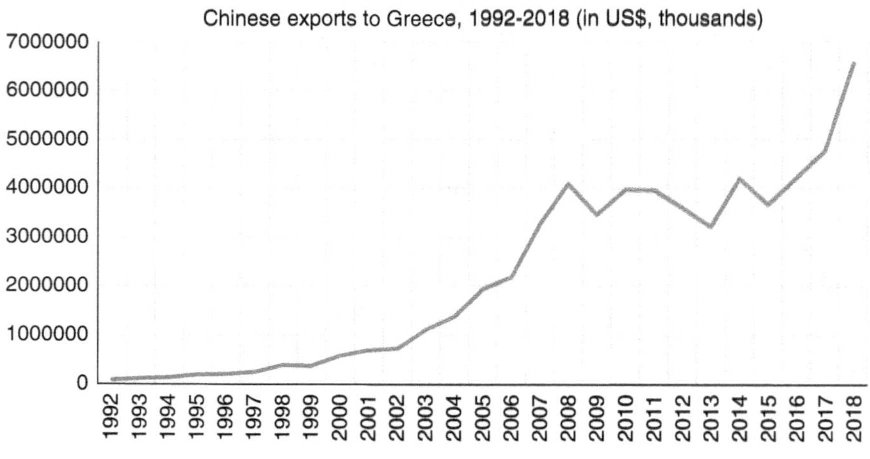

Figure 12.2 Chinese exports to Greece, 1992–2018 (in US$). Source: World Integrated Trade Solution, https://wits.worldbank.org/CountryProfile/en/Country/CHN/StartYear/1992/EndYear/2018/TradeFlow/Export/Partner/GRC/Indicator/XPRT-TRD-VL#

foreign capital created uncertainties and vulnerability, especially when businesses had to borrow in foreign currency. Nevertheless, the vast Chinese market provided opportunities for Greek businesses. The political climate in

Athens has overall been conducive to Chinese investments in Greece with some limits inherent in Greeks' attitude towards foreign investments and entrepreneurship in general.

Despite economic considerations, there are constants in Greek foreign policy since the beginning of the 20th century that neither Greece nor China could afford to ignore. Greece's orientation to the West has been quintessential for its political and economic development. However, Greek policymakers entertained the idea, from time to time, of reorienting Greek foreign policy away from the West. Eventually, the anti-Americanism of the 1980s failed to detach Greece from the West (Litsas 2017, 9). But the West's financial crisis that engulfed the EU and Greece has left Greeks questioning the country's place in the world. The question then is whether the current political and economic context provides opportunities for increased Chinese influence on Greek foreign policy. What topics may lead to an alignment between the two countries? And conversely, are there any foreign policy issues that could derail Sino-Greek relations?

BRI objectives and the Mediterranean/Balkans region

The essence of the Belt and Road Initiative (BRI) is the construction of viable economic belts, including a land 'belt' stretching from China through Central Asia, West Asia, the Middle East reaching Europe, and a maritime 'road' starting from the Chinese ports linking the Indian Ocean and ending in the Mediterranean Sea (Li 2019a, 6).

Chinese discourse has resisted the representation of the BRI as a 'Chinese Marshall Plan' citing three points: a) the Marshall Plan was a US-led effort to curtail Soviet expansionism in Europe and Asia; b) the BRI has no apparent political or military agenda; and c) BRI has no political strings attached (Li 2019a, 12). However these points can be countered: a) the BRI is a Chinese-led effort to overcome the US containment strategy targeting China; b) the BRI seems to be accompanied by the venturing out of the Chinese navy as it tries to transform into a blue water navy (Len 2015; Ploberger 2017; Wang 2016); and c) as cases in Kenya and Sri Lanka (Abi-Habib 2018; Niba 2019) have demonstrated, BRI loan terms can be onerous, leading to ownership change of the infrastructure to Chinese interests. In sum, the launch of the BRI signifies the ambition of China to shift from a rule-follower to a rule-shaper (Li 2019b).

To reach Europe, China relies on the China-Mongolia-Russia Corridor, the New Eurasian Land Bridge, the China-Central Asia-West Asia Corridor, and the Maritime Silk Road (Grieger 2016). The BRI converges on the Eastern Mediterranean over land and by sea. The China-Central Asia-West Africa Corridor ends up in Istanbul, while the Maritime Silk Road creates a hub at Piraeus on its way to the endpoint of Venice. In light of this, the Eastern Mediterranean and the Balkans are of interest to China because they are the starting point connecting the BRI to Central and

Eastern Europe. The alternatives to connecting to these countries are the China-Mongolia-Russia Corridor and the New Eurasian Land Bridge. What is more, the enlargement of the Suez Canal makes the Mediterranean a prime route of commerce because it reduces the transit time between Asia and Europe, making the Mediterranean ports more critical.

Greek expectations from China

On January 19, 2006, the center-right New Democracy-led Greek government signed with China the Joint Communiqué on the Establishment of Comprehensive Strategic Partnership (USC US-China Institute 2006). This communiqué signaled the significant upgrade of Sino-Greek relations and the success of persistent lobbying by the Greek shipping industry, which favored closer economic relations with China (Huliaras and Petropoulos 2014). At that time, Greece wanted to become a gateway for Chinese products to the Balkans and the rest of Europe. An implicit hope was that Chinese products would be assembled in Greece before getting shipped to their final destination. Additionally, the Greek merchant fleet could transport Chinese goods to international markets, while Greece could export high-quality agricultural products to the Chinese market. Gradually, Chinese investment in Greece concentrated in transport infrastructure, energy, telecommunications, and increasingly in real estate and tourism (Tonchev and Davarinou 2017, 16). In 2008, China Ocean Shipping Co (COSCO), a Chinese state-owned enterprise, acquired a 35-year lease of two container terminals (Piers II and III) in Piraeus from the Greek government (Huliaras and Petropoulos 2014; Stamouli, 2016a).

The Eurozone crisis hit the EU periphery hard and Greece the hardest when the country had to sign, in 2010, a bailout agreement with painful conditions with its EU creditors. As part of the bailout conditions, the PASOK government announced its plans to privatize public property in April 2011. COSCO succeeded in the bidding process for the 51% of the Piraeus Port Authority (PPA) and gained permission to build and operate a third terminal.

Following the imposition of crippling austerity measures, the cash-strapped Greek economy was in great need of new investments in order to build new and upgrade existing infrastructure and to reduce unemployment. In this context came the investment in the Port of Piraeus that has drawn much attention, as a major Chinese investment in an EU country involving a major transportation hub. In his 2014 visit to Athens, the Chinese Premier Li Keqiang described the Port of Piraeus as ‘a pearl in the Mediterranean Sea’, vowing that COSCO will make it ‘one of the most competitive ports of the world’ (BBC News 2014).

The Chinese government and companies appeared to have a comprehensive plan to invest in infrastructure. Despite COSCO’s failure to win the tender for the Greek national railway due to the European Commission’s objections over creating a transportation monopoly, another Chinese company, China State Grid International Development, acquired 24% of Greece's Independent Power Transmission Operator in 2016 (Tonchev and Davarinou 2017, 18–20). Chinese companies have also been very active in renewable energy projects, most prominently Shenhua, which has invested in four wind parks in Thrace, Evia, the Peloponnese, and Crete (Ibid). In the telecommunication sector, cooperation has focused mainly on research and development, paving the way for a partnership between Chinese telecom giants and Greek service providers, in the form of share acquisition by the Chinese companies (Ibid).

Economic dimensions of Chinese investments in Greece

The most prominent story capturing peoples' imagination regarding China's entry to Greece has unambiguously been the investment in Piraeus by COSCO. It has been presented variously as a story of success (Alderman 2012), mixed feelings (Stamouli 2016a), grievance (Horowitz and Alderman 2017), and envy and anxiety (van der Putten 2014).

The COSCO-owned container terminals operate differently than the pier belonging to the Greek-owned terminal. Pressured by the debt crisis and austerity, successive Greek governments loosened the tight labor regulations that protected workers and unions. As early as 2011, COSCO handled 1.05 million containers (or 1.7 million 20-foot Equivalent Units—TEU), 2.7 million TEU in 2012, 3.471 million TEU in 2016, and 5.65 million TEU in 2019 (Alderman 2012; Glass 2020; van der Putten 2014). COSCO also plans to build a fourth pier increasing the total capacity of the Piraeus Port Authority (PPA), which the Chinese company owns since 2016 after offering €368.5 million for a 51% stake, contingent on additional investments—to 10.3 million TEU (Stamouli 2016a; Glass 2019). The privatization of the PPA was supposed to be completed by 2021, conditional on mandatory investments up to €300 million. Upon fulfillment of this condition in 2021 by paying an additional amount of €88 million to the Hellenic Republic Asset Development Fund (HRADF), COSCO will increase its stake to 67% (Hellenic Republic Asset Development Fund 2016; Liu and Davarinou 2019, 109). The involvement and investments of COSCO at the Piraeus port have significantly increased its importance in the Mediterranean, making it 'the faster [sic] growing container port in the world, the second largest in the Mediterranean, and the seventh largest in Europe' (Liu and Davarinou 2019, 111).

There have been optimistic projections of the medium-term impact of the PPA privatization. In a 2016 study, the Foundation for Economic and Industrial Research stated that 'the level of GDP would be higher by 0.8% in 2025', '[t]he demand factors related to construction works and the operation of the port create more than 31,000 new jobs overall', and 'the investment in the port contributes to a long-term reduction of public debt by 2.3

percentage points of GDP' (Foundation for Economic and Industrial Research 2016, 4).

A side-effect of COSCO's presence in Piraeus is the spillover effect for other businesses directly or indirectly related to the freight industry (Meunier 2015). COSCO stabilized its position in Piraeus by investing capital, modernizing idle infrastructure, installing new loading cranes, and expanding the container terminal, planning to place Piraeus on par with Rotterdam, Antwerp, and Hamburg in terms of capacity (Granitsas and Paris 2014).

There are some indications that COSCO's increased interest in the logistics sector, the tourism industry, and recreation may create friction between the company and the local community, which sees such activities as an infringement on local interests (Glass 2019; Liu and Davarinou 2019). Chinese companies investing in Greece caused concerns about social dumping, environmental degradation, and labor rights. These fears have not yet materialized.

Beyond these domains, Chinese investments in telecommunications across the globe have come under scrutiny from the US, the EU, and other authorities. Such a development could not leave Chinese investments in the Greek telecommunications industry out of controversy. While Chinese telecommunication companies started cooperating with Greek companies, the US and the EU started pushing back. This pressure led Cosmote (the largest telecommunication company owned by Deutsche Telecom) to join other companies in the European telecommunication market, such as Telefonica in Spain and O2 in the UK, to part ways with ZTE (Mandravelis 2020; Reuters 2017; The Week 2020).

Political dimensions of Chinese investments in Greece

Worried observers should view the reception of Chinese investments in Greece from the perspective of a country whose creditors forced it to open up and privatize public corporations, traditionally a suspect process for both the Greek political class and people. It is against this backdrop that Greeks responded positively to COSCO and other Chinese investments. It is worth remembering that at the beginning of the 2000s, it was common for Greek businesspeople to worry about Chinese-owned shops popping up in downtown Athens. This created trepidation that 'the Chinese will swarm the Greek market' with cheap, low-quality products. Nonetheless, the economic crisis and China's constructive interaction with Greece changed Greek perceptions. As a result, Greeks viewed China more favorably than other Europeans did (Tonchev and Davarinou 2017).

The start of the privatization process in 2014, under the New Democracy-PASOK coalition government led by then Prime Minister Samaras, was met with resistance from pressure groups and leftist parties like the Coalition of the Radical Left (SYRIZA) and the Greek Communist Party (KKE), which felt that the Greek state was ceding parts of its sovereignty to foreigners. Moreover, SYRIZA found common ground with the populist, right-wing party Independent Greeks (ANEL), thanks to their rejection of the austerity program and anti-globalization rhetoric (Tonchev and Davarinou 2017).

In crisis-era elections, SYRIZA and KKE performed well in the districts that comprise the Piraeus port and the nearby shipbuilding zone. This excellent electoral performance made leftist politicians receptive to the objections of local trade unions that rightly feared that they would lose privileges emanating from strict labor laws. COSCO wanted to take over Pier II free of obligations. COSCO executives felt that Greek labor laws were overly strict, stifled effectiveness, and prevented competition with other ports in the Mediterranean and Northern Europe (Alderman 2012). The Chinese company started upgrading the infrastructure by bringing in new machinery and hiring non-unionized workers through a third-party employment agency pitting itself against dockworkers (Meunier 2015; van der Putten 2014).

Following the January 2015 elections, SYRIZA formed a new government with ANEL as its junior coalition partner. Following an adventurous renegotiation of bailout terms with the Eurozone, the government led by Alexis Tsipras relented and accepted a third adjustment program that renewed Greece's commitment to privatizations. Soon, however, SYRIZA ministers started dragging their feet and tried to undermine what the SYRIZA-ANEL government had agreed to in the summer of 2015, leading to a momentary stalling of the privatization program (Stamouli 2016b). New Democracy returned to power in 2019 with an aggressively pro-free market leadership favoring further privatizations of state assets. It will be interesting to see how the relaunching of privatizations will interplay with relations with China, given the party's leadership is also strongly pro-European and its leading elites traditionally harbor close relations with the US.

Greece-China relations in a European context

Chinese companies started investing in Europe well before Xi Jinping announced the BRI in 2013 (Ministry of Foreign Affairs: People's Republic of China 2013). Since 2000, China has invested in sectors and businesses that can provide energy and raw materials and participation or ownership in infrastructure, high technology, and brand names (Le Corre 2017, 162). The EU is alluring to China because it is one of the three most prominent global players for international trade (the other two being the United States and China), has a high per capita income, and implements an open or non-protectionist trade policy. Until 2015, China had invested US$ 65 billion in listed companies on European stock markets, surpassing Japan (Casarini 2015, 6). The European project also had a political appeal, as it constitutes a model of regional policy, accomplishes a political economy of social capitalism, and expresses a preference for multilateralism.

The EU did not disregard the prospects of the BRI, but nor could it let the Chinese establish standards of transportation. Therefore, the two sides established the EU–China Connectivity Platform in 2015, which aspired to form a synergy between the EU and China transportation networks of the Trans-European Transport Network and the BRI (see Su, Chapter 8).

EU countries initially welcomed Chinese investments up until 2016. But when Chinese companies tried to push ahead with acquisitions of businesses or critical infrastructure, European governments started scrutinizing, delaying, or blocking initial deals. Not only European governments but also the US put pressure against deals involving Chinese companies in sectors deemed critical for national security, as in the Aixtron case, a chip equipment maker (Sheahan 2016). As Chinese companies increasingly bid for utility infrastructure across Europe, questions are being raised about the risks of China controlling the national infrastructure of European countries, and whether Chinese ownership will serve political goals (Le Corre 2017, 171).

In this context, Greece has tried to strike an intricate balance between its EU membership and its relations with China. On the one hand, Greece has to honor the obligations towards its European and international partners and creditors (European Commission, ECB, and IMF) by repaying the loans Greece took from the ECB and the IMF to service its debt. Close Sino-Greek economic relations help the Greek economy under the proviso that such closeness will not raise the ire of Brussels and Washington against Athens. Some European politicians expressed concerns that '[t]he Greek government needs to choose where its alliances lie and realize the EU is not only a market, but first and foremost a community of values' (Horowitz and Alderman 2017). But to many Greeks, the punishing terms of the austerity programs imposed on them by their European partners left them no choice but to draw investments from whoever is willing to invest in Greece (Horowitz and Alderman 2017). The shifting geographic focus of China from northwest Europe to the southern and eastern periphery may also contribute to the annoyance of erstwhile privileged partners of China, as the ports of Rotterdam, Hamburg, and Antwerp, are in danger of being displaced as the primary gateways of China to Europe (van der Putten 2014, 24).

Some commentators alleged that the increasing political clout that China enjoys in Greece led Athens to act as the mouthpiece of China in the EU (Horowitz and Alderman 2017). It is true that the economic crisis endangered Greece's position in the core of the EU and destabilized the region (Chryssogelos 2019; Dokos 2012). However, the use of Chinese investments to nudge Greek diplomacy towards pro-China positions would be risky and counter-productive for China in the long run. If China used COSCO as the bargaining chip in its relations with Greece, then automatically prospective host countries would start looking at Chinese overtures suspiciously (van der Putten 2019). The lack of a common EU–China policy has permitted

Greece and other Member States to interact with China largely independently, promoting their economic interests (Arduino 2016; Casarini 2015; de Jonquières 2015). But at the same time, EU membership offers Greece much leeway vis-à-vis China. Greek policymakers are well aware that the country is not alone in its endeavors with China. Greece can punch above its weight because it belongs to the largest and most prosperous bloc in the world, while not denying itself opportunities such as the one COSCO offered when crisis made it imperative to capitalize on them (Casarini 2015).

Conclusion

In this chapter, we discussed how a small European country could become significant for Chinese economic and political objectives. Greece has served as China's gateway to southern, central, and eastern Europe. This has put Athens in a delicate position in that it has to strike a balance between its national interests and its membership of the EU as well as NATO. Greece offers a gateway for Chinese products to Europe, the means of transportation by sea, logistics support in times of a regional crisis, and a receptive voice in decision-making in EU institutions. On the other hand, China has provided Greece with investments and a market to export its products.

However, there are red lines that Greece cannot cross. Despite the absence of a China-oriented communicated European Common Security and Foreign Policy, Greece has limited freedom of action when it comes to its relationships with China within the EU–China framework, as illustrated by the inability to accept COSCO's bidding for the national railways due to the European Commission's objections. At the same time, EU legislation can protect Greece from excessive Chinese demands. As the Commission's 2019 strategic outlook on EU–China relations clearly flagged, there are limits in the EU–China relationship beyond which Greece should not venture.

A conundrum that Greek policymakers might face in the future is the transformation of competition between China and the West from purely economic goals into geopolitical and strategic ones. Over the last four years, the EU sheltered Greece from being caught in the middle of the emerging US-China competition for global primacy as Brussels tried to deflect Donald Trump's disruptive attacks on the international order. But soon it may be the EU as a whole, not Greece, that will be forced to choose between economic benefits from China and the security and political alliance with the US. For a country in Greece's geographical position and economic needs, the EU framework may soon turn from an amplifier of international influence into a source of pressure regarding relations with China.

The BRI offers opportunities and challenges to the countries participating in this gigantic project. However, they should always carefully read Chinese intentions and position themselves according to their mid- and long-term interests. It is on the basis of considerations described above that Greece should decide how to engage with BRI and China. Thankfully, despite the crisis that befell it, Greece still possesses political, diplomatic, and military capital that it can use to pursue its goals in the future. With a firm understanding of their position in the world, Greeks can navigate the waters of the EU–China relationship and promote their own interests.

Bibliography

Abi-Habib, M., (2018). How China Got Sri Lanka to Cough Up a Port. *New York Times* [online]. 25 June. Available from: https://www.nytimes.com/2018/06/25/world/asia/china-sri-lanka-port.html.

Alderman, L., (2012). Under Chinese, a Greek Port Thrives. *New York Times* [online]. 10 October. Available from: https://www.nytimes.com/2012/10/11/business/global/chinese-company-sets-new-rhythm-in-port-of-piraeus.html.

Arduino, A., (2016). China's One Belt One Road: Has the European Union Missed the Train?. S. Rajaratnam School of International Studies, Singapore. Available from: http://hdl.handle.net/11540/6511.

Baldwin, D. A., (1985). Economic Statecraft. Princeton University Press, Princeton.

BBC News., (2014). China and Greece Sign Deals Worth $5bn During Li Visit [online]. *BBC*. 21 June. [Viewed 20 August 2020]. Available from: https://www.bbc.com/news/world-asia-china-27960661.

Brewster, D., (2017). Silk Roads and Strings of Pearls: The Strategic Geography of China's New Pathways in the Indian Ocean. *Geopolitics* 22(2): 269–291.

Casarini, N., (2015). Is Europe to Benefit from China's Belt and Road Initiative? Istituto Affari Internazionali, Rome.

Chan, S. and Drury, A. C. (Eds.). (2000). Sanctions as Economic Statecraft: Theory and Practice. Basingstoke, Palgrave.

Chourchoulis, D., (2019). Greece and the People's Republic of China in the Cold War, 1972–1989. In: J. M. Schaufelbuehl, M. Wyss and V. Zanier, eds. Europe and China in the Cold War: Exchanges Beyond the Bloc Logic and the Sino-Soviet Split. Brill, Leiden, pp. 62–84.

Chourchoulis, D., Koumas, M. and Panoutsopoulos, A., (2020). Beyond the Bipolar World: Greece's Relations with China, Israel and Africa, 1967–73. In: A. Klapsis, C. Arvanitopoulos, E. Hatzivassiliou and E. G. H. Pedaliu, eds. The Greek Junta and the International System: A Case Study of Southern European Dictatorships, 1967-74. Routledge, London, pp. 71–83.

Chryssogelos, A., (2019). Europeanisation as De-politicisation, Crisis as Re-politicisation: The Case of Greek Foreign Policy During the Eurozone Crisis. *Journal of European Integration* 41(5): 605–621.

Council of the European Union., (2014). EU Maritime Security Strategy (EUMSS) - Action Plan. Council of the European Union, Brussels. 16 December. [Viewed 20 August 2020]. Available from: https://ec.europa.eu/maritimeaffairs/sites/maritimeaffairs/files/docs/body/20141216-action-plan_en.pdf.

de Jonquières, G., (2015). The European Union's China Policy: Priorities and Strategies for the New Commission. European Centre for International Political Economy, Brussels.

Dokos, T., (2012). Who Lost Greece? The Geopolitical Consequences of the Greek Crisis. Hellenic Foundation for European and Foreign Policy ELIAMEP, Athens.

Drezner, D. W., (1999). The Sanctions Paradox: Economic Statecraft and International Relations. Cambridge University Press, Cambridge.

European Commission., (2018). EU-China Summit: Deepening the Strategic Global Partnership for Transport. European Commission, Brussels. 16 July. [Viewed 8 August 2020]. Available from: https://ec.europa.eu/transport/themes/international/news/2018-07-16-eu-china-summit_en.

European Commission., (2019a). EU-China – A Strategic Outlook. European Commission and HR/VP Contribution to the European Council. European Commission, Strasbourg. 12 March.

European Commission., (2019b). EU-China Summit: Rebalancing the Strategic Partnership. European Commission, Strasbourg. 4 April. [Viewed 8 August 2020]. Available from: https://ec.europa.eu/transport/themes/international/news/2019-04-09-eu-china-summit_en.

Foundation for Economic and Industrial Research., (2016). The Economic Impact of the Privatisation of the Piraeus Port Authority. Foundation for Economic and Industrial Research, Athens. Available from: http://iobe.gr/docs/research/en/RES_03_08032016_PRE_EN.pdf.

Glass, D., (2019). Cosco Plans New Pier to Expand Piraeus Capacity to Over 10m TEU. *Seatrade Maritime News*. 15 August. [Viewed 10 August 2020]. Available from: https://www.seatrade-maritime.com/europe/cosco-plans-new-pier-expand-piraeus-capacity-over-10m-teu.

Glass, D., (2020). Piraeus Port Container Volumes Continue to Grow in 2019. *Seatrade Maritime News*. 27 May. [Viewed 9 August 2020]. Available from: https://www.seatrade-maritime.com/ports-logistics/piraeus-port-container-volumes-continue-grow-2019.

Granitsas, A. and Paris, C., (2014). Chinese Transform Greek Port, Winning Over Critics: Cosco-Built Container Terminal in Piraeus Marks Public-Relations Victory for Beijing. *Wall Street Journal* [online]. 20 November [Viewed 8 August 2020]. Available from: https://www.wsj.com/articles/chinese-transform-greek-port-winning-over-critics-1416516560.

Grieger, G. (2016). One Belt, One Road (OBOR): China's Regional Integration Initiative. Briefing. European Parliament Research Service, Brussels.

Hellenic Republic Asset Development Fund., (2016). Press Release: Cosco (Hong Kong) Group Limited 51% Shareholder of PPA. 10 October. Hellenic Republic Asset Development Fund, Athens.

Horowitz, J. and Alderman, L., (2017). Chastised by E.U., a Resentful Greece Embraces China's Cash and Interests. *New York Times* [online]. 16 August. [Viewerd 9 August 2020]. Available from: https://www.nytimes.com/2017/08/26/world/europe/greece-china-piraeus-alexis-tsipras.html.

Huliaras, A. and Petropoulos, S., (2014). Shipowners, Ports and Diplomats: The Political Economy of Greece's Relations with China. *Asia Europe Journal* 12(3): 215–230.

Kassimeris, C., (2010). Greece and the American Embrace: Greek Foreign Policy Towards Turkey, the US and the Western Alliance. Tauris, London.

Le Corre, P., (2017). Chinese Investments in European Countries: Experiences and Lessons for the "Belt and Road" Initiative. In: M. Mayer, ed. Rethinking the Silk Road: China's Belt and Road Initiative and Emerging Eurasian Relations. Palgrave Macmillan, Basingstoke, pp. 161–175.

Len, C., (2015). China's 21st Century Maritime Silk Road Initiative, Energy Security and SLOC Access. *Maritime Affairs: Journal of the National Maritime Foundation of India* 11(1): 1–18.

Li, X., (2019a). China's Pursuit of the "One Belt One Road" Initiative: A New World Order with Chinese Characteristics?. In: X. Li, ed. Mapping China's 'One Belt One Road' Initiative. Palgrave Macmillan, Basingstoke, pp. 1–27.

Li, X., (2019b). Understanding the Multiple Facets of China's "One Belt One Road" Initiative. In: X. Li, ed. Mapping China's 'One Belt One Road' Initiative. Palgrave Macmillan, Basingstoke, pp. 29–56.

Litsas, S. N., (2017). From Sentimental Idealism and Incompetent Realism Towards a New Greek Grand Strategy: Searching for Ariadne's Thread. In: S. N. Litsas and A. Tziampiris, eds. Foreign Policy Under Austerity: Greece's Return to Normality?. Palgrave Macmillan, London, pp. 1–28.

Liu, Q. and Davarinou, P., (2019). Sino-Greek Economic Cooperation: COSCO's Investment in the Port of Piraeus. *IDS Bulletin* 50(4): 109–124.

Mandravelis, V., (2020). Greece Caught in US-China Conflict on 5G. *Kathimerini* [online]. 24 November 2019. [Viewed 19 September 2020]. Available from: https://www.ekathimerini.com/246807/article/ekathimerini/business/greece-caught-in-us-china-conflict-on-5g.

Meunier, S., (2015). A Tale of Two Ports: The Epic Story of Chinese Direct Investment in the Greek Port of Piraeus. Council for European Studies, New York. Available from: https://mnccenter.org/sites/default/files/publication_files/Meunier%20A%20Tale%20of%20Two%20Ports%20CritCom.pdf.

Ministry of Foreign Affairs: Hellenic Republic., (n.d.). Greece's Bilateral Relations: China. [Viewed 4 August 2020]. Available from: https://www.mfa.gr/en/blog/greece-bilateral-relations/china/.

Ministry of Foreign Affairs: People's Republic of China., (2013). President Xi Jinping Delivers Important Speech and Proposes to Build a Silk Road Economic Belt with Central Asian Countries. 7 September. [Viewed 8 August 2020]. Available from: https://www.fmprc.gov.cn/mfa_eng/topics_665678/xjpfwzysiesgjtfhshzzfh_665686/t1076334.shtml.

Niba, W., (2019). Will Kenya's Mombasa port be taken over by the Chinese?. *RFI*. 15 January. [Viewed 28 August 2020]. Available from: https://www.rfi.fr/en/africa/20190114-kenya-mombasa-port-china-debt-default.

Pedaliu, E. G. H., (2016). Human Rights and International Security: The International Community and the Greek Dictators. *International History Review* 38(5): 1014–1039.

Ploberger, C., (2017). One Belt, One Road – China's New Grand Strategy. *Journal of Chinese Economic and Business Studies* 15(3): 289–305.

Reuters., (2017). Forthnet Teams Up with Chinese Firms to Fund Greek Telecoms Network. 13 May [Viewed 19 September 2020]. Available from: https://in.reuters.com/article/greece-china-telecoms/forthnet-teams-up-with-chinese-firms-to-fund-greek-telecoms-network-idUSL8N1IF0JX.

Sheahan, M., (2016). China's Fujian Drops Aixtron Bid after Obama Blocks Deal. *Reuters*. 8 December. [Viewed 8 August 2020]. Available from: https://www.reuters.com/article/us-aixtron-m-a-fujian/chinas-fujian-drops-aixtron-bid-after-obama-blocks-deal-idUSKBN13X16H.

Stamouli, N., (2016a). Greece Signs Deal to Sell Stake in Port of Piraeus to China's Cosco. *Wall Street Journal* [online]. 8 April. [Viewed 5 August 2020]. Available from: https://www.wsj.com/articles/greece-signs-deal-to-sell-stake-in-port-of-piraeus-to-chinas-cosco-1460130394.

Stamouli, N., (2016b). What's Derailing Greece's Plan to Sell State Assets? Its Own Government. *Wall Street Journal* [online]. 3 October. [Viewed 9 August 2020]. Available from: https://www.wsj.com/articles/the-greek-government-is-both-for-and-against-its-own-privatization-plan-1475428917.

State Council: People's Republic of China., (2013). The Diversified Employment of China's Armed Forces. [Viewed 10 August 2020]. Available from: http://english.www.gov.cn/archive/white_paper/2014/08/23/content_281474982986506.htm.

The Editorial Board., (2020). Europe's Huawei Stumbling Block. *Wall Street Journal* [online]. 26 July. [Viewed 13 August 2020]. Available from: https://www.wsj.com/articles/europes-huawei-stumbling-block-11595797992.

The Week., (2020). US Agency Classifies Chinese Huawei, ZTE as 'Security Threats'. 1 July. [Viewed 19 September 2020]. Available from: https://www.theweek.in/news/biz-tech/2020/07/01/us-agency-classifies-chinese-huawei-zte-as-security-threats.html.

Tonchev, P. and Davarinou, P., (2017). Chinese Investment in Greece and the Big Picture of Sino-Greek Relations. Institute of International Economic Relations, Athens.

USC US-China Institute., (2006). Joint Communiqué Between the People's Republic of China and the Republic of Greece on the Establishment of Comprehensive Strategic Partnership. [Viewed 9 August 2020]. Available from: https://china.usc.edu/joint-communiqu%C3%A9-between-peoples-republic-china-and-republic-greece-establishment-comprehensive.

van der Putten, F.-P., (2014). Chinese Investment in the Port of Piraeus. The Relevance for the EU and the Netherlands, Greece. The Hague: Clingendael Institute.

van der Putten, F.-P., (2019). European Seaports and Chinese Strategic Influence: The Relevance of the Maritime Silk Road for the Netherlands. Clingendael Institute, The Hague.

Wang, Y., (2016). Offensive for Defensive: The Belt and Road Initiative and China's New Grand Strategy. *The Pacific Review* 29(3): 455–463.

13 Italy's embrace of BRI and the role of internal political dynamics

Alessia Amighini[1]

[1] *The author would like to thank Lorenzo Bencivelli and Flavia Tonelli for useful comments on a previous draft of the chapter.*

2020 was intended to be a very special year in bilateral relations between Italy and China, being the 50th anniversary since the establishment of diplomatic relations between the two countries. Before the COVID-19 pandemic forced the cancellation of most of the public events, the planning for official celebrations had gathered a lot of attention and efforts within the diplomatic community. When the 45th anniversary of diplomatic relations was celebrated in 2015, the opportunity was seized upon to reflect on next steps. The then Italian Minister of Foreign Affairs, Paolo Gentiloni, developed a strategic vision of Italian-Chinese relations that was called "Road-to-50" (Pacifici 2018).

That road reached rather unexpected heights when the two countries signed a Memorandum of Understanding (MoU) on the Belt and Road Initiative (BRI) on March 23, 2019, during the first state visit to Italy by President Xi Jinping. The MoU states bilateral willingness to cooperate in the fields of connectivity, transports, logistics and infrastructure, trade and investment, financial cooperation, people-to-people exchanges, as well as 'green' development (similarly to other BRI MoUs signed by China with other partner countries, but with a slightly reduced scope, as explained below).[i]

This MoU came as a rather shocking outcome from the point of view of international relations, as the prospect that a NATO member and G7 country might consider joining the BRI was astonishing. Therefore, the Italian MoU was considered an unexpected and rushed result, largely unforeseen by the international community, despite some unheeded rumours circulated in autumn 2018 that such an option was on the table, during an official visit to China by Italian Foreign Minister Luigi Di Maio. How it was that Italy eventually decided to sign the MoU, despite mounting concerns of the United States and other European countries in the weeks before the signature, is due to the rather peculiar circumstances related to the governing coalition in Italy at that time.

Fifty years of diplomatic relations

Well ahead of 2019, in May 2017, the then Italian Prime Minister, Gentiloni, and the Chinese Prime Minister, Li Keqiang, revised the so-called Action

Plan, a fundamental document envisioning the aim to further raise the profile of the Sino-Italian strategic partnership, extending its scope from the economic, commercial and financial sectors to cultural, scientific-technological, environmental, and tourism collaboration, in the years 2017–2020. The new Action Plan between Italy and China also aimed at promoting complementarity between the two economies, their respective industrial innovation strategies ("Industry 4.0" and "Made in China 2025" respectively) and the processes of financial harmonization and integration, with particular attention to the theme of investment and logistical-infrastructural development.

In anticipation of the 50th anniversary of diplomatic relations, the Gentiloni government had already expended a lot of energy over the previous two years in the hope that a deeper link could be established between Italy and China in 2020, which was also the year in which the Chinese Communist Party's (CCP) 13th five-year plan would come to an end. In particular, it was speculating that 'the time was approaching to relaunch the rebirth of the "new silk road". Along the same lines that for centuries have linked Europe and the Far East, we believe that the "new silk routes of knowledge" can also prosper, of which Italy and China represent not only the geographical landing places, but also the ideal inspirers' (Pacifici 2018).

It was such a view that eventually inspired Italy's gradual embrace of BRI, which was intended to become a milestone in Sino-Italian relations. Under the BRI umbrella, China has organised most of its diplomatic relations since 2013, developing bilateral infrastructure, trade, and finance agreements with more than 70 countries that have partnered on that Initiative (Amighini 2017; Blanchard and Flint 2017). However, BRI is not only a geopolitical and geo-economic initiative but also a major 'exercise in geo-cultural power' (Winters 2020), as confirmed by the specific developments in March 2019. Similarly, celebrations for the 50th anniversary in 2020 were organized within a joint project called 'the year of culture and tourism between Italy and China', foreseeing a series of events, shows, and exhibitions in the two countries (severely reduced due to the COVID-19 pandemic lockdowns). 'China and Italy are two symbolic nations, respectively of the East and the West', said Zheng Hao, deputy director of the Chinese Ministry of Culture (and fluent in Italian) (as reported by the Italian newspaper *La Repubblica* on January 17 2020 in Santelli (2020)).

The two countries are global leaders *ex aequo* for UNESCO World Heritage Sites, with 55 each (although Italy is far above, both for geographical density and in per capita terms). Italy was the favourite European destination for Chinese tourists in 2018, with approximately three million visitors, a figure that is estimated to have increased by 20% in 2019 (Italy-China Foundation 2019). A recent agreement signed by ENAC, the Italian Civil Aviation Authority, and its Chinese counterpart, has increased the slots on China-Italy routes from 56 to 164 per week, the highest number among European countries (again, suspended since the end of January 2020, due to COVID-19).

At the plenary session of the ninth meeting of the Italy-China Governmental Committee held at the Italian Ministry of Foreign Affairs (which has always been the main driver and forum for bilateral relations) on January 25, 2020, the two foreign ministers restated their strong and consolidated bilateral relationship. The two ministers stressed the ambitious aim of promoting a solid and balanced growth in the exchange of goods and services and in the flow of investments. They encouraged fair competition between companies so as to secure mutual benefits, including through the protection of intellectual property and strengthening the fight against counterfeiting in the field of electronic commerce, both at bilateral and multilateral levels. In line with the 2017–2020 bilateral Action Plan signed in 2015, the two ministers also confirmed the following areas as the priorities for sectoral collaboration: environment and sustainable energy; agriculture; sustainable urbanization; health; aviation; space technologies and their applications; infrastructure; and transportation.

At the same time, however, this meeting came against a backdrop of mounting concerns across the entire Italian political spectrum about the geopolitical consequences of a rising and widespread partnership between Italy and China. Despite the strong emphasis on cultural exchanges that dominate the narrative about Italy and China cooperating along the BRI (reminiscent of the ancient silk road linking Venice to Xi'an), China's increasing geopolitical interest in the Mediterranean (Ekman 2018; Lin 2015; van der Putten 2016) has put Italy in a very special position. On the one hand, the country has a geographical advantage as a southern point of entry into Europe and a central location in the Mediterranean; on the other hand, the need for China to maintain and possibly improve its relations with Europe as a whole requires that Beijing try to reach a balance in its bilateral relations with the largest EU Member States (Germany and France, besides Italy).

This is why 2020 would likely prove to be a year that answers a lot of the questions that were raised around the increased assertiveness of China's relations in Europe, and possibly also in the rest of the world, especially after the remarkable developments in Rome in March 2019.

The most prominent among those questions is whether China's increased assertiveness in its pursuit of both formal (i.e. official support for BRI, as in the case of the Italian MoU) and substantive (i.e. general economic and business exchanges with countries like France and Germany) support in Europe, in times of geopolitical turbulence with the US, is likely to jeopardise traditional NATO alliances. Closely linked to this is the question of whether Italy's embrace of BRI should be considered as a milestone in China's strategy in Europe, to the extent that, as was suggested in the past (Pompili 2019) by former Italian Undersecretary of State Michele Geraci (whose efforts to contribute to the MoU were significant (Davide et al. 2019), it might fuel deeper relations between Italy and possibly other European Member States in the future. Furthermore, the international community has been speculating about the regional and global geopolitical and geo-economic consequences of Italy supporting the BRI, both officially—through a formal MoU—and operatively partnering with China over specific infrastructure projects at home and abroad.

In this chapter, an effort is made to disentangle the internal political dynamics that led to the MoU, while assessing whether it really marked a crossroads in Italy-China and in EU–China relations. In order to do so, we will first examine the Italian domestic context at the time of the MoU's signing. Then we will review the lively debate that surrounded the memorandum, which was subject to several diverging interpretations, both at home and abroad. We will then compare the Italian government's take on the MoU with the actual scope and significance of the document from a Chinese perspective. Finally, a set of concluding remarks will be offered, focusing on the overall geopolitical implications of the Italian BRI MoU on EU–China relations.

The Italian approach towards the BRI: Great expectations

Italy started considering, although very distantly, the possibility of engaging with the BRI back in 2015, at a time when the government was headed by the centre-left Democratic Party. Gentiloni attended the first BRI Forum in Beijing in 2017, a high-level forum that drew 29 foreign heads of state and government and representatives from more than 130 countries and 70 international organizations. This in turn led to an Italian 'MoU for cooperation with China in third countries' negotiated in September 2018. It was only after the visit of PRC Foreign Minister Wang Yi to Italy in January 2019 that diplomatic efforts accelerated towards a fully-fledged MoU focusing on BRI.

Overall, the circumstances that made Italy sign this MoU with China are very peculiar. The Italian rationale was mostly based on economic motivations, which largely outweighed other considerations and certainly overlooked the overall implications on wider EU–China relations. When the Italian government started talking about its membership in the BRI, this was based on hopes that such a move would improve bilateral trade and investment relations with China, primarily compared to those that Germany and France had enjoyed throughout the last four decades. Some members of the government argued that such a bold move would upgrade Rome's position vis-à-vis China compared to other national capitals, possibly to a point where it would eventually become a model for other EU Member States in their own bilateral relations with Beijing. However genuine or not, the belief that agreeing to such an MoU would be a vehicle for deepening business and trade relations with China was offered as a major justification for moving forward with this initiative vis-à-vis the Italian Parliament and public opinion. Although business deals were formally separated from the MoU, the latter was presented as a way to unlock or speed up (for those that were already in the pipeline for a long time, as in the area of orange exports) the signing of ten of them worth potentially around €7 billion (Carli 2019). The expectation was that this would provide significant stimulus to several sectors of the Italian economy.

An additional factor that convinced the government at that time that such a move would be a way forward in bilateral relations concerned trade. Rome was hoping to reduce part of its trade deficit with China, and the general idea was not only that trade relations could be significantly improved as a result of the MoU, but also that such a decision would put Rome in a position to become Beijing's favourite EU partner.

Although the MoU signed is not a treaty—and it therefore has no legally binding effect between the parties—it sets very ambitious targets of cooperation on a broad range of areas. These include trade, investment, finance, transportation, logistics, infrastructure, connectivity, sustainable development, mobility, and international cooperation (where the BRI MoU suggests avenues for cooperation between Italy and China in third countries with the aim to implement the BRI), including telecommunications (while 5G is not explicitly mentioned). One of the document's most ambitious claims is that there would be 'open, transparent and non-discriminatory procurement procedures' between the two countries (as if a simple statement in a non-legally binding document could solve a very delicate issue—i.e. dumping—that has concerned all foreign partners in China since the 1980s). As such, the document was intended, according to the narrative that dominated public discourse in early 2019, to pioneer a deepening in the bilateral relations that individual EU members had had thus far with China.

Notwithstanding the fact that the allure of bridging the gap with the largest European competitors vis-à-vis China could eventually convince even the most skeptical among the members of the Italian Parliament, the Italian signature eventually became possible due to the peculiar political and ideological conditions within the government coalition at that time. The Gentiloni government was followed by a coalition government formed by the 5 Stars Movement (5S) and the League (previously the Northern League) parties. The government was nominally led by prime minister Giuseppe Conte but was essentially controlled by the two deputy prime ministers—the leader of the League, Matteo Salvini, and the leader of the 5S, Luigi Di Maio—who both aimed at influencing the government's international political agenda. While Salvini has always been very skeptical of deepening Italy's relations with China, Di Maio (also serving as Minister for Economic Development) took the lead in initiating discussions on the BRI MoU—together with one of his undersecretaries, Michele Geraci. Geraci had been very close to the 5S political program during the Gentiloni government, but a couple of days before his appointment, he joined the League, as an expert in foreign markets.

Di Maio and Geraci both tried hard to convince the Parliament and the public that 'the Memorandum was a simple commercial agreement without political values, as if the economy were separate and independent from the logic of government' (Scarpari 2019b). Yet, all evidence suggested the opposite (based on the widely acknowledged political implications of the 123 cooperation documents on the Belt and Road development that China signed until that time with 105 countries in Asia, Africa, Europe, Latin America, and the South Pacific). The debate surrounding this was so lively that the Foreign Affairs Ministry eventually took the lead on drafting the document, which was partly amended (in line with suggestions by Italy's President of the Republic Mattarella) to smooth out the most critical issues, most notably the possibility that Italy would welcome investment by Chinese telecommunication companies (a highly strategic sector for the country's national security).

The various criticisms that were raised at that time (e.g. Amighini 2019b, 2019c, 2019d; Scarpari 2019a, 2019b) insisted on a number of delicate issues at stake. These primarily related to the global geopolitical significance of a NATO founding member backing BRI—a chief goal of the PRC, enshrined in the CPC's constitution during the 19th Party Congress in October 2017—and subscribing to one of its long-term goals, 'the community with a shared future for humanity', which was added as an amendment to the PRC constitution in March 2018 (Lu 2018). Critics raised what appears to be an intrinsic inconsistency between being a member of NATO, whose essential purpose is to safeguard the freedom and security of all its members by political and military means, and of the G7, and being a partner of Beijing on the BRI.

BRI's direct purpose—i.e. to 'promote the economic prosperity of the countries along the Belt and Road, promote regional economic cooperation, strengthen exchanges and mutual learning between civilizations, and promote world peace and development' (Rolland 2017b)—is peaceful in principle. However, China as its chief promoter has other economic and geopolitical goals whose nature and long-term implications are potentially more confrontational, such as the plan to become a high-tech country by 2025 (as included in the 'Made in China 2025' program) in direct competition with the US.

Besides the global geopolitical significance of the MoU, Rome's backing of the Initiative also raised an issue of consistency concerning individual EU Member States' relations with China, at a time when the European Commission's approach to China shifted from unconditional openness to a more cautious position. This position was encapsulated in the 'Strategic Outlook' document that was released by Brussels in 2019, which recognizes China as 'an economic competitor in pursuit of technological leadership and a systemic rival promoting alternative models of governance' (European Commission 2019).

A number of other specific concerns raised at the time referred to the fact that China aimed at expanding total bilateral trade while providing no assurances of increased imports from partner countries (actually China has shown a preference for expanding Chinese exports more than Chinese imports, except for some partner countries that are rich in natural resources), and that an MoU would be no guarantee that things could develop differently for Italy (as confirmed by the lack of any significant increase in Italian exports to China).

In spite of uncertain economic benefits, the MoU also implied a risk of upsetting political relations both within the EU and with the US. A significant example of the political consequences of excessive Chinese economic presence in individual European countries was the inability to reach a common EU position on human rights in China, due to the abstention of Greece, which blocked a joint EU statement at the United Nations criticizing China's human rights record in June 2017 (Emmott and Koutantou 2017).

Yet, with the exception of its embrace of the BRI in the spring of 2019, Rome did not follow the same path when it supported the EU Parliament's motion for the resolution calling for the Hong Kong government to formally withdraw its highly unpopular extradition bill in July 2019 (European Parliament 2019). This suggests that signing a BRI MoU is not necessarily a step towards unrestricted political support and an unconditional show of friendship towards China. At the same time, this episode confirms the widespread perception among observers and scholars that the domestic circumstances that led Italy to fondly embrace BRI were quite 'opaque', in that many of the reasons offered supporting this move were insufficiently explained and unsupported by facts.

Speculation about the rationale of Italy's embrace of BRI

President Xi's imminent state visit to Italy ahead of the MoU's signature in Rome was extensively covered by media from all over the world. What is more, the diverging interpretations of the Italian backing of the BRI led to a lively debate within the country, all across Europe, and in the US early in 2019. Domestically, those supporting the move were mostly within the Italian government and the country's business community, whereas detractors primarily included the right-wing opposition parties in Parliament and a number of scholars who were very critical of Italian support of the BRI.

Many observers were convinced by the idea that the main driver behind the decision to sign the MoU was the intention to compensate for the relative disadvantage of Sino-Italian trade relations compared to those of France and Germany. A large number of op-eds and interviews were published, including one by Romeo Orlandi (the Italy-ASEAN Association vice-president), in which he argued that the aim behind the Italian government's endorsement of BRI was 'to regain some ground lost in the commercial relationship with China. Twenty years ago, Italy had a 1.9% share of Chinese imports. Today, the share is a mere 0.9%' (Kuo 2019). In hindsight, it is now evident that the narrative that some members of the government employed at that time about the economic benefits expected from the MoU had convinced the 5S that joining BRI would offer an opportunity to rebalance bilateral economic relations in favour of Italy. But Orlandi went much further than that, offering his personal opinion of why Washington should understand that Rome had no option but to sign the MoU. As reasons for this, he mentioned that Italy's 'technological edge with China, originally and still in favor of Italy, is losing ground', which would imply the need to 'sell its jewels' (i.e. its high-tech small and medium companies] to China, which 'needs to improve its industry and move from a quantitative model to a qualitative one, as envisaged in the 'Made in China 2025' plan' (Ibid).

In an effort to figure out the rationale for Italy's MoU with China, many observers and scholars outside Italy (including Bindi 2019) believed that this decision was based on a *de facto* agreement that must have been made within Italy's political class concerning the need to deepen relations with Beijing. However, that belief could not be further from the truth. Actually, deep divergences were evident between the incumbent government at that time and the opposition, and also within the two parties of the governing coalition (5S and the League).

A further misunderstanding that has long been widespread among scholars (Bindi 2019; Fardella and Prodi 2017) is that Italy would have missed huge opportunities in the logistics and shipping sectors were it not to join the BRI. According to this argument, Chinese seaborne merchandise trade from the Suez Channel would normally reach the Port of Piraeus in Greece (where Chinese COSCO acquired a minor stake in 2008 and a majority stake in 2016) and then transit to Central Europe by railway (the Belgrade-Budapest rail, which the Chinese have already started building) (Kafkadesk 2020). However, this railway project had long been hindered by legal difficulties, due to the need to open public tenders in the Hungarian part of the route—as it represents a big EU infrastructure project, and therefore cannot be directly financed by a single party without a proper tender being open. Therefore, the idea was that Italy would be allowed to become a major hub for China's trade in Europe instead, since it already had a number of ports connected by rail to Central Europe, and signing the MoU would likely accelerate the process. Unfortunately, the ability of any of the Italian ports to serve as a significant hub was and is still lagging far behind the scale of existing Northern European ports, namely, Antwerp and Rotterdam (and will always be, due to the geomorphological peculiarities of Italian ports, which lack proper and efficient rail connections from the ports' facilities). Moreover, the overall idea that Italy could become a hub linking China's trade with Europe overlooked the ability of China to eventually unlock the Hungarian route by securing a loan covering 85% of the total costs of the project (the details of which the Hungarian government has recently designated state secret status for ten years) (Kafkadesk 2020).

Among most prominent commentators, just a few provided a more balanced depiction of the circumstances at that time. Among those, Tiezzi

(2019) offered an unbiased interpretation of the Italian decision by comparing the economic outcomes of Xi's visits to Rome and to Paris, a couple of days later. Indeed, were it true that Italy chose to sign the MoU in order to improve its bilateral business with China, then it was rather surprising that deals signed in Italy were only worth 2.5 billion euros—compared to previous rumours suggesting up to 7—compared to 40 billion euros in France a couple of days later.

What seems to be clear beyond all speculation is that Italy and China had rather diverging expectations on the implications of signing the MoU. This is confirmed by the leading Chinese narrative on the role of Europe, and more specifically Italy, in the BRI.

Italy in the BRI: A Chinese perspective

Since its announcement in 2013, the BRI has become the focal point of China's whole economic and political diplomacy and has exerted a deep influence on diplomatic activities in the rest of the world as well (Lin et al. 2019; Sidaway and Woon 2017). BRI aims at integrating China into the global economy along much deeper avenues than ever before, far beyond trade and investment (Yong 2016; Yuan 2018). Along with the flourishing of bilateral agreements signed by the Chinese government with individual partner countries (at the time of writing, up to 202 international investment agreements and 14 free trade agreements) with the objective of reducing institutional barriers to trade and investment flows, the BRI intends to build a great Eurasian continent along lines that are very different from any other traditional paradigm of regional integration (Fallon 2015; Rolland 2017a). While the world has so far experienced rules-based regional integration arrangements (largely within the framework of the World Trade Organization's regional preferential trade agreements), the Chinese way to regional integration tends to be less rules-based and more coalition-based along country-specific interests. As such, the BRI may have considerable implications on international economic and political relations for the rest of the world and more specifically for Europe, the final geographic destination of the vast network of land routes and sea-lanes starting from various Chinese provinces (Chan 2018).

Italy is the historic and geographically natural endpoint of the BRI maritime route from the Suez Canal to the heart of Europe (Amighini 2016, 2019a). This was evident to China when they first approached the port of Gioia Tauro in Southern Italy back in 2008, with the goal of making it become the major hub for China's seaborne trade with Europe. The unsuccessful outcome of that plan diverted China to the Greek Port of Piraeus as a second-best option compared to Gioia Tauro, which would have averted the need to plan and build an entire railway connection from Athens to Budapest.

Nonetheless, today there is still some interest by Chinese shipping companies (most notably COSCO) and port authorities (such as the Port of

Qingdao), which have invested in a number of Italian ports and in Italy's logistics sector: most notably Vado Ligure near Genoa and Savona in Liguria (the Northern region facing the Tyrrhenian Sea). On the Adriatic side, Trieste is part of the Trihub project, a framework agreement between the EU and China to promote reciprocal infrastructure investments; and in the port of Ravenna, the China Merchant Group invested 10 million euros in 2018 to make the Byzantine city the European hub of naval engineering. The possibility of facing more favourable political and economic conditions when investing in Italy, in order to be able to pursue its own interests in the Mediterranean region, was therefore one of the reasons for China's diplomatic efforts regarding the MoU.

However, China's view on the role of Italy within BRI seems to be rather different from the great expectations of the Italian government in March 2019. An interesting perspective that sheds light on this discrepancy comes from a recent analysis (Wen 2019), according to which:

> ... the pattern of China's cooperation in Europe differs amongst individual European countries based on their different interests in the BRI. The relatively backward economic development level of Central and Eastern European countries explains why they are the most active in participating in the BRI, hoping to attract Chinese investment, and especially to obtain policy loan support from the AIIB and other institutions, and expand exports to China at the same time (Wen 2019).

Another group of countries in southern and southwestern Europe (including Italy) 'are highly competitive in the fields of organic food, and hope to further open up the Chinese market and export more green agricultural products such as olive oil, dairy products and wine' (Ibid). According to this analysis, the same group of southern European countries would also benefit from the increasingly dynamic Chinese tourism market. In contrast, Western European countries with a higher level of economic and industrial development seem to have more reservations about the BRI *inter alia* based on concerns that the concept of 'community of common destiny' advocated by China might become a Chinese tool to 'export' its values to Europe.

This analysis confirms why China has been carefully targeting countries in Southern and Central Europe on the basis of a comprehensive long-term strategy. Thirteen other EU Member States before Italy had signed bilateral agreements to support the BRI. Moreover, starting in 2012, 11 EU Member States and five EU candidate countries—all in Central and Eastern Europe—started meeting with China on a regular basis, within what was known as '16+1' (meaning 16 countries plus China) Initiative, which became '17+1' after Greece became a partner country of the BRI by signing a BRI MoU in August 2018 and joined 17+1 in 2019 (Zeneli 2019; see also Snyder, Chapter 4).

The diverging views between Rome and Beijing about the significance of Italy joining the BRI added to the confusion within the Italian government in 2019 and explain the variety of different views that have since developed about the implications of the MoU on EU-China relations.

Implications of the MoU from a European perspective

The MoU suggested that Italy was prepared to change its attitude in economic relations with China from skepticism to support, within a larger European context that seemed to be taking the opposite direction. While that does not imply a change either in Italy's foreign policy or its major alliances, the move raised serious concerns in Brussels and Washington, because Italy was the first NATO country to formalize its participation in the BRI project, albeit not the first EU Member State to do so. While the MoU is legally non-binding, it is still not clear what would be the informal consequences of whatever could be perceived by Beijing as a breach of friendship.

Following the above analysis of the internal political circumstances that led to the MoU, what is now quite clear is that it was purely economic considerations (rather than geopolitical motives) that drove the somewhat naive Italian approach to the BRI.

Nonetheless, the evolution of Italian relations with China exerted a certain (maybe just indirect) pressure on Brussels, which eventually led to a shift in the overall European approach to China. Already on the eve of the Italian signature, on March 22, 2019, the EU Council started to discuss a common EU strategy toward China, in preparation for the EU–China Summit which was planned to be held on April 9 that year. Before that time, efforts to follow a common strategy had not been agreed upon amongst larger European Member States, which only started to discuss a common China approach towards the end of 2016.

The vast majority of analysts are inclined to consider Italy as a milestone in China's EU strategy. Following the well-established experience of tightening relations with several countries in Central and Eastern Europe, China moved a step forward by strengthening ties with Greece and Portugal, both of which eventually decided to sign a BRI MoU, and Italy was intended to be the next step in that strategy. This supported the view that a rising Chinese presence in some European economies would lead to stronger bilateral relations with specific Member States to the detriment of a united EU approach. As the Italian MoU started to be discussed at a time when the EU had just shifted its approach to China (no longer just an economic partner but also a strategic competitor), a widespread view considers the Italian approach on China as a critical strategic trend to observe. As Chatzky (2019) observed, 'many believe that this economic cooperation will inevitably turn into a greater geopolitical understanding between the two countries—thus reinforcing Beijing's influence in Europe and the Mediterranean region'.

Detractors feared that Italy might become more than just a milestone (Turak 2019), but a real Trojan horse for Chinese influence in Europe. In support of this view, they point to a partial shift in the Italian position within the EU with regard to China, when Rome abstained from a vote on a new screening mechanism for foreign direct investments in strategic sectors in Europe. This, despite the fact that this mechanism was first requested by Italy together with France and Germany in a letter submitted to the European Commission in February 2017.

In principle, there should be no doubts about the geopolitical consequences of the MoU, as it is in accordance with EU rules and policies, and in full agreement with the United Nations 2030 Agenda for Sustainable Development (United Nations 2015), the 2020 EU–China Cooperation Agenda (European External Action Service 2020b) and the EU Strategy for Eurasian Connectivity (European External Action Service 2020a). This is why Prime Minister Conte denied in March 2019 that Italy will become a Trojan horse for China in Europe (Fontana and Franco 2019), a statement that has recently been confirmed by the Italian decision to fully back the EU motion to support pro-democracy protesters in Hong Kong, which clarifies that Italy's alleged political closeness to China is no longer unambiguous.

Conclusion

Looking ahead, what might prove true in the future is that the MoU could turn out to be more a misstep than a milestone in China's EU strategy. Although Italy is one of the most important EU Member States, its bargaining power vis-à-vis China also depends on the extent to which it will be pursued through the EU, as outlined in the EU's 2019 Strategic Outlook on China (European Commission 2019). This was reinforced on March 12, 2019, when the Commission issued a decalogue of actions suggested to Member States in their relations with Beijing, under the significant name of China Strategy. This includes, among other things, an explicit reference to the need to safeguard the most strategic sectors, such as telecommunications, from excessive Chinese interference.

This development seems to have been inspired by the then-impending signature of the Italian MoU, and this can be seen as a first positive effect of the document in the process of defining a clearer and more robust EU position. The MoU actually accelerated the building of a common approach at the European level that was not seen before, as suggested by Emmanuel Macron's clever move to invite Angela Merkel and the then EU Commission President Jean-Claude Juncker to Paris to meet Xi during the Chinese president's visit, just days later after his visit to Rome.

At the time of writing, the COVID-19 pandemic was still causing a heavy death toll around the world while forcing countries to implement strict social distancing and lockdown measures to prevent the further spread of the virus. Originating in Wuhan, the virus hit Italy faster and harder than the rest of

Europe, plunging the country into a deep public health crisis. One of the most serious issues when the virus started circulating broadly was the lack of sufficient stocks of sanitary equipment, including masks and ventilators, whose production had been heavily concentrated in a few countries over the last decades, with China being the top producer.

This is when China started to leverage one of the pillars of the BRI—the Health BRI or the so-called 'Health Silk Road'—to expand its soft power further into Europe, through deeper cooperation and economic exchanges. China even exploited the tragic situation in Italy for propaganda purposes, with state-owned media even claiming that the coronavirus originated in Italy, not China (Ferraresi 2020).

Against this peculiar backdrop, the virus exerted an unexpected twist to Italy-China relations, in directions that have further added to the confusion that had prevailed one year earlier (Lamperti 2020). Foreign Minister Di Maio and the 5S movement have tried their best to leverage their support for the MoU, trying to convince public opinion that it would help Italy to fight the pandemic. However, China's 'mask diplomacy', i.e. the showing off of donations of medical equipment, was found lacking as a means of restoring the country's international reputation as a responsible power, since many of those transfers of equipment actually proved to be actually sales under standard business contracts.

As the first wave of the pandemic gradually abated in Italy in the summer of 2020, developments like this meant that there was no perception in the Italian public opinion that China had helped in any way. Instead, the public's awareness of China's business objectives and wider political goals to increase its presence in Europe was heightened. What happened in the spring of 2020 provided a chance to see that the MoU did not in fact change the previous course of Italy-China relations in any substantial way.

Note

i The English version of the Italian MoU can be found here: http://www.governo.it/sites/governo.it/files/Memorandum_Italia-Cina_EN.pdf.

Bibliography

Amighini, Alessia, (2016), Porti italiani lungo la via della seta, Lavoce.info, https://www.lavoce.info/archives/42060/porti-italiani-lungo-la-via-delle-seta/

Amighini, Alessia, (2017), China's Belt and Road: a game changer? ISPI.

Amighini, Alessia, (2019a), Il ruolo dell'Italia nella BRI, Inchiestaonline, http://www.inchiestaonline.it/lavoro-e-sindacato/alessia-arrighini-il-ruolo-dellitalia-nella-bri-belt-and-road-initiative/

Amighini, Alessia, (2019b), Risultati concreti, ma solo per la Cina, Huffington Post, https://www.huffingtonpost.it/2019/03/23/risultati-concreti-ma-solo-per-la-cina_a_23699087/

Amighini, Alessia, (2019c), Non basta un Memorandum per conquistar la Cina, Lavoce.info, https://www.lavoce.info/archives/62023/non-basta-un-memorandum-per-conquistare-la-cina/

Amighini, Alessia, (2019d), Italia-Cina: quel Memorandum è un pasticcio, Lavoce.info, https://www.lavoce.info/archives/58076/italia-cina-quel-memorandum-e-un-pasticcio/

Amighini, Alessia, (2019e), Europa in cerca di una strategia comune verso la Cina, Lavoce.info, https://www.lavoce.info/archives/58230/europa-in-cerca-di-una-strategia-comune-verso-la-cina/

Bindi, Federiga, (2019), Why did Italy embrace Belt and Road Initiative, Carnegie Endowment, https://carnegieendowment.org/2019/05/20/why-did-italy-embrace-belt-and-road-initiative-pub-79149

Blanchard, Jean-Marc F. and Flint, Colin, (2017), The Geopolitics of China's Maritime Silk Road Initiative. *Geopolitics*, 22(2): 223–245.

Carli, Andrea, (2019), Italia-Cina, i contenuti del Memorandum e i 29 accordi per (almeno) sette miliardi di euro, Il Sole24ore, https://www.ilsole24ore.com/art/italia-cina-contenuti-memorandum-e-trenta-accordi-almeno-sette-miliardi-euro--ABPvc3gB?refresh_ce=1

Chan, Man Hung Thomas, (2018), The Belt and Road Initiative – the New Silk Road: A Research Agenda. *Journal of Contemporary East Asian Studies*, 7(2): 104–123.

Chatzky, Andrew, (2019), China's Belt and Road gets a win in Italy, Council for Foreign Relations, https://www.cfr.org/in-brief/chinas-belt-and-road-gets-win-italy

Coratella, Teresa, (2019), Italy's Chinese dilemma, European Council for Foreign Relations, https://www.ecfr.eu/article/commentary_italys_chinese_dilemma

Cristiani, Dario, (2019), Italy Joins the Belt and Road Initiative: Context, Interests, and Drivers. *China Brief*, 19(8), https://jamestown.org/program/italy-joins-the-belt-and-road-initiative-context-interests-and-drivers/

Davide, Ghiglione, Sevastopulo, Demetri, Peel, Michael and Hornby, Lucy, (2019), Italy set to formally endorse China's Belt and Road Initiative, Financial Times, March 6, https://www.ft.com/content/17f91d24-3f60-11e9-b896-fe36ec32aece

Ekman, Alice, (2018), China in the Mediterranean: An Emerging Presence, Notes de l'Ifri, Ifri, February 2018, https://www.policycenter.ma/sites/default/files/Ekman_China_Mediterranean_2018_0.pdf

Emmott, Robin and Koutantou, Angeliki, (2017), Greece blocks EU statement on China human rights at U.N., World News, https://www.reuters.com/article/us-eu-un-rights-idUSKBN1990FP

European Commission, (2019), EU-China: A strategic outlook, European Commission, https://ec.europa.eu/commission/sites/beta-political/files/communication-eu-china-a-strategic-outlook.pdf

European External Action Service, (2020a), Connecting Europe & Asia: The EU strategy, European External Action Service, https://eeas.europa.eu/headquarters/headquarters-homepage/50699/connecting-europe-asia-eu-strategy_en

European External Action Service, (2020b), EU-China 2020 strategic agenda for cooperation, European External Action Service, https://eeas.europa.eu/archives/docs/china/docs/eu-china_2020_strategic_agenda_en.pdf

European Parliament, (2019), European Parliament resolution on the situation in Hong Kong, European Parliament, https://www.europarl.europa.eu/doceo/document/RC-9–2020-0169_EN.html

Fallon, Theresa, (2015), The New Silk Road: Xi Jinping's Grand Strategy for Eurasia. *American Foreign Policy Interests*, 37(3): 140–147.

Fardella, Enrico and Prodi, Giorgio, (2017), The Belt and Road Initiative Impact on Europe: An Italian Perspective. *China & World Economy*, 25(5): 125–138.

Ferraresi, Mattia, (2020), China isn't helping Italy. It's waging information warfare, Foreign Policy, https://foreignpolicy.com/2020/03/31/china-isnt-helping-italy-its-waging-information-warfare/

Fontana, Luciano and Franco, Massimo, (2019), Via della Seta, Conte: «Italia-Cina, intesa limpida: l'obiettivo è crescere», Corriere della Sera, https://www.corriere.it/politica/19_marzo_13/via-seta-conte-italia-cina-intesa-limpida-nostro-obiettivo-crescere-0b5a29ac-450d-11e9-b3b0–2162e8762643.shtml

Italy-China Foundation, (2019), X Rapporto annuale CeSIF, Italy-China Foundation, https://www.fondazioneitaliacina.it/m/cesif/rapporto-annuale/2019/

Kafkadesk, (2020), Belgrade-Budapest high-speed train: Highway to rail?, Kafkadesk.org, https://kafkadesk.org/2020/05/15/belgrade-budapest-high-speed-train-highway-to-rail/

Kuo, Mercy A., (2019), China-Italy Relations: The BRI effect, Thediplomat.com, https://thediplomat.com/2019/04/china-italy-relations-the-bri-effect/

Lamperti, Lorenzo, (2020), Coronavirus, l'Italia molla la Cina. Dalla Via della Seta alla sinofobia, https://www.affaritaliani.it/esteri/coronavirus-italia-cina-via-della-seta-m5s-ripensamento-650077.html

Lin, Christina, (2015), The Dragon's Rise in the Great Sea: China's Strategic Interests in the Levant and the Eastern Mediterranean, in Aristotle Tziampiris, Spyridon N. Litsas (eds), The Eastern Mediterranean in Transition: Multipolarity, Politics and Power, Ashgate.

Lin, Shaun, Sidaway, James D. and Woon, Chih Yuan, (2019), Reordering China, Respacing the World: Belt and Road Initiative (一带一路) as an Emergent Geopolitical Culture. *The Professional Geographer* 71(3): 507–522.

Lu, Hui, (2018), China Focus: China's national legislature adopts landmark constitutional amendment, Xinhua.

Mitchell, David, (2020), Making or Breaking Regions: China's Belt Road Initiative and the Meaning for Regional Dynamics. *Geopolitics*, 1–21.

Pacifici, Paola, (2018), Nel 2020 Il 50° Anniversario Relazioni Italo-Cinesi, Mondo Italiano, https://www.mondoitaliano.net/ettore-sequi-lambasciatore-italiano-a-pechino/

Pompili, Giulia, (2019), Il sottosegretario italiano che gira l'Europa per promuovere la Cina, Il Foglio, https://www.ilfoglio.it/esteri/2019/05/11/news/il-sottosegretario-italiano-che-gira-leuropa-per-promuovere-la-cina-254189/

Rolland, Nadège, (2017a), China's "Belt and Road Initiative": Underwhelming or Game-Changer? *The Washington Quarterly* 40(1): 127–142.

Rolland, Nadège, (2017b), China's Eurasian Century? Political and strategic implications of the Belt and Road Initiative, National Bureau of Asian Research.

Santelli, Filippo, (2020), Italia-Cina, iniziative e scambi per "l'anno della cultura e del turismo, La Repubblica, https://www.repubblica.it/esteri/2020/01/17/news/

italia-cina_iniziative_e_scambi_per_l_anno_della_cultura_e_del_turismo_-245982109/?refresh_ce

Scarpari, Maurizio, (2019a), In margine alla visita di Xi Jinping in Italia, Inchiesta online, http://www.inchiestaonline.it/osservatorio-internazionale/maurizio-scarpari-in-margine-alla-visita-di-xi-jinping-in-italia/

Scarpari, Maurizio, (2019b), Timeo danaos et dona ferentes. Timori e speranze sulla Via della seta, Inchiesta online, http://www.inchiestaonline.it/osservatorio-internazionale/maurizio-scarpari-timeo-danaus-et-dona-ferentes-timori-e-speranze-sulla-via-della-seta/

Sidaway, James D. and Woon, Chih Yuan, (2017), Chinese Narratives on "One Belt, One Road" (一带一路) in Geopolitical and Imperial Contexts. *The Professional Geographer* 69(4): 591–603.

Tiezzi, Shannon, (2019), Xi Jinping in Europe. A tale of two countries, The Diplomat, https://thediplomat.com/2019/03/xi-jinping-in-europe-a-tale-of-2-countries/

Turak, Natasha, (2019), Italy joining China's Belt and Road project is 'geopolitically unwise,' former prime minister says, CNBC, https://www.cnbc.com/2019/03/25/italy-joining-chinas-belt-and-road-project-is-unwise-former-pm.html

United Nations, (2015), Transforming our World: The 2030 Agenda for Sustainable Development, United Nations, https://sustainabledevelopment.un.org/post2015/transformingourworld/publication

van der Putten, Frans Paul, (2016), Infrastructure and Geopolitics: China's Emerging Presence in the Eastern Mediterranean. *Journal of Balkan and Near Eastern Studies* 18(4).

Wen, Wang, 2019. Pragmatic Cooperation: China and Europe's Best Choice, ISPI, https://www.ispionline.it/it/pubblicazione/pragmatic-cooperation-china-and-europes-best-choice-22789

Winter, Tim (2020), Geocultural Power: China's Belt and Road Initiative, *Geopolitics*, 1–24, DOI: 10.1080/14650045.2020.1718656.

Yong, Wang, Offensive for defensive: the belt and road initiative and China's new grand strategy (2016) *The Pacific Review*, 29(3): 455–463.

Yuan, Jingdong, Beijing's institutional-balancing strategies: rationales, implementation and efficacy (2018) *Australian Journal of International Affairs*, 72(2): 110–128.

Zeneli, Valbona (2019), Italy signs on to Belt and Road Initiative, *The Diplomat* available online at https://thediplomat.com/2019/04/italy-signs-on-to-belt-and-road-initiative-eu-china-relations-at-crossroads/

14 China and the Belt and Road Initiative in Europe: The case of Portugal

Laura C. Ferreira-Pereira and Paulo Afonso B. Duarte

Introduction[i]

The incursions of the Chinese Belt and Road Initiative (BRI) across Europe have generated broad concern and controversy in addition to heterogeneous reactions within the European Union and amongst its member states. Within academia, the expansion of the BRI in Europe has attracted increased interest, especially in relation to Central and Eastern Europe focusing on the 17+1 forum (Pavlićević 2018; Jakimow 2019; Song and Song 2020; Szczudlik 2019). Yet, when it comes to Southern Europe, there is little scholarly work explicitly focused on Portugal-China relations in connection with the BRI (Duarte 2018a; Ilhéu 2019; Duarte and Leandro 2020), especially in the context of the post-2008 Eurozone crisis and the subsequent Portuguese economic and financial crisis.

Thus, this chapter will seek to fill in such a gap by analyzing the contours and implications of the BRI in Portugal, in the context of a growing presence of China in Europe. The Portuguese case is a very interesting one since it helps to illuminate the medium- to long-term interests of Beijing under BRI regarding the use of other critical policy areas to achieve foreign policy aims. This becomes all the more interesting given the increasingly open stance that the Portuguese authorities have demonstrated vis-à-vis Chinese initiatives and proposals, which developed not only against the background of warnings from Washington about succumbing to Chinese influence, but also of German and French suspicions over Chinese investments and contracts with various EU member states. These developments hint at emergent novel elements in the country's foreign policy, considering that the latter has been traditionally characterized both by unconditional alignment to the United States (US)—inside and outside the realm of NATO—and the pivotal importance of the EU (Ferreira-Pereira 2007, 2014).

The present study will focus mostly, albeit not exclusively, on the period between the Portuguese international bailout in 2011 and the general elections held in October 2019. This delimitation is justified by the need to take into account several domestic challenges posed by the financial assistance program of severe austerity implemented by Lisbon between 2011 and 2014;

and also the new political cycle initiated with the government led by the Socialist António Costa elected in 2015 and reelected in 2019.

This chapter aims to analyze both the increase of Chinese interests and investments in Portugal amidst the geographical expansion of the BRI in Europe and Lisbon's leaning towards exploring and taking advantage of diverse opportunities resulting from a closer relationship with China. It begins with a brief overview of the origins and core tenets of the BRI before exploring the principal contours and approaches characterizing China's engagement in Europe. It then looks at how the post-2008 Portuguese economic and financial crisis and the ensuing economic hardship functioned as a catalyst for China's pull on Portugal; and how this fostered a sort of red *passerelle* for the increase of Chinese presence and influence in the country.

This analysis concludes that Portugal has adopted pragmatically a very receptive stance towards BRI-related projects. However, the eventual overstretching of this stance is likely to make China's penetration in the national economy even more noticeable. All this is not without implications for the implementation of Portuguese foreign policy, which cannot escape from the effects of the growing role played by Beijing in the aforementioned domains (Duarte 2020; Duarte and Leandro 2020).

Contextualizing the Belt and Road Initiative: Origins and core tenets

Since its launch, the BRI's scope of intervention has considerably widened. Besides economic and trade considerations, it has placed emphasis upon physical infrastructure development and security concerns (Casarini 2016). China's National Development and Reform Commission (NDRC) acknowledged that in 2015 by identifying five axes of connectivity, notably, policy communication, road connectivity, unimpeded trade, monetary circulation and understanding between peoples, including intellectual exchanges and flows of tourists and students (China's National Development and Reform Commission 2015).

Whilst officially depicted with altruistic contours as a 'win-win' initiative for all countries involved[ii], in practice, the BRI has been devised to ensure national, regional and global stability to back up China's re-emergence (Callahan 2016; Li 2018) and also the restoration of its geopolitical and cultural centrality in the 21st-century international arena. By creating a series of maritime and land routes, promoting economic interdependence, and facilitating the projection of Beijing's soft and hard power, the BRI, like the Old Silk Road, aims to bring China back to the center of the world (Duarte 2018a,b).

Both as a narrative and a policy tool, the BRI has been imbued with pragmatic assertiveness and patriotism[iii]; and it has operated both at the internal and external level. Domestically, it has aimed to meet concerns and needs not only related to food, environmental and economic security, but also to internal stability, and even the survival of the political regime (Fang and Nolan 2019; Weidong 2019). On the external front, as a foreign policy instrument, the BRI has encapsulated efforts to project Chinese soft power worldwide and promote the country's image of a responsible stakeholder within the international community thereby allaying the perception of acting as a disruptor at the global and regional level (Callahan 2016; Li 2018). Although Chinese soft power is not limited to the BRI, it is to a great extent encapsulated in the initiative. In light of this, closing the gap between China's own self-perception of its international role and third parties' role expectations about it has been of critical importance under Xi Jinping (Lams 2018).

China and the European Union against the backdrop of the Belt and Road Initiative: Contours and approaches

When the BRI was launched in 2013, the EU was under intense strain. It was muddling through the eye of the post-2008 economic and financial storm that fiercely hit the Eurozone and especially the economies of Southern Europe, namely, Greece, Portugal and Spain. This crisis led to intra-EU breaches of solidarity as well as divisions between different 'Europes': 'Northern' versus 'Southern' and 'Western' versus 'Eastern'. Initially, there was no common response to the BRI on the part of the EU. The lack of a collective response was further indicated by the different approaches displayed by EU member states regarding accession to the Asian Infrastructure Investment Bank (AIIB), which was a by-product of the BRI. The same can be said regarding the rush with which 14 EU countries joined the AIIB, in April 2015, despite the criticism voiced by Washington (Menegazzi 2017; Bustillo and Andoni 2018). Portugal was one of the founding members of the AIIB, and since then it has begun to look to this institution alongside the European Bank for Reconstruction and Development, the Asian Development Bank and the World Bank, 'to form synergy and provide each other support' (Macao Magazine 2019, para. 6).

In order to overcome the lack of a coordinated approach towards the BRI, the European Commission established in September 2015 the EU–China Connectivity Platform. The Platform's official goal was to deepen strategic planning synergies between China's BRI and the EU's connectivity initiatives, such as the Trans-European Transport Network (TEN-T) (European Commission 2015a). In practice, however, the EU–China Connectivity Platform showed difficulties in establishing effective cooperation given the two actors' diverging perceptions on connectivity and economic development, as well as their resorting to distinct working methods to achieve these goals. One major roadblock has been the lack of reciprocity, insofar as 'Chinese and other foreign companies are welcome to bid on tenders related to the EU-Asia Connectivity Strategy, but only as long as European construction companies have equal access to Chinese-funded infrastructure projects such as the BRI' (BusinessEurope 2020, 6). Yet, beyond connectivity, China has adopted several different approaches in dealing both with the EU as a whole and its member states, individually considered. Literature has called attention to three major approaches, namely, bilateralism, multilateralism and multilateralism 'à la carte' (Wuthnow et al. 2012; Szczudlik 2019).

A relevant manifestation of a Chinese multilateral strategy engaging with the EU can be found in Beijing's interest in supporting the Investment Plan for Europe, known as the Juncker Plan, which was launched in November 2014. Given China's substantial financial reserves resulting from trade surpluses, as well as the significant expansion of Chinese banks, Brussels expected this financial support to reinforce the European Fund for Strategic Investments (EFSI) by synergizing economic cooperation. Thus, the European Commission welcomed the money coming from China, which became the first non-EU country to participate in the Juncker Plan (European Commission 2015b). In August 2018, the first EU–China investment platform backed by the Plan was inaugurated, with China injecting €600 million into the venture (European Commission 2018). This amount was relatively modest given the initial high expectations and also when compared to investments made by Chinese billionaires (e.g. Huang Nubo and Jack Ma) elsewhere in the world (Casarini 2016; Duarte 2018a,b). That being said, this developing economic cooperation has not evolved without European suspicions, especially concerning what were seen as Beijing's attempts to instrumentalize its engagement in the Juncker Plan in order to boost more or less stealthily BRI's political intrusion, economic impact and geopolitical influence in Europe (Valero 2015; Casarini 2016; EU Observer 2020).

In addition to the multilateral approach, Beijing has shown a preference for bilateralism and multilateralism 'à la carte', which Maher describes as reflecting a 'divide-and-rule strategy' since relations with national capitals to the detriment of the EU have stirred up political division across Europe (Maher 2016, 976). As concrete examples of such divisions, one can point out two revealing episodes. In February 2017, Hungary was seen as the main responsible country for derailing consensus among 11 countries (seven of them EU member states), which prevented them from signing a letter criticizing Beijing for torturing Chinese activists and lawyers (Benner et al. 2018). Furthermore, in June 2017, Greece reportedly blocked an EU statement at the United Nations criticizing China's human rights record, a decision that according to EU diplomats 'undermined efforts to confront Beijing's crackdown on activists and dissidents' (Reuters 2017, para. 1).

The view of China as a source of economic growth and infrastructure development created a set of conditions whereby various European states sought to reap these perceived benefits and take advantage of these growth opportunities. Under these circumstances, bilateralism emerged as China's preferred option to further unleash the potential of BRI. Portugal provides an illustrative example of this, given Beijing's interest in converting the country into a case study in Europe—and in the EU for that matter—when it comes to exploring diverse possibilities related to critical components pertaining to the BRI, namely, the fields of space and ocean exploration, as well as that of the so-called 'Panda Bonds' (i.e. the issue of public debt in renminbi). In response, Lisbon has also tried 'to make full use of existing bilateral cooperation mechanisms, multilateral mechanisms and institutions' to deepen its relations with China (Macao Magazine 2019, para. 6)[iv].

Finally, as for the multilateralism 'à la carte', which implies dealing differently with certain parts of the whole (i.e. the EU), the most paradigmatic example is that of the 16+1 forum that China set up in 2011, which became instrumental for China's efforts to deepen its relations with the countries of Central and Eastern Europe (CEE). Regardless of their being EU member states or not, these countries have shared amongst them a willingness to catch up with European levels of economic and social development. The Chinese investment made available within this framework has been considered of critical importance especially by smaller states like the Czech Republic, Slovakia, Hungary and Romania (European Council on Foreign Relations 2016; Pepermans 2018; Hanemann et al. 2019).

This varied approach underlying China's growing presence in Europe resulted in criticisms by specific EU member states about the BRI's negative implications. Major concerns have been associated with the impact of Chinese financial investments, economic competition and Europe-focused geopolitical ambitions upon the EU's internal cohesion and international role (Casarini 2016; Minghao 2016; Pepermans 2018). The stance adopted by the French and German leadership is a revealing example of this. In March 2019, French President Macron called for the end of 'the period of European naivety' vis-à-vis Beijing, while blaming some EU countries for 'the strategic error' of 'letting Chinese companies buy up EU infrastructure such as ports' (Reuters 2019, paras. 4–5). Similarly, German Chancellor Angela Merkel warned that 'Europe should consider China as much a competitor as a partner' (Ibid, para. 7). As will be shown below, this stance can be contrasted with Lisbon's increasingly accommodative posture vis-à-vis Chinese economic projects and strategic priorities, considering them as a source of opportunity, rather than a source of challenge.

China in Portugal before and after the launch of the Belt and Road Initiative

The Portuguese government's austerity packages in 2010 and 2011 were undertaken against the background of the growth of wider spreads on sovereign debt to unsustainable levels, which had made it impossible to avoid Portugal's bailout. This took the form of an emergency assistance program of €78 billion led by a troika composed of the European Central Bank, the European Commission and the International Monetary Fund (Ferreira-

Pereira 2014). Between 2011 and 2014, the implementation of this programme under the 'Memorandum of Understanding on Specific Economic Policy Conditionality' agreed with the troika, became the driving force in the policy of the government led by the (center-right) Social Democrat Pedro Passos Coelho. Embodying an economic, financial, budgetary and fiscal 'straightjacket' (Gorjão 2012), this rescue package brought with it stringent austerity measures, which had dramatic social costs. In fact, Portugal became quickly enmeshed in deep trouble, having to cut its spending while not having access to international markets to finance its economy and the State; and asking people, particularly workers and pensioners, to bear numerous hardships (Ferreira-Pereira and Groom 2014). This critical political, economic and social juncture made the country more vulnerable to the gradual penetration of Chinese interests in various domains, since foreign investment became crucial for obtaining financial resources (Gaspar and de Haro 2019; Duque apud Deutsche Welle 2019).

This meant that the previously 'protectionist economic attitude' towards China that prevailed in Lisbon prior to the outbreak of the economic crisis eroded gradually (Pareja-Alcaraz 2017, 701). As a consequence, the 'foul weather' of the Portuguese recession and the desire to overcome the economic crisis and eventually get rid of the troika's austerity measures created favorable conditions for the Chinese presence that started to be particularly felt as of 2012. During the international bailout period (2011–2014), 'Chinese firms [...] invested around 10 billion euros in Portugal' (CNBC 2020a, para. 11). The aftermath of the financial assistance program in 2014 saw further overtures to Chinese economic interests, contracts and acquisitions. The diversification of Chinese presence across various domains became noticeable. New areas like real estate and banking, but also innovating sectors like strategic communications gained increased importance in China's eyes; and Chinese private actors (other than the purely public ones) become more active and relevant.

The overall presence of Chinese investors and companies in Portugal was clearly facilitated by the Golden Visa scheme, which was launched a few months after the agreement of the emergency assistance programme (May 2012). Officially known as Residence Permit for Investment Activity, its implementation began on 8 October 2012, by the Passos Coelho led-government. Intended 'to attract foreign investment and boost the domestic economy' (EXPATICA 2020, para. 8), the scheme provided non-EU citizens with a residence permit in Portugal on the condition that they would invest at least half a million euros either in business or real estate within Portuguese territory. Data shows that '8466 gold visas were granted by the Portuguese Foreign and Borders Service, between October 2012 and the end of April 2020' (Dinheiro Vivo 2020, para. 1), with the Chinese being 'by far the nationality that obtained the most gold visas, totalling more than half of the total, that is, 4518 [visas]' (Ibid, para. 7). The Golden Visa has been often associated with the idea of 'fast-tracking Portuguese residency at a cost', or seen as a means of 'buying citizenship' (EXPATICA 2020, para. 8). This situation raised, over time, 'questions of national sovereignty, since Portuguese national issues could be indirectly controlled by a foreign government' (Gaspar and de Haro 2019, 67).

Boosted by the Golden Visa scheme, the Chinese presence and influence, in the form of new investments and investors/residents, became more noticeable since the early days of the economic recession. The sector of energy is a good example of this emerging tendency. Here, as had been the case elsewhere in the world, the *modus operandi* of China in Portugal has been based on important acquisitions usually carried out by large Chinese state-owned enterprises. In 2012, the Chinese State Grid invested €290 million to purchase 25% of the Portuguese REN (National Electricity Network) (AICEP 2018). In the same year, the Chinese state-owned power company China Three Gorges bought 21.35% of the capital of Electricity of Portugal (EDP) for €2.7 billion. In 2014, Portugal became the EU country with the highest weight of Chinese investment (Público 2017).

In the aftermath of the international bailout and financial aid program, the 2015 general elections initiated a new political cycle with the coming to power of a Socialist minority government led by Prime Minister António Costa. The new government was determined to put an end to austerity politics and find a different path to economic growth and development. Therefore, this political transition brought about the deepening and widening of the ties with China as part of a strategy mainly directed at attracting foreign capital and stimulating economic growth. In reality, this strategy was also aided by a lack of substantive domestic political debate about how far the rising Chinese economic presence contributed to the eventual national prosperity and social stability, and about its long-term implications.

The years between 2015 and 2019 saw the expansion of Chinese investment in areas beyond that of energy, such as real estate, banking, health and well-being. Besides the involvement of Chinese state-owned companies in those sectors, Chinese private actors also gained significant importance in terms of acquisitions in the Portuguese market. In October 2017, FOSUN, a Chinese privately owned company known for its investments in the sectors of health and well-being, acquired the health service provider company Luz Saúde, after having become the owner of the most important insurance company in Portugal, Fidelidade (May 2014) and the largest shareholder of Banco Comercial Português, the largest private bank (November 2016) in the country (Jornal Económico 2018). In the financial sector, the acquisition of the investment bank BANIF in July 2016 by Bison Capital, owned by private Chinese capital from Hong Kong, is also worth mentioning (Ibid). On 31 August 2015, China's Anbang attempted (but failed) to purchase Novo Banco; and China Three Gorges launched a takeover bid for EDP on 11 May 2018 (Jornal Económico 2019), which also failed to materialize given the main shareholders' opposition in an official decision taken in 2019.

Despite these two failures, Portugal did become the first country of the Eurozone to issue public debt[v] in renminbi (the so-called 'Panda Bonds'). This initiative was 'part of Portugal's strategy to promote itself as a gateway for Chinese investment in Europe' (Financial Times 2019a, para. 2; and below). According to the Portuguese State Secretary for Finance, Ricardo Félix, 'the purpose of the issue is to be present in larger markets, with abundant liquidity, with high savings, and thus to broaden an investor's base' (cit. by Jornal de Negócios 2019a, para. 4). Moreover, the private bank Millennium BCP also became the first European bank to issue Union Pay[vi] credit cards (Jornal de Negócios 2019b). This assertive policy of Chinese acquisitions and Portuguese concessions made to Chinese interests and preferences was only possible due to Lisbon's willingness to keep up a sort of grace or honeymoon period with China (Duarte 2020).

Concerning the energy sector, particular attention should be drawn to two dimensions, notably, renewable energy and the so-called 'blue partnership'. Regarding the former, an interesting example is the purchase of plots of land located in the Southern village of Alcoutim by China Triumph International Engineering for around €200 million to build a photovoltaic solar power plant, described as 'the largest solar energy project in the country and one of the largest in Europe' (Expresso 2017, para. 2). Here it is worth noting that according to Pareja-Alcaraz (2017), investments made by Chinese firms in the energy sector in Portugal and also in Greece, Italy and Spain were mainly driven by strategic economic calculations, rather than by China's need to secure energy availability. When it comes to the blue partnership, Portugal was the first country to launch such a partnership with China in 2017. The objective was to develop cooperation in the fields of 'maritime governance, marine ecology, marine renewable energy and marine culture' (Xinhua 2018a, para. 8).

Chinese private companies have also invested in land for various purposes. This is the case of the acquisition of a plot of approximately 10,000 square meters in *Oeiras* for €14.4 million (Eco 2019) by *Índice Plural*[vii] in October 2019. In these lands, which once formed one of the largest slums in Lisbon's metropolitan area, *Índice Plural* plans to build several housing, parking, services and commerce facilities (Ibid). Also, the Chinese group EMGI is investing about €300 million in the old quarry of *Alvito* (Monsanto) for the construction of housing, services and commerce facilities (Diário de Notícias 2019a). In the Alentejo region, near *Estremoz*, other plots of land have captured the attention of a Chinese private company, Prospect Time International Investment Limited, for the construction of a complex devoted to health and well-being. The project called Concorde Enclave was described by the city's mayor, Luís Mourinha, as the 'largest investment ever in Estremoz' (Jornal de Negócios 2018, para. 1).

In many of these ventures, the Chinese investors' *modus operandi* has been marked by pragmatism, in the sense that 'the majority of [medium] business investors do their homework even before contacting consultants and law firms based in Portugal, which they call upon to validate their assessment and to set up the financial operation' (Sábado 2018, para. 13). These efforts have often been facilitated by all the exploratory work undertaken by the Chinese embassy in Lisbon as well as individuals belonging to the diaspora living in Portugal who have enabled exposure to potential investment opportunities (Ibid.). This pattern of investment resembles Chinese investment and business engagement opportunities in other EU countries as well: 'buy [ing] it is quicker than building it' (CNBC 2020b, para. 6).

Interestingly enough, China's investments in Portugal, as facilitated by the launch of the BRI, have further explored economic and cultural opportunities beyond the Portuguese borders as well, focusing on the historical, cultural and linguistic affinities of the country in the African continent. Indeed, the President of the League of Chinese in Portugal, Y Ping Chow, once acknowledged that '[Chinese companies] look not only to Portuguese territory, but also to the capacity of influence that Portugal has in Portuguese-speaking African countries' (AICEP 2019, para. 7). To this, he added that: 'Portugal is important, but the Community of Portuguese-Speaking Countries is considerably more' (Ibid.). During his visit to China in October 2016, Prime Minister Costa seized the opportunity of his participation in the Ministerial Conference of the Forum of Macao to stress the need to reinforce a "trilateral cooperation between China, Portugal and the rest of the Lusophone countries", comprising areas such as agriculture, education, environmental sustainability, infrastructure and renewable energy (Governo da República Portuguesa 2016, para. 4). What is more, in an interview given to Chinese state television (CCTV), Costa affirmed that Portugal was willing to participate actively in the 21st Maritime Silk Road, which would enable the country to capitalize on its strategic location as a 'big bridge between Europe, Africa, Latin America and Asia' (Ibid). Eager to attract Chinese capital, he also explicitly described his country as an entrance door for Chinese investors into the EU, by emphasizing that, '... investing in Portugal, having a visa to enter or living in Portugal is the same as investing, exporting or living in any country of the European Union' (Ibid). Implicit in this statement, one can detect the Portuguese government's concern with diversifying its sources of foreign investment. This is of utmost importance as it contributes towards decreasing dependency upon neighboring Spain and provides national companies with the means to fulfill their ambitions and expand beyond European borders (Le Monde 2019).

The acceleration of Chinese presence and influence in Portugal, on the one hand, and Portuguese receptiveness towards BRI-related projects and investments, on the other, gained further momentum during President Xi Jinping's visit in December 2018. The visit resulted in the signing of a memorandum of understanding for the development of logistical, air, land and maritime cooperation within the framework of the BRI; and the signing of 17 bilateral agreements covering sectors as comprehensive as trade, culture and science (Xinhua 2018b). Indeed, Xi's visit to Portugal paved the way for interesting developments that accentuated the deepening and widening of the Luso-Chinese relationship at the end of the 2010s. The two countries became engaged in an attempt to build a laboratory in charge of producing microsatellites for monitoring space as well as the Atlantic Ocean. This laboratory, known as STARLAB, is currently under development and would set a precedent in a highly strategic area (i.e. ocean monitoring) (Duarte and Leandro 2020). Considering that Portugal has the third-largest Exclusive Economic Zone of the EU, the North Atlantic might provide China with a crucial foothold in terms of information, surveillance and access to resources (Duarte and Leandro 2020; Duarte 2020), especially if the United Nations endorses the Portuguese claim submitted in 2009 to double its continental shelf. Such a development should be understood against the backdrop of the EU's suspension of cooperation with China in the framework of the development of the Galileo Programme in view of the growing perception of this country as a cybersecurity threat (Kirchner et al. 2016; Financial Times 2019b; Kaska et al. 2019). Thus, the Luso-Chinese cooperation on the production of microsatellites to monitor space and the Atlantic seems to contrast with Brussels' reluctance in sharing critical know-how with China.

Stronger cooperation between the two sides has also taken place in the telecommunications sector. This was so despite repeated warnings by representatives of the Trump administration against the involvement of Huawei, the Chinese technology group, in the rollout of 5G networks in Europe on the basis of being perceived as a potentially coercive foreign policy tool of the Chinese Communist Party (Público 2019). For example, during his visit to Portugal, in December 2019, the Secretary of State, Mike Pompeo, said: 'The Chinese Communist Party will not hesitate to use all tools at its disposal to oppress its people and others around the world, be it in Portugal, in Europe or the United States' (Público 2019, *author's translation*). Similarly, in May 2019, the US Ambassador to Portugal, George Glass, who since 2018 has publicly expressed concerns about China's investment in Portugal, warned Portuguese authorities that 'this Xi is not the China with whom the Portuguese have been trading for 500 years' (*apud*Diário de Notícias 2019b, para. 1, author's translation). Such warnings should be associated with the signature of a memorandum between the Portuguese national mobile operator MEO and Huawei, on 5 December 2018, for the development of an advanced generation of wireless technology communications (Duarte and Leandro 2020). Despite US admonitions about the security risks such a move would eventually pose, Portuguese Foreign Minister Augusto Santos Silva admitted that, 'Lisbon has no plans to curtail the Portuguese operations of Huawei, the Chinese telecoms group […] as long as [Huawei] complies with Portuguese law' (apud Financial Times 2020, paras. 17–19).

As indicated above, the growing accommodative approach of Portugal regarding Chinese initiatives and projects has been reflected in the receptive environment offered to Chinese public and private investors. The aggregate effect of this led commentators such as Le Corre (2018) to ask: 'Why is it that other countries fear such Chinese initiatives more than Portuguese public opinion or the political elites themselves?' Lisbon's stance of continuing openness vis-à-vis Beijing can be plausibly linked to two aspects. The first aspect is the perceived positive assessment made by the Socialist government regarding Portugal's economic relations with China. As Prime Minister Costa asserted in March 2019: 'Our experience with Chinese investment has been very positive'. He also stressed that: 'The Chinese have shown complete respect for our legal framework and the rules of the market' (Wise and Hall 2019). Similarly, Foreign Minister Santos Silva rejected claims that '[Portugal] is China's "special friend" in EU' or that '[Lisbon] is developing a problematic reliance on Beijing' (*apud*Financial Times 2020, para. 1).

The second aspect is the relative 'commercialization' of Portuguese foreign policy for the sake of capital attraction, economic gains and technological innovation. This has required Portuguese foreign policymakers to implement a policy of mitigating any negative effects Lisbon's closer engagement with Beijing has had on the country's relations with the US and key EU member states, notably, Germany and France. Thus, while ensuring its Western allies that Portugal was 'listening' and shared the concerns over potential risks arising from the engagement of Huawei in the development of 5G networks, Prime Minister Costa, for instance, advocated that it was 'important not to stop the modernization of Europe's digital infrastructure'; and not to close European border 'to innovation coming from abroad' (Wise and Hall 2019, paras. 9–10). Moreover, in the face of German and French insistence on other EU countries to follow their lead in endorsing robust national legislation on foreign investment screening, he also conceded to the usage of screening to protect national strategic sectors but warned against using it 'to open the door to protectionism' (Ibidem).

Conclusion

In placing its focus on Portugal, this chapter has attempted to demonstrate that the South European country represents an intriguing case concerning the implementation of the BRI in Europe for two main reasons. Similar to other EU member states, the first reason is linked to Beijing's preference for bilateralism in dealing with Lisbon in order to advance its BRI-related priorities and interests. The second reason, however, rests on the collaborative approach exhibited by Portuguese national authorities vis-à-vis Chinese bilateral initiatives since the beginning of the sovereign debt crisis. Eventually, such a bilateral approach enabled Beijing's authorities to explore possibilities and initiatives outside the framework of the existing cooperative multilateral arrangements like the Galileo Programme. The issuing of public debt in yuan and the monitoring of space as well as the Atlantic Ocean are cases in point.

The preceding analysis has outlined the rise of Chinese-led activities and projects in Portugal before and after the launch of the BRI, which has been largely due to Lisbon's growing realization of the multiple opportunities derived from a closer economic relationship with China. The international bailout period (2011–2014), which was marked by severe austerity politics, ignited China's pull on Portugal for financial and economic motivations. With the impetus of the Gold Visa scheme, Chinese investments started to emerge and flourish, whilst the center-right government led by Passos Coelho strived to fulfill the demands of the financial assistance programme agreed with and monitored by the troika. After such a traumatic experience for the country's politics, economy and society, the center-left Socialist government has further deepened Portugal's openness to Chinese companies and investors and adopted an increasingly receptive stance towards BRI-related projects and opportunities. This was primarily driven by the need for the country to achieve sustainable economic growth and international competitiveness thereby escaping from its chronic underdog position among the Eurozone economies.

Consequently, China's presence in Portugal grew over time and Luso-Chinese relations reached a major milestone in December 2018, as evinced by Xi Jinping's visit to Portugal. Several agreements signed at the time paved the road for furthering Chinese engagement, namely, in critical and strategic areas such as satellite construction, ocean monitoring and 5G communications. The issue of Portuguese sovereign debt in Chinese currency also became symptomatic of the deepening relations between the two countries.

China's growing presence and influence in Portugal constitutes a somewhat innovative factor in the country's contemporary foreign policy. This is so since the latter has been characterized by long-standing advocacy of US strategic interests inside and outside NATO, and also a politico-diplomatic alignment to preferences and concerns of leading European players such as Germany and France. Despite this traditional posture, Lisbon's collaborative approach towards Chinese bilateral initiatives expanded in the midst of caution and suspicions by both German and France regarding China's strategic investments in Europe. Equally important, such expansion took place despite Washington's vocal warnings against Portuguese exposure to Huawei, perceived by the US Administration as a sort of *longa manus* of the Chinese Communist Party.

The COVID-19 outbreak in March 2020 brought the Portuguese economy—still recovering from the effects of the 2011 international bailout—to a halt. The ensuing devastating socio-economic consequences it has had is likely to leave the country with no viable alternative to engaging with China even more actively than in recent years for the sake of national economic survival. Therefore, there is a strong potential that the 'Chinese factor' becomes a real predicament for contemporary Portuguese foreign policy, if and when Luso-Chinese collaboration further expands to encompass a multiplicity of connections with national strategic sectors, including critical technology and infrastructure.

Notes

i The authors acknowledge that this study was conducted at the Research Center in Political Science (UIDB/CPO/00758/2020), University of Minho/University of Évora, and was supported by the Portuguese Foundation for Science and Technology and the Portuguese Ministry of Education and Science through national funds.

ii Note, for instance, that the action plan released by China's NDRC stated that the initiative 'is open to all countries, and international and regional organizations for engagement', whilst 'advocat[ing] peace and cooperation, openness and inclusiveness, mutual learning and mutual benefit' (China's National Development and Reform Commission 2015, 3–4).

iii Patriotism in China was largely affected by a period marked by the repression of injustices and unequal treaties imposed by the West. Chinese authorities usually describe this period, ranging from 1839 to 1949, as the 'Century of Humiliation'.

iv The authors note that the Chinese bilateral approach has been also cultivated in the framework of the EU–China Strategic Partnership (SP) since the Sixth China–EU Summit, held in Beijing in October 2003. This SP has incrementally institutionalized multisectoral cooperation between the two partners. Yet, due to space limitations, this subject is not addressed in this section.

v Around €260 million of Portuguese public debt during three years (Expresso 2019).

vi A Chinese company that leads electronic payments in China.

vii This is a real estate company whose headquarters are located in Portugal, albeit its shareholders are Chinese.

Bibliography

AICEP. (2018). http://www.portugalglobal.pt/PT/PortugalNews/Paginas/NewDetail.aspx?newId=%7B6D7A7847-AA7A-4405-A55C-1182E8EB6F26%7D

AICEP. (2019). http://www.portugalglobal.pt/PT/PortugalNews/Paginas/NewDetail.aspx?newId=%7B4397E86E-AAEC-4F9A-8480–141989D21773%7D

Benner, T., Gaspers, J., Ohlberg, M., Poggetti, L. and Shi-Kupfer, K. (2018). "Authoritarian Advance: Responding to China's Growing Political Influence in Europe". https://www.merics.org/sites/default/files/2018-02/GPPi_MERICS_Authoritarian_Advance_2018_1.pdf

BusinessEurope. (2020). "The EU and China: Addressing the Systemic Challenge". https://www.businesseurope.eu/sites/buseur/files/media/reports_and_studies/2020-01-16_the_eu_and_china_-_addressing_the_systemic_challenge_-_full_paper.pdf

Bustillo, R. and Andoni, M. (2018). "China, the EU and Multilateralism: The Asian Infrastructure Investment Bank". *Revista Brasileira de Política Internacional*, 61(1). DOI: 10.1590/0034-7329201800108

Callahan, W. (2016). "China's 'Asia Dream': The Belt Road Initiative and the New Regional Order". *Asian Journal of Comparative Politics*, 1(3): 226–243. DOI: 10.1177/2057891116647806

Casarini, N. (2016). "When All Roads Lead to Beijing. Assessing China's New Silk Road and its Implications for Europe". *The International Spectator*, 51(4): 95–108. DOI: 10.1080/03932729.2016.1224491

China's National Development and Reform Commission [In conjunction with the Ministry of Foreign Affairs and the Ministry of Commerce]. (2015). "Vision and Actions on Jointly Building Silk Road Economic Belt and 21stCentury Maritime Silk Road". https://reconasia-production.s3.amazonaws.com/media/filer_public/e0/22/e0228017-7463-46fc-9094-0465a6f1ca23/vision_and_actions_on_jointly_building_silk_road_economic_belt_and_21st-century_maritime_silk_road.pdf

CNBC. (2020a). https://www.cnbc.com/2020/02/12/reuters-america-us-firms-keen-to-expand-portugals-sines-port-for-lng-trade-energy-secretary.html

CNBC. (2020b). https://www.cnbc.com/2020/04/16/chinese-takeover-of-europe-tech-firms-face-increased-scrutiny.html

Diário de Notícias. (2019a). https://www.dn.pt/edicao-do-dia/28-ago-2019/investimento-chines-de-300-milhoes-vai-fazer-nascer-casas-em-monsanto-11243425.html

Diário de Notícias. (2019b). https://www.dn.pt/mundo/este-xi-nao-e-a-china-com-quem-os-portugueses-tem-comerciado-durante-500-anos-10878774.html

Dinheiro Vivo. (2020). https://www.dinheirovivo.pt/economia/vistos-gold-investimento-recua-46-para-28-milhoes-em-abril/

Duarte, P. (2018a). La Nouvelle Route de la Soie: vers une (re)configuration de l'intégration régionale et globale. Presses Universitaires de Louvain. Collection Scène Internationale, Louvain.

Duarte, P. (2018b). "China's Momentum: The "One Belt One Road" Triple's Securitisation". In Xing, L. (ed.). Mapping China's 'One Belt One Road' Initiative. Palgrave Macmillan, Cham. 143–165.

Duarte, P. (2020). "Quando os extremos se tocam: Portugal na Faixa e Rota chinesa". *Revista Oriente-Ocidente*, (37): 18–29.

Duarte, P. and Leandro, F. (2020). "The Ultimate European Border: The Belt and Road Initiative Discovers Portugal". In Duarte, P. and Leandro, F. (eds.). The Belt and Road Initiative - International Perspectives on an Old Archetype of a New Development Model. Palgrave MacMillan, Singapore. 363–388.

Duque, J. (2019). "Portugal: A China-friendly EU nation driven by need". In Deutsche Welle. https://www.dw.com/en/portugal-a-china-friendly-eu-nation-driven-by-need/a-47872582

Eco. (2019). https://eco.sapo.pt/2019/10/30/chineses-compram-terrenos-de-antigo-bairro-de-lata-em-oeiras-por-145-milhoes/

EU Observer. (2020). https://euobserver.com/coronavirus/148295?utm_source=euobs&utm_medium=email&utm_source=EUobserver+Newsletter&utm_campaign=088b215f49-EMAIL_CAMPAIGN_2020_05_09_05_30&utm_medium=email&utm_term=0_8f318ca8da-088b215f49–114905277

European Commission. (2015a). https://ec.europa.eu/transport/sites/transport/files/2018-07-13-eu-china-connectivity-platform-action-plan.pdf

European Commission. (2015b). https://europa.eu/rapid/press-release_IP-15–5723_en.htm

European Commission. (2018). https://ec.europa.eu/commission/news/cathay-capital-completes-first-closing-cathay-midcap-ii-eur-600-million-2018-aug-06_en

European Council on Foreign Relations. (2016). https://www.ecfr.eu/page/-/ECFR174_Absorb_and_Conquer.pdf

EXPATICA. (2020). https://www.expatica.com/pt/moving/visas/golden-visa-portugal-1042263/

Expresso. (2017). https://expresso.pt/economia/2017-03-01-Conglomerado-chines-constroi-em-Alcoutim-a-maior-central-solar-do-pais

Expresso. (2019). https://expresso.pt/economia/2019-05-30-Portugal-paga-409-em-obrigacoes-em-moeda-chinesa

Fang, C. and Nolan, P. (eds.). (2019). Routledge Handbook of the Belt and Road. Routledge, London.

Ferreira-Pereira, L. C. (2007). "Portugal and ESDP", In Brümmer, K. (ed.). The South and ESDP: Greece, Italy, Portugal and Spain. Bertelsmann Stiftung, Gütersloh. 32–49. http://www.bertelsmann-stiftung.org

Ferreira-Pereira, L. C. (2014). "Introduction". In Ferreira-Pereira, L.C. (ed.). Portugal in the European Union: Assessing Twenty-Five Years of Integration Experience. Routledge, London. 1–10.

Ferreira-Pereira, L. C. and Groom, J. R. (2014). "Conclusion". In Ferreira-Pereira, L.C. (ed.). Portugal in the European Union: Assessing Twenty-Five Years of Integration Experience. Routledge, London. 143–159.

Financial Times. (2019a). https://www.ft.com/content/0240c8b0–81ff-11e9–9935-ad75bb96c849

Financial Times. (2019b). "EU Eyes Tougher Scrutiny of China Cyber Security Risks". https://www.ft.com/content/3d13c208–0545-11e9–99df-6183d3002ee1

Financial Times. (2020). https://www.ft.com/content/862c633e-393b-11ea-a6d3–9a26f8c3cba4

Gaspar, S. and de Haro, A. (2019). "Buying Citizenship? Chinese Golden Visa Migrants in Portugal". *International Migration*, 58(3): 58–72. DOI: 10.1111/imig.12621

Gorjão, P. (2012). "Portugal and the Straitjacket of the European Financial Crisis". *The International Spectator*, 47(4): 64–68, DOI: 10.1080/03932729.2012.743644

Governo da República Portuguesa. (2016). https://www.portugal.gov.pt/pt/gc21/comunicacao/noticia?i=20161010-pm-china

Hanemann, T., Huotari, M. and Kratz, A. (2019). "Chinese FDI in Europe: 2018 Trends and Impact of New Screening Policies". A report by Rhodium Group (RHG) and the Mercator Institute for China Studies (MERICS).

Ilhéu, F. (2019). "Portugal and China's Cooperation for the New Maritime Silk Road of the 21st Century. In Duarte, P., Ilhéu, F. and Leandro, F. (eds.). The New Silk Road and the Portuguese Speaking Countries in the New World Context. International Institute of Macau, Lisbon. 15–35.

Jakimow, M. (2019). "Desecuritisation as a Soft Power Strategy: the Belt and Road Initiative. European fragmentation and China's Normative Influence in Central-Eastern Europe". *Asia Europe Journal*, 17(4): 369–385. DOI: 10.1007/s10308-019-00561-3.

Jornal Económico. (2018). https://jornaleconomico.sapo.pt/noticias/os-principais-investimentos-da-china-em-portugal-352999

Jornal Económico. (2019). https://jornaleconomico.sapo.pt/noticias/a-historia-da-opa-a-edp-em-quinze-capitulos-436840

Jornal de Negócios. (2018). https://www.jornaldenegocios.pt/empresas/detalhe/empresa-chinesa-investe-64-milhoes-em-complexo-de-saude-e-bem-estar-em-estremoz

Jornal de Negócios. (2019a). https://www.jornaldenego cios.pt/mercados/obrigacoes/detalhe/portugal-vai-colocar-divida-em-moeda-chinesa-na-proxima-semana

Jornal de Negócios. (2019b). https://www.jornaldenegocios.pt/empresas/banca---financas/detalhe/bcp-quer-emitir-220-mil-cartoes-da-unionpay-em-cinco-anos

Kaska, K., Beckvard, H. and Minárik, T. (2019). "Huawei, 5G and China as a Security Threat". NATO Cooperative Cyber Defence Centre of Excellence. https://ccdcoe.org/uploads/2019/03/CCDCOE-Huawei-2019-03-28-FINAL.pdf

Kirchner, E., Christiansen, T. and Dorussen, H. (2016). Security Relations between China and the European Union: From Convergence to Cooperation. Cambridge University Press, Singapore.

Lams, L. (2018). "Examining Strategic Narratives in Chinese Official Discourse under Xi Jinping". *Journal of Chinese Political Science*, 23(3): 387–411. DOI: 10.1 007/s11366-018-9529-8

Le Corre, P. (2018). https://carnegieendowment.org/2018/11/24/china-s-golden-era-in-portugal-pub-77789

Li, X. (ed.). (2018). Mapping China's 'One Belt One Road' Initiative. Palgrave Macmillan.

Macao Magazine. (2019). https://macaomagazine.net/portugals-place-in-chinas-belt-and-road-initiative/

Maher, R. (2016). "The Elusive EU-China Strategic Partnership". *International Affairs*, 92(4): 959–976. DOI: 10.1111/1468-2346.12659

Menegazzi, S. (2017). "Global Economic Governance between China and the EU: The Case of the Asian Infrastructure Investment Bank". *Asia Europe Journal*, 15(2): 229–242.

Michalski, A. and Pan, Z. (2017). "Role Dynamics in a Structured Relationship: The EU-China Strategic Partnership". *Journal of Common Market Studies*, 55(3): 611–627. DOI: 10.1111/jcms.12505

Minghao, Z. (2016). "The Belt and Road Initiative and its Implications for China-Europe Relations". *The International Spectator*, 51(4): 109–118. DOI: 10.1080/03 932729.2016.1235819

Lee Monde. (2019). https://www.lemonde.fr/economie/article/2019/05/21/le-portugal-deroule-le-tapis-rouge-pour-les-investisseurs-chinois_5464971_3234.html

Pareja-Alcaraz, P. (2017). "Chinese Investments in Southern Europe's Energy Sectors: Similarities and Divergences in China's Strategies in Greece, Italy, Portugal and Spain". *Energy Policy,* (101): 700–710.

Pavlićević, D. (2018). "China Threat' and 'China Opportunity: Politics of Dreams and Fears in China-Central and Eastern European Relations". *Journal of Contemporary China*, 27(113): 688–702. DOI: 10.1080/10670564.2018.1458057

Pepermans, A. (2018). "China's 16+1 and Belt and Road Initiative in Central and Eastern Europe: Economic and Political Influence at a Cheap Price". *Journal of Contemporary Central and Eastern Europe*, 26(2–3): 181–203. DOI: 10.1080/2573 9638.2018.1515862

Público. (2017). https://www.publico.pt/2015/04/26/economia/noticia/portugal-foi-o-pais-da-ue-com-maior-peso-de-investimento-chines-em-2014-1693637

Público. (2019). https://www.publico.pt/2019/12/05/politica/noticia/pompeo-avisa-governo-portugues-perigos-investimento-chines-1896300

Reuters. (2017). https://www.reuters.com/article/us-eu-un-rights/greece-blocks-eu-statement-on-china-human-rights-at-u-n-idUSKBN1990FP

Reuters. (2019). https://www.reuters.com/article/us-eu-china/eu-leaders-call-for-end-to-naivety-in-relations-with-china-idUSKCN1R31H3

Sábado. (2018). https://www.sabado.pt/dinheiro/detalhe/a-china-os-novos-donos-de-portugal

Song, W. and Song, L. (2020). "Assessing China's '16+1 Cooperation' with Central and Eastern Europe: A Public Good Perspective". In Duarte, P. and Leandro, F. (eds.). The Belt and Road Initiative – International Perspectives on an Old Archetype of a New Development Model. Palgrave MacMillan. 411–431.

Szczudlik, J. (2019). "Seven Years of the 16+1: An Assessment of China's 'Multilateral Bilateralism' in Central Europe". Institut Français des Relations Internationales. *Asie. Visions*, No. 107, April.

Valero, J. (2015). "China Uses Juncker Plan to Boost Involvement in Europe". https://www.euractiv.com/section/global-europe/news/china-uses-juncker-plan-to-boost-involvement-in-europe/

Weidong, L. (2019). The Belt and Road Initiative. Routledge, London.

Wise, P. and Hall, B. (2019). "Portugal PM Warns on EU protectionism over China Investment Screening", *Financial Times*, 3 March. https://www.ft.com/content/8bb21cf6-3ab6–11e9-b72b-2c7f526ca5d0

Wuthnow, J., Li, X. and Qi, L. (2012). "Diverse Multilateralism: Four Strategies in China's Multilateral Diplomacy". *Journal of Chinese Political Science*, (17): 269–290. DOI: 10.1007/s11366-012-9202-6

Xinhua. (2015). http://www.xinhuanet.com/english/2015-03/28/c_134105435.htm

Xinhua. (2018a). http://www.xinhuanet.com/english/2018-12/04/c_137650888.htm

Xinhua. (2018b). http://www.xinhuanet.com/english/2018-12/06/c_137653556.htm

Part V

Conclusion

15 Conclusion: The EU's Belt and Road challenge: Coherence, consolidation and connectivity

Vassilis Ntousas and Stephen Minas

This book has illustrated the ongoing challenge of pinning down the essence of the Belt and Road Initiative. In different chapters, the BRI has been identified as 'a development strategy' which 'aims to enhance China's role in global governance' (Zhao and Chen, Chapter 2); as 'more of a grand geopolitical strategy than an economic blueprint' (Blockmans and Hu, Chapter 5); and as 'deeply rooted' in the aim of 'engender[ing] new economic stimulus' (Su, Chapter 8). This is unsurprising for a project of this scope, yet it has in part been the reason behind the plethora of unresolved questions that have been raised over time concerning the initiative's motivations.

Despite these questions, however, some generalisations can be drawn from the preceding chapters. First, the BRI is not just or even primarily about infrastructure. It is more about setting global standards and agendas and channelling global economic activities and relationships. Second, the BRI, either directly or indirectly, has been a key element of China's international relations so far in the Xi Jinping years. At the same time, its core rationale of serving as a vehicle for Beijing's external action and interstate relationship management will likely remain a crucial element in the years ahead, even if the initiative's exact contours are continuously rethought, not least due to lessons learned from the first years of implementation and the impact of external developments, such as the COVID-19 pandemic. Third, in developing EU responses to the BRI, EU officials need to make an effort to perceive the BRI through the eyes of others—not just their Chinese counterparts, but also people in participating countries (including European countries).

Given competing interpretations of the BRI, diverging Member State perceptions of interest, the distribution of competences between Brussels and national capitals and the multiple crises that have preoccupied the EU in the last decade, it may be unsurprising that the EU's response to the BRI has been 'rather incoherent' (Blockmans and Hu, Chapter 5). There is much debate over whether the BRI is a vehicle for EU–China collaboration, a threat to be fended off or some uneasy combination of the two. There is furious agreement among many European policymakers and analysts that a more unified EU approach to the BRI would be beneficial. Rather than simply adding to this chorus, this book has examined the reasons why such unity is absent; why different EU institutions and Member States see different things 'in the BRI kaleidoscope' (Snyder, Chapter 4).

Some tentative conclusions can be ventured on this point. First, the domestic politics of European countries have been an important factor in shifting attitudes to the BRI. For example, Italy's BRI MoU was signed during an unprecedented and short-lived correlation of populist forces in the Italian government (Amighini, Chapter 13). The second Conte cabinet, with ongoing participation of the populist 5 Stars Movement but with the far-right League sent into opposition and replaced in government by Social Democrats, moved closer to the EU policy mainstream.

Second, either by choice or need, each EU Member State sees in the BRI a different balance of economic opportunity and risk. EU Member States and candidate countries can be divided not only by their particular political dynamics, but also by the type of Chinese financing on offer, whether predominantly foreign direct investment or debt (Bastian, Chapter 6), by their degree of reliance on the Chinese export market and the depth and width of their institutionalized relations with Beijing (Mair and Schaff, Chapter 11). Some Member States, moreover, see in Chinese capital and technology opportunities for their further development, while others are more concerned about unfair Chinese competition and forced technology transfer to Chinese competitors.

The varying Member State responses to the BRI must also be placed in the context of the EU's political economy. In 2013, when the BRI was launched, the eurozone crisis had 'led to intra-EU breaches of solidarity as well as divisions between different "Europes": "Northern" versus "Southern" and "Western" versus "Eastern"' (Ferreira-Pereira and Duarte, Chapter 14). The eurozone crisis and the 'austerity' regimes that followed resulted in mass business failures, skyrocketing unemployment and the inability of many public authorities to maintain basic services. Cast into this depression, the hardest-hit nations of Europe's South were desperate to attract new capital and naturally as receptive to investment from China as from elsewhere (Kokoromytis and Chryssogelos, Chapter 12; Ferreira-Pereira and Duarte, Chapter 14). Nevertheless, some of the same northern politicians who, as creditors, insisted on the dogma of austerity, have demanded that crisis-hit countries refuse Chinese investment and financing. Such a perspective myopically misses the important ramifications of how the eurozone crisis was handled for ownership of critical infrastructure, not just for the countries in the South but for the Union as a whole as well. The lesson from these difficult years is that, even more so than in the past, the EU's domestic socio-economic settings directly affect its ability to act in the world. The social catastrophe of austerity weakened the EU's ability to reach common economic positions, including with respect to Belt and Road.

A more coherent EU approach to the BRI will require a Europe of solidarity: 'the Europe that protects' not only economically and strategically, but also socially.

Notwithstanding the plurality of EU approaches to the BRI, multiple chapters discerned a welcome trend towards a more sceptical response in recent years. This tendency appears to have been strengthened and/or accelerated by the events of the COVID-19 pandemic. The result has been not a resurgent 'Health Silk Road', as the Chinese leadership might have wished, but rather mixed reactions to Beijing's domestic handling of COVID-19, EU pushback against assertive Chinese public diplomacy and intensified practical difficulties for the BRI in Europe (Esteban and Armanini, Chapter 9) and beyond.

Within the European Commission, perceptions of the BRI reversed dramatically within the space of a few years, from a potential source of finance for the EU's economic recovery through the 'Juncker Plan' to an economic challenge, promoting different standards of economic development, threatening EU competitiveness and targeting EU technologies for transfer (Men, Chapter 3). The EU has entered 'uncharted waters' in relating to China simultaneously as partner and rival (Men, Chapter 3). This change is likely not just a result of updated assessments of the BRI, as the initiative became decreasingly amorphous over time, but also evidences a much broader agenda underway to develop EU strategic autonomy: 'if we as Europeans are to safeguard our way of life, then Europe as a whole must think more strategically and be able to engage in power-play among the other players' (Van Middelaar 2019, 3). The EU is learning to 'speak geopolitics' as it aspires to be an autonomous actor in a multipolar world, and this is reflected in the EU's relationships with the world's major powers, including but not only China. An approach to economic matters that seeks to build strategic autonomy is also necessary. The EU has repeatedly witnessed China deploy economic coercion as an instrument of foreign policy against smaller nations, such as Norway and Australia. The EU therefore can have no illusions that its Chinese interlocutors separate economic and geopolitical concerns.

Nevertheless, it may be that a focus on 'systemic rivalry' blinds EU actors to other challenges. For example, in September 2020, the European Court of Auditors (ECA) published its assessment of 'EU risks from China's investment strategy'. One such risk is '[l]ack of coordination' between EU and Chinese investment programmes, potentially resulting in connectivity gaps or duplication. The ECA noted that the Commission and the External Action Service 'do not consider this risk to be relevant due to the political reality and consider the issue of infrastructure coordination to go against the EU's current policy' (ECA 2020, 25). This reveals quite a stark disconnect from the perspectives of many Member States, as well as business sectors. Faced with a global (and European) shortage in infrastructure investment (Oxford Economics/Global Infrastructure Hub 2017), risks of costly duplication and infrastructure gaps seem worth taking seriously. (The position cited by the ECA also follows a different logic to Commission warnings against 'politicizing' competition policy (Svetlicinii, Chapter 7), suggesting divergences between the newly 'geopolitical' and the resolutely technocratic among Commission services.)

Overall, however, the noted transition from a 'naïve' to a more 'sceptical' approach to the BRI indicates less interest in engagement for its own sake and greater awareness of the risks posed by the BRI to EU economic interests.

Evidently, this should not prevent sober appraisal of any opportunities for EU–China cooperation, including through the BRI. From an EU perspective, the practical challenge is to frame a response to the BRI that captures core, shared EU interests while acknowledging legitimate differentiation at Member State level. Attaining a higher degree of freedom to choose autonomously means cooperation with China (and other international partners) that is genuinely 'win-win', but resisting a type of engagement that does not defend the bloc's interests, values and standards: 'open where possible and protective when necessary' (Nicolas, Chapter 10).

Crafting such a common EU position requires not Procrustean homogeneity (which is anyway not a realistic prospect) but, rather, agreement on fundamental principles and a pertinent policy approach. The BRI is seen in different ways by 'actors in three semi-autonomous European social fields': the EU, Member States and the now 16+1 (Snyder, Chapter 4). The Commission has grown louder in how it approaches China, but, as shown throughout this volume, Member States have naturally (and legitimately) opted for different responses to the very real dilemma of what concerns to prioritise vis-à-vis Beijing. A completely unified EU response to the BRI—as a vital piece of crafting a unified 'China policy'—may therefore not be feasible in the foreseeable future. After all, EU strength in the world derives not just from weight, but also from its diversity. EU Member States run the gamut from an Indo-Pacific military power and permanent UN Security Council member in France to a former member of the Non-Aligned Movement in Cyprus, whose first president attended the Bandung Asian-African conference alongside Zhou Enlai. The EU is large and contains multitudes. As such, the bloc should focus on common core interests in its dealings with the BRI and then utilise the diverse Member State economic and diplomatic resources in pursuing these interests.

While the details of such a stance cannot be developed here, economic reciprocity clearly merits a place at its centre. The absence of a 'level playing field' is a major challenge in two senses: first, the mismatch between Chinese access to the EU market and restrictions on European firms in the Chinese market; and second, the fact that many Chinese SOEs compete in the EU market with the advantage of public support that essentially amounts to state aid (ECA 2020, 15–16). Though much remains to be done, the EU has had some success in building up 'legal bulwarks' against such market distortions (Blockmans and Hu, Chapter 5), notably in the areas of state aid and FDI screening. The case of infringements proceedings concerning the Belgrade-Budapest rail project demonstrated that the Commission succeeded in upholding EU procurement norms, but without affecting the project's 'end result' (Bastian, Chapter 6). Chinese state-owned enterprises have also featured prominently in the ongoing debate over reforming EU competition policy (Svetlicinii, Chapter 7). At the same time, Blockmans and Hu are right to warn that 'Europe must not fall into the trap of protectionism'. The EU–China Comprehensive Agreement on Investment, agreed in principle in December 2020, has the potential to improve economic reciprocity, although the ultimate fate of the deal remains to be determined (European Commission 2021).

On the BRI beyond the borders of the EU, a policy of 'conditional engagement' is an appropriate position (Nicolas, Chapter 10). The mechanism of third-party market cooperation (3PMC), while 'complicated' in implementation, indicates selective participation on the basis of consistency with EU standards (Nicolas, Chapter 10). Importantly, as the debate in Germany has moved closer to the French position on selective BRI participation (Mair and Schaff, Chapter 11), a more solidified common EU approach along the lines of what has been presented above may be beginning to emerge.

Recent research indicates a dramatic reduction of overseas financing by China's two main policy banks, from $75 billion in 2016 to $4 billion in 2019, in a sign that regulators are reining in overextended lenders (Wheatley and Kynge 2020). Such a reduction is likely linked to the Chinese leadership's new economic concept of 'dual circulation', encompassing domestic and international circulation. The stated goal is to make domestic circulation the 'main body', i.e. reorient China's economy to domestic consumption and innovation (CCP 2020, para. 4). If this domestic reorientation is confirmed in practice, it is likely to disrupt the plans of states which have come to rely on BRI financing. In such a new context, the EU approach to connectivity that insists on high environmental, social and governance standards would attain a stronger competitive position, including in the EU's neighbourhood.

The EU's approach should be informed by close examination of BRI's legal development, despite the fact that at this stage, the BRI is not so much a legal order as a latticework of bilateral agreements (Drache et al. 2019, 37ff). Zhao and Chen have proposed a new agreement for 'BRI dispute settlement', as well as greater EU–China judicial cooperation (Chapter 2). In contrast, Bastian has highlighted the potential role of the recently established China International Commercial Court as a challenge for EU Member States and candidate countries in South-Eastern Europe (Chapter 6). In any case, the initiative's wider legal underpinnings, consequences and complications should be a focal point in the continuous analysis undertaken at the EU and Member State levels, given the importance attached by the Union to its own legal order and the influential nature of this order globally—at least in some sectors.

The transition to an environmentally sustainable global economy should also be at the heart of the EU's future approach to the BRI. The big picture is that China is an indispensable partner for the EU when it comes to climate change and related challenges, despite the gulf of values and interests that separates the two sides in various fields. This is based on China's status as the largest emitter of greenhouse gases (GHGs), the largest exporter of renewable energy technologies and a major financier of new fossil fuel capacity through the BRI. By virtue of its design and magnitude, the BRI has the potential to influence the climate trajectories of dozens of countries, for better or worse (Harlan 2020, 2). Therefore, constructive engagement with it should remain a vital part of the EU's calculus. The mismatch between Beijing's climate ambitions and the carbon footprint of BRI projects is now widely acknowledged. Nevertheless, early experiences of EU–China cooperation in the Connectivity Platform and the Asian Infrastructure Investment Bank (whose participating EU members collectively account for the second-largest shareholding after China) lead Su to suggest that 'cooperation contingent on pragmatic interests could transcend norm contestation and conceptual gaps, contributing to regional sustainable development under the BRI' (Chapter 8). The Chinese government's September 2020 announcement of new targets to peak GHG emissions in 2030 and achieve carbon neutrality by 2060, while lacking in detail, are important commitments to achieving the goals of the Paris Agreement. Climate cooperation will therefore be a key test of the thesis that 'Beijing can be a constructive partner, especially in view of an unpredictable trading partner across the Atlantic' (Blockmans and Hu, Chapter 5). EU actors should therefore support efforts to 'green' the BRI as a matter of urgency. Work to seek convergence on standards for 'sustainable' or 'green' finance has particular potential in this regard (European Investment Bank (EIB) 2018). Additionally, an accelerated climate transition within China should create new opportunities for the 'greening' of BRI cooperation, while attempts to export redundant fossil fuel capacity to BRI participants (Magnus 2018, 182) should be discouraged.

Framing a core EU response to the BRI that also encompasses the position of the EU's near neighbours, many of whom aspire to EU accession, will also be vital. The European Commission president was correct to note that the 'Western Balkans are part of Europe—and not just a stopover on the Silk Road' (von der Leyen 2020). However, the Western Balkan countries also host Chinese institutions as welcome financiers and commercial partners. Rather than attempting to wish the Chinese presence away, the EU should focus on improving the compliance of China-backed projects with EU substantive and procedural standards (including, as Snyder emphasises in Chapter 4, norms of participation, consultation, accountability and transparency). If, as a Chinese Academy of Social Sciences report stated, '[d]ealing properly with the Western Balkans' is perceived in Beijing as 'a good opportunity for China to develop good relations with the EU and its members like Germany' (Liu 2017, 84), there should be opportunities for improvement on this score. Bastian argues that 'as a non-EU external actor China is learning the rules of engagement with EU member states and candidate countries' (Chapter 6). At the same time, BRI's appeal on the EU's periphery is a wake-up call to the EU. The 'Brussels effect' on autopilot is not enough; more is required to consolidate the European space within the EU normative framework.

Intimately linked to this, EU responses to the BRI cannot be left to governments and public institutions alone. As Snyder notes (Chapter 4), companies are 'more powerful than European governments in the BRI'. While European businesses (and foreign businesses trading in the EU market) are subject to EU and Member State regulation, they also retain significant agency in the environmental, social, governance and labour standards they observe. While acknowledging EU–China competition over standards, EU authorities and businesses have every incentive to engage in a 'race to the top' rather than its opposite. People-to-people links should also continue to be encouraged in fields such as education, tourism and culture. Friendly relations between peoples add valuable ballast to political relationships, which can assist in realising opportunities, but also enduring the challenges, connected to the Belt and Road.

Bibliography

Chinese Communist Party (CCP), (2020). 中共中央关于制定国民经济和社会发展第十四个五年规划和二〇三五年远景目标的建议, http://www.gov.cn/zhengce/2020-11/03/content_5556991.htm

Drache, D., Kingsmith, A.T., and Qi, D., (2019). One Road, Many Dreams: China's Bold Plan to Remake the Global Economy. Bloomsbury China, London.

European Commission, (2021). EU – China Comprehensive Agreement on Investment (CAI): list of sections, https://trade.ec.europa.eu/doclib/press/index.cfm?id=2237

European Court of Auditors (ECA), (2020). The EU's response to China's state-driven investment strategy. Review No 03. https://www.eca.europa.eu/en/Pages/DocItem.aspx?did=54733

European Investment Bank (EIB), (2018). Towards a common language in Green Finance: progress is made at COP24 in Katowice, https://www.eib.org/en/press/all/2018-327-towards-a-common-language-in-green-finance-progress-is-made-at-cop24-in-katowice?media=rss&language=EN

Harlan, T., (2020). Green development or greenwashing? A political ecology perspective on China's green Belt and Road. *Eurasian Geography and Economics*, 62(2), 202–226. DOI: 10.1080/15387216.2020.1795700 (online first).

Liu, Z., (2017). Europe and the Belt and Road Initiative: Responses and Risks. China Social Sciences Press, Beijing.

Magnus, G., (2018). Red Flags: Why Xi's China Is in Jeopardy. Yale University Press, New Haven.

Oxford Economics/Global Infrastructure Hub, (2017). Global Infrastructure Outlook. https://cdn.gihub.org/outlook/live/methodology/Global+Infrastructure+Outlook+-+July+2017.pdf

Van Middelaar, L., (2019). Alarums and Excursions: Improvising Politics on the European Stage. Agenda, Newcastle upon Tyne.

Von der Leyen, U., (2020). State of the Union Address by President von der Leyen at the European Parliament Plenary. European Commission, https://ec.europa.eu/commission/presscorner/detail/en/SPEECH_20_1655

Wheatley, J., and Kynge, J., (2020). China curtails overseas lending in face of geopolitical backlash. Financial Times, https://www.ft.com/content/1cb3e33b-e2c2–4743-ae41-d3fffffa4259

Index

D

For Product Safety Concerns and Information please contact our EU
representative GPSR@taylorandfrancis.com
Taylor & Francis Verlag GmbH, Kaufingerstraße 24, 80331 München, Germany

www.ingramcontent.com/pod-product-compliance
Lightning Source LLC
LaVergne TN
LVHW021121300926
849160LV00010B/817

9781032045467